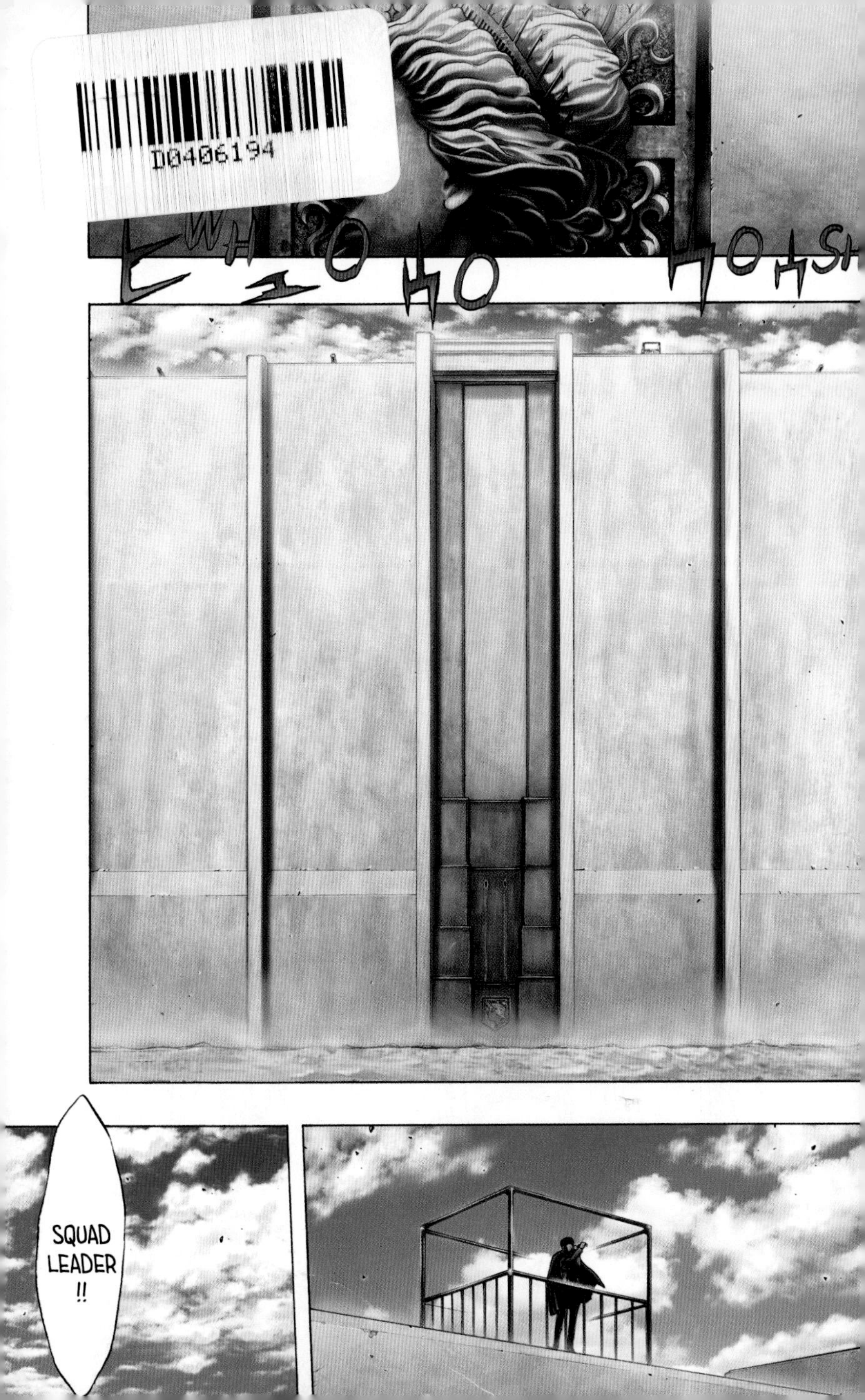
SQUAD LEADER !!

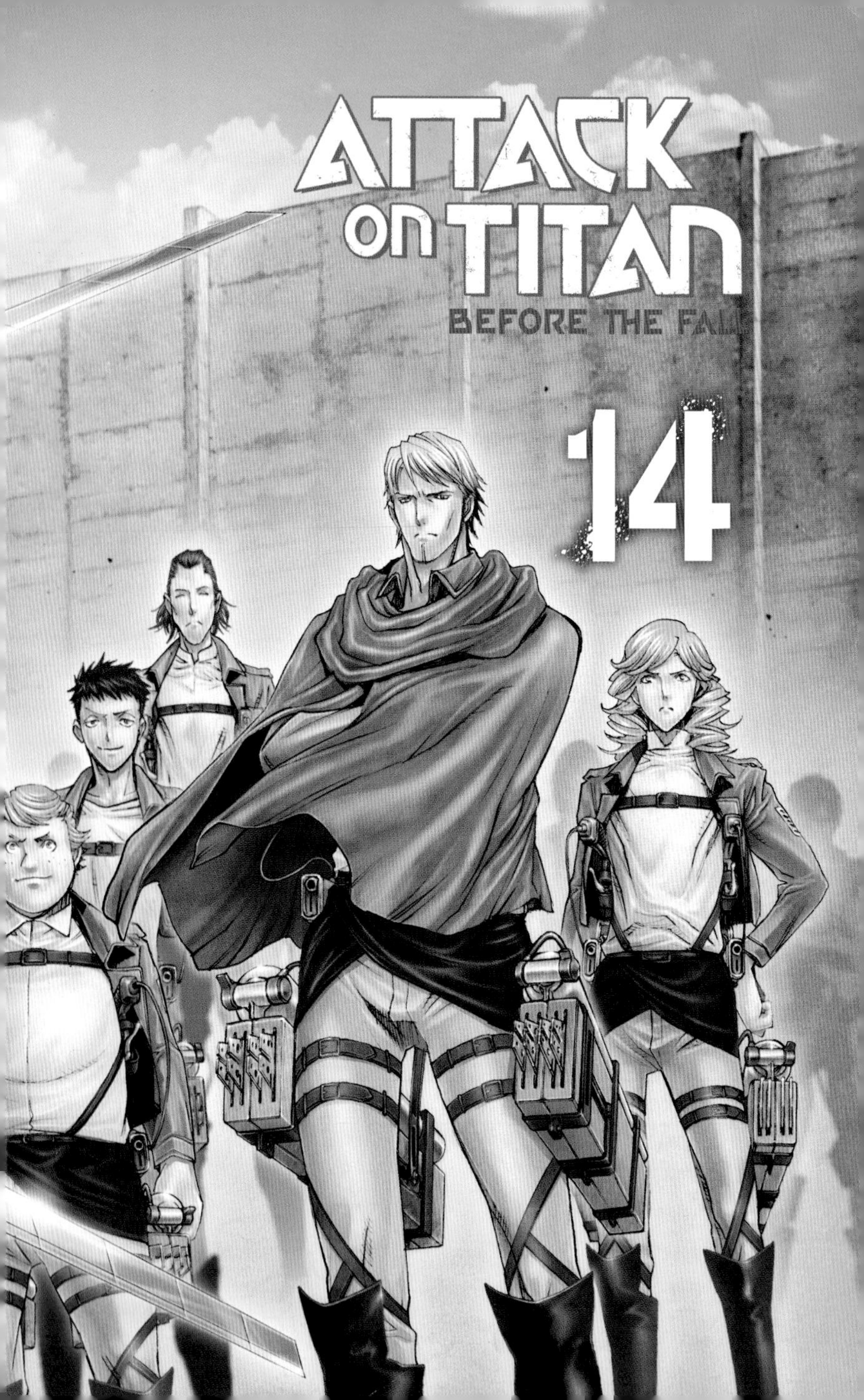
ATTACK on TITAN
BEFORE THE FALL
14

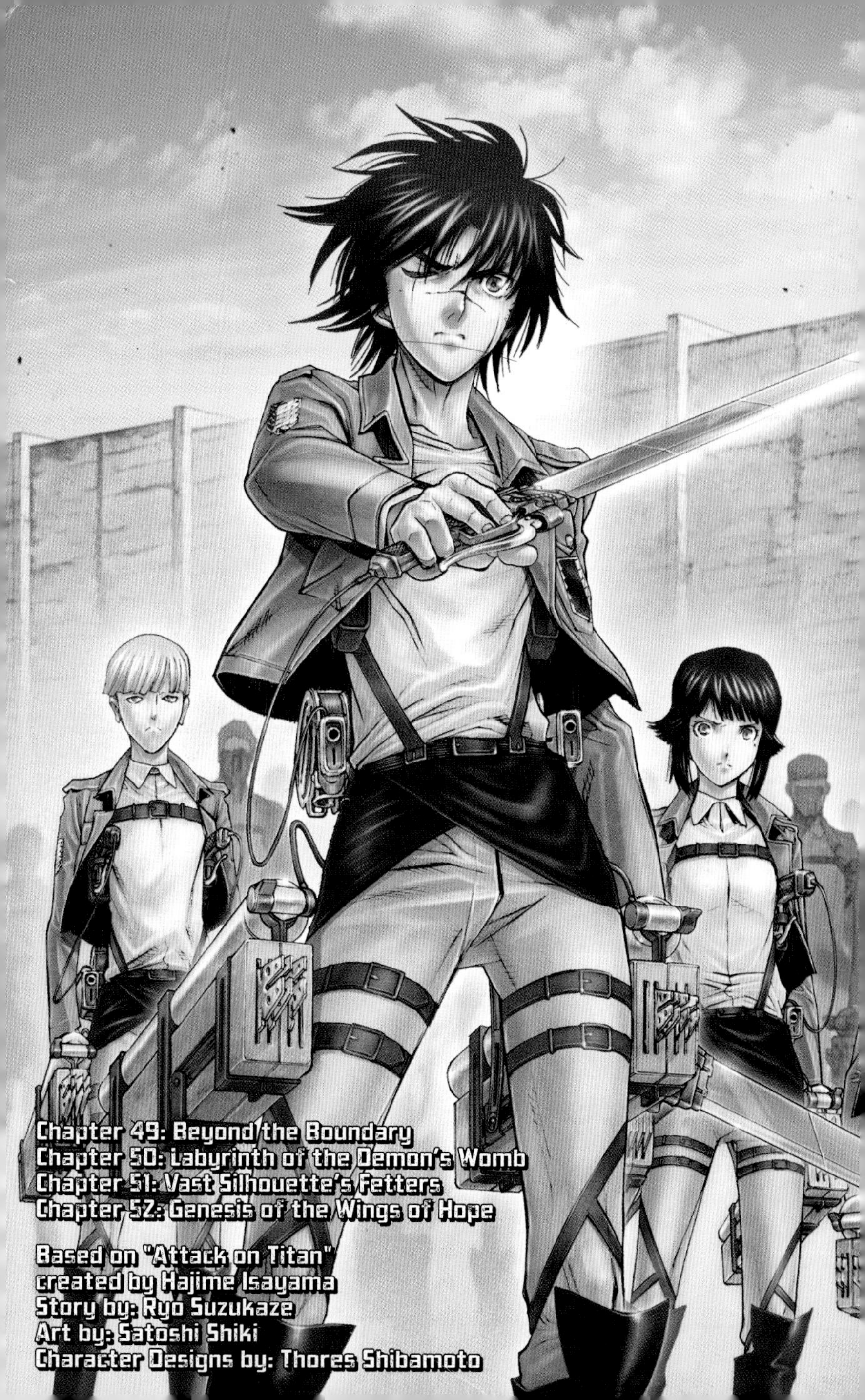

Chapter 49: Beyond the Boundary
Chapter 50: Labyrinth of the Demon's Womb
Chapter 51: Vast Silhouette's Fetters
Chapter 52: Genesis of the Wings of Hope

Based on "Attack on Titan"
created by Hajime Isayama
Story by: Ryo Suzukaze
Art by: Satoshi Shiki
Character Designs by: Thores Shibamoto

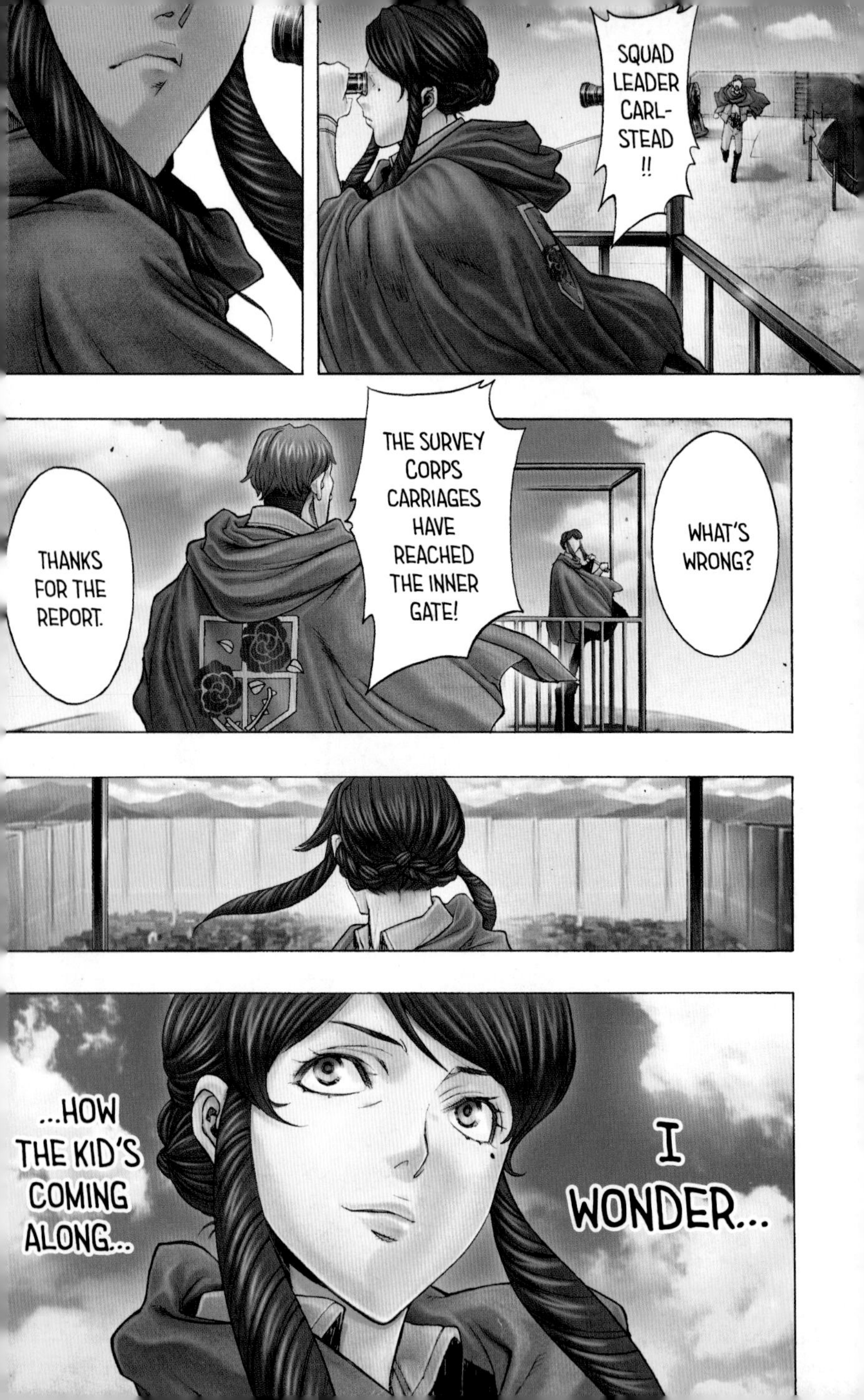
SQUAD LEADER CARL-STEAD !!
WHAT'S WRONG?
THE SURVEY CORPS CARRIAGES HAVE REACHED THE INNER GATE!
THANKS FOR THE REPORT.
I WONDER...
...HOW THE KID'S COMING ALONG...

Before the fall Character Profiles

Kuklo

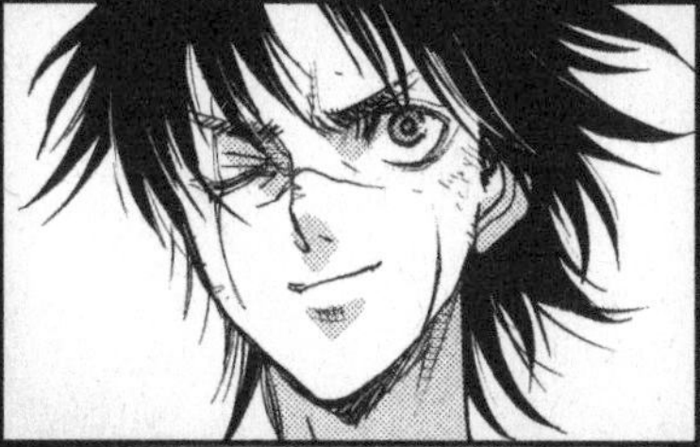

A 15-year-old boy born from a dead body packed into the vomit of a Titan, which earned him the moniker, "Titan's Son." He is fascinated with the Device as a means to defeat the Titans. Xavi defeated him in battle and left him for dead, until Rosa's group found and rescued him.

Sharle Inocencio

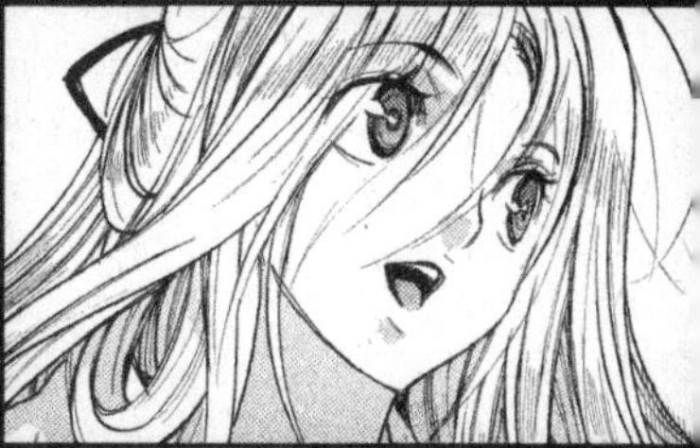

First daughter of the Inocencios, a rich merchant family within Wall Sheena. When she realized that Kuklo was a human, she taught him to speak and learn. She escaped her family home and went into the underground ward in search of Angel, inventor of the Device.

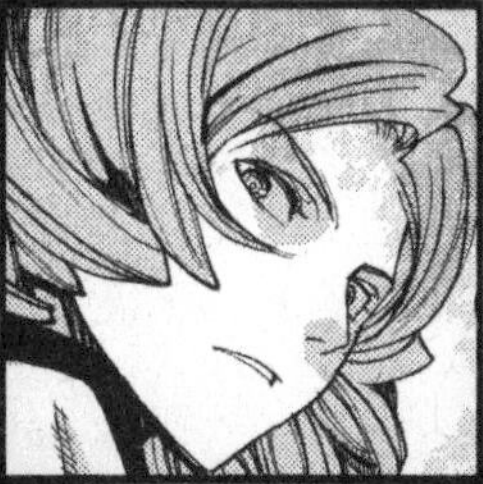

Cardina Baumeister

Kuklo's first friend in the outside world, and his companion in developing the Device.

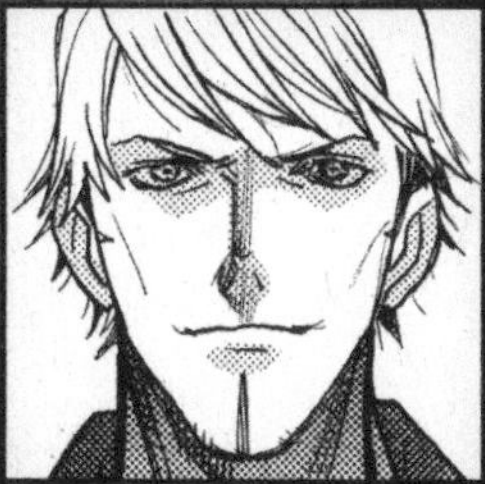

Carlo Pikale

Jorge's son and current captain of the Survey Corps. After they battled Titans together, he has great respect for Kuklo.

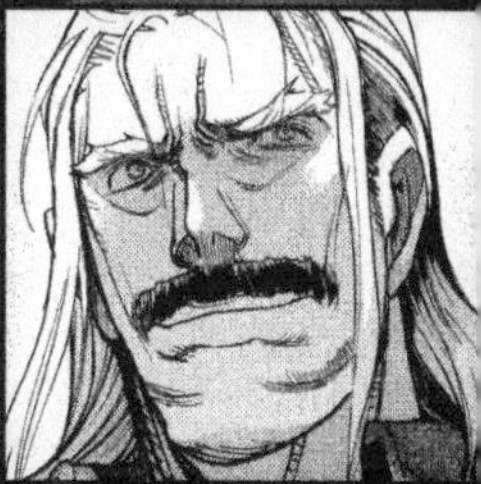

Jorge Pikale

Training Corps instructor. A former Survey Corps captain who was hailed as a hero for defeating a Titan.

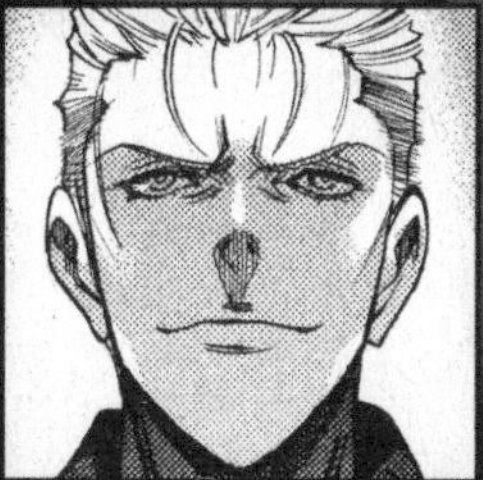

Xavi Inocencio

Head of the Inocencio family and Sharle's brother. Member of the Military Police in Shiganshina District.

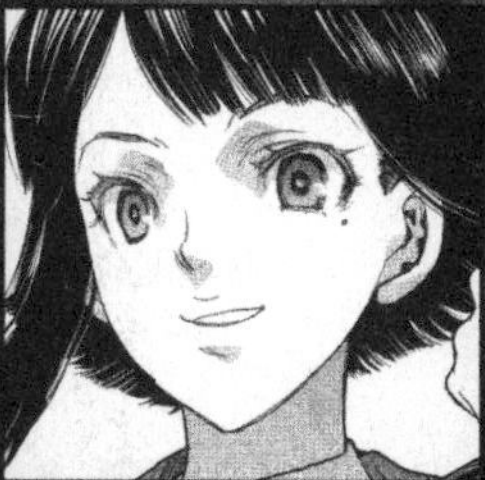

Rosa Carlstead

The daughter of Maria and Sorum, Angel's longtime friends. She's in training now, hoping to enter the Survey Corps.

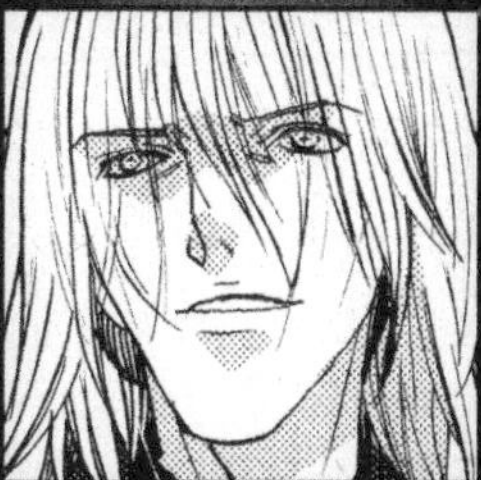

Angel Aaltonen

A former inventor who developed a tool to fight the Titans 15 years ago, known simply as "The Device."

The Story So Far

When a Titan terrorized Shiganshina District and left behind a pile of vomit, a baby boy was miraculously born of a pregnant corpse. This boy was named Kuklo, the "Son of a Titan," and treated as a sideshow anomaly. Eventually the wealthy merchant Dario Inocencio bought Kuklo. Dario's daughter Sharle learned that Kuklo was human and not the son of a Titan, and decided to teach him the words and knowledge of humanity. Two years later, Kuklo escaped from the mansion along with Sharle, who was being forced into a marriage she did not desire.

In Shiganshina District, the Survey Corps was preparing for its first expedition outside of the Wall in 15 years. Kuklo snuck into the expedition's cargo wagon, but the Titan they ran across was far worse of a monster than he expected. He helped the Survey Corps survive, but inside the Walls he was greeted by the Military Police, who wanted the "Titan's Son" on charges of murdering Dario. In prison, he met Cardina, a young man jailed over political squabbles. They hoped to escape to safety when exiled beyond the Wall, but found themselves surrounded by a pack of Titans. It was through the help of Jorge, former Survey Corps Captain and first human to defeat a Titan, that the two boys escaped with their lives. The equipment that Jorge used was the very "Device" that was the key to defeating the Titan those 15 years ago. Kuklo and Cardina escaped the notice of the MPs by hiding in the Industrial City, where they found Sharle. It is there that the three youngsters learned the truth of the ill-fated Titan-capturing expedition 15 years earlier, and swore to uphold the will of Angel, the inventor of the Device.

Next, Kuklo and Cardina headed back to Shiganshina to test out a new model of the Device developed by Xenophon, Angel's friend and rival, but while they were gone, a rebellion by anti-establishment dissidents broke out in the Industrial City. Kuklo was able to slip through the chaos to rescue Sharle from the dissidents, but then Sharle's brother Xavi arrived, now a member of the Military Police, and turned his sword on Kuklo. Xavi won the battle by inflicting a grievous blow on Kuklo, who fell into the river. Ultimately, Kuklo survived his ordeal thanks to the help of Rosa, the daughter of Sorum, who lost his life in the fateful expedition 15 years earlier.

After a month and a half of recovery, Kuklo accepted Jorge's offer of an assistant instructor position with the Survey Corps. Sharle escaped Xavi's grasp and visited Angel, inventor of the Device, who unveiled the finished version, the Vertical Maneuvering Equipment. But not all of their news was good: the Survey Corps would have to run an expedition in just two months' time, and bring back proof that the Vertical Maneuvering Equipment vanquished a Titan, or the Corps would be disbanded. Captain Carlo was forced to speed up his schedule and choose trainees of high aptitude to use the equipment. In order to give Rosa and the other potential Survey Corps members a certain kind of "baptism," he took them to Shiganshina Ward.

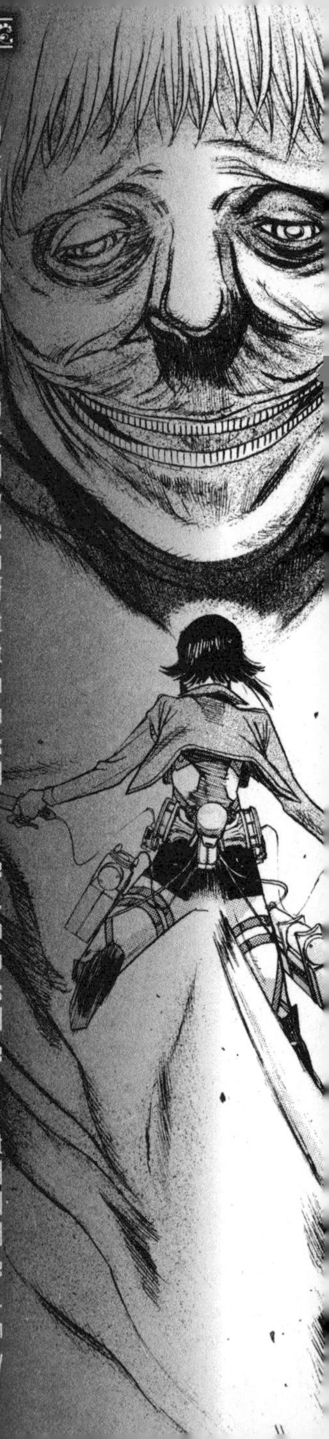

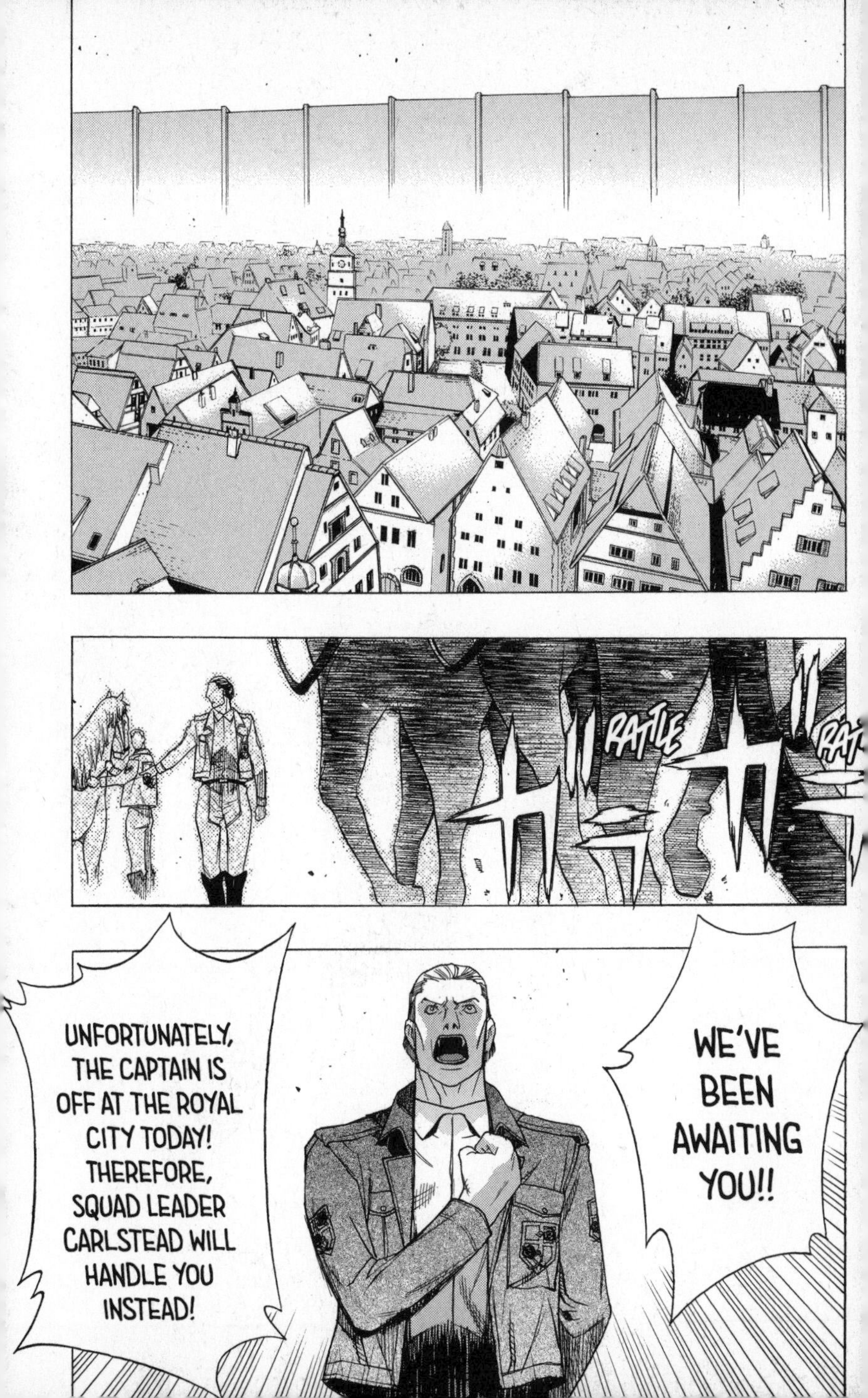
RATTLE
WE'VE BEEN AWAITING YOU!!
UNFORTUNATELY, THE CAPTAIN IS OFF AT THE ROYAL CITY TODAY! THEREFORE, SQUAD LEADER CARLSTEAD WILL HANDLE YOU INSTEAD!

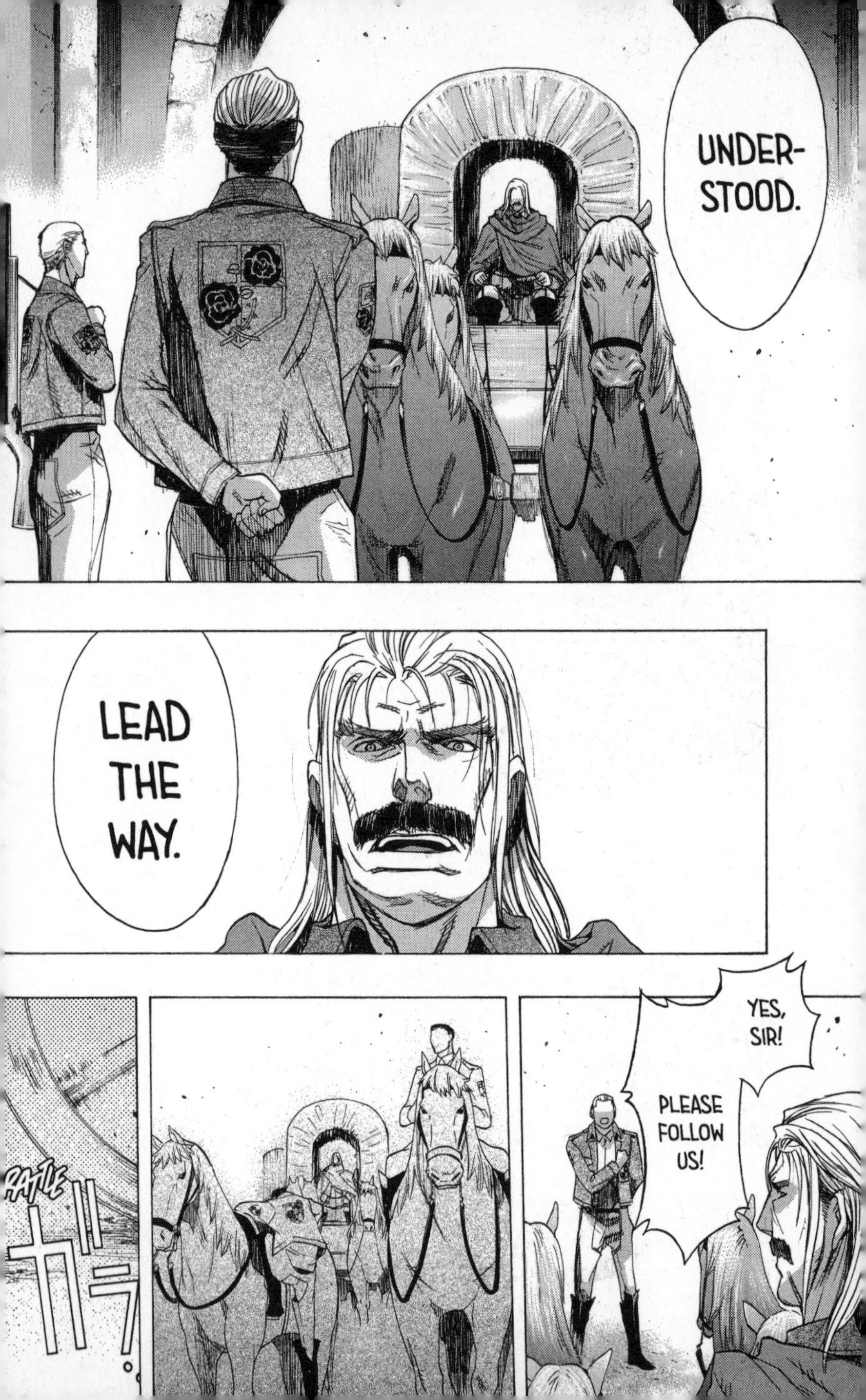
UNDER-
STOOD.
LEAD THE WAY.
YES, SIR!
PLEASE FOLLOW US!
RATTLE

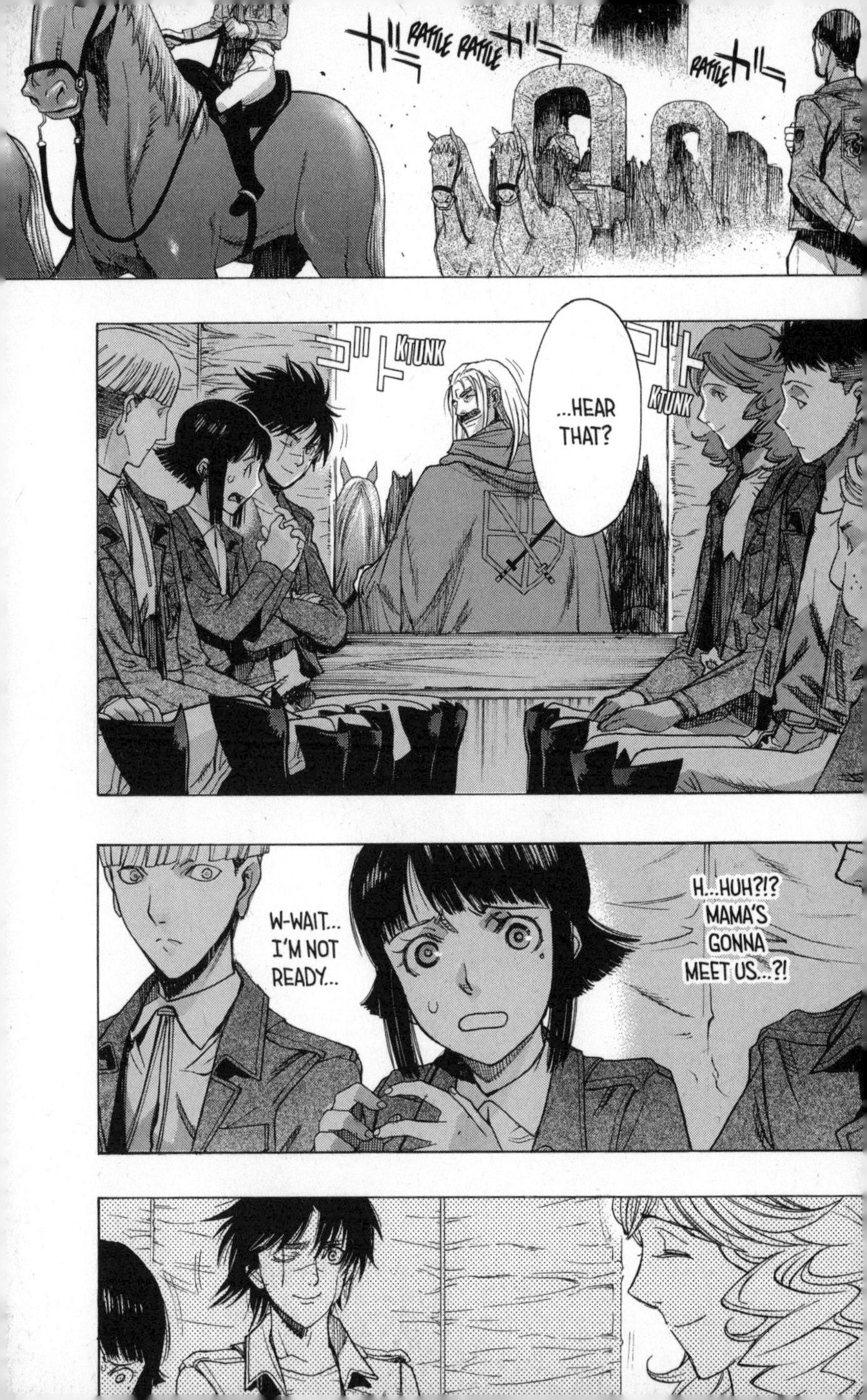
RATTLE
RATTLE RATTLE
KTUNK
...HEAR THAT?
KTUNK
H...HUH?!? MAMA'S GONNA MEET US...?!
W-WAIT... I'M NOT READY...

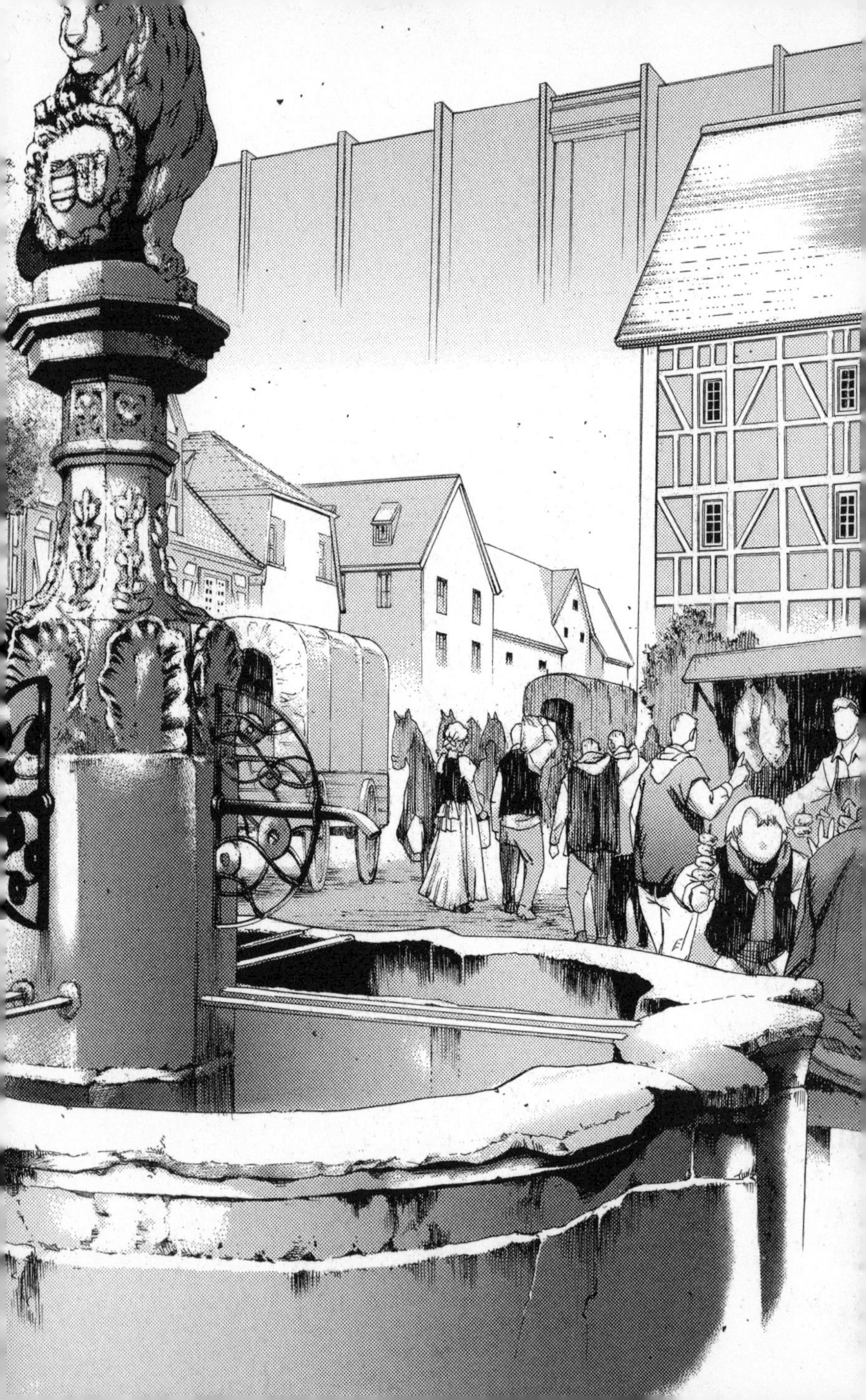

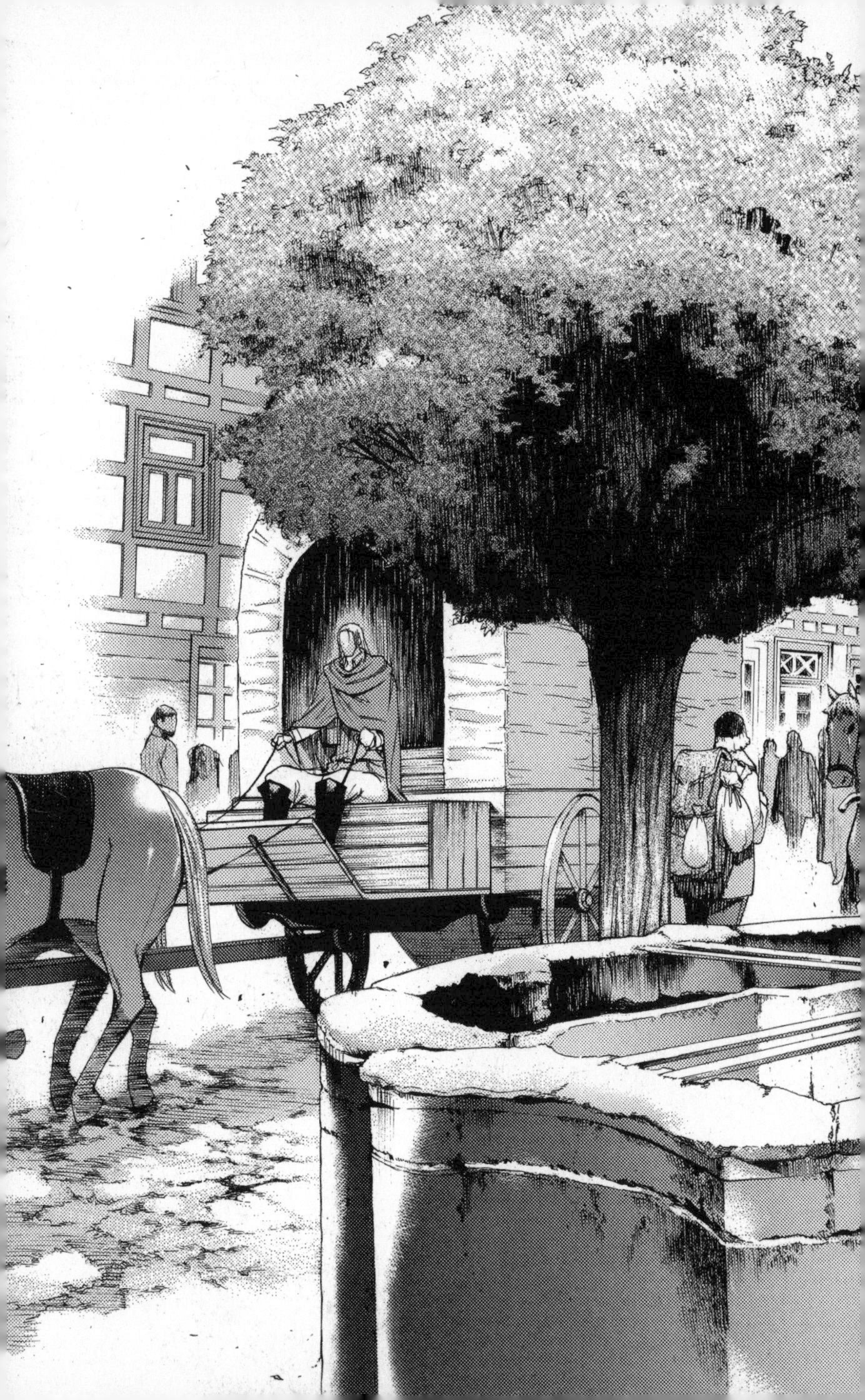

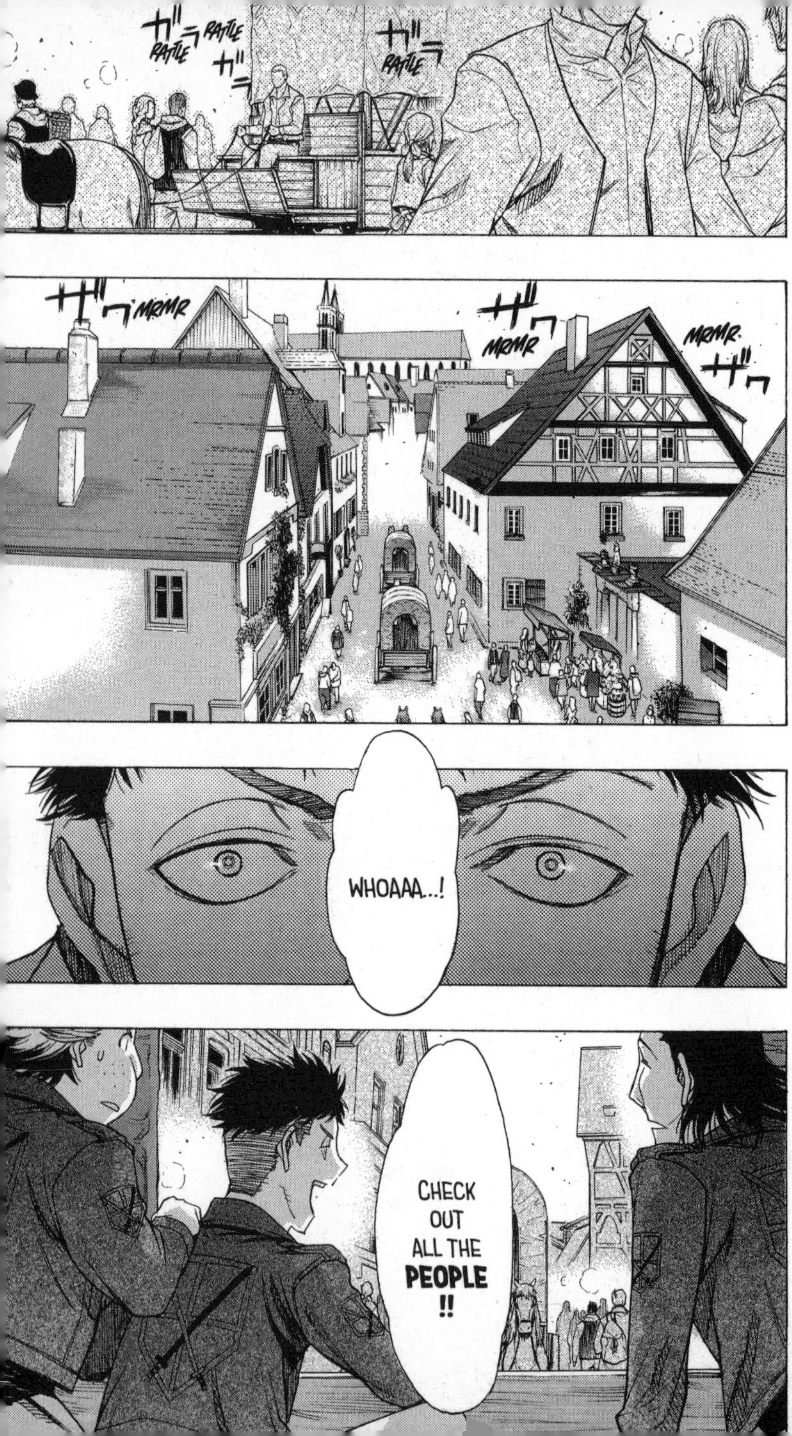
ガラ RATTLE
RATTLE
ガラ
ガラ RATTLE
ザワ MRMR
ザワ MRMR
MRMR. ザワ
WHOAAA...!
CHECK OUT ALL THE **PEOPLE** !!

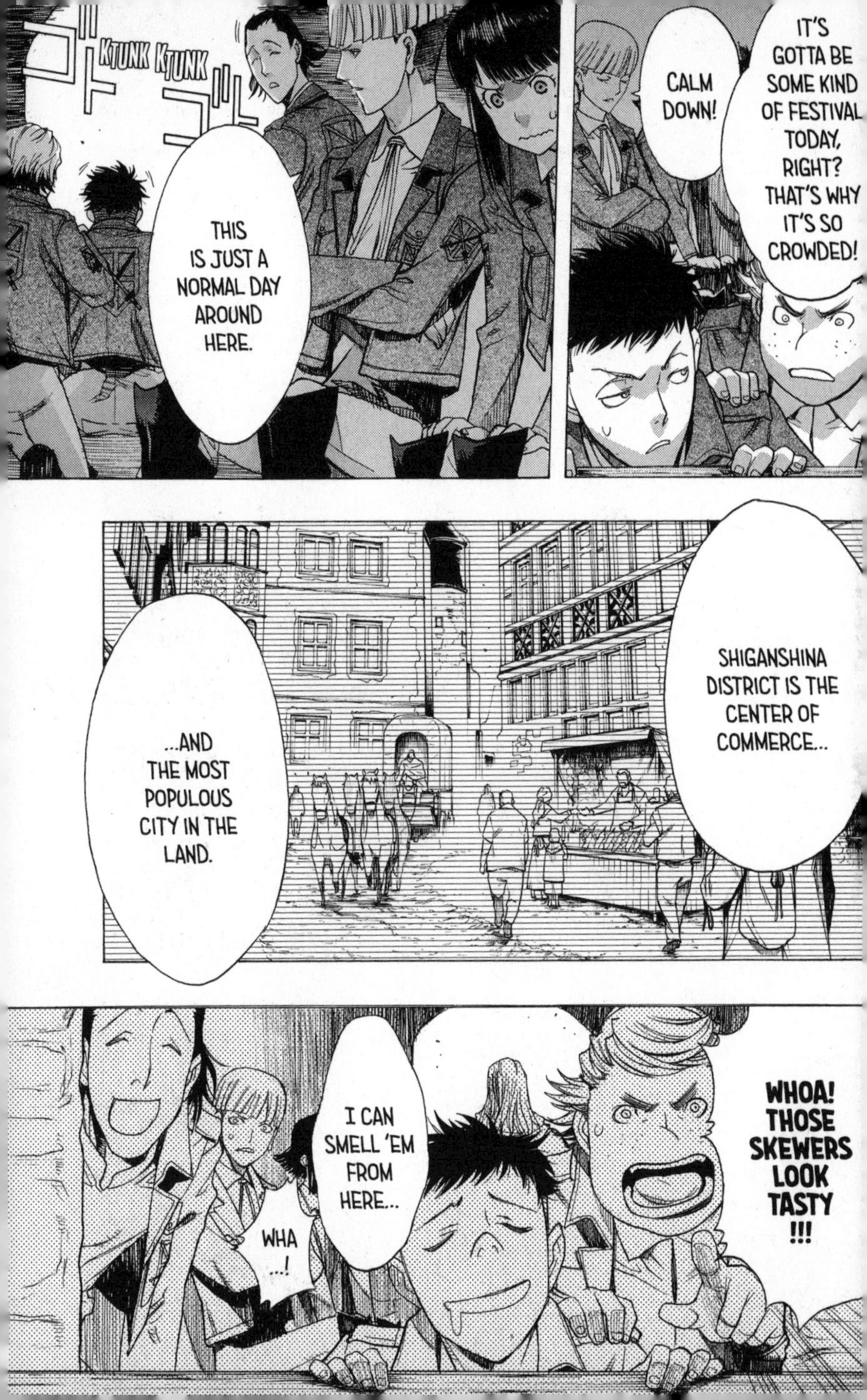
IT'S GOTTA BE SOME KIND OF FESTIVAL TODAY, RIGHT? THAT'S WHY IT'S SO CROWDED!
CALM DOWN!
KTUNK KTUNK
THIS IS JUST A NORMAL DAY AROUND HERE.
SHIGANSHINA DISTRICT IS THE CENTER OF COMMERCE...
...AND THE MOST POPULOUS CITY IN THE LAND.
WHOA! THOSE SKEWERS LOOK TASTY !!!
I CAN SMELL 'EM FROM HERE...
WHA ...!

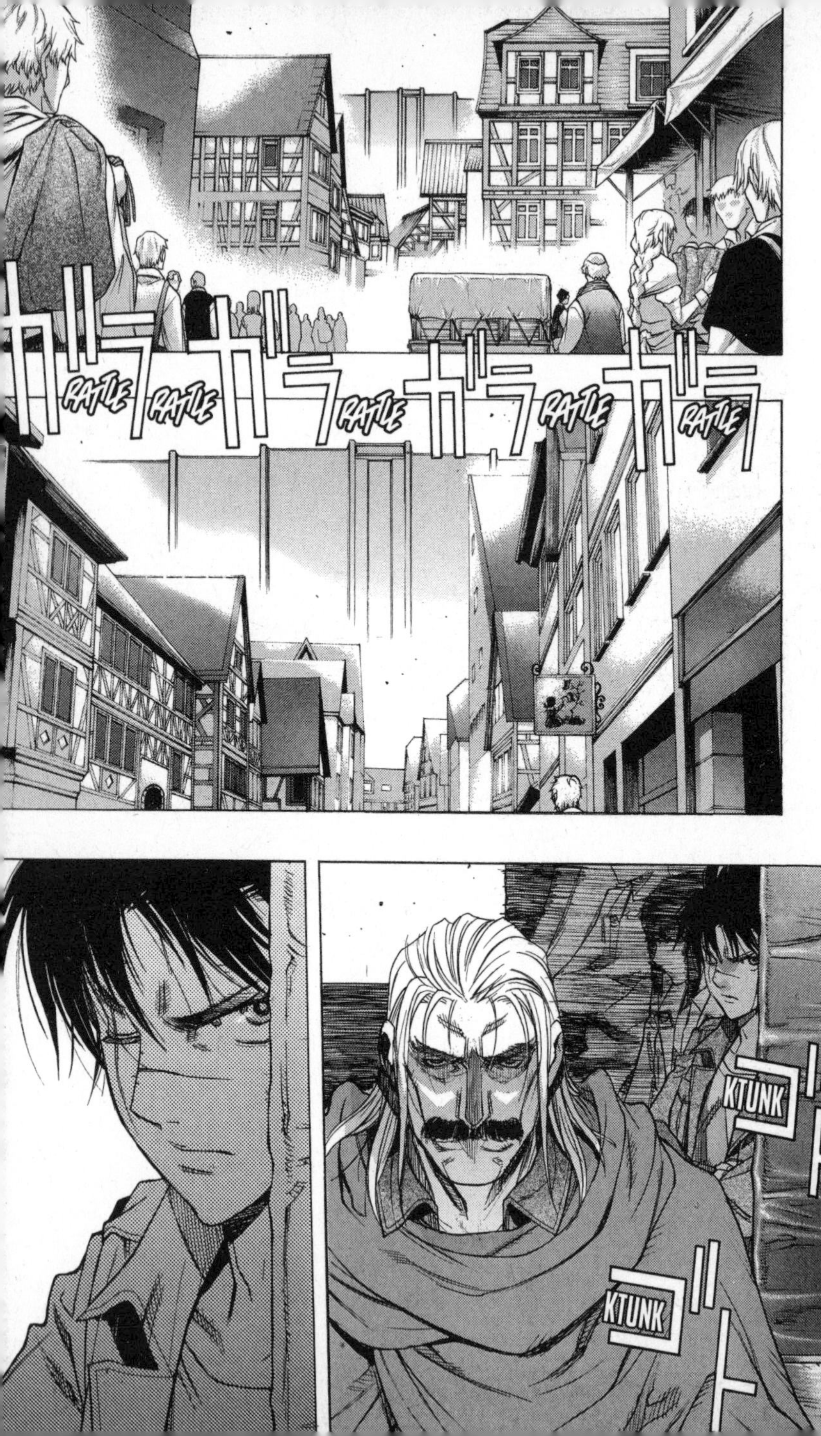

ガラ
RATTLE
ガラ
RATTLE
ガラ
RATTLE
ガラ
RATTLE
カラ
RATTLE
KTUNK
ゴト
KTUNK
ゴト

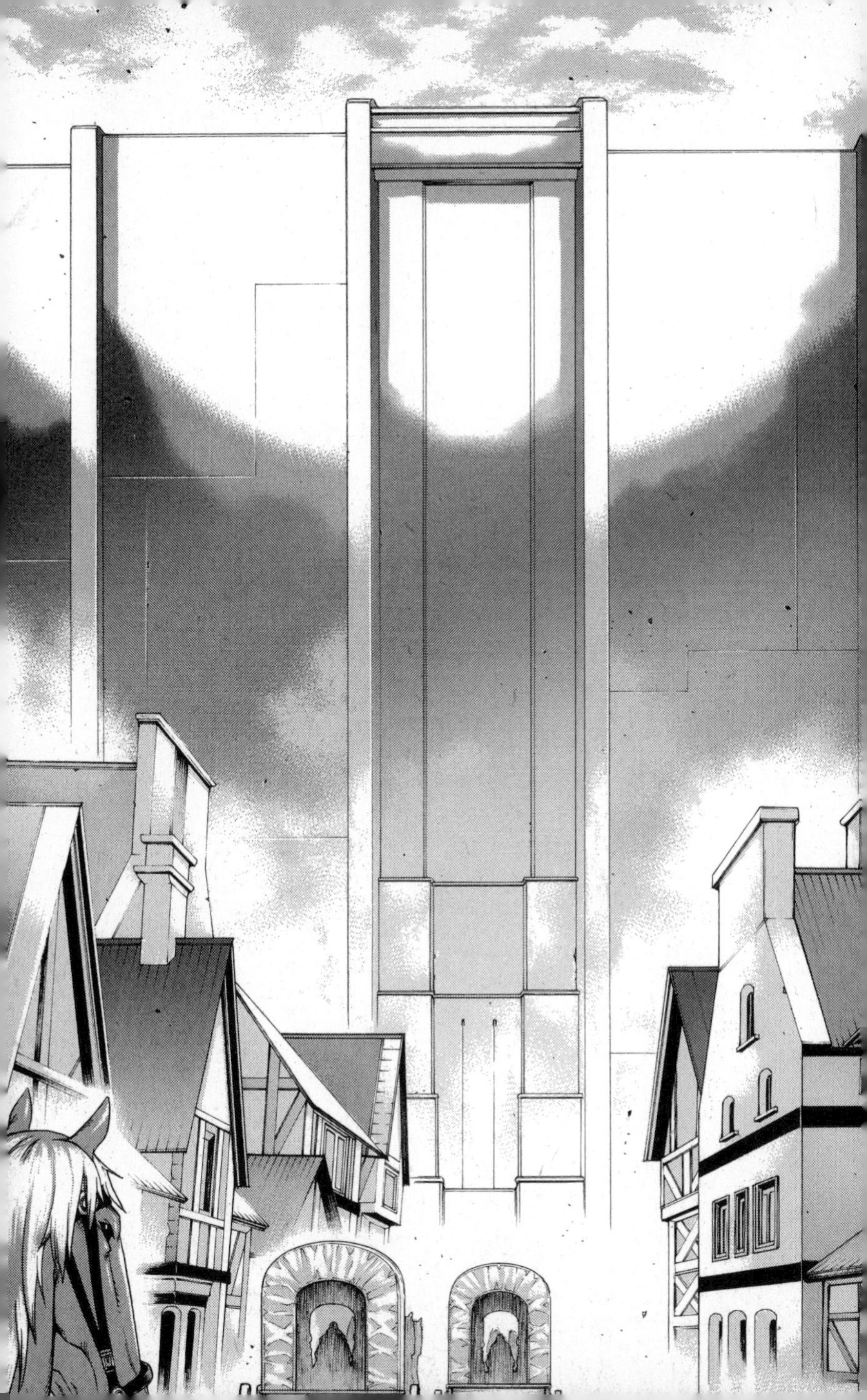

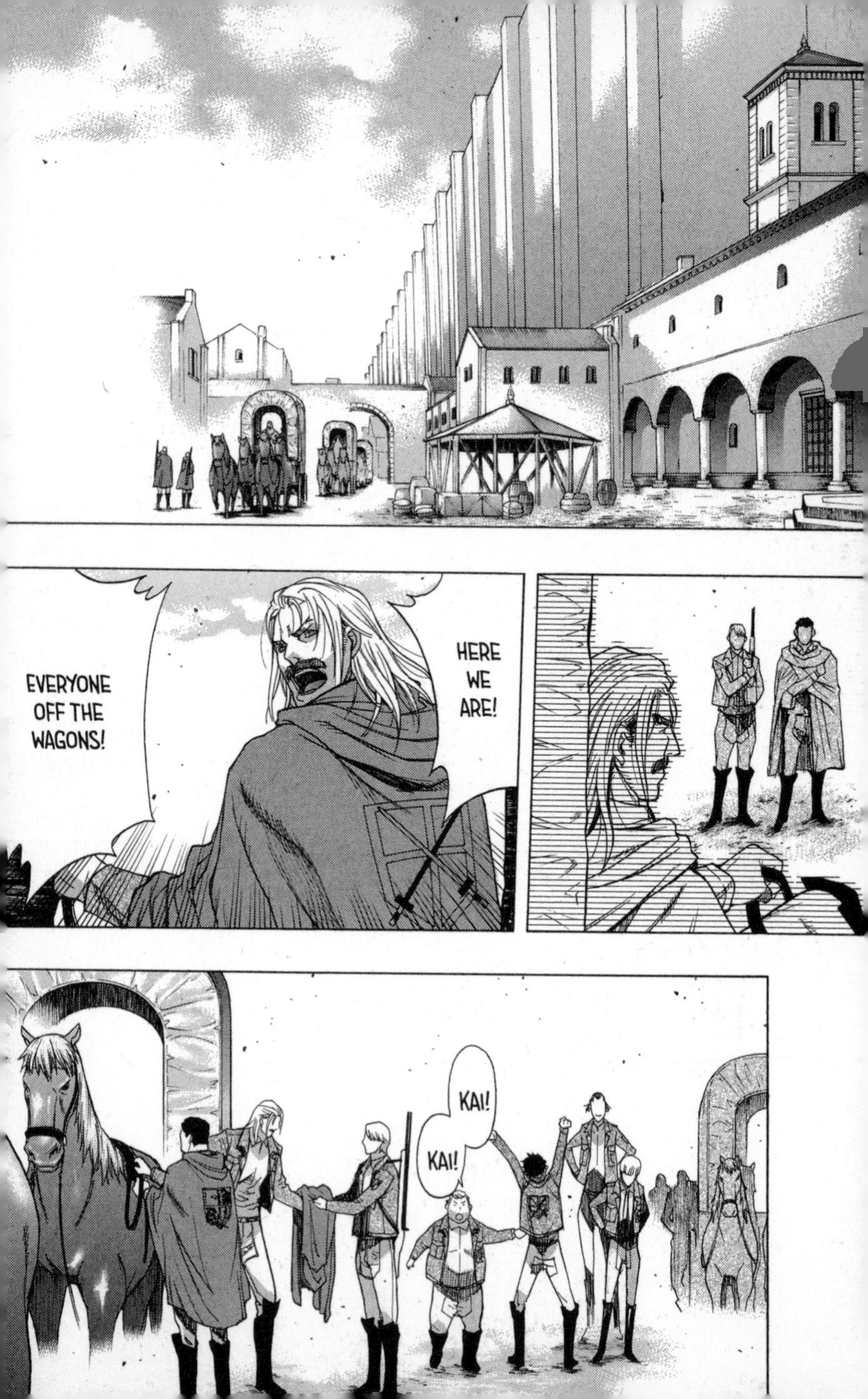
HERE WE ARE!
EVERYONE OFF THE WAGONS!
KAI!
KAI!

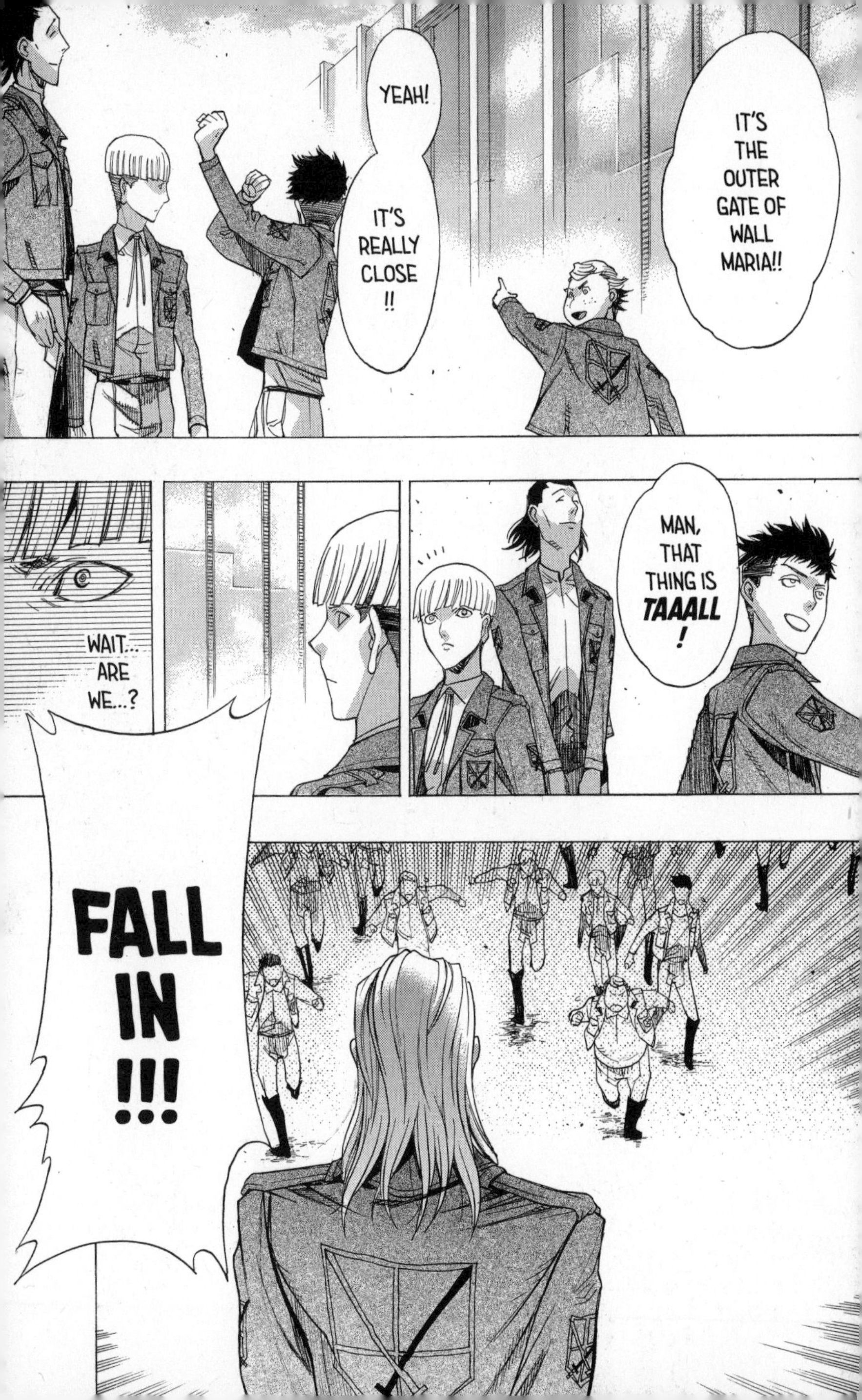
IT'S THE OUTER GATE OF WALL MARIA!!
YEAH!
IT'S REALLY CLOSE!!
MAN, THAT THING IS TAAALL!
WAIT... ARE WE...?
FALL IN!!!

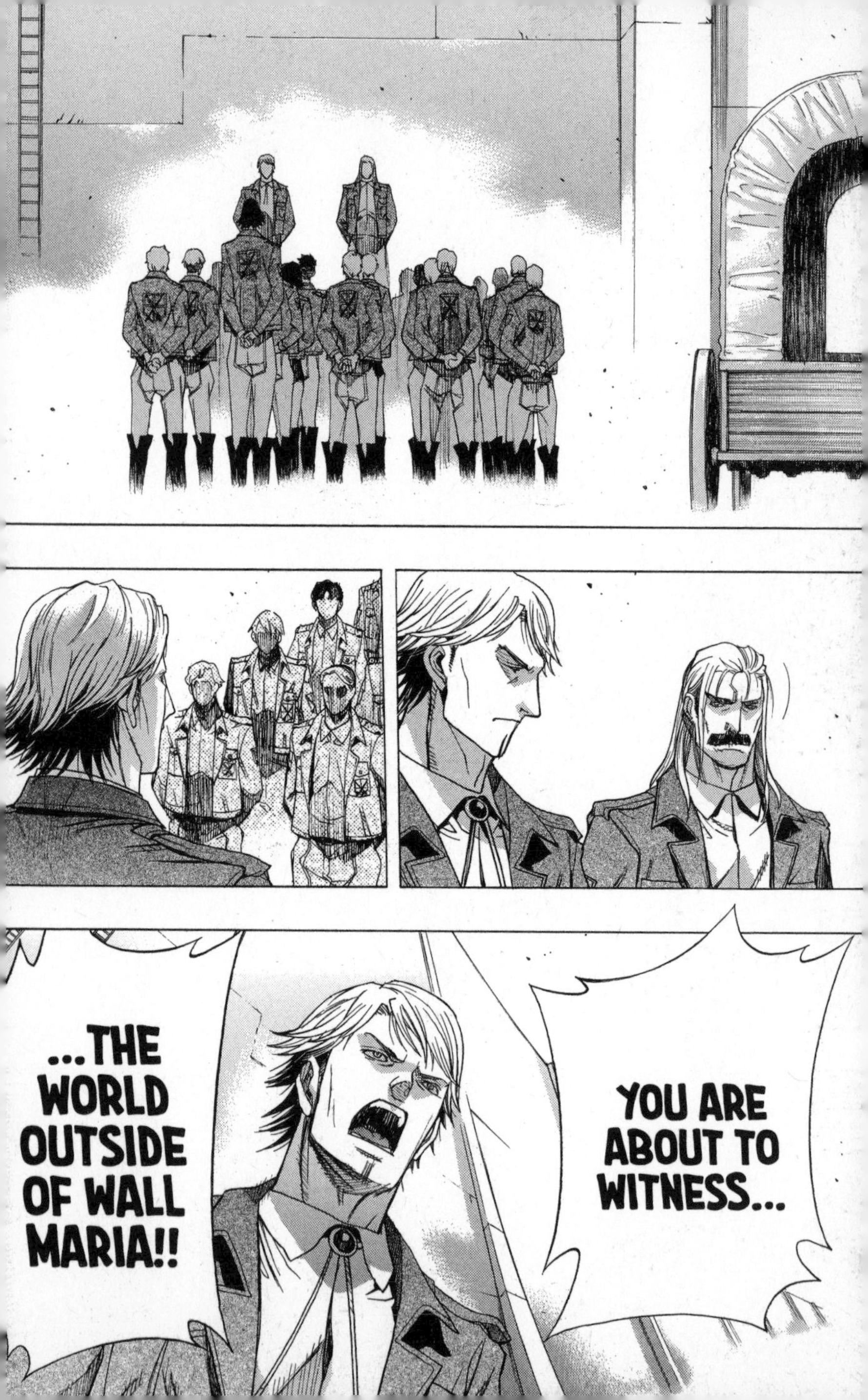
YOU ARE ABOUT TO WITNESS...
...THE WORLD OUTSIDE OF WALL MARIA!!

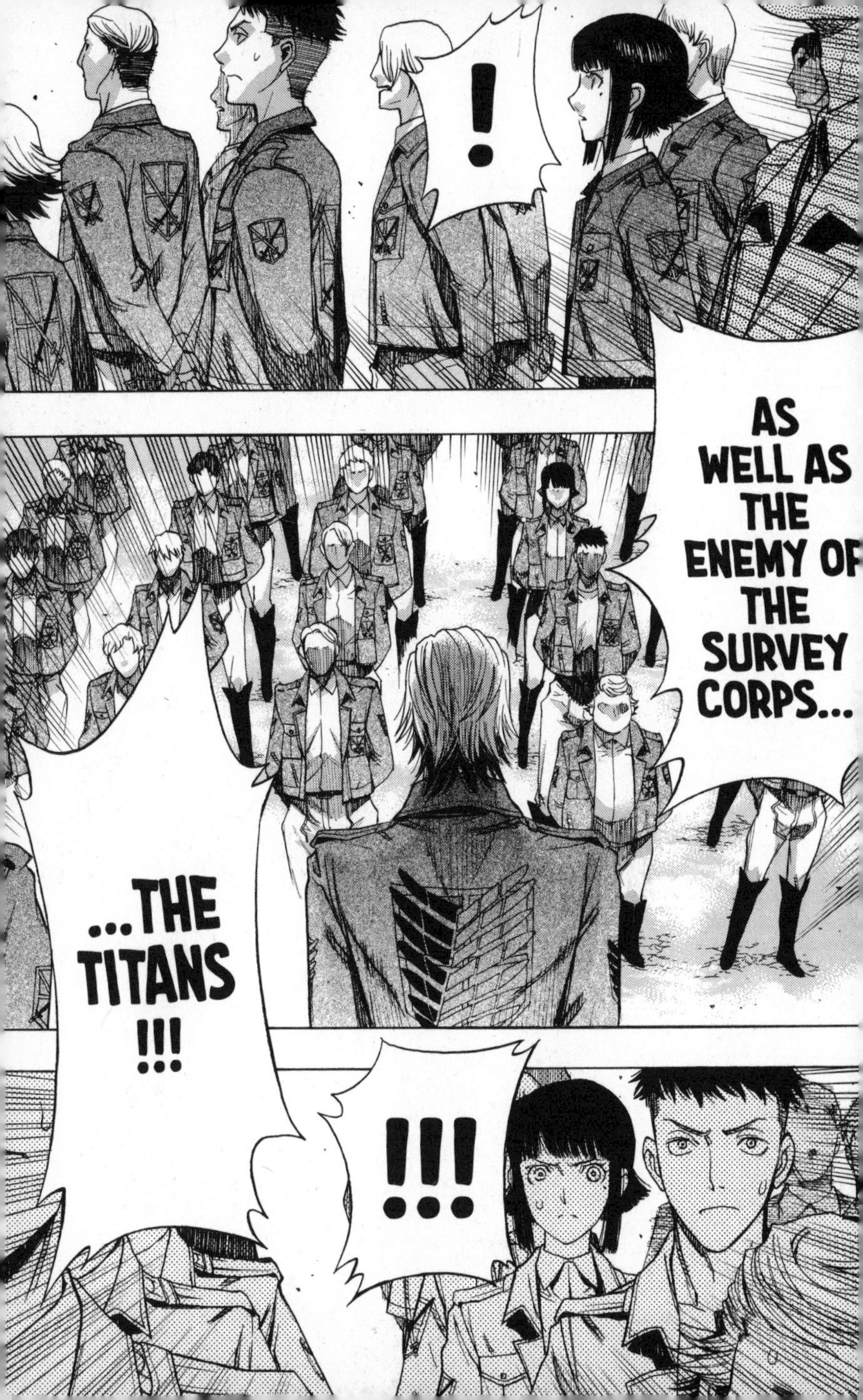
!
AS WELL AS THE ENEMY OF THE SURVEY CORPS...
...THE TITANS !!!
!!!

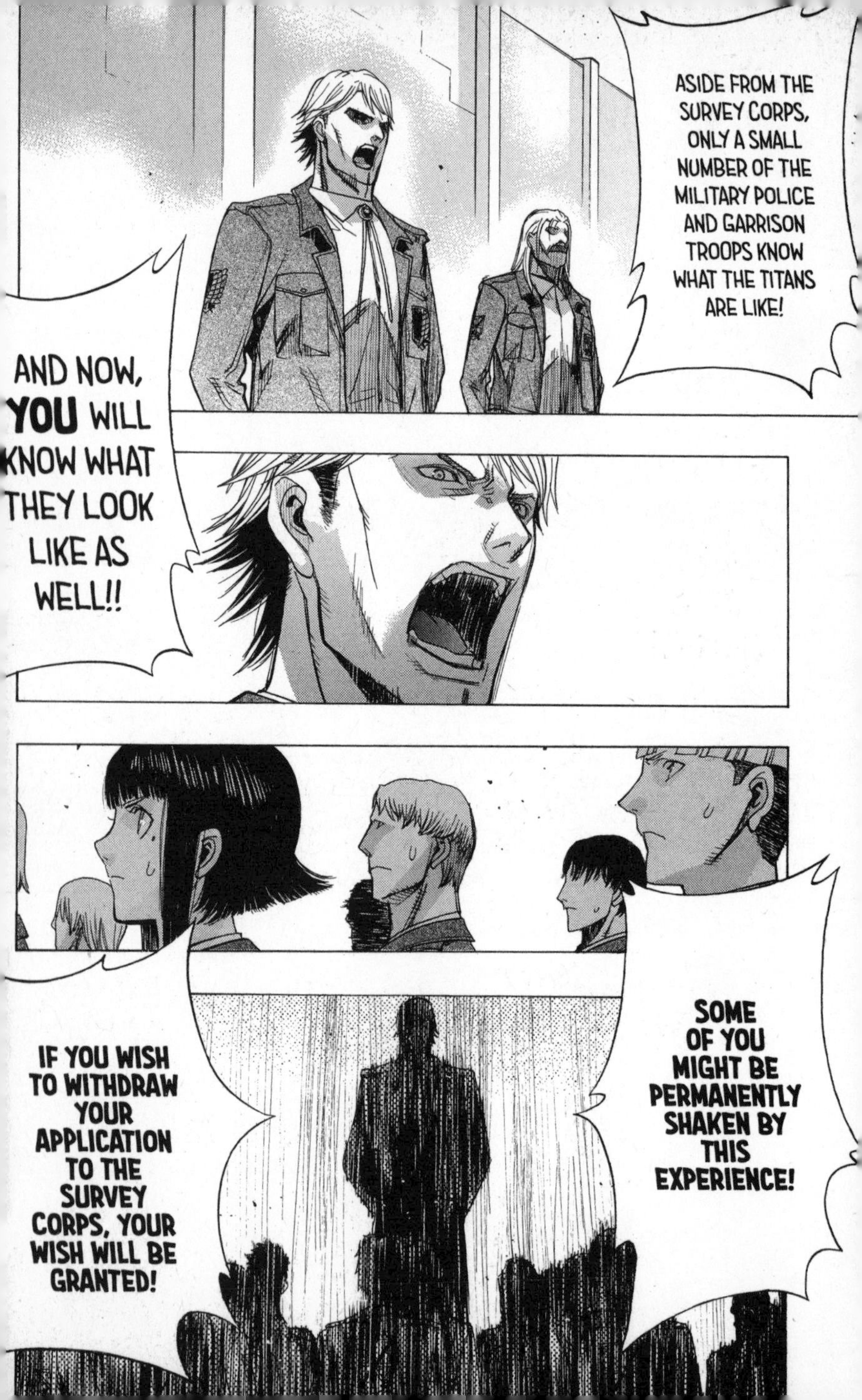
ASIDE FROM THE SURVEY CORPS, ONLY A SMALL NUMBER OF THE MILITARY POLICE AND GARRISON TROOPS KNOW WHAT THE TITANS ARE LIKE!
AND NOW, **YOU** WILL KNOW WHAT THEY LOOK LIKE AS WELL!!
SOME OF YOU MIGHT BE PERMANENTLY SHAKEN BY THIS EXPERIENCE!
IF YOU WISH TO WITHDRAW YOUR APPLICATION TO THE SURVEY CORPS, YOUR WISH WILL BE GRANTED!

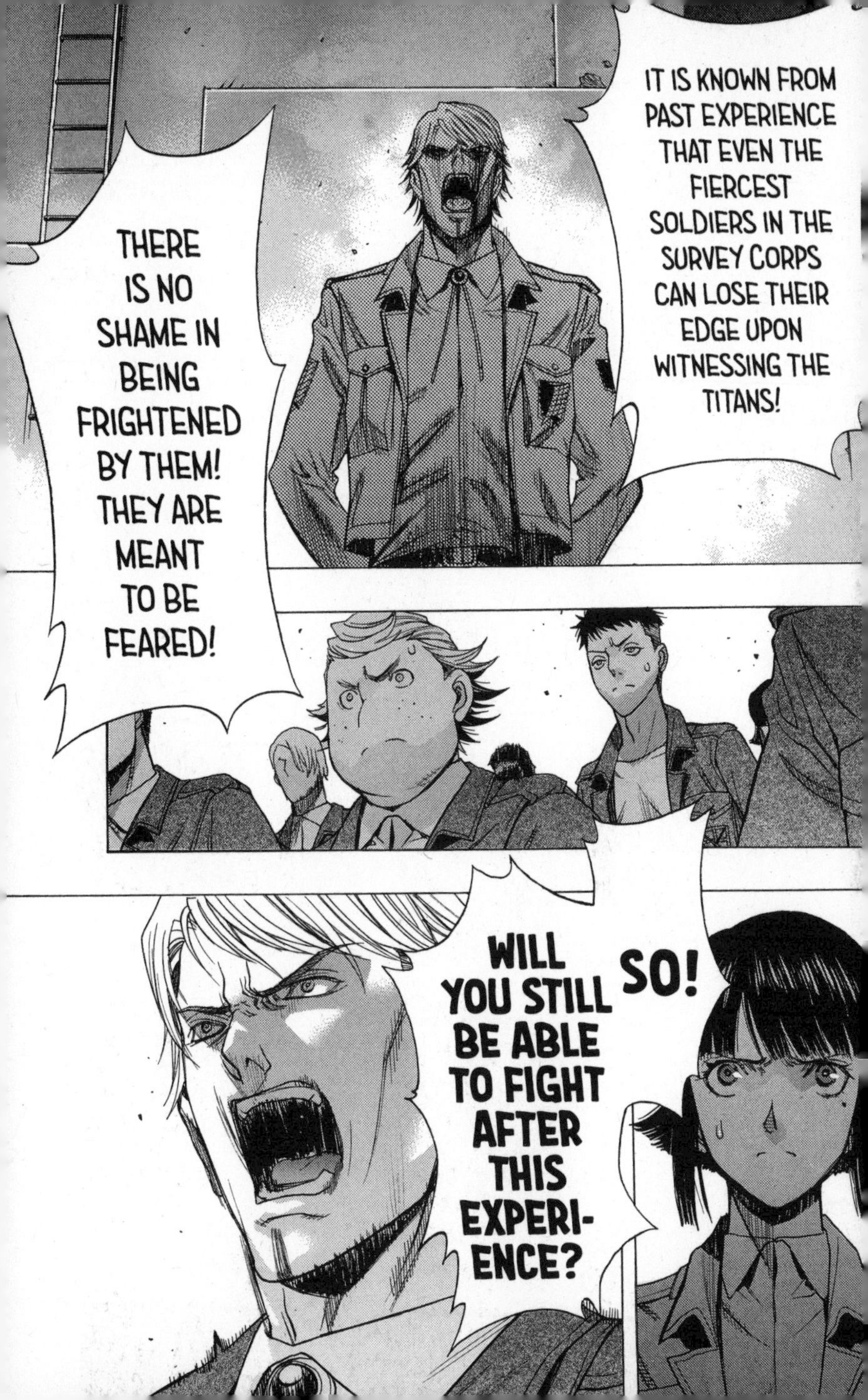
IT IS KNOWN FROM PAST EXPERIENCE THAT EVEN THE FIERCEST SOLDIERS IN THE SURVEY CORPS CAN LOSE THEIR EDGE UPON WITNESSING THE TITANS!
THERE IS NO SHAME IN BEING FRIGHTENED BY THEM! THEY ARE MEANT TO BE FEARED!
SO!
WILL YOU STILL BE ABLE TO FIGHT AFTER THIS EXPERI-ENCE?

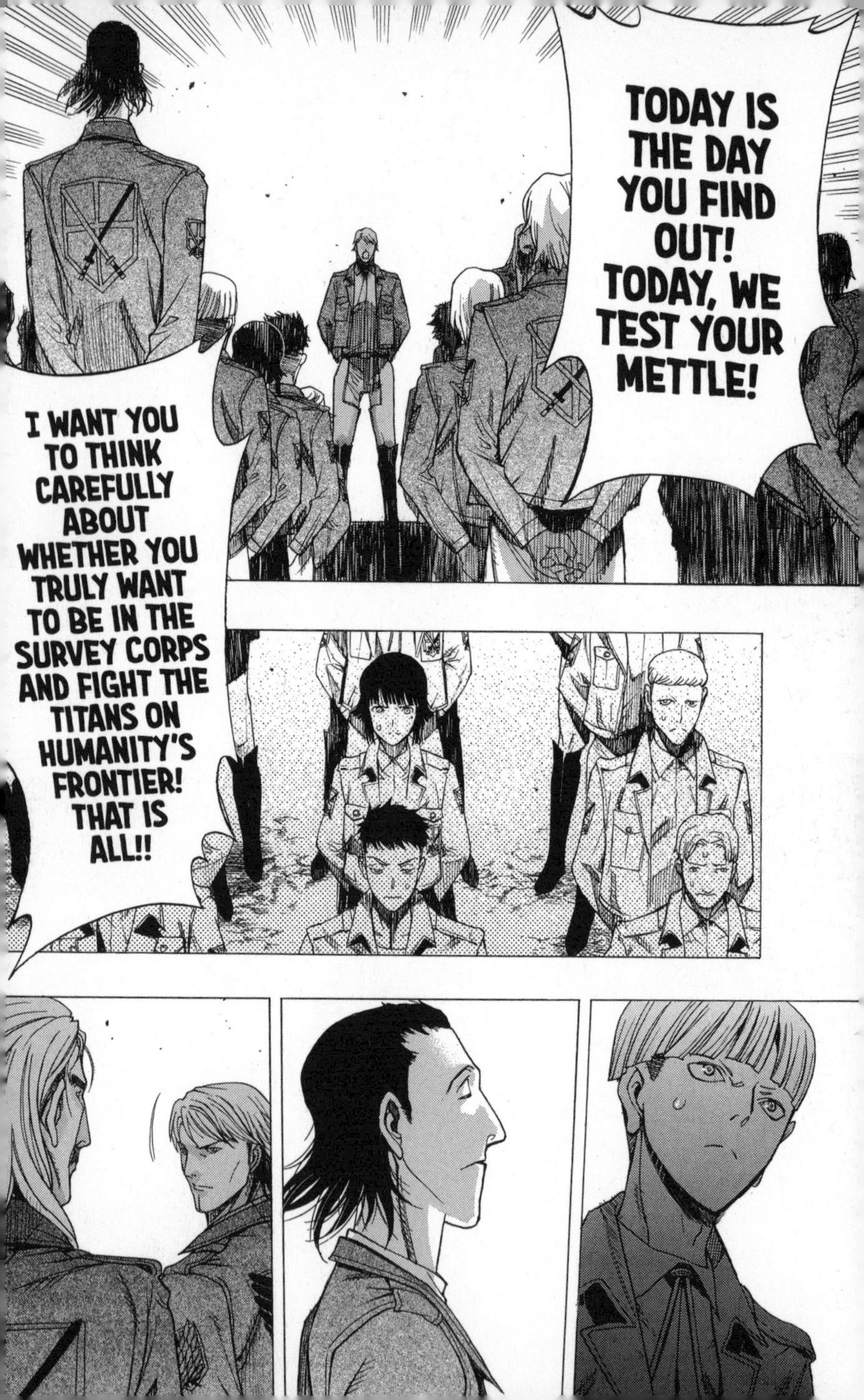
TODAY IS THE DAY YOU FIND OUT! TODAY, WE TEST YOUR METTLE!
I WANT YOU TO THINK CAREFULLY ABOUT WHETHER YOU TRULY WANT TO BE IN THE SURVEY CORPS AND FIGHT THE TITANS ON HUMANITY'S FRONTIER! THAT IS ALL!!

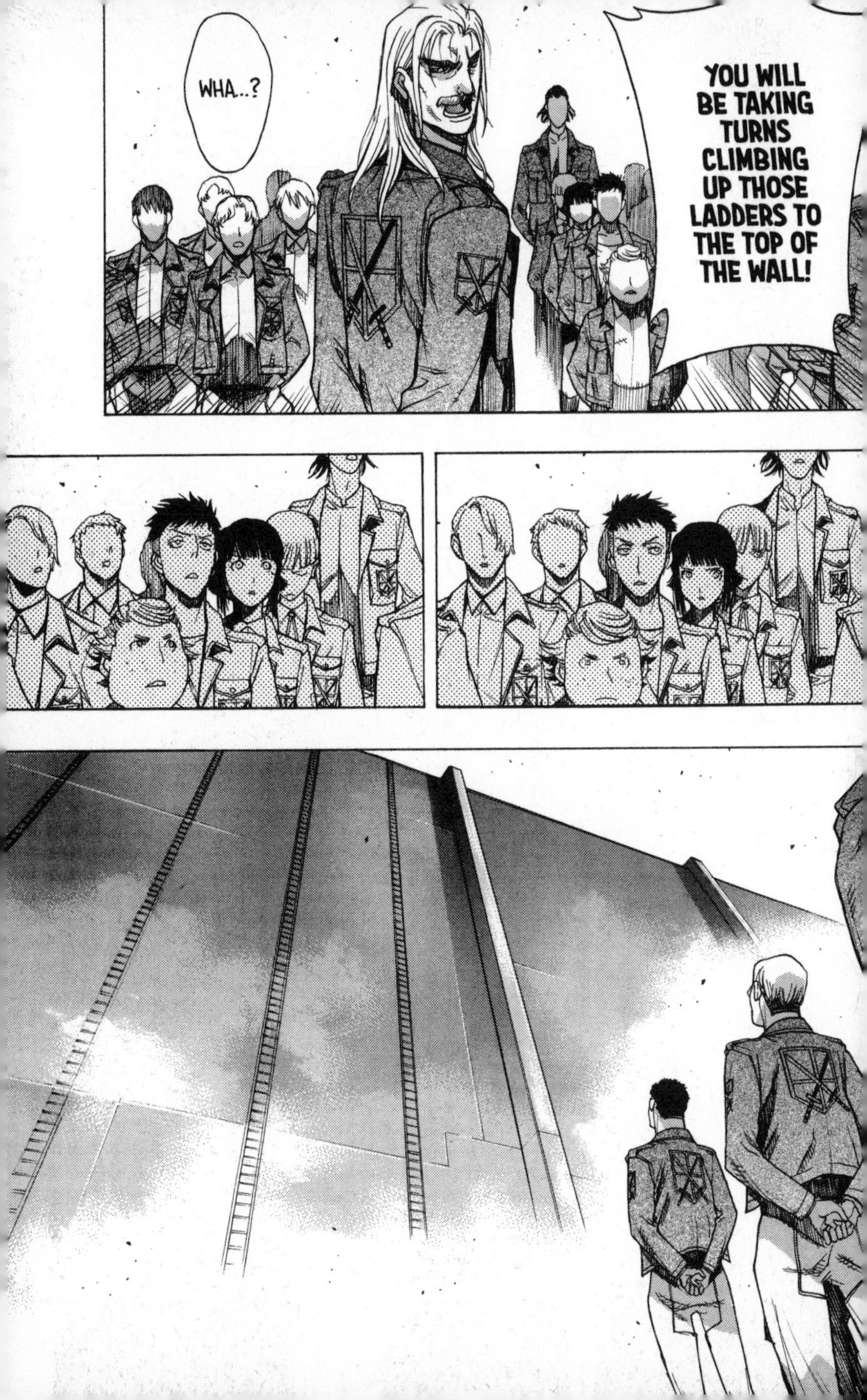
YOU WILL BE TAKING TURNS CLIMBING UP THOSE LADDERS TO THE TOP OF THE WALL!
WHA...?

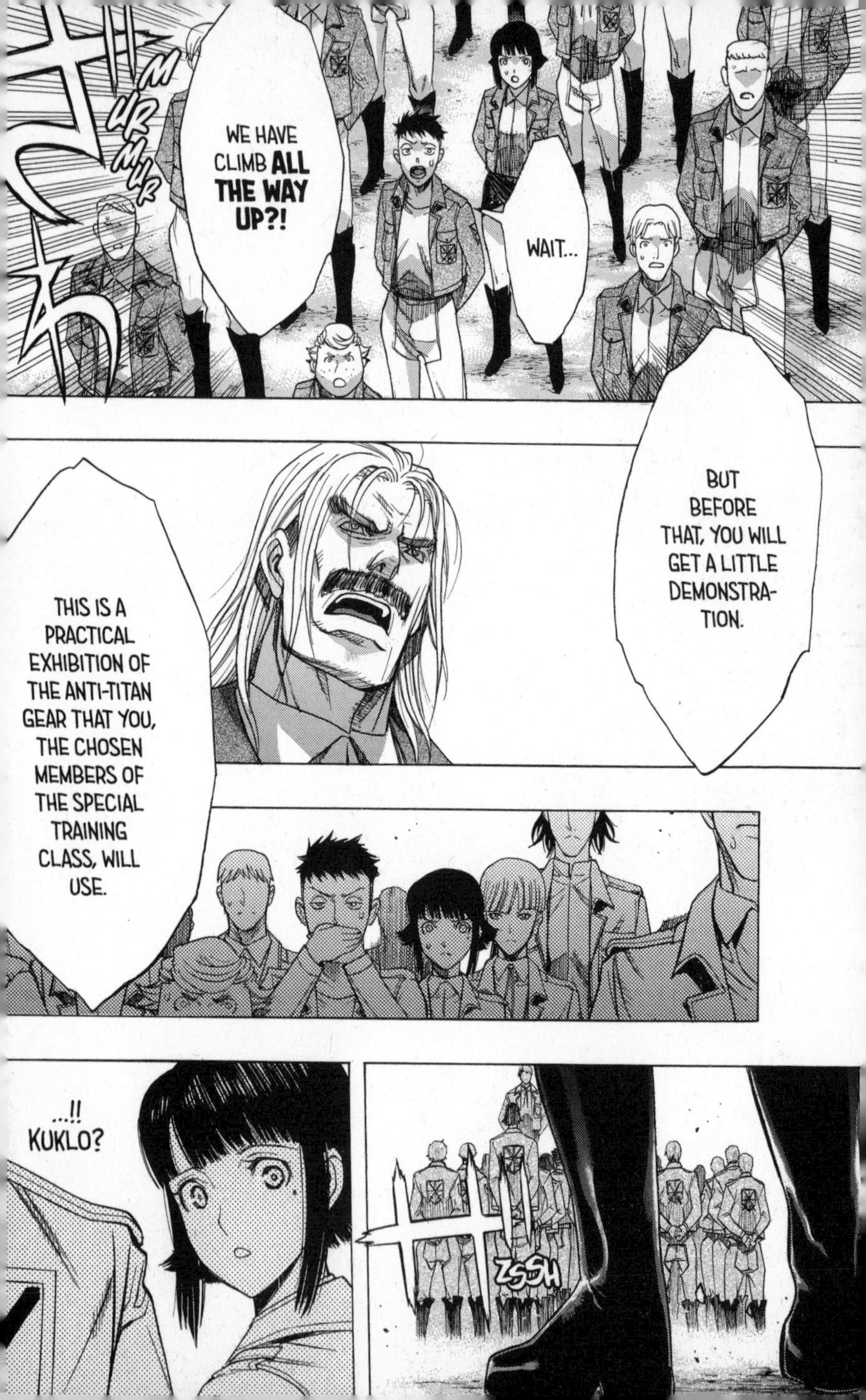

WAIT...
WE HAVE CLIMB **ALL THE WAY UP?!**
MURMUR
BUT BEFORE THAT, YOU WILL GET A LITTLE DEMONSTRA-TION.
THIS IS A PRACTICAL EXHIBITION OF THE ANTI-TITAN GEAR THAT YOU, THE CHOSEN MEMBERS OF THE SPECIAL TRAINING CLASS, WILL USE.
ZSSH
...!! KUKLO?

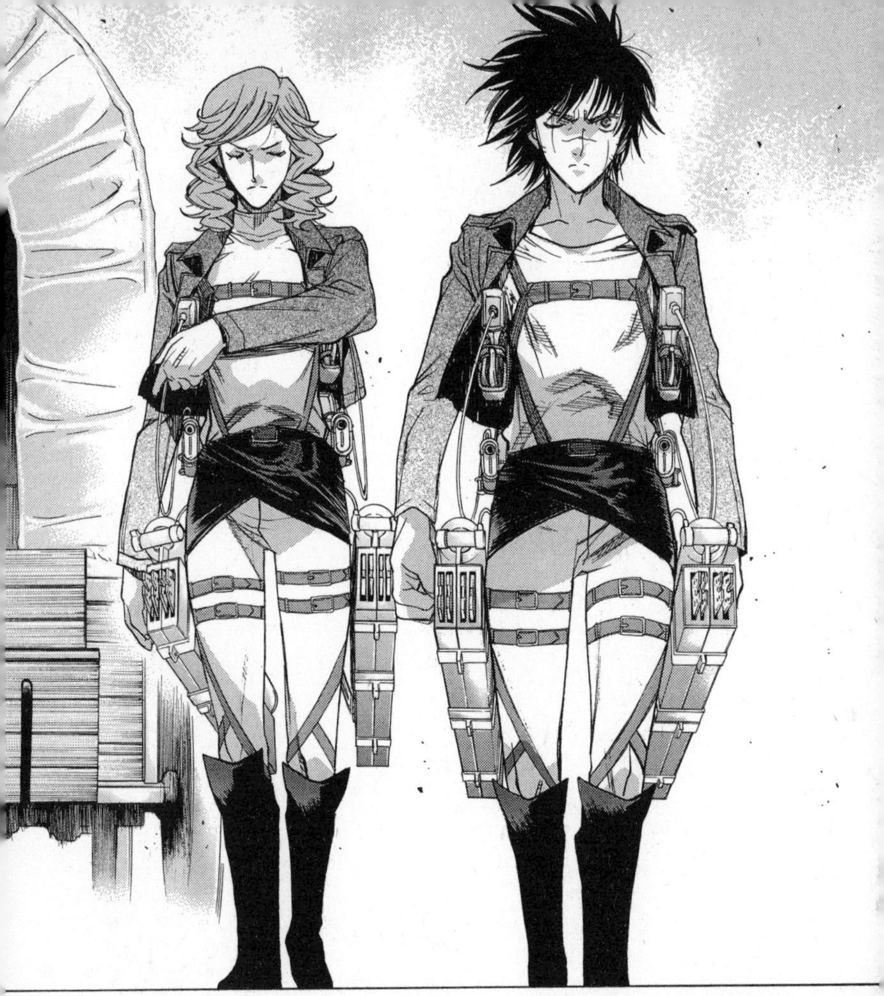
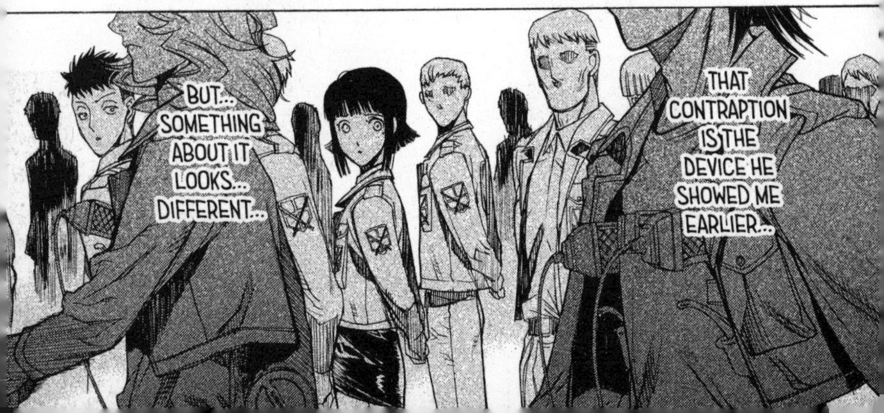
THAT CONTRAPTION IS THE DEVICE HE SHOWED ME EARLIER...
BUT... SOMETHING ABOUT IT LOOKS... DIFFERENT...

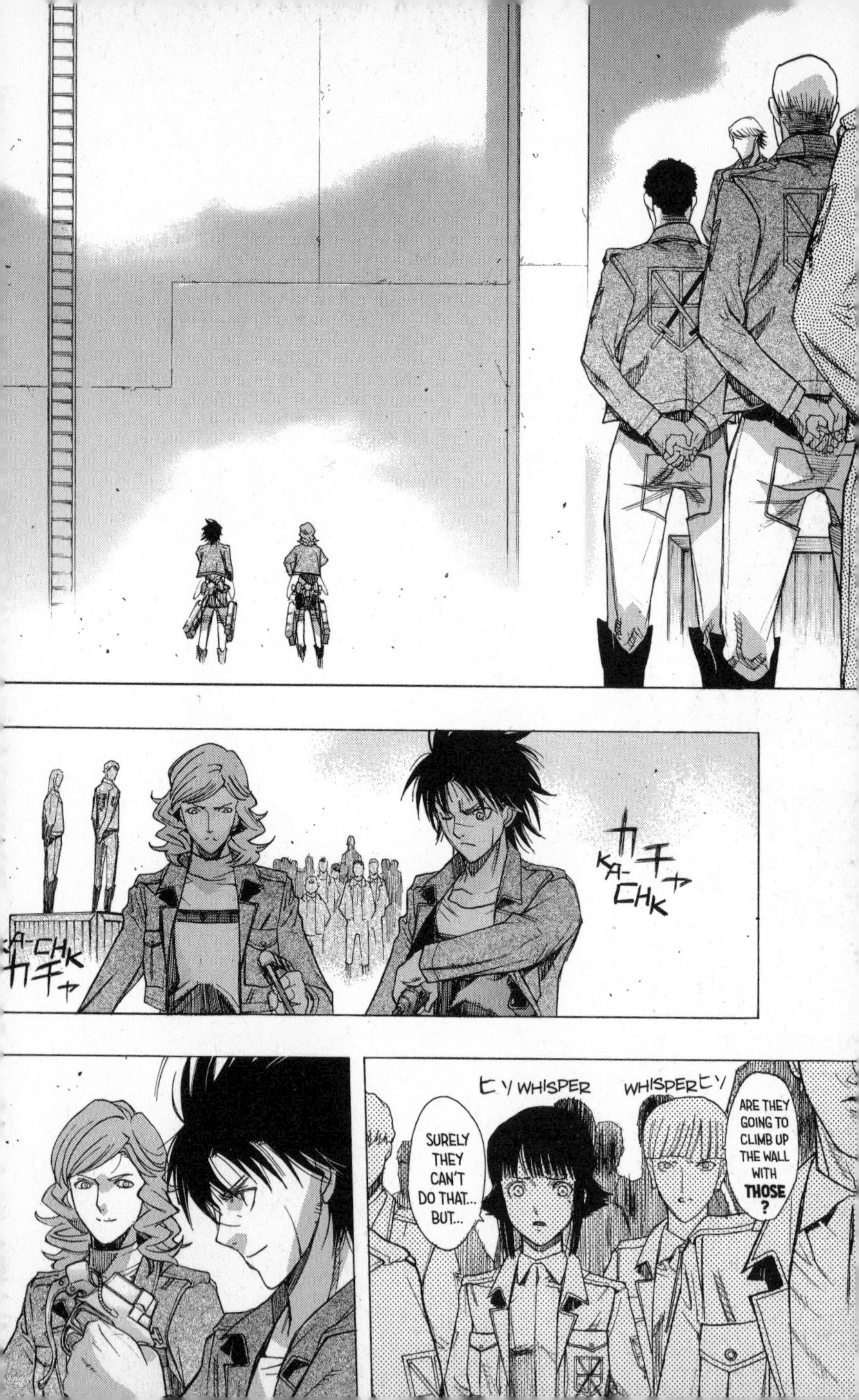
カチャ
KA-CHK
KA-CHK
カチャ
WHISPER ヒソ
ヒソ WHISPER
ARE THEY GOING TO CLIMB UP THE WALL WITH **THOSE**?
SURELY THEY CAN'T DO THAT... BUT...

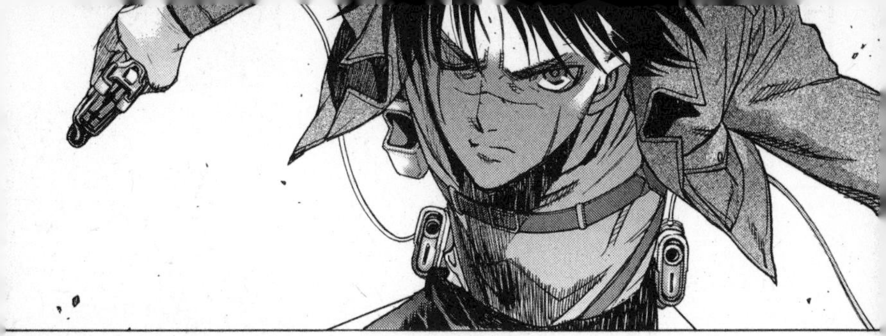
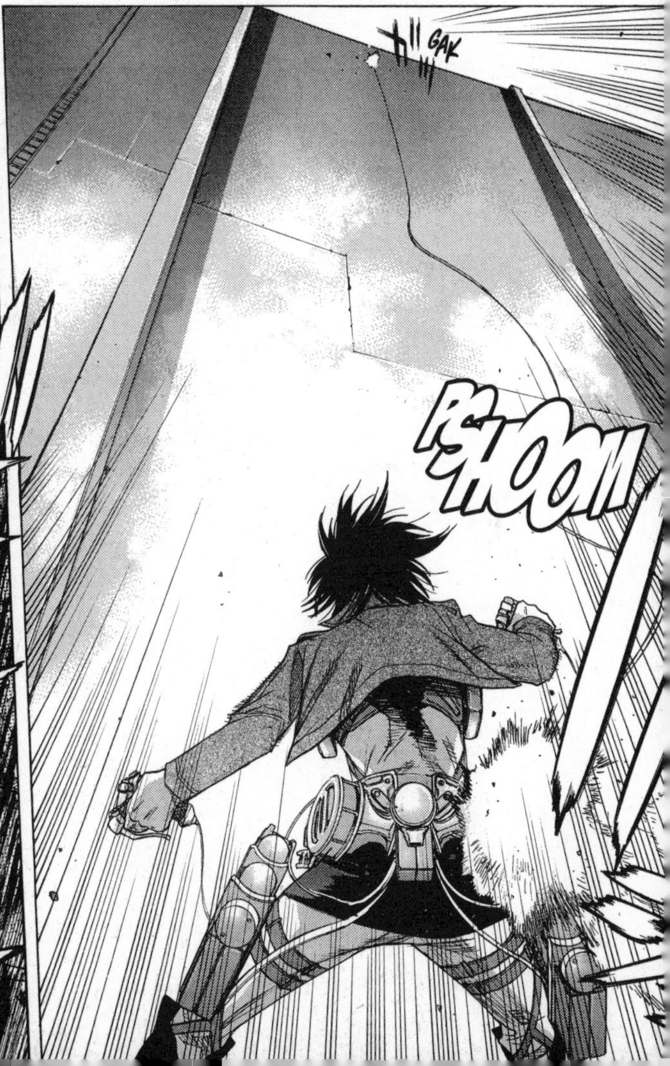
GAK
PSHOOM
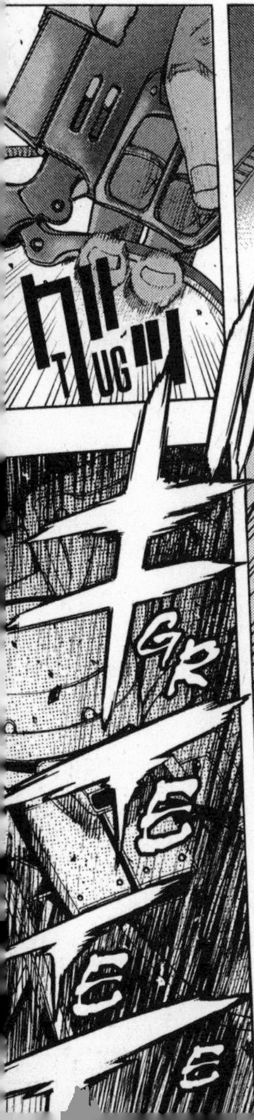
TUG
GREEE

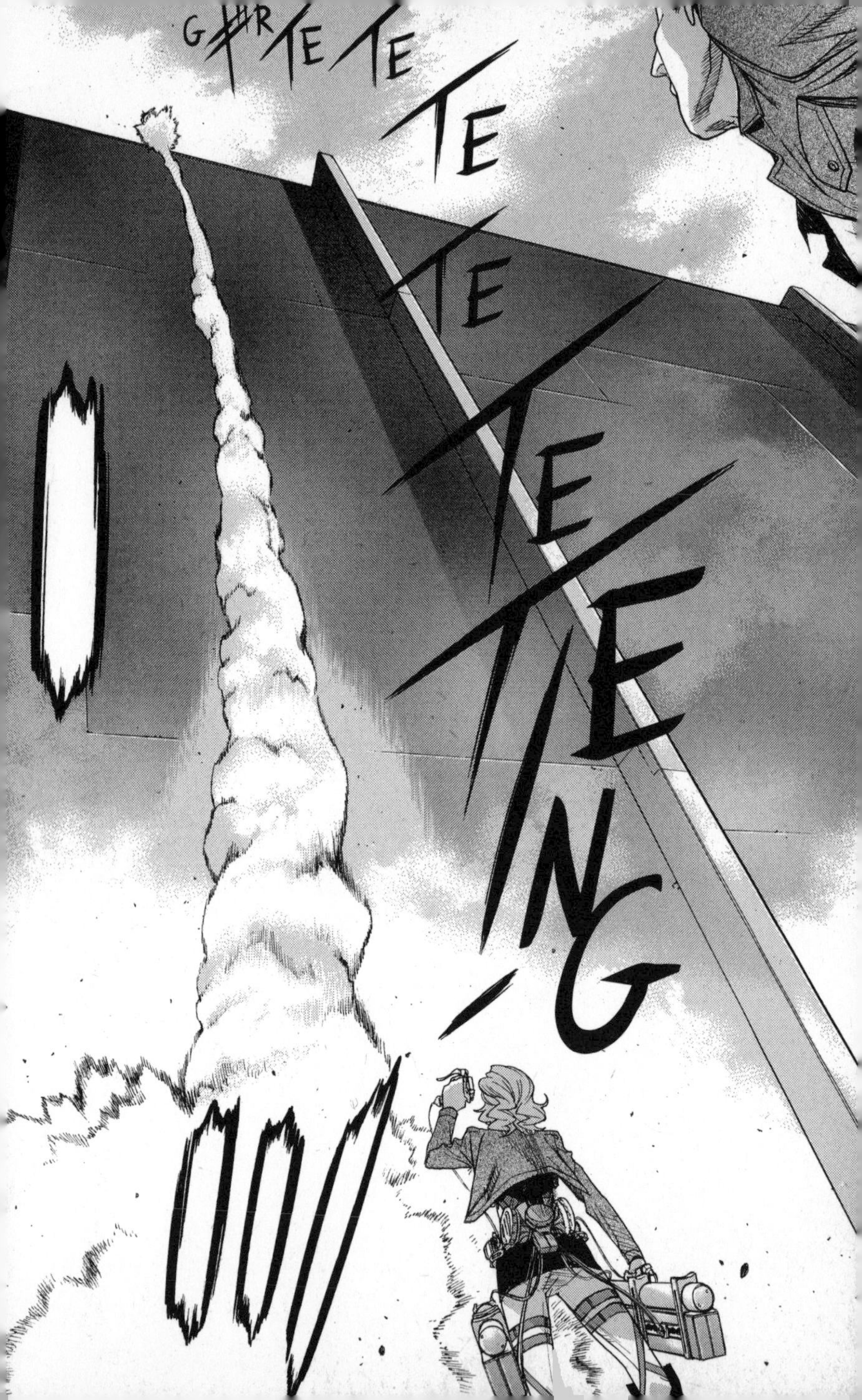

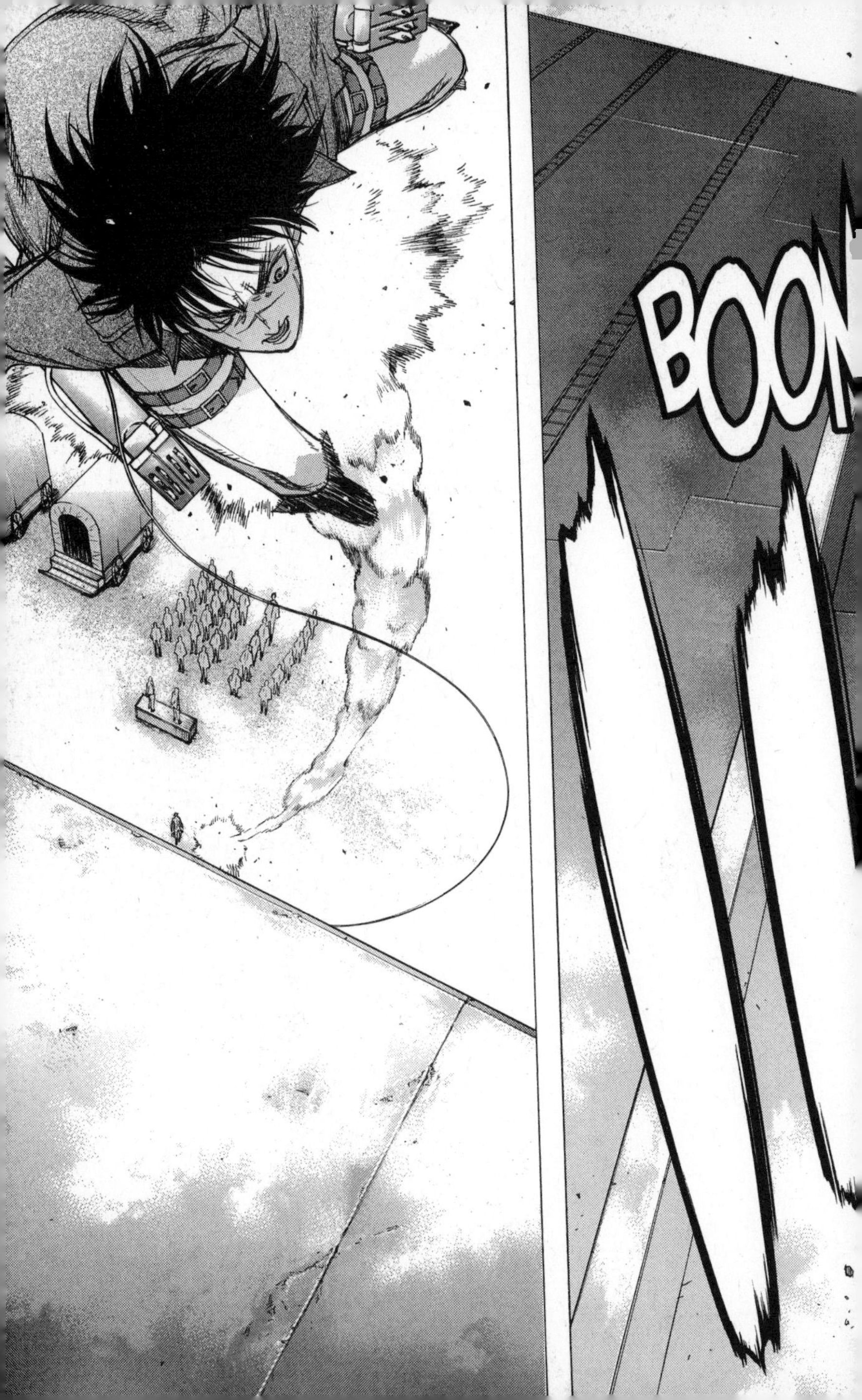
BOOM

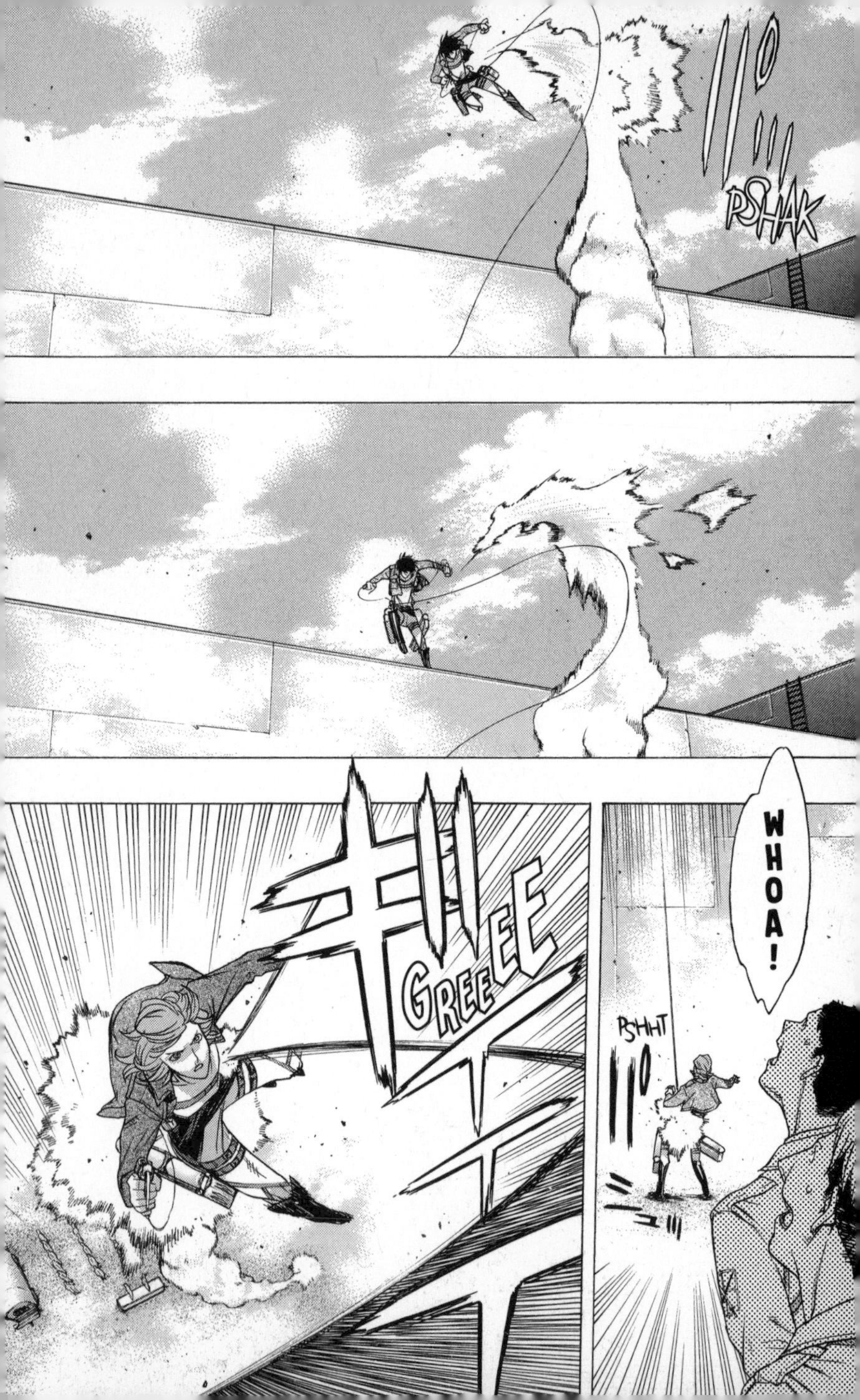
PSHAK
WHOA!
PSHHT
GREEEE

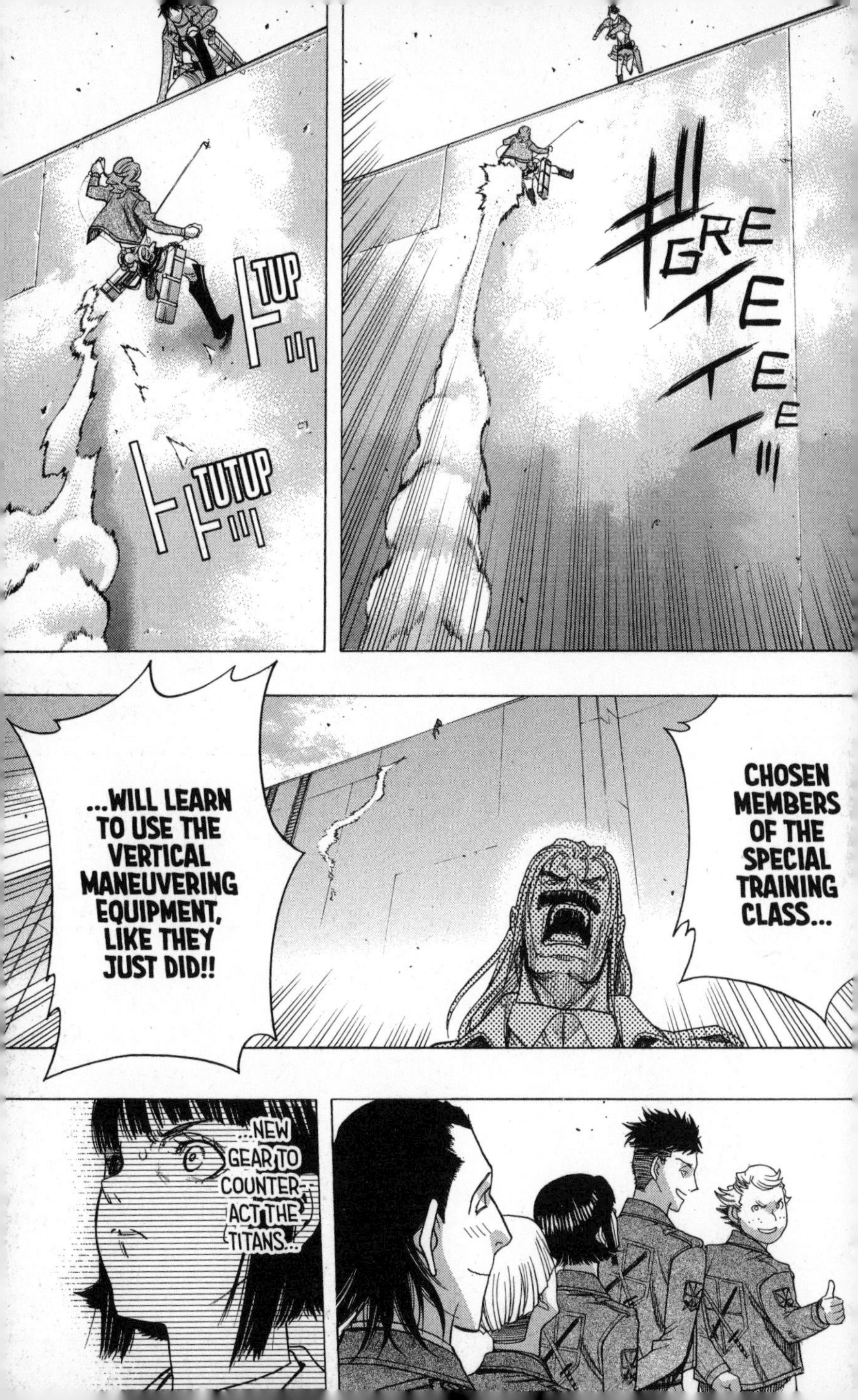
GREEEE
TUP
TUTUP
CHOSEN MEMBERS OF THE SPECIAL TRAINING CLASS...
...WILL LEARN TO USE THE VERTICAL MANEUVERING EQUIPMENT, LIKE THEY JUST DID!!
...NEW GEAR TO COUNTER-ACT THE TITANS...

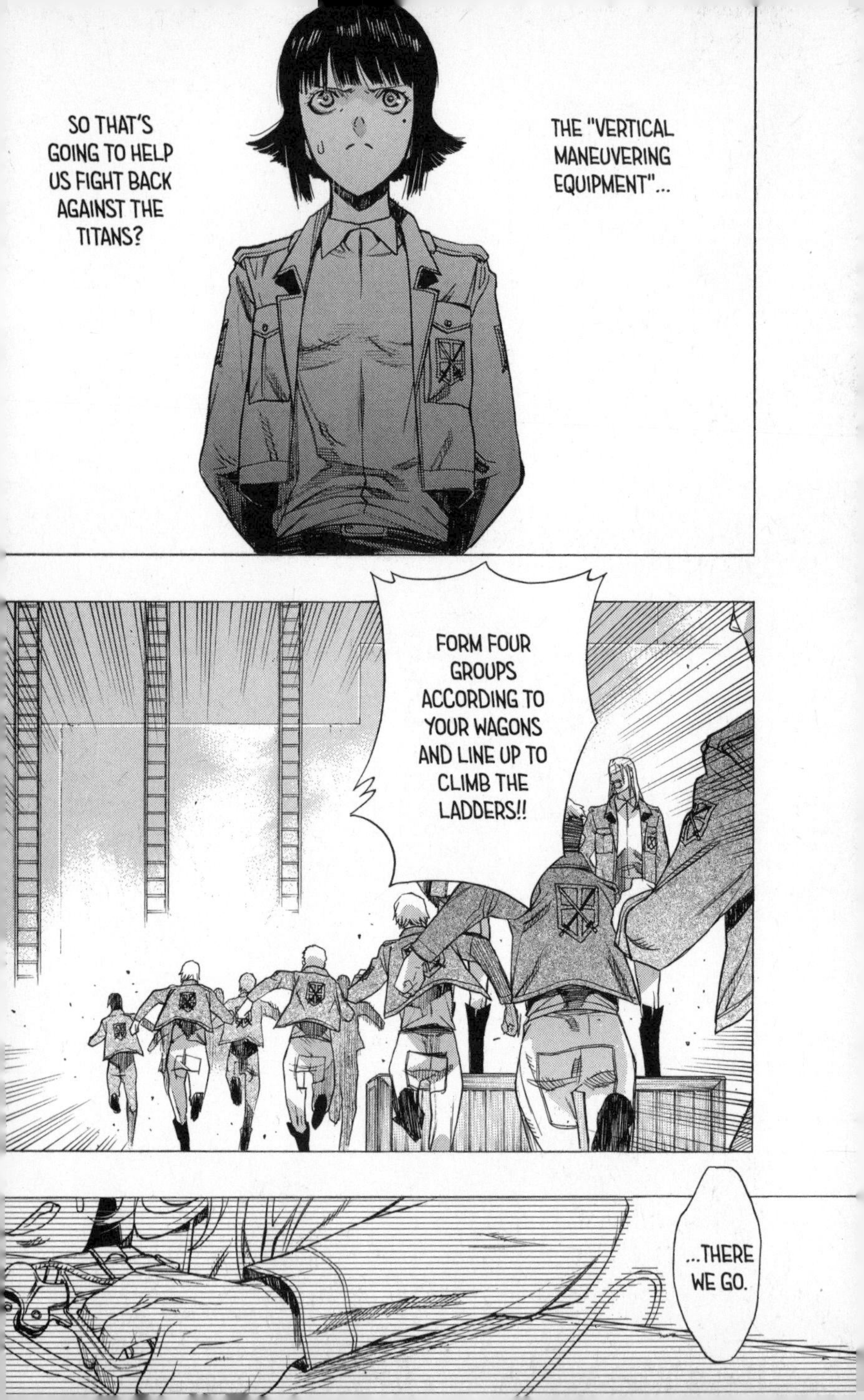
THE "VERTICAL MANEUVERING EQUIPMENT"...
SO THAT'S GOING TO HELP US FIGHT BACK AGAINST THE TITANS?
FORM FOUR GROUPS ACCORDING TO YOUR WAGONS AND LINE UP TO CLIMB THE LADDERS!!
...THERE WE GO.

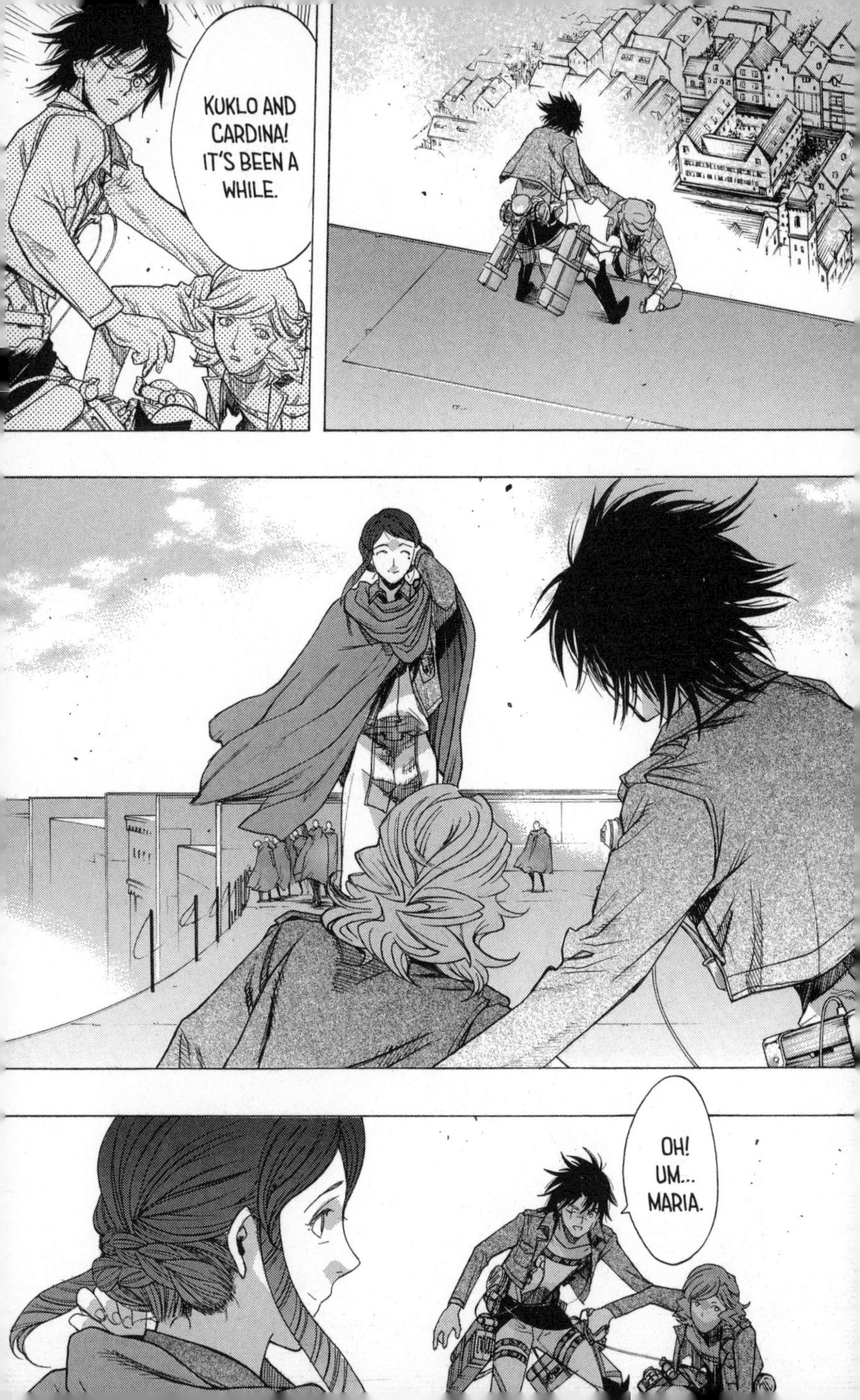
KUKLO AND CARDINA! IT'S BEEN A WHILE.
OH! UM... MARIA.

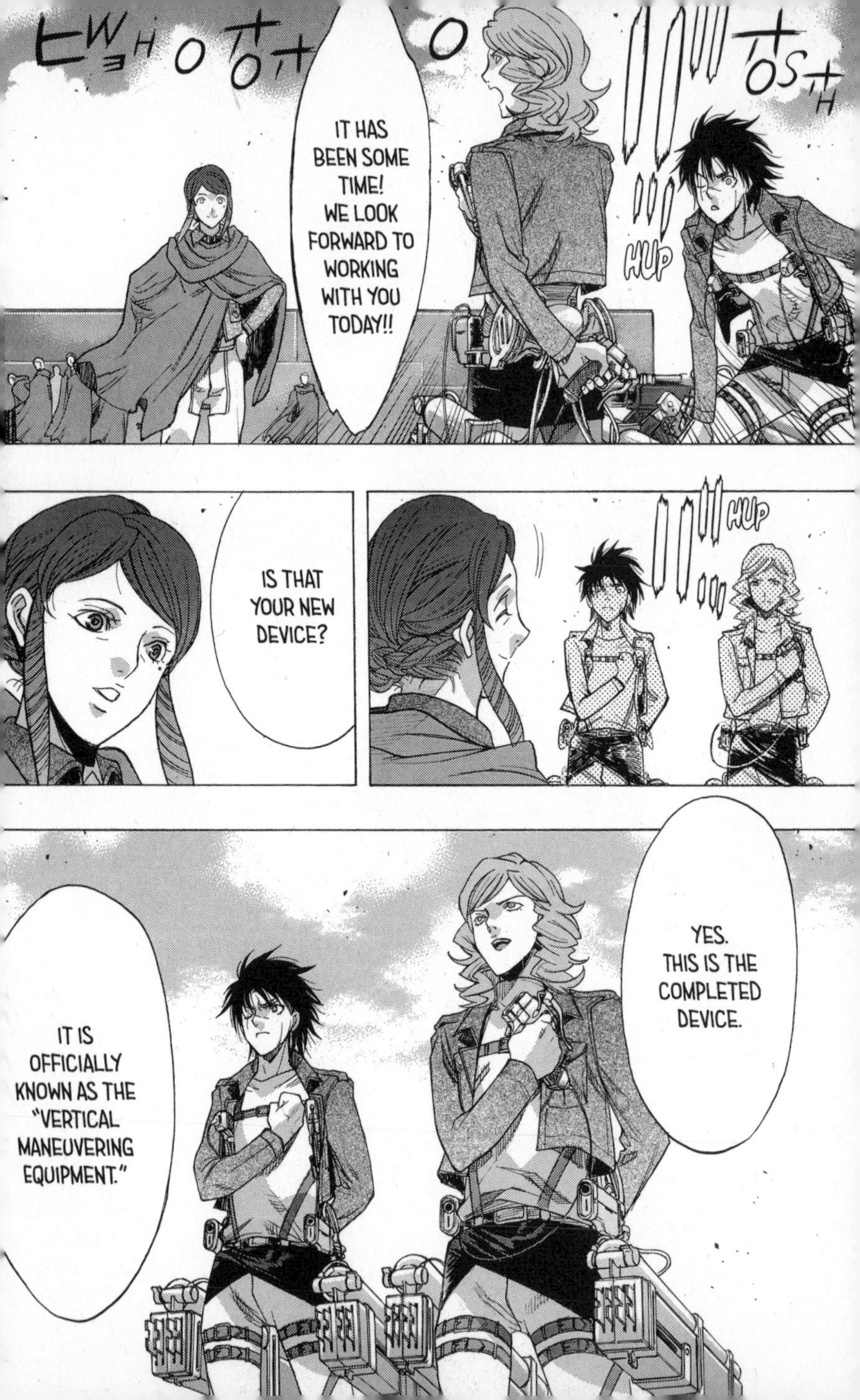
HUP
IT HAS BEEN SOME TIME! WE LOOK FORWARD TO WORKING WITH YOU TODAY!!
HUP
IS THAT YOUR NEW DEVICE?
YES. THIS IS THE COMPLETED DEVICE.
IT IS OFFICIALLY KNOWN AS THE "VERTICAL MANEUVERING EQUIPMENT."

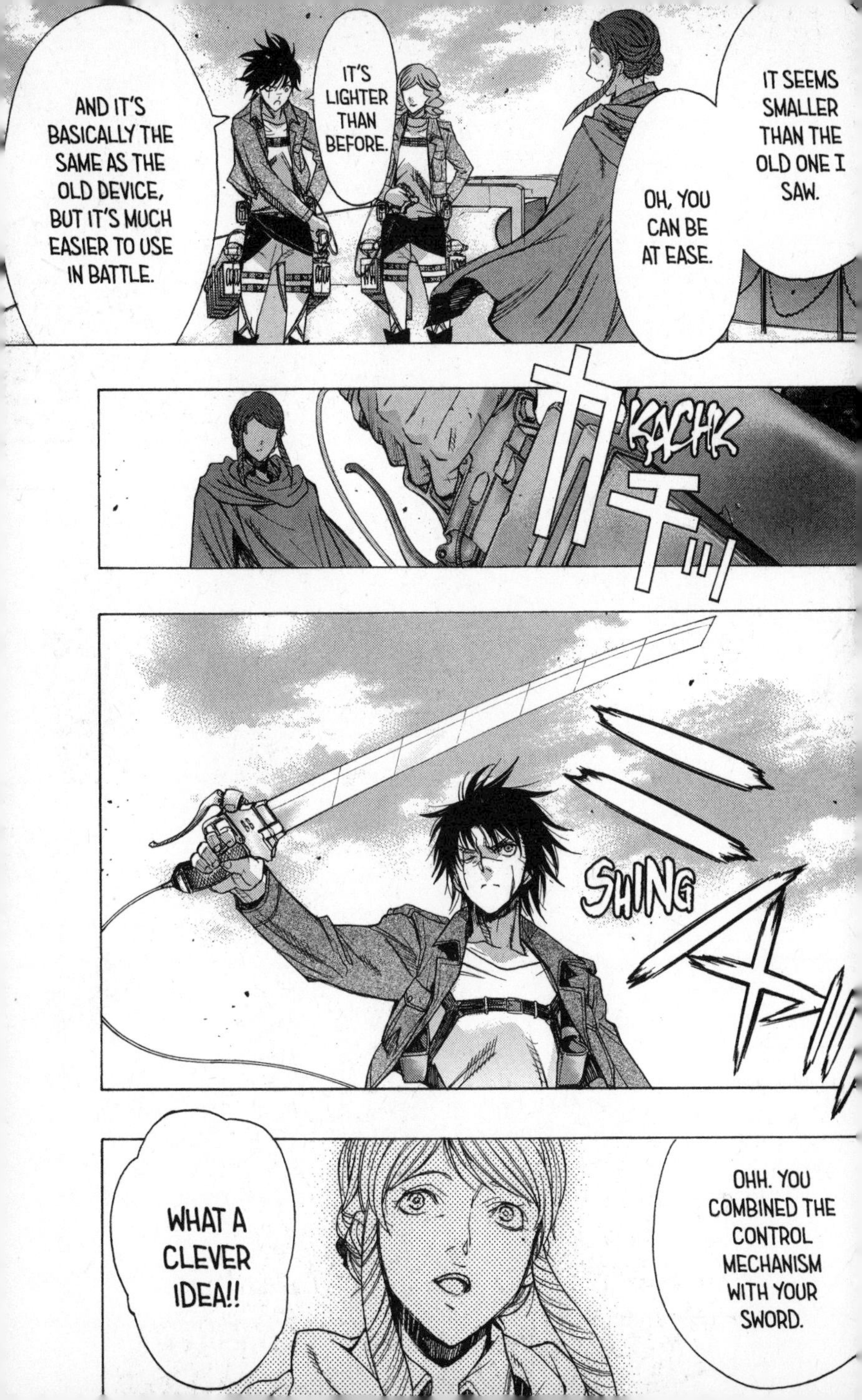
IT SEEMS SMALLER THAN THE OLD ONE I SAW.
OH, YOU CAN BE AT EASE.
IT'S LIGHTER THAN BEFORE.
AND IT'S BASICALLY THE SAME AS THE OLD DEVICE, BUT IT'S MUCH EASIER TO USE IN BATTLE.
KACHIK
カチッ
SHING
OHH. YOU COMBINED THE CONTROL MECHANISM WITH YOUR SWORD.
WHAT A CLEVER IDEA!!

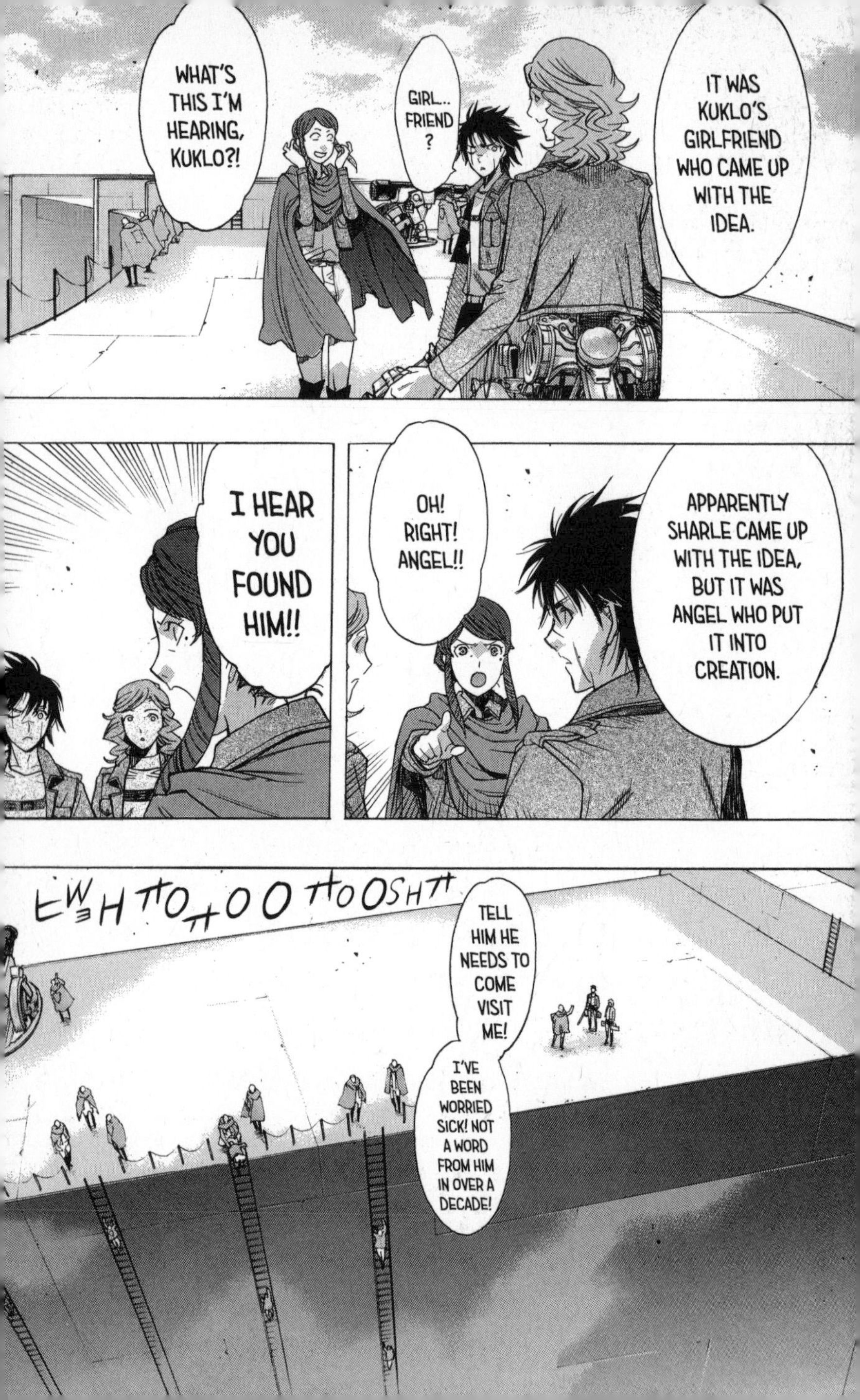
IT WAS KUKLO'S GIRLFRIEND WHO CAME UP WITH THE IDEA.
GIRL.. FRIEND ?
WHAT'S THIS I'M HEARING, KUKLO?!
APPARENTLY SHARLE CAME UP WITH THE IDEA, BUT IT WAS ANGEL WHO PUT IT INTO CREATION.
OH! RIGHT! ANGEL!!
I HEAR YOU FOUND HIM!!
TELL HIM HE NEEDS TO COME VISIT ME!
I'VE BEEN WORRIED SICK! NOT A WORD FROM HIM IN OVER A DECADE!

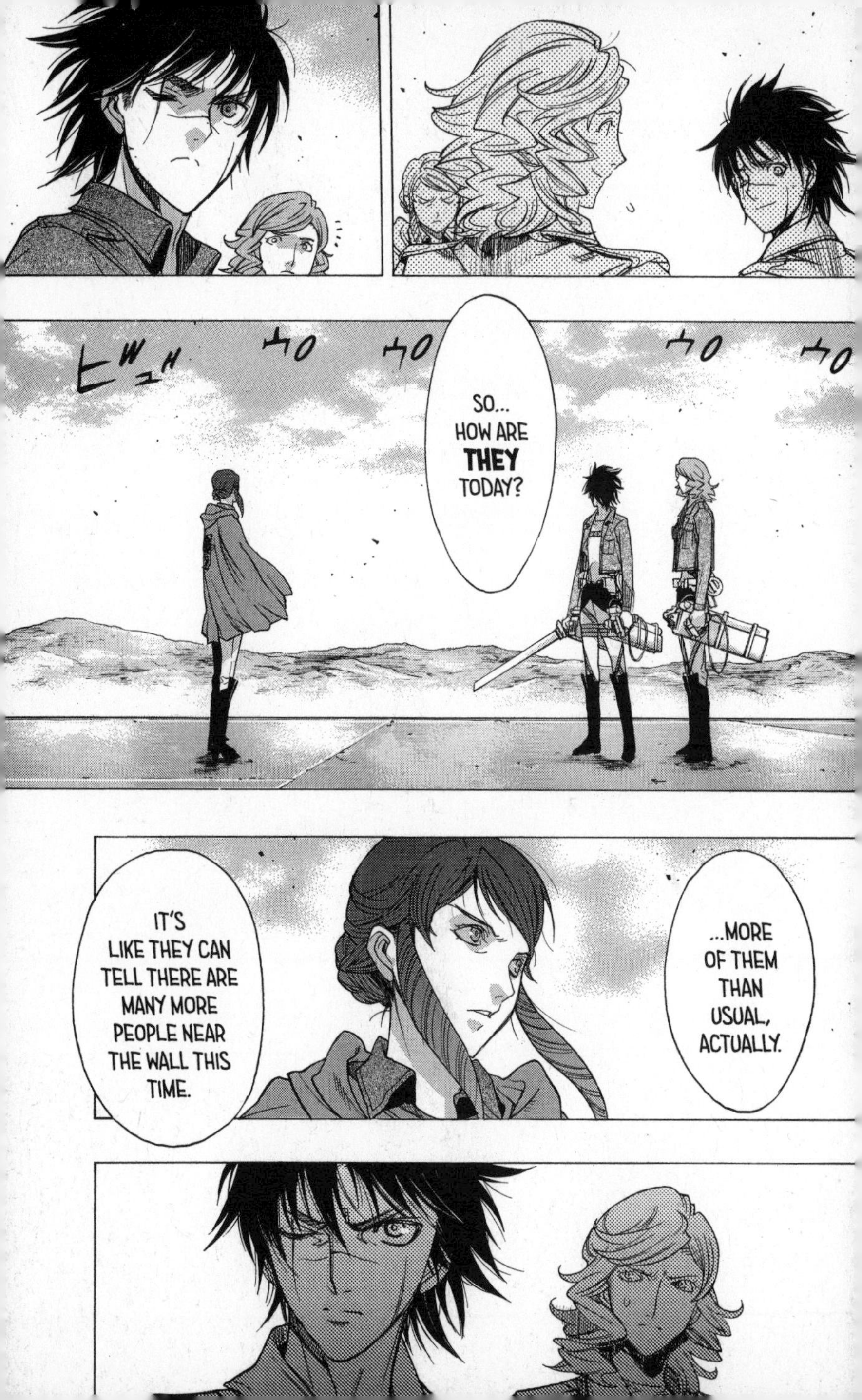
SO... HOW ARE **THEY** TODAY?
...MORE OF THEM THAN USUAL, ACTUALLY.
IT'S LIKE THEY CAN TELL THERE ARE MANY MORE PEOPLE NEAR THE WALL THIS TIME.

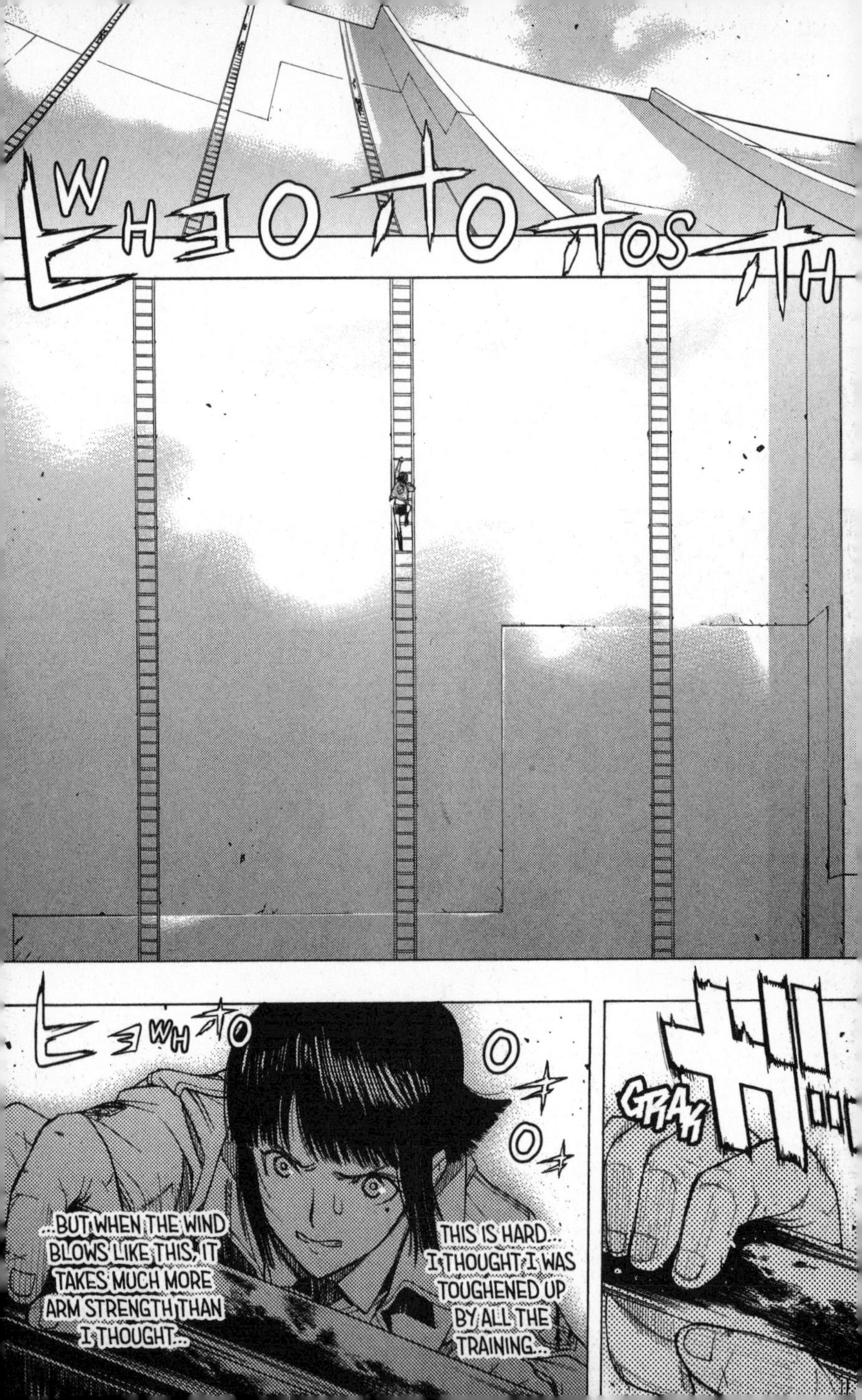
GRAK
THIS IS HARD... I THOUGHT I WAS TOUGHENED UP BY ALL THE TRAINING...
...BUT WHEN THE WIND BLOWS LIKE THIS, IT TAKES MUCH MORE ARM STRENGTH THAN I THOUGHT...

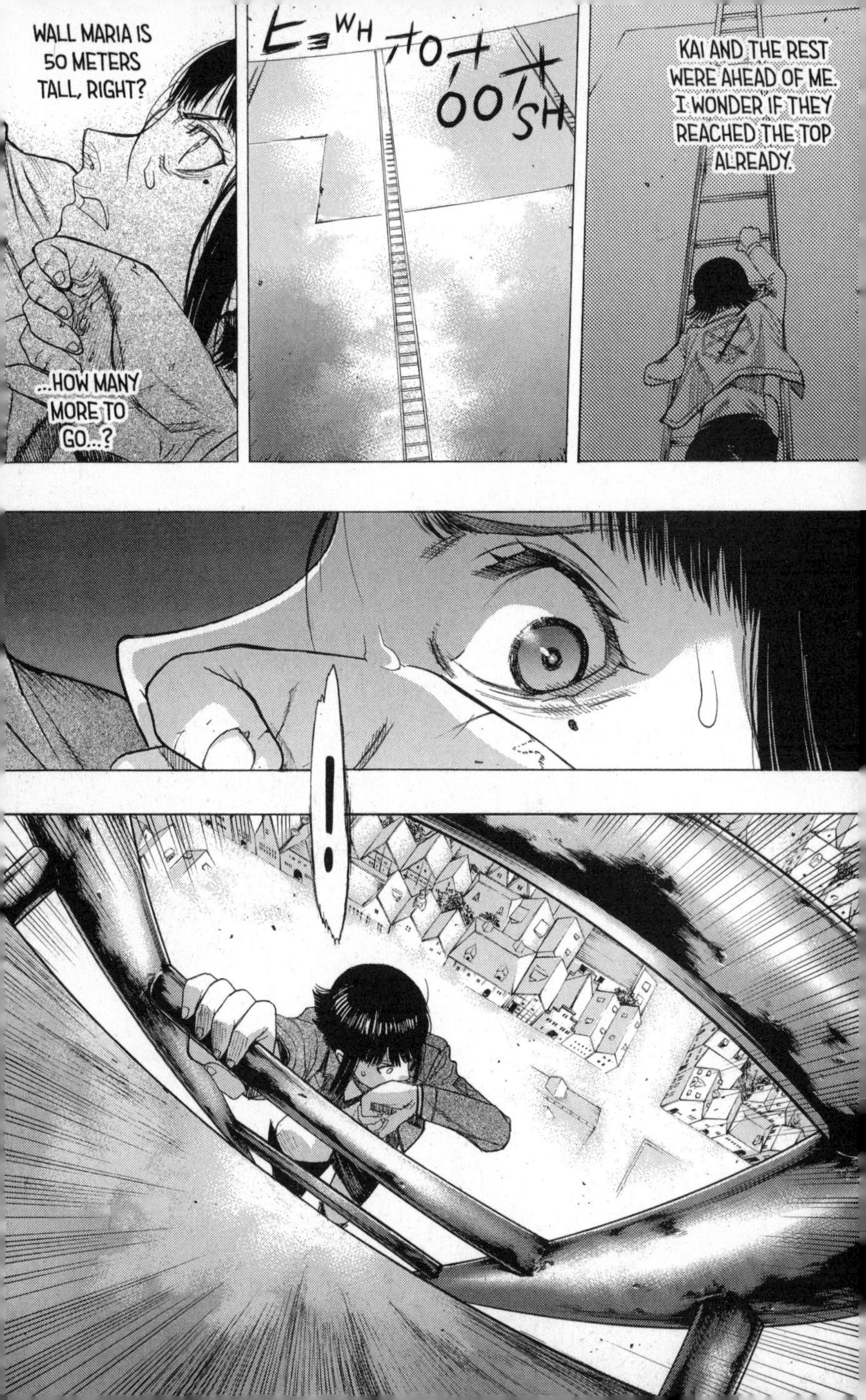
KAI AND THE REST WERE AHEAD OF ME. I WONDER IF THEY REACHED THE TOP ALREADY.
WHOOSH
WALL MARIA IS 50 METERS TALL, RIGHT?
...HOW MANY MORE TO GO...?
!

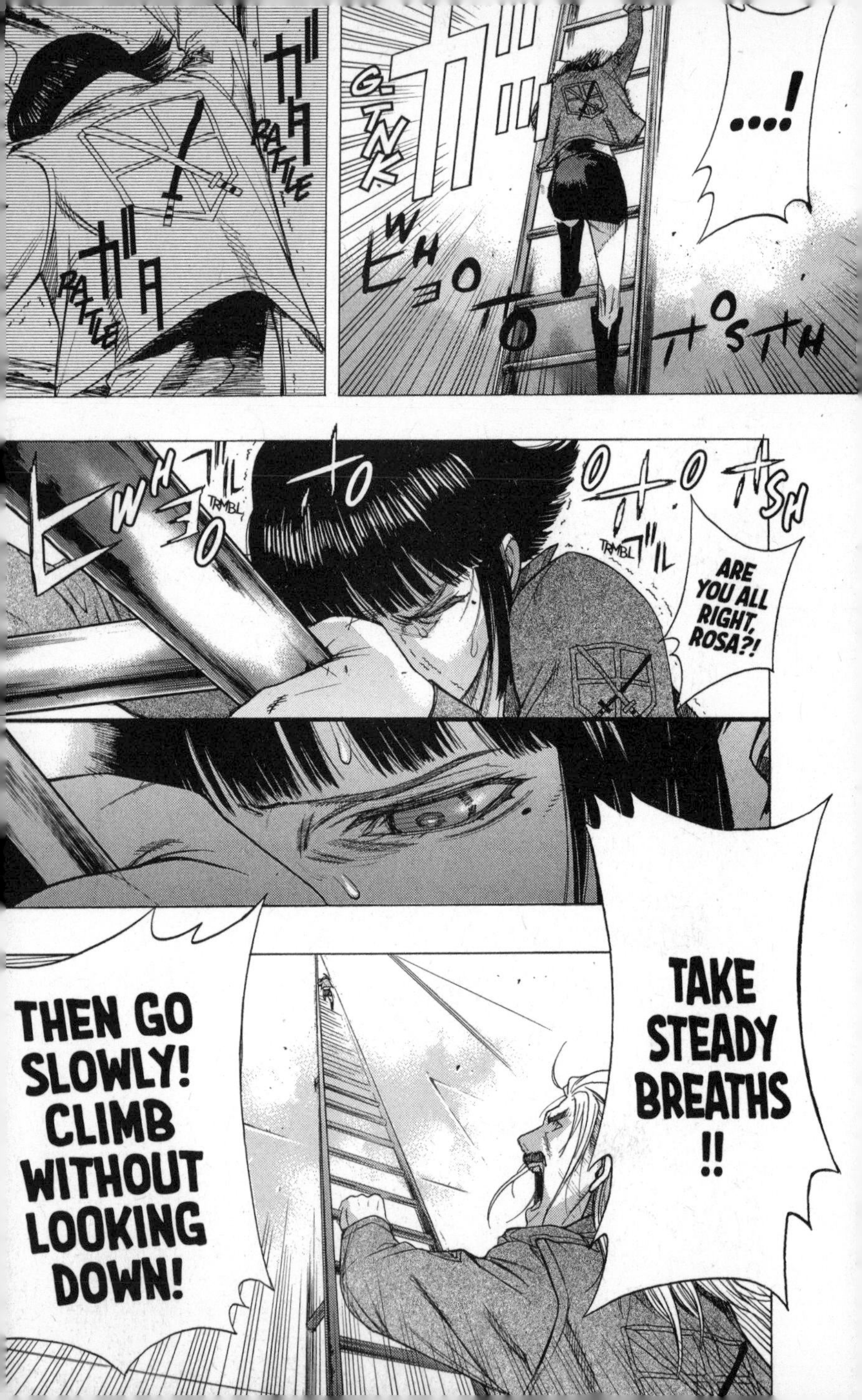
...!
G-TNK
RATTLE
RATTLE
TRMBL
TRMBL
ARE YOU ALL RIGHT, ROSA?!
TAKE STEADY BREATHS!!
THEN GO SLOWLY! CLIMB WITHOUT LOOKING DOWN!

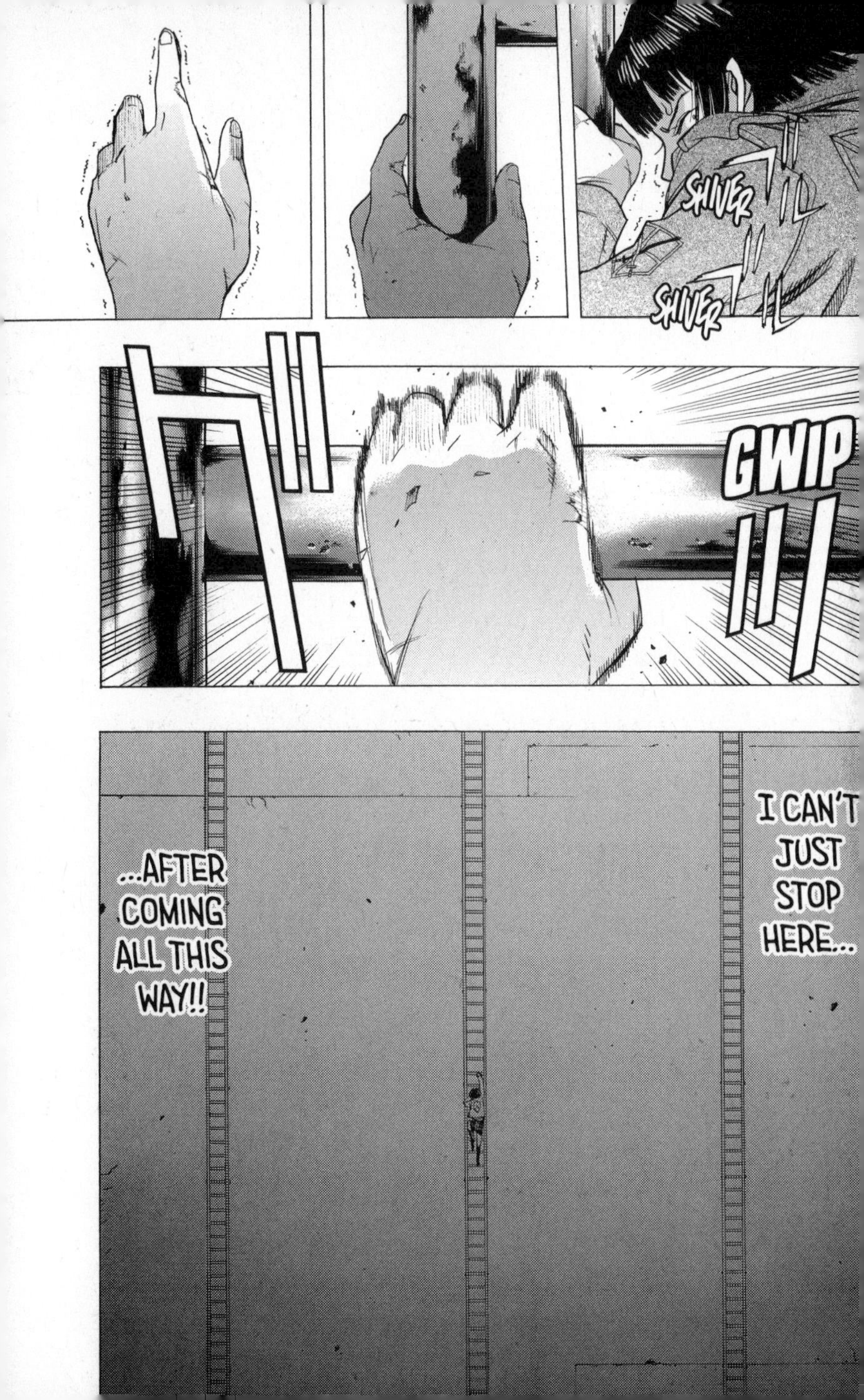
SHIVER
SHIVER
GWIP
I CAN'T JUST STOP HERE...
...AFTER COMING ALL THIS WAY!!

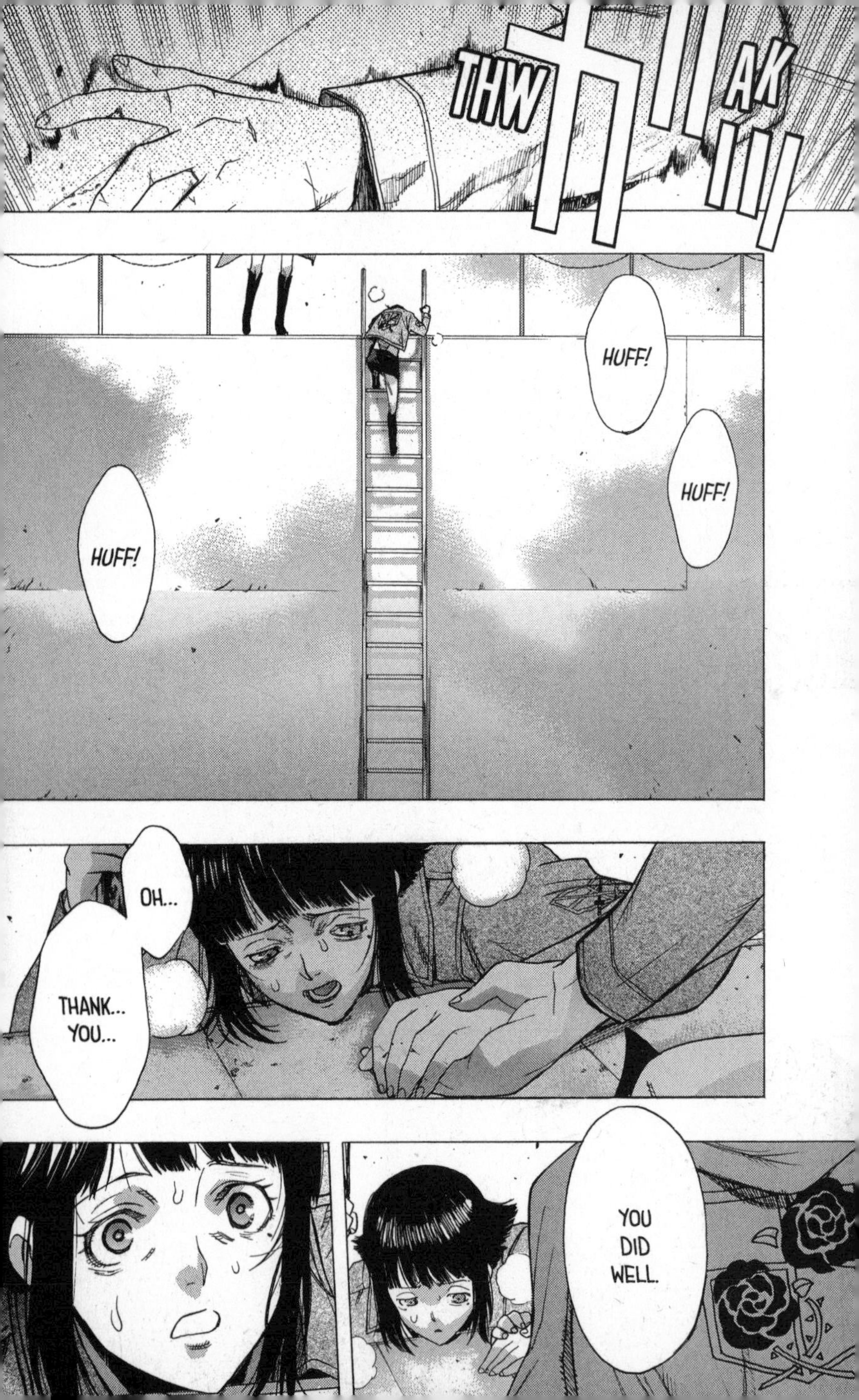
THWAK!!!
HUFF!
HUFF!
HUFF!
OH...
THANK... YOU...
YOU DID WELL.

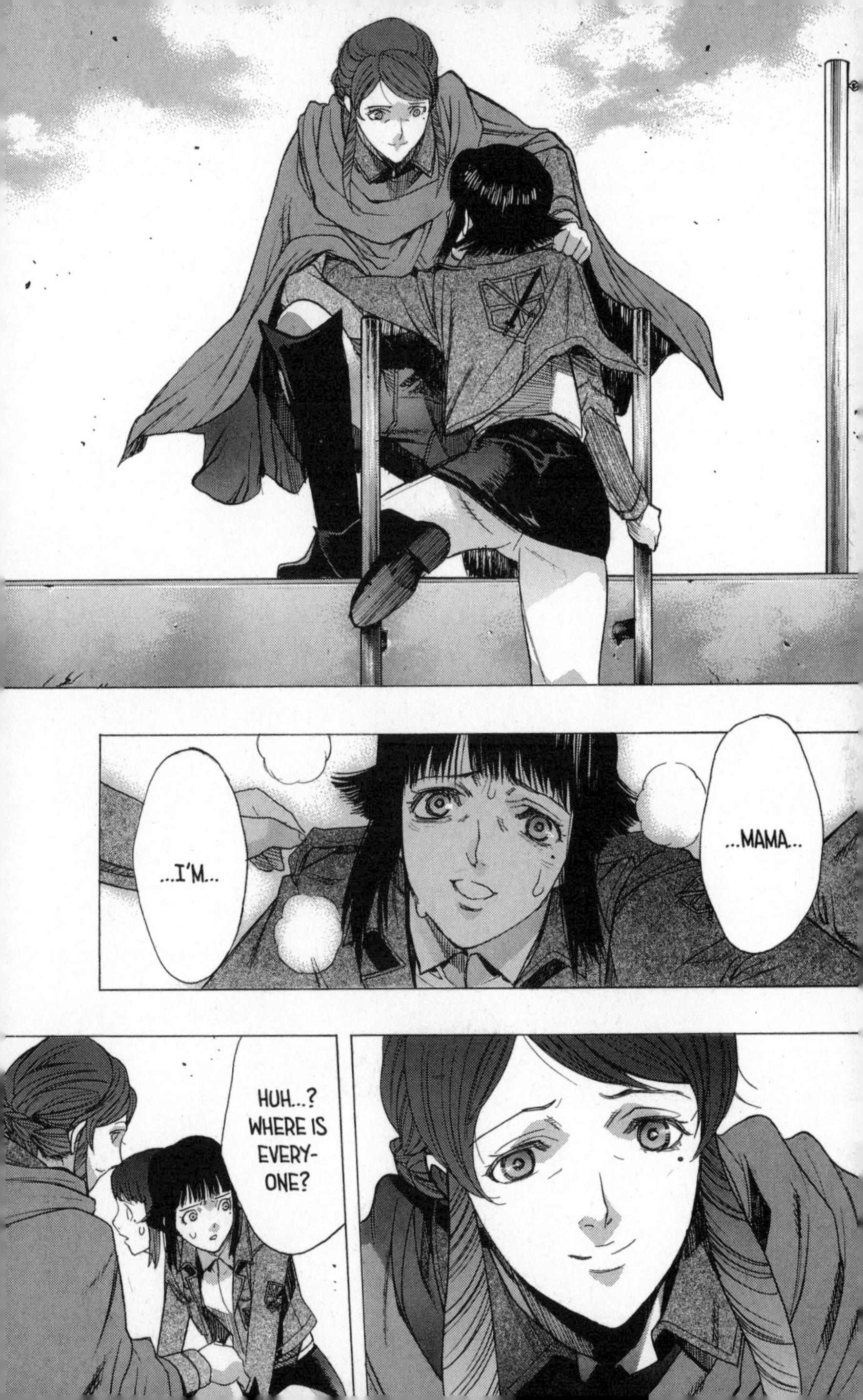
...MAMA...
...I'M...
HUH...? WHERE IS EVERY-ONE?

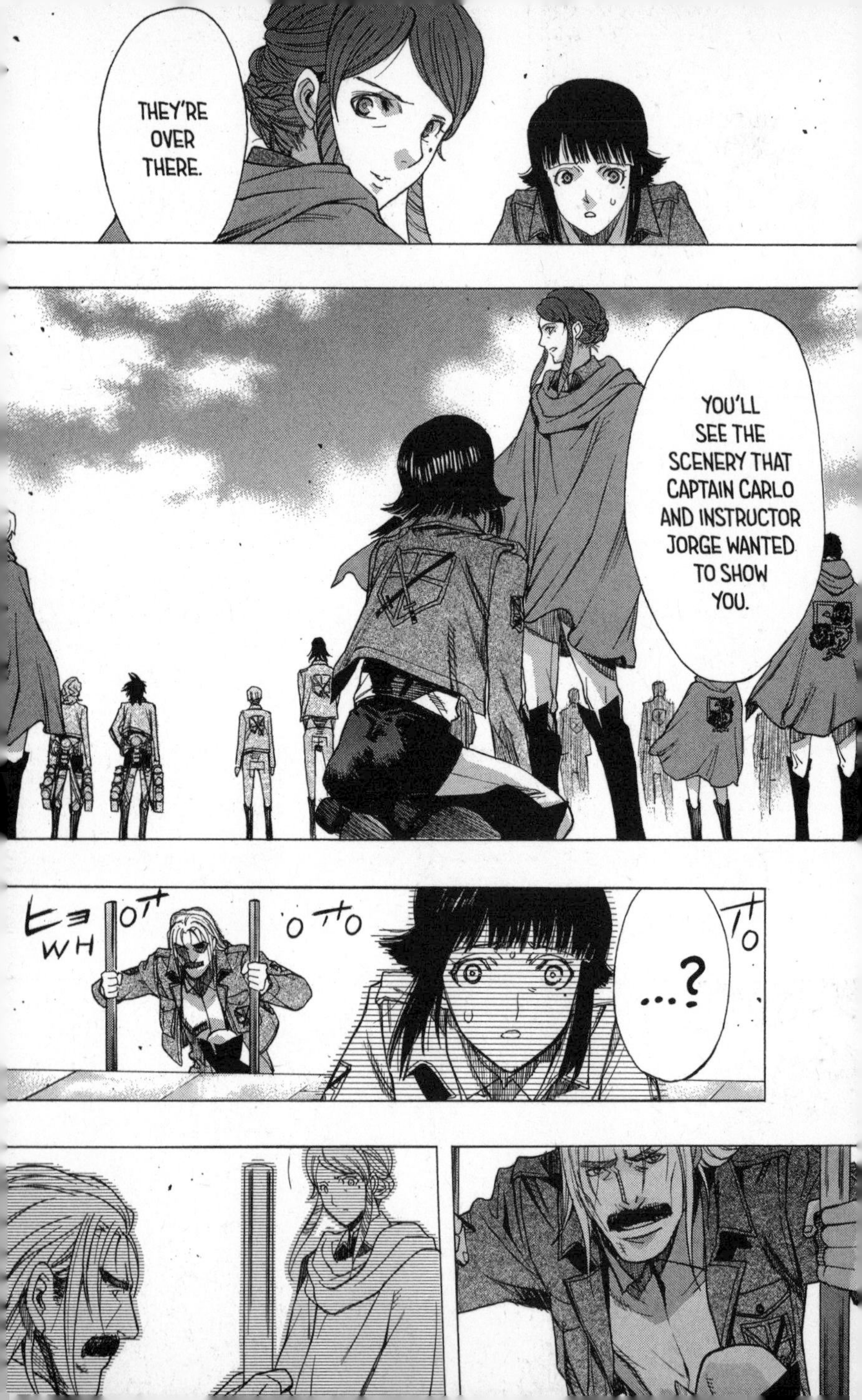
THEY'RE OVER THERE.
YOU'LL SEE THE SCENERY THAT CAPTAIN CARLO AND INSTRUCTOR JORGE WANTED TO SHOW YOU.
...?
WHOA

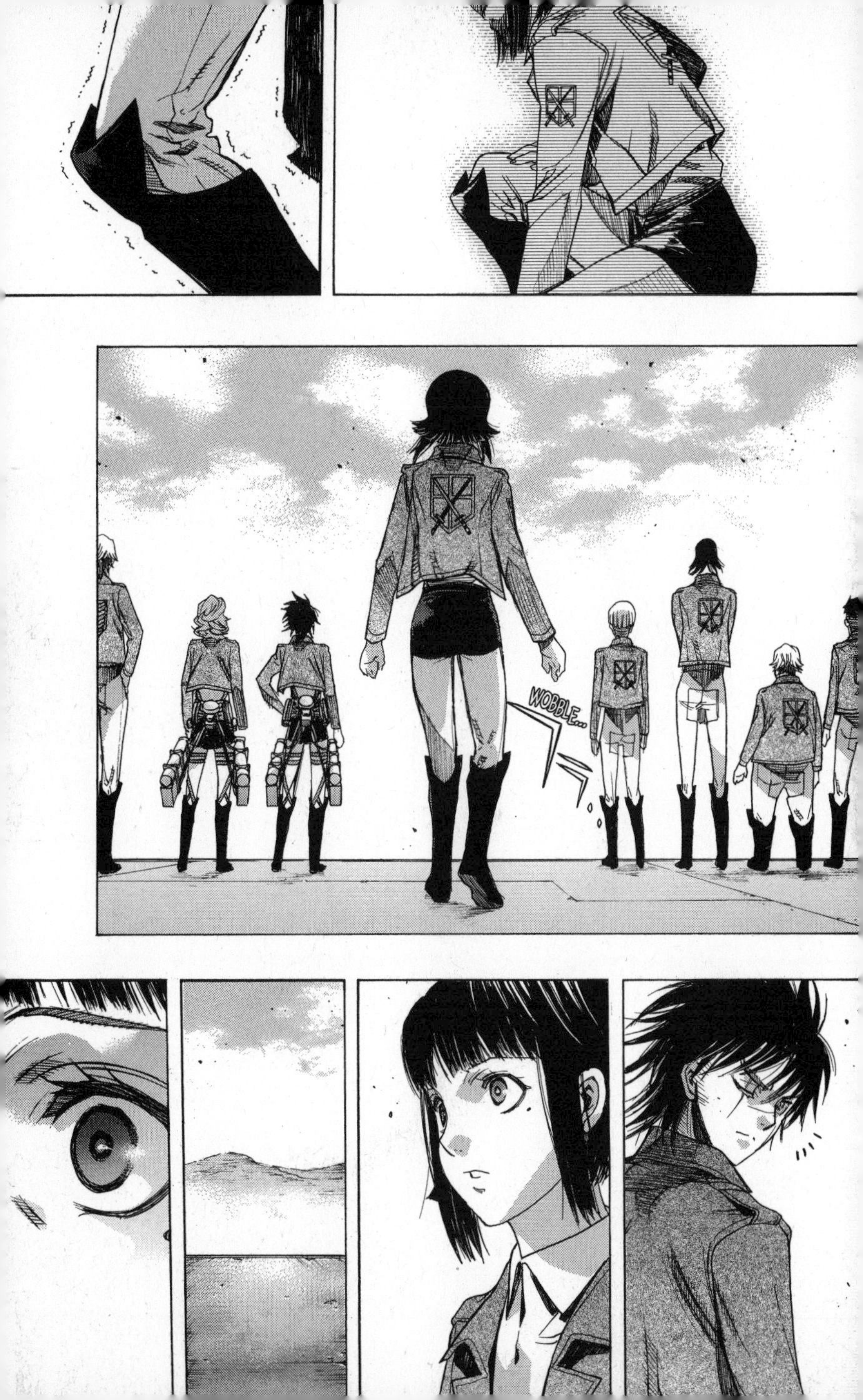
WOBBLE...

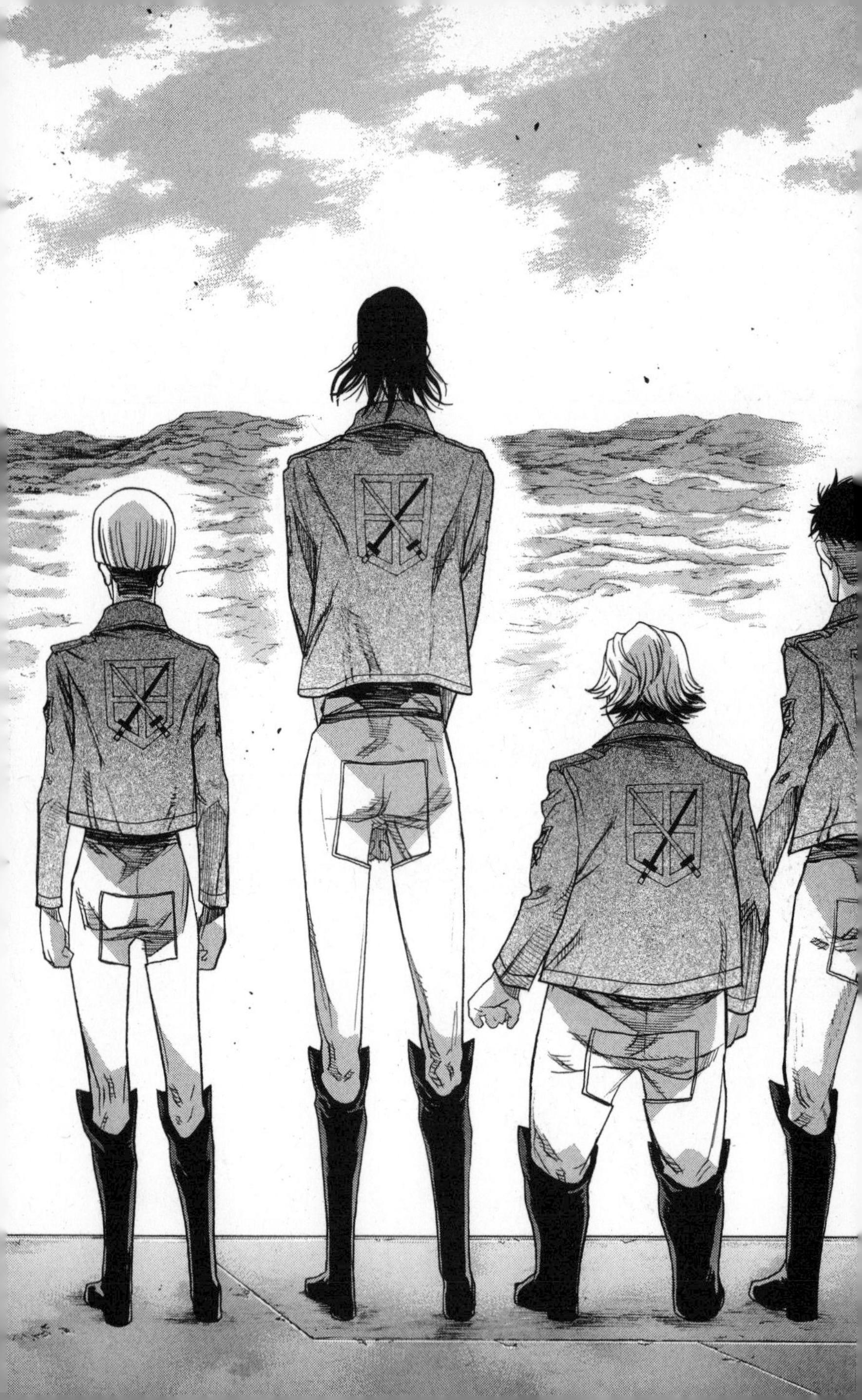

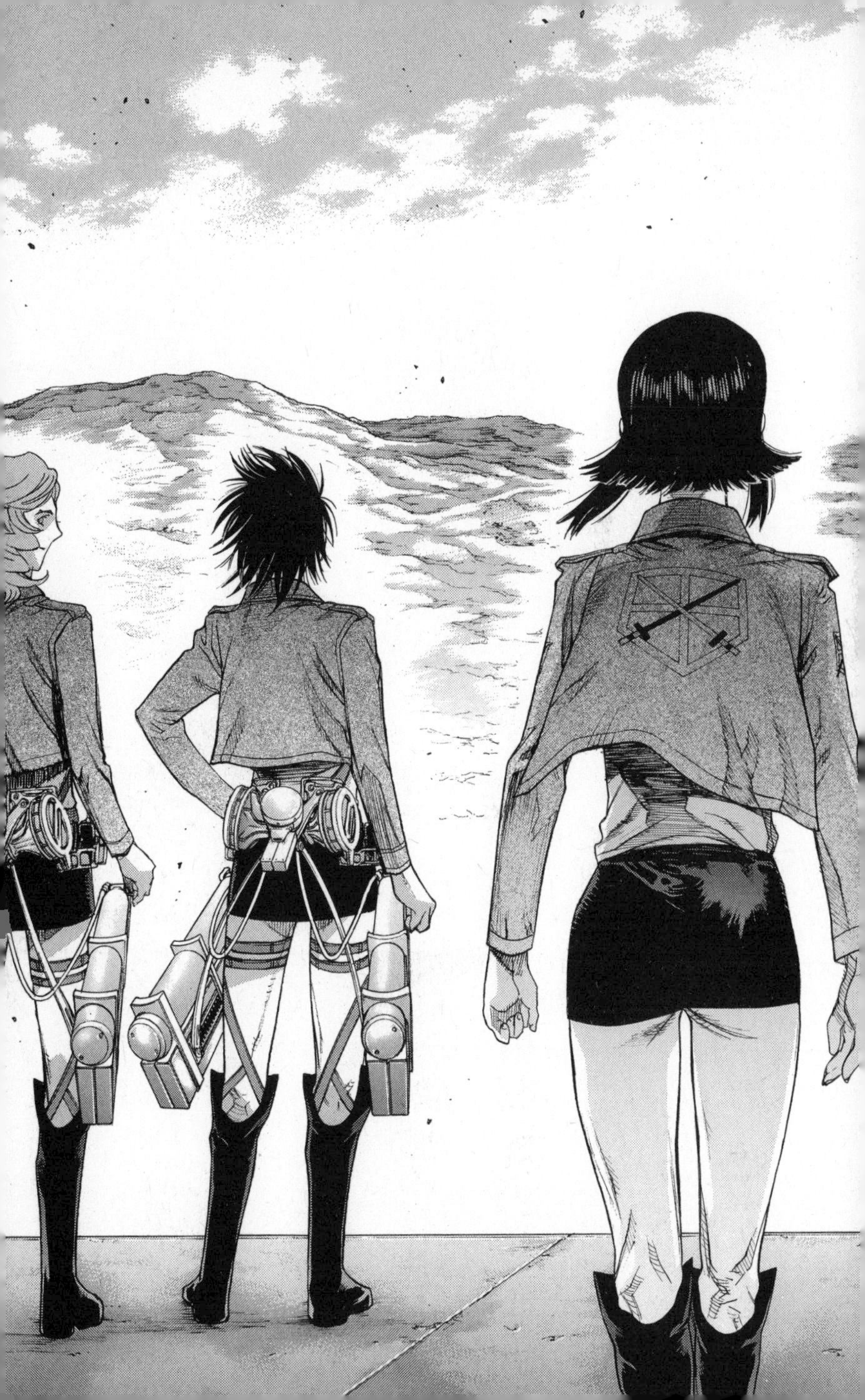

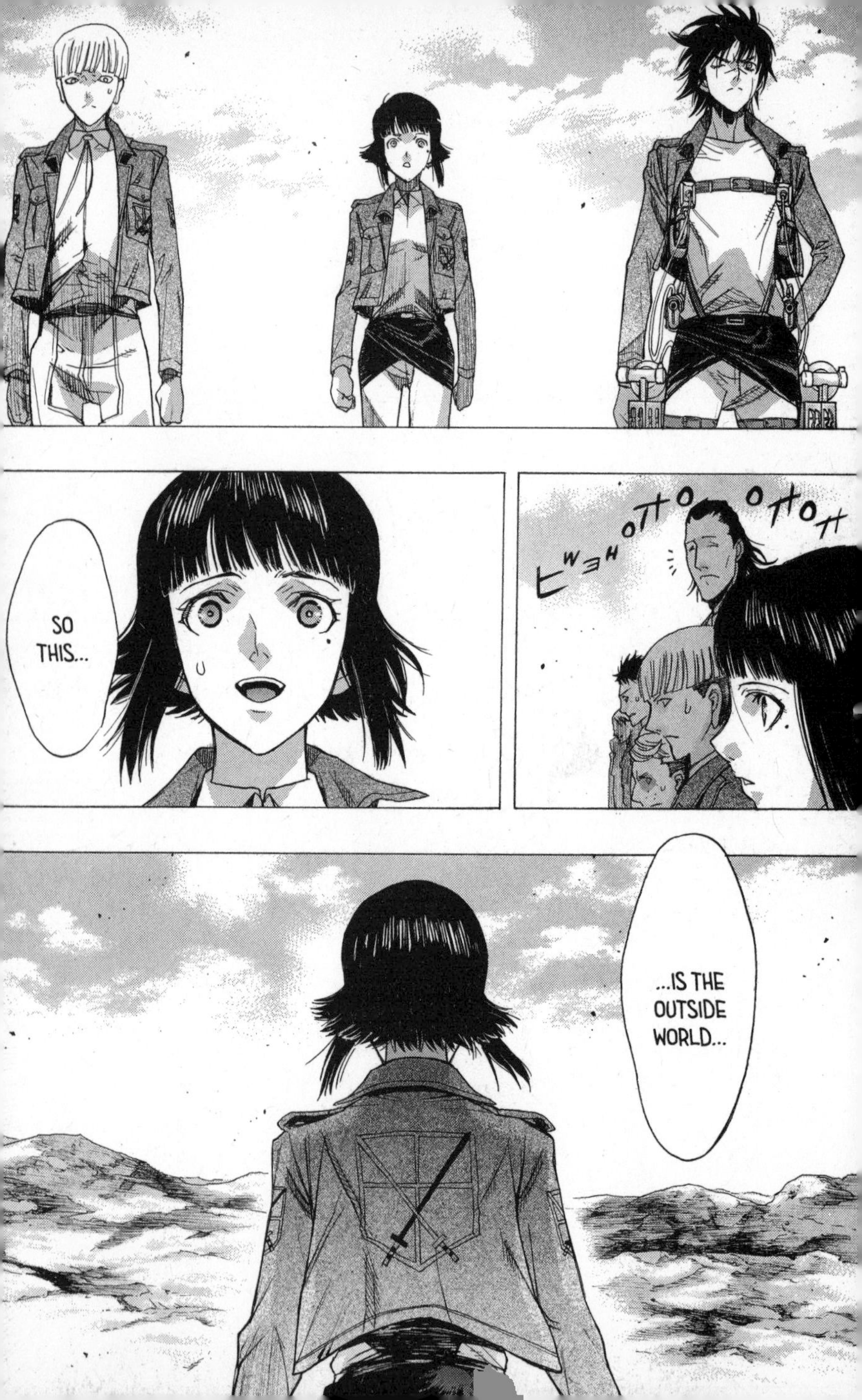
SO THIS...
...IS THE OUTSIDE WORLD...

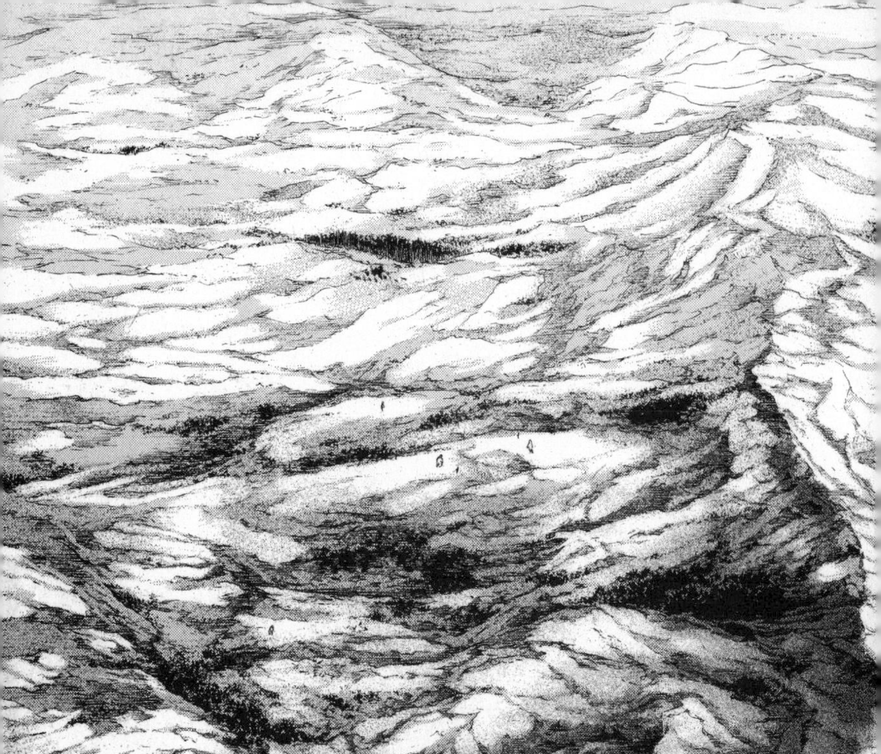
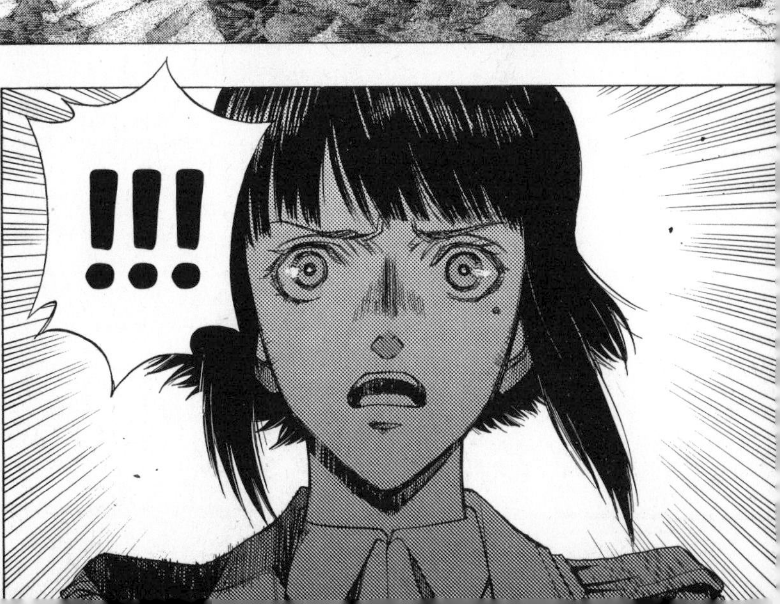
!!!

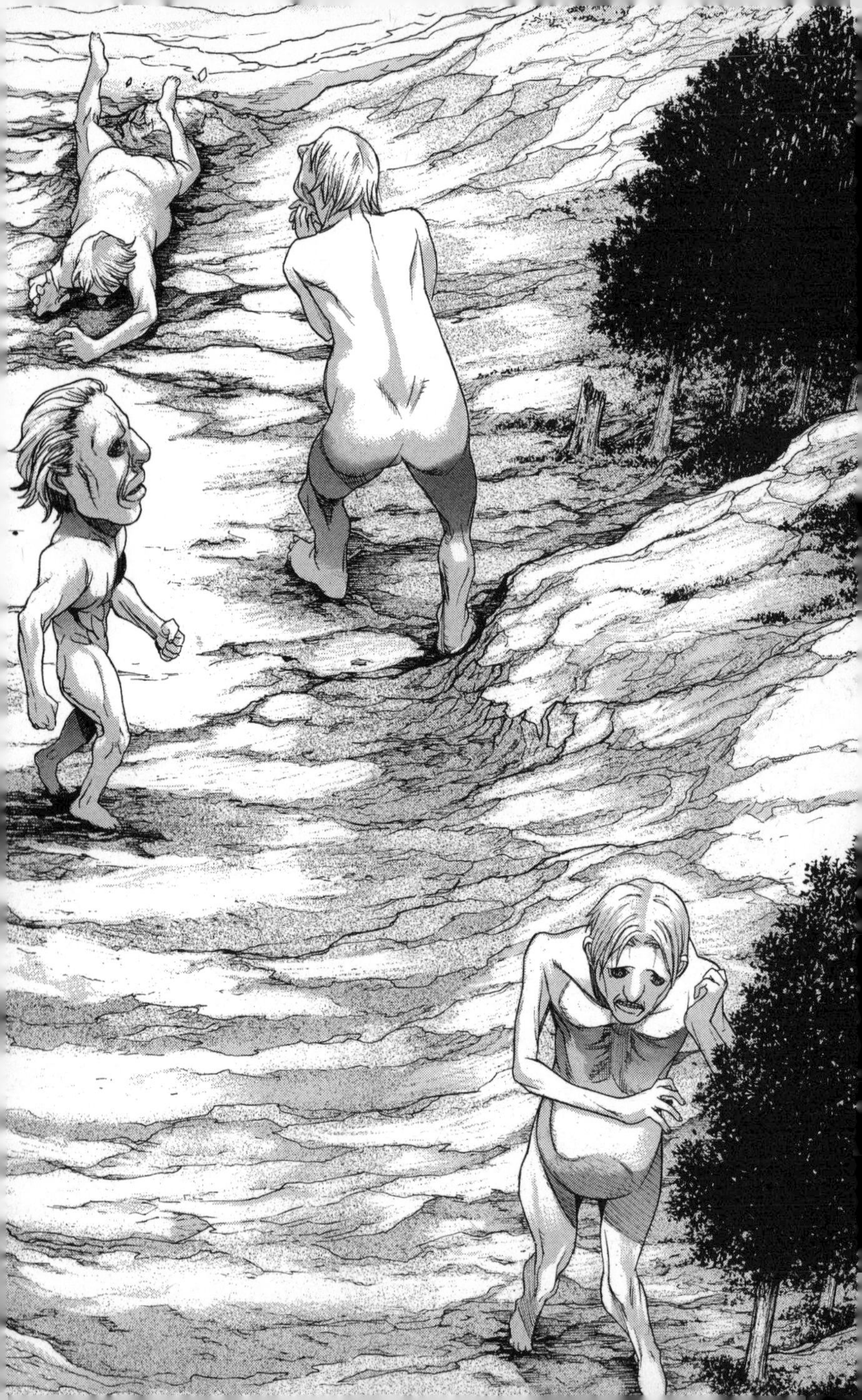

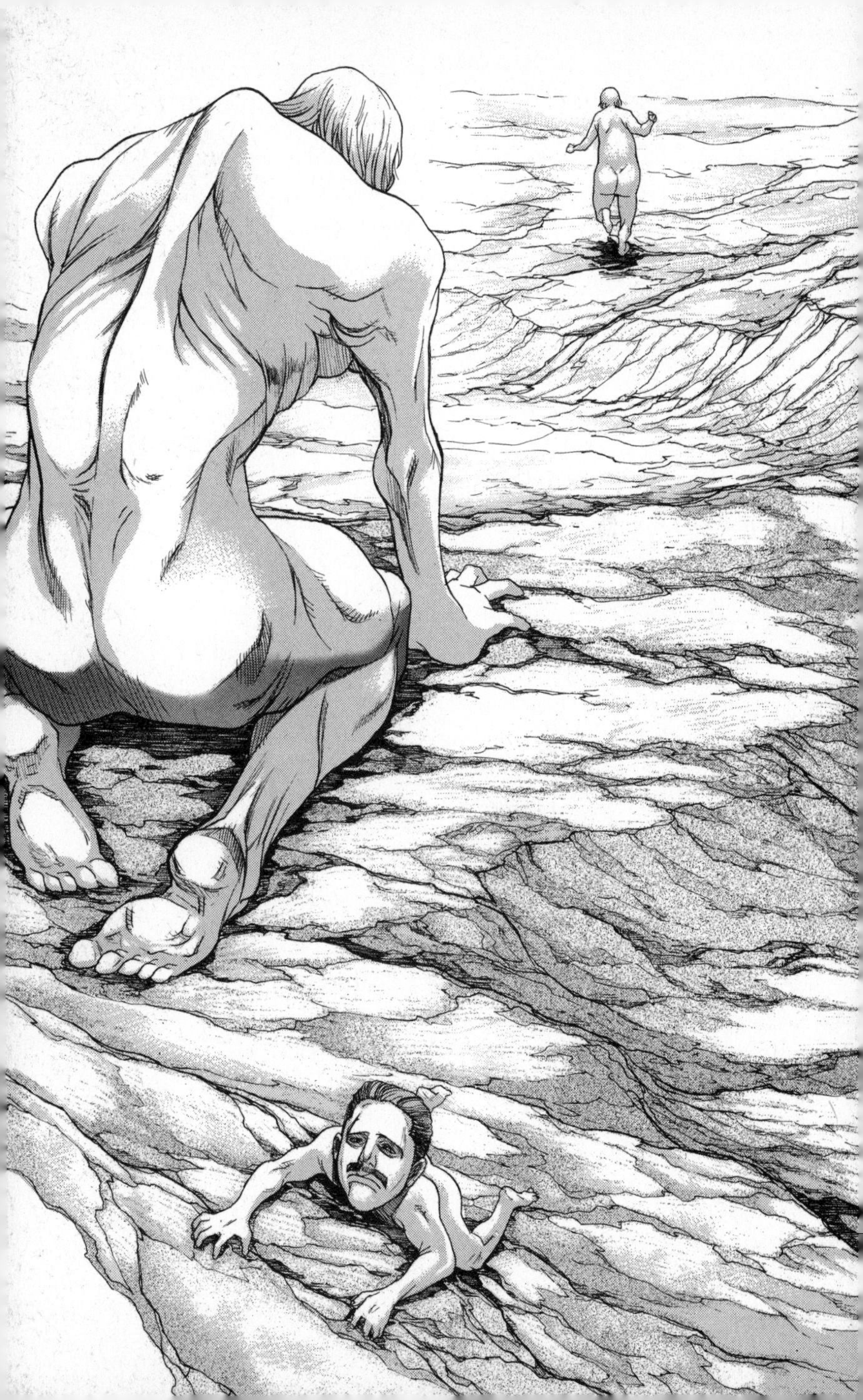

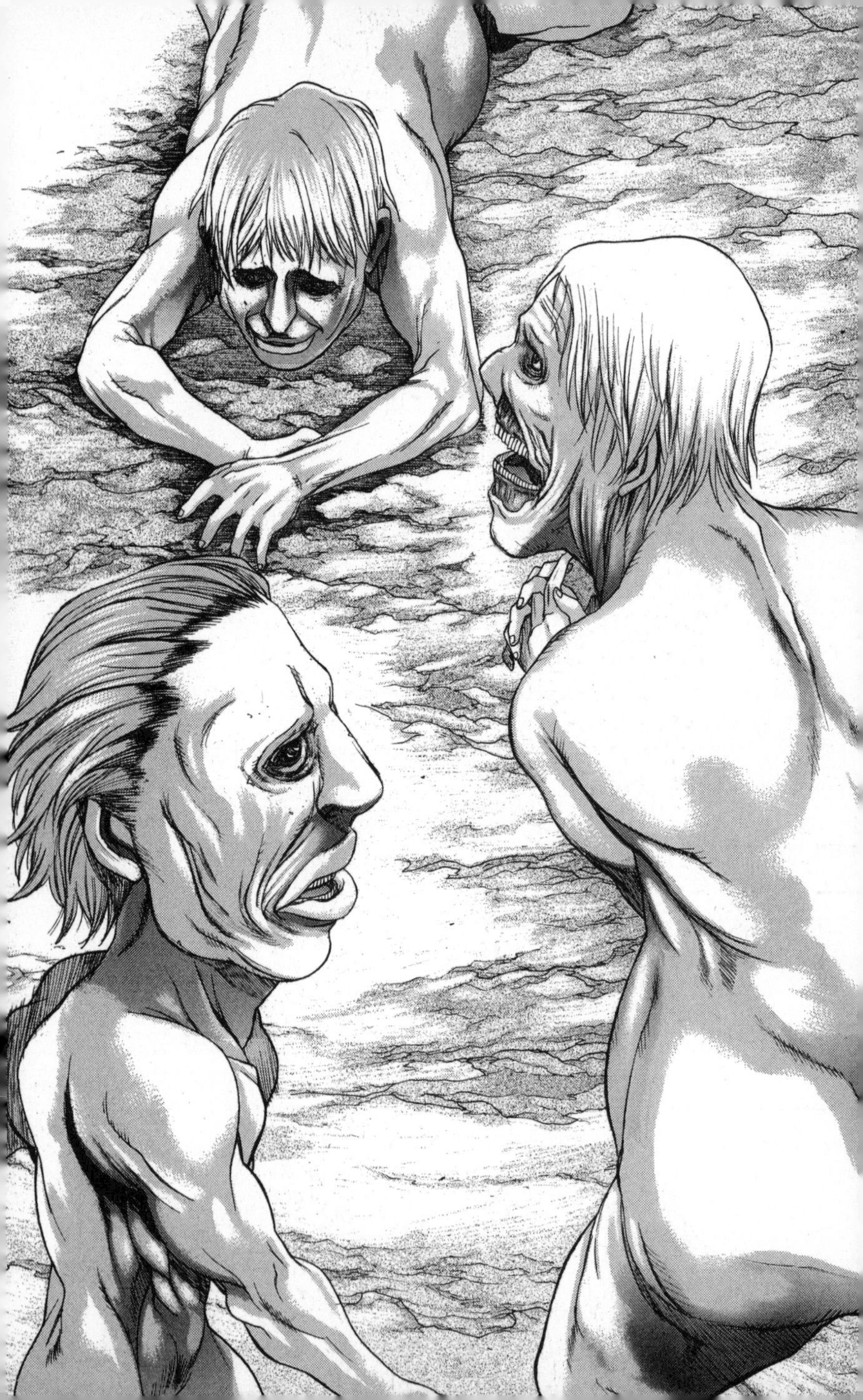

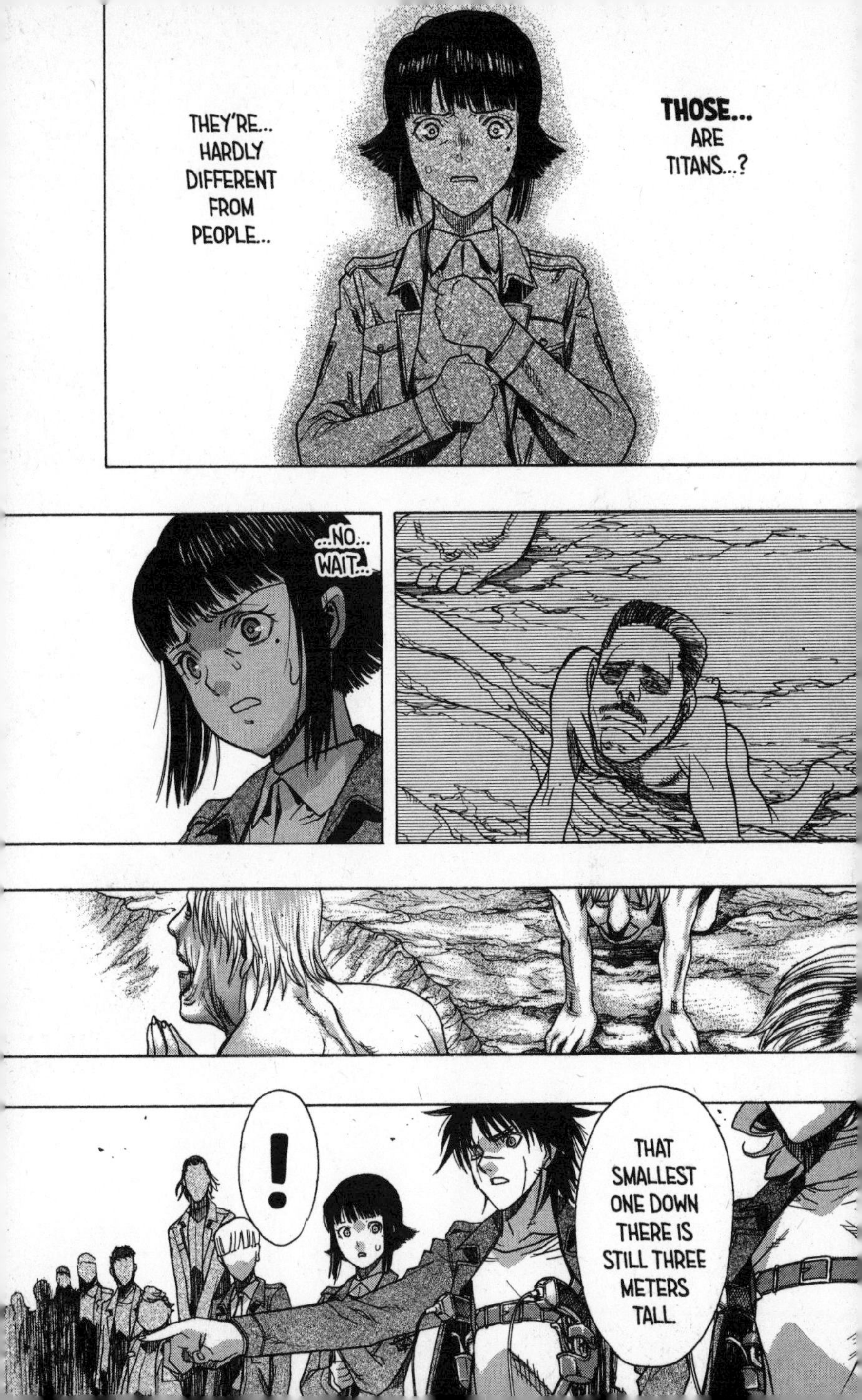
THOSE... ARE TITANS...?
THEY'RE... HARDLY DIFFERENT FROM PEOPLE...
...NO... WAIT...
THAT SMALLEST ONE DOWN THERE IS STILL THREE METERS TALL.
!

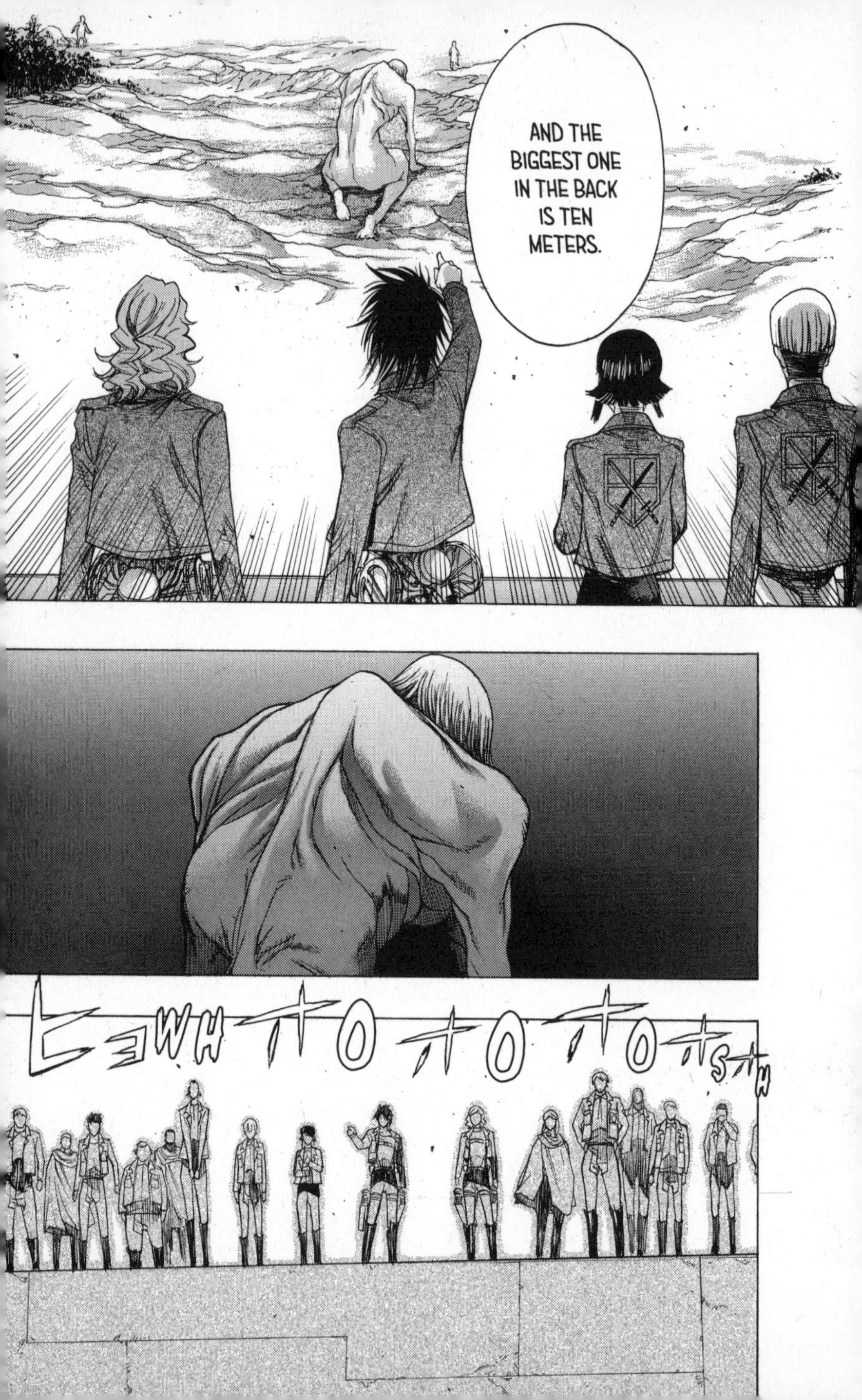
AND THE BIGGEST ONE IN THE BACK IS TEN METERS.

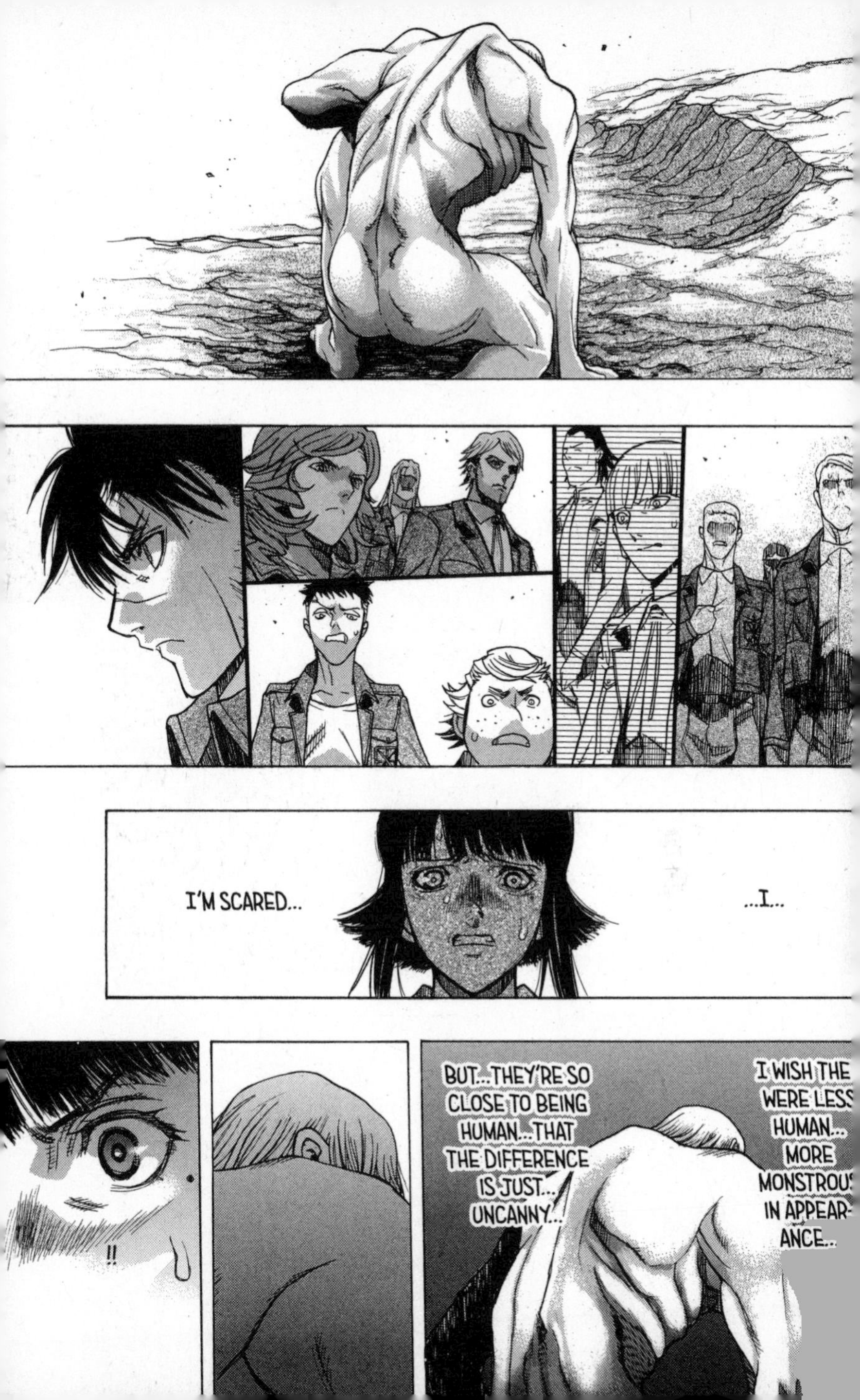
...I...
I'M SCARED...
I WISH THE WERE LESS HUMAN... MORE MONSTROUS IN APPEAR-ANCE...
BUT...THEY'RE SO CLOSE TO BEING HUMAN...THAT THE DIFFERENCE IS JUST... UNCANNY...
!!

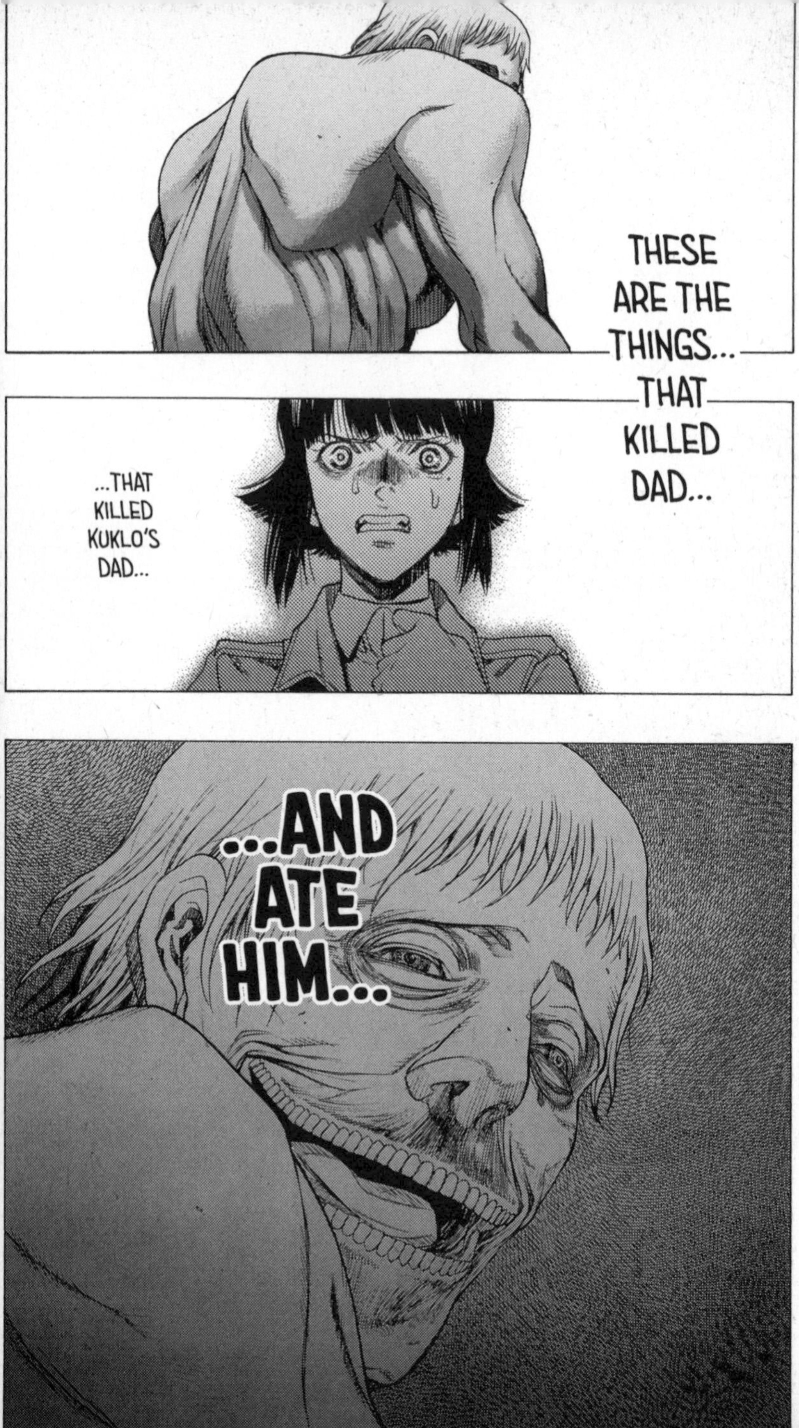
THESE ARE THE THINGS... THAT KILLED DAD...
...THAT KILLED KUKLO'S DAD...
...AND ATE HIM...

Chapter 49: Beyond the Boundary · End

ATTACK on TITAN
BEFORE THE FALL

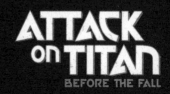

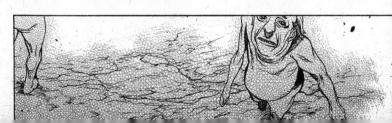

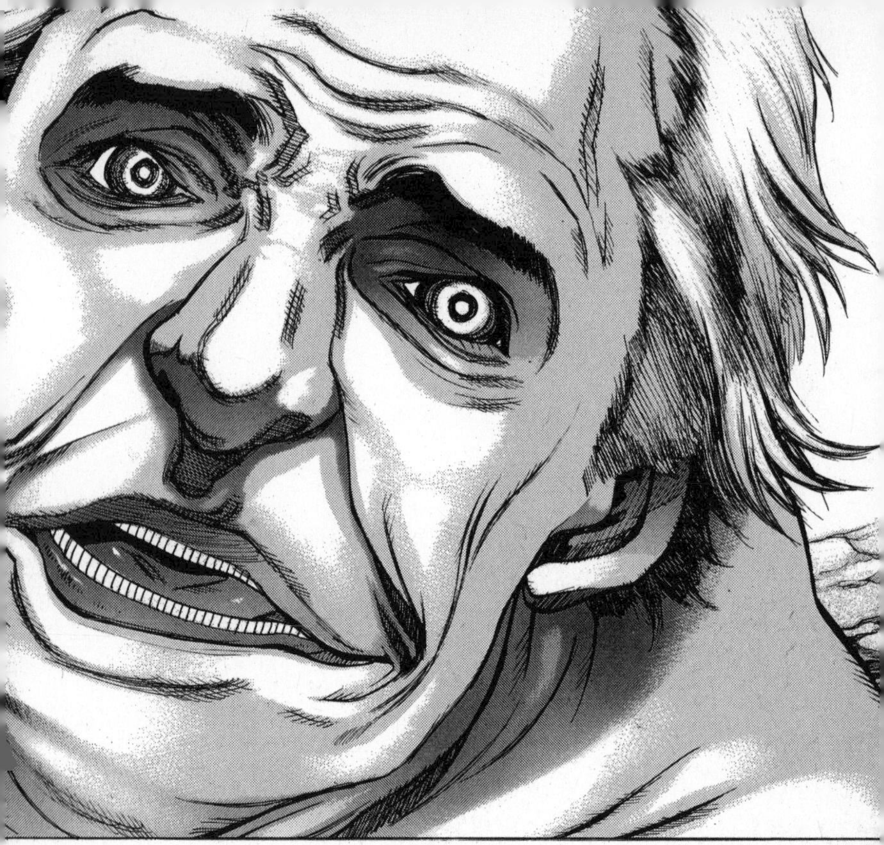
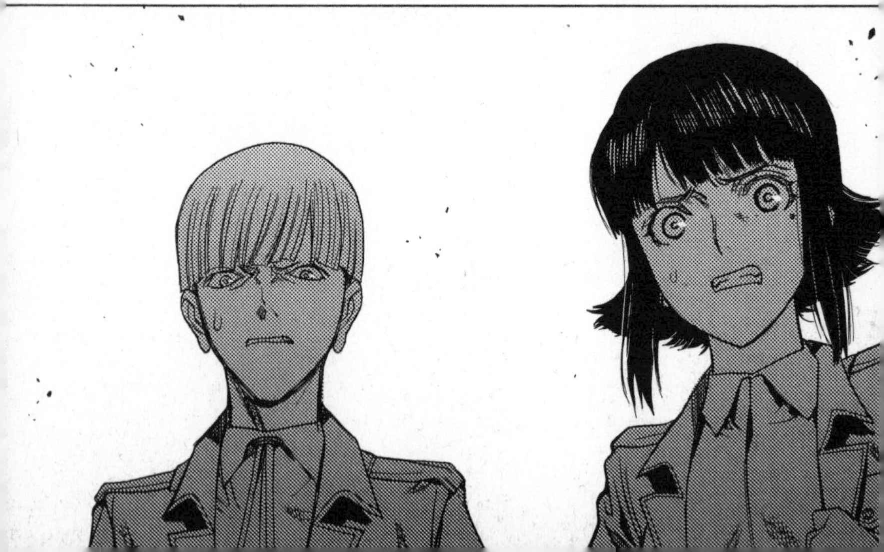

Chapter 50: Labyrinth of the Demon's Womb

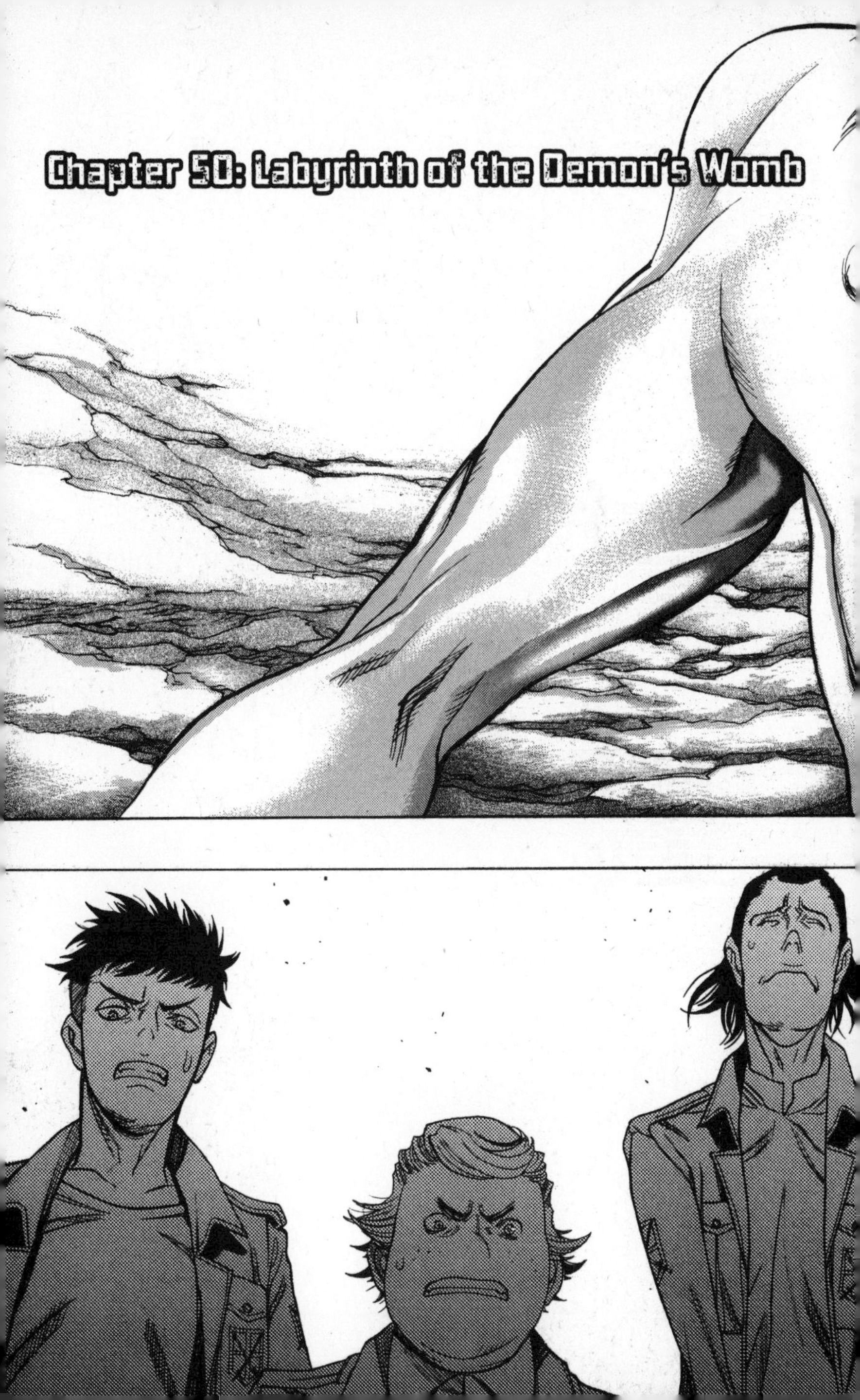

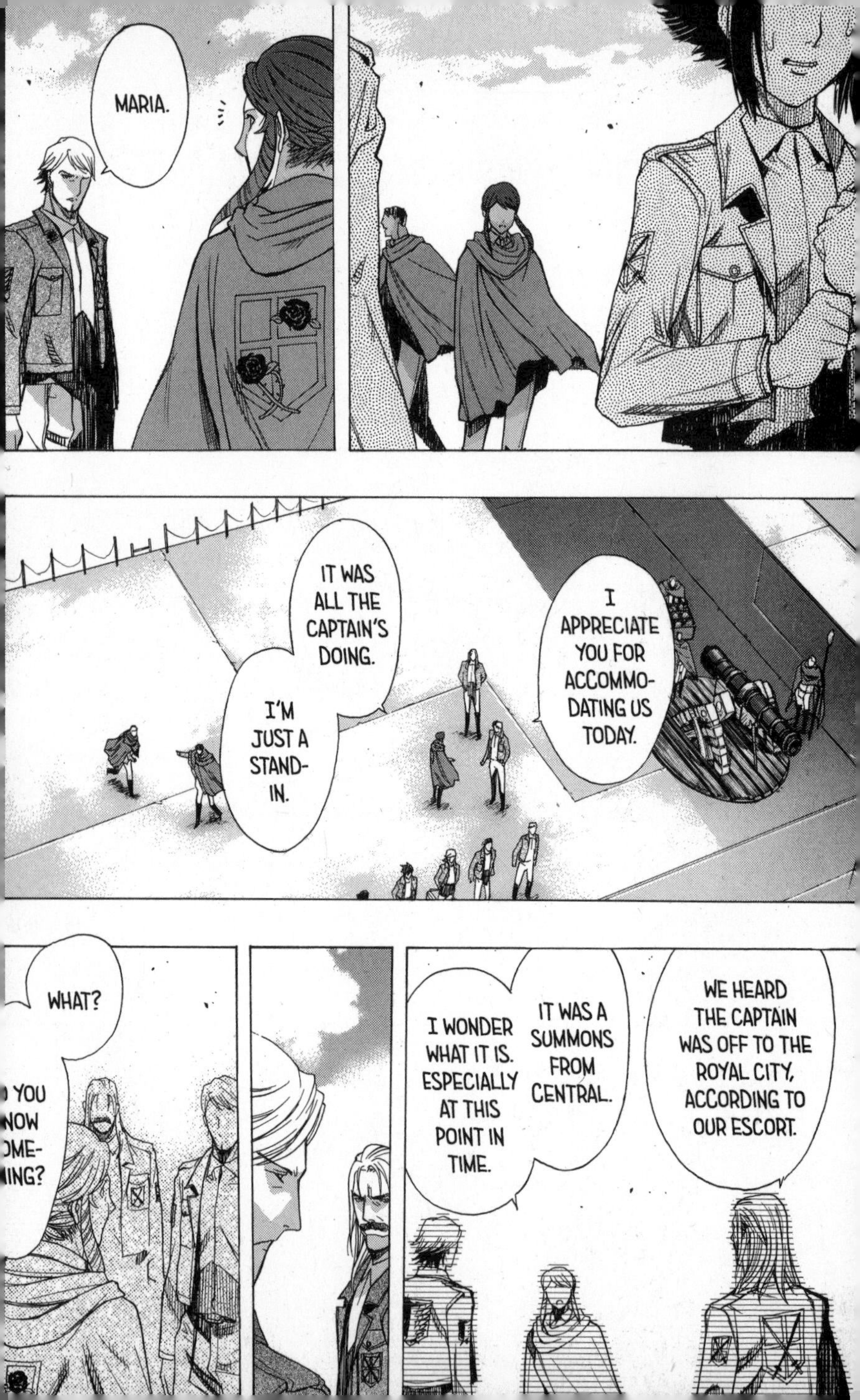
MARIA.
I APPRECIATE YOU FOR ACCOMMODATING US TODAY.
IT WAS ALL THE CAPTAIN'S DOING.
I'M JUST A STAND-IN.
WE HEARD THE CAPTAIN WAS OFF TO THE ROYAL CITY, ACCORDING TO OUR ESCORT.
IT WAS A SUMMONS FROM CENTRAL.
I WONDER WHAT IT IS. ESPECIALLY AT THIS POINT IN TIME.
WHAT?

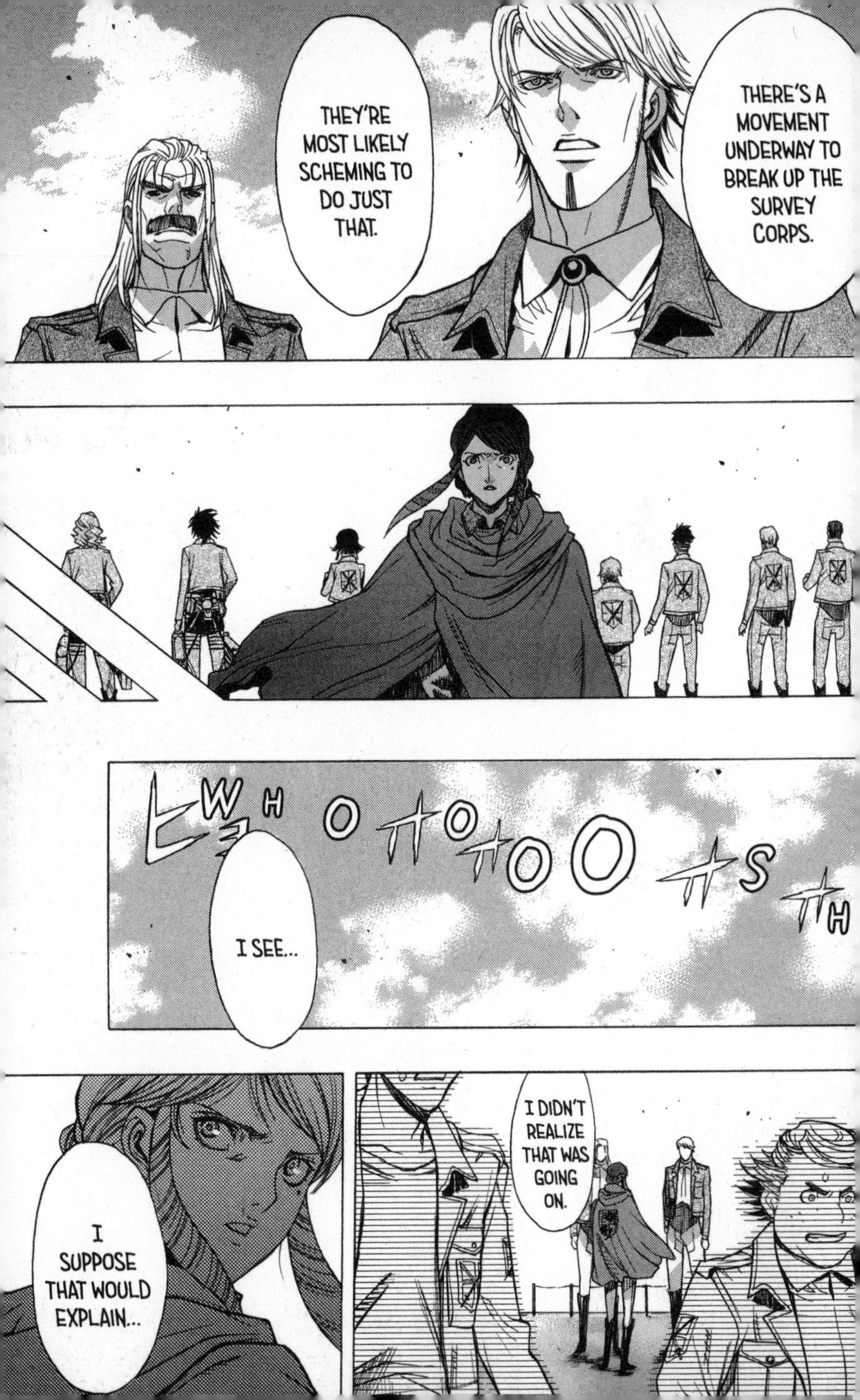
THERE'S A MOVEMENT UNDERWAY TO BREAK UP THE SURVEY CORPS.
THEY'RE MOST LIKELY SCHEMING TO DO JUST THAT.
WHOOOOSH
I SEE...
I DIDN'T REALIZE THAT WAS GOING ON.
I SUPPOSE THAT WOULD EXPLAIN...

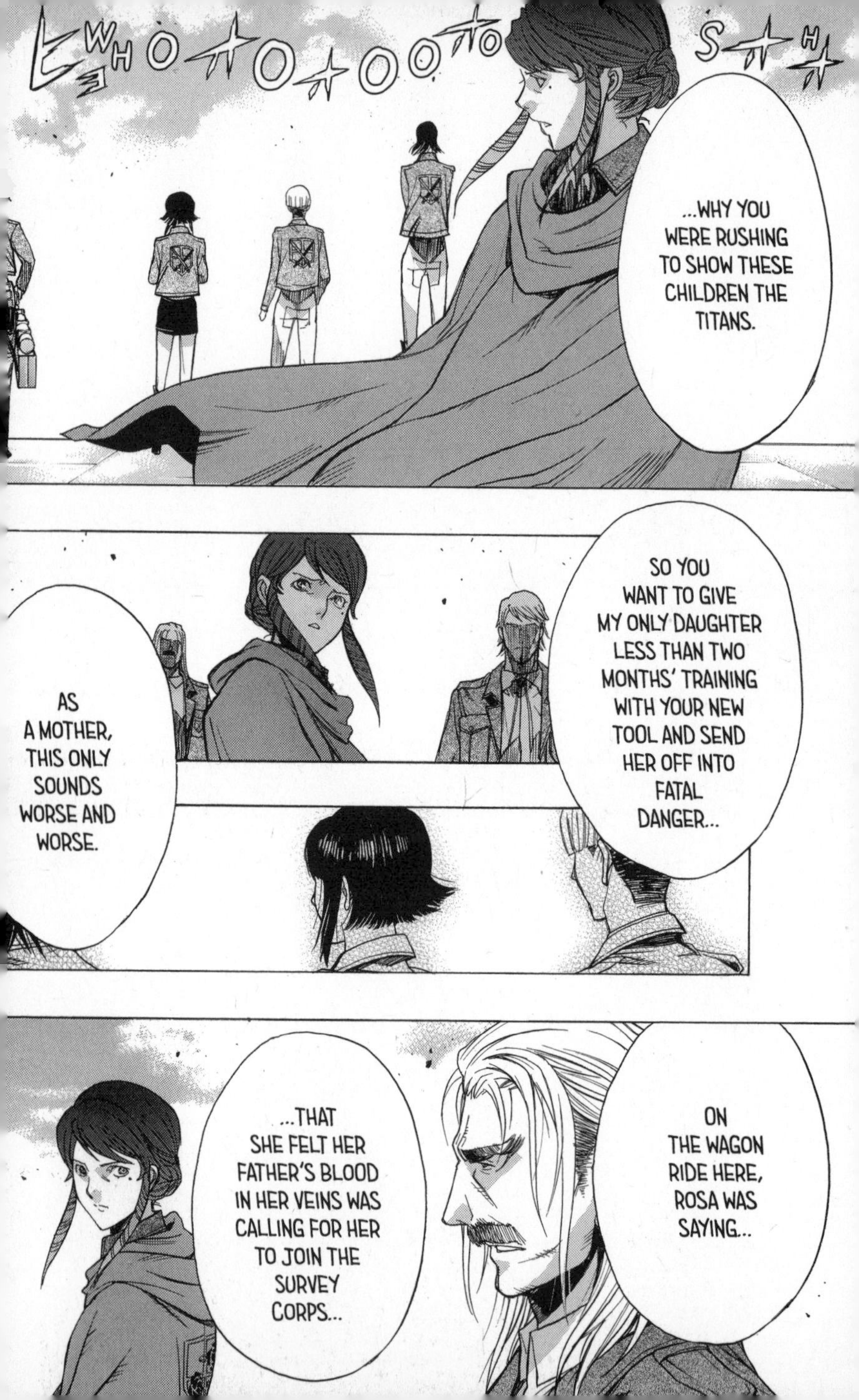
WHOOOOOSH
...WHY YOU WERE RUSHING TO SHOW THESE CHILDREN THE TITANS.
SO YOU WANT TO GIVE MY ONLY DAUGHTER LESS THAN TWO MONTHS' TRAINING WITH YOUR NEW TOOL AND SEND HER OFF INTO FATAL DANGER...
AS A MOTHER, THIS ONLY SOUNDS WORSE AND WORSE.
ON THE WAGON RIDE HERE, ROSA WAS SAYING...
...THAT SHE FELT HER FATHER'S BLOOD IN HER VEINS WAS CALLING FOR HER TO JOIN THE SURVEY CORPS...

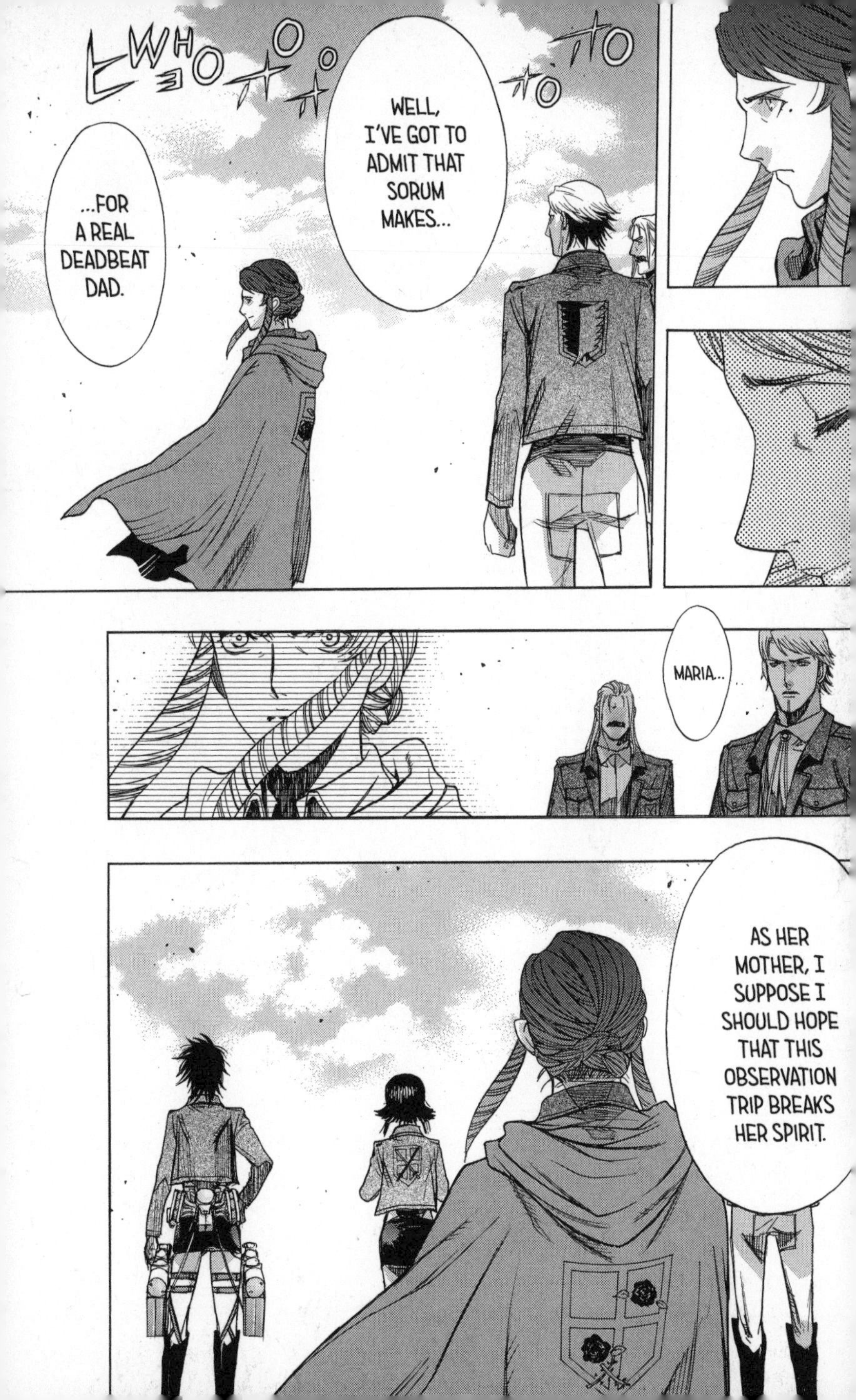
WELL, I'VE GOT TO ADMIT THAT SORUM MAKES...
...FOR A REAL DEADBEAT DAD.
MARIA...
AS HER MOTHER, I SUPPOSE I SHOULD HOPE THAT THIS OBSERVATION TRIP BREAKS HER SPIRIT.

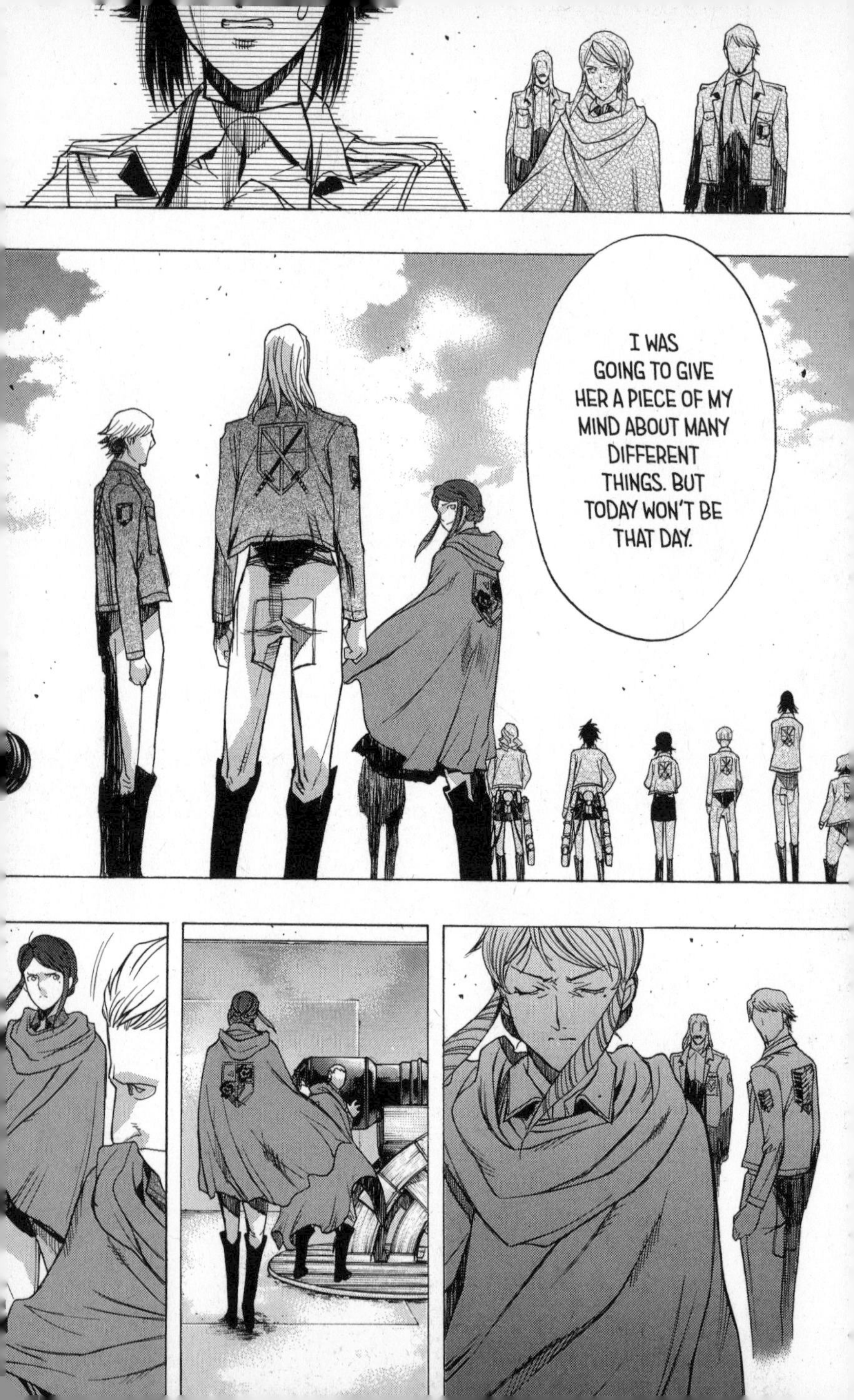
I WAS GOING TO GIVE HER A PIECE OF MY MIND ABOUT MANY DIFFERENT THINGS. BUT TODAY WON'T BE THAT DAY.

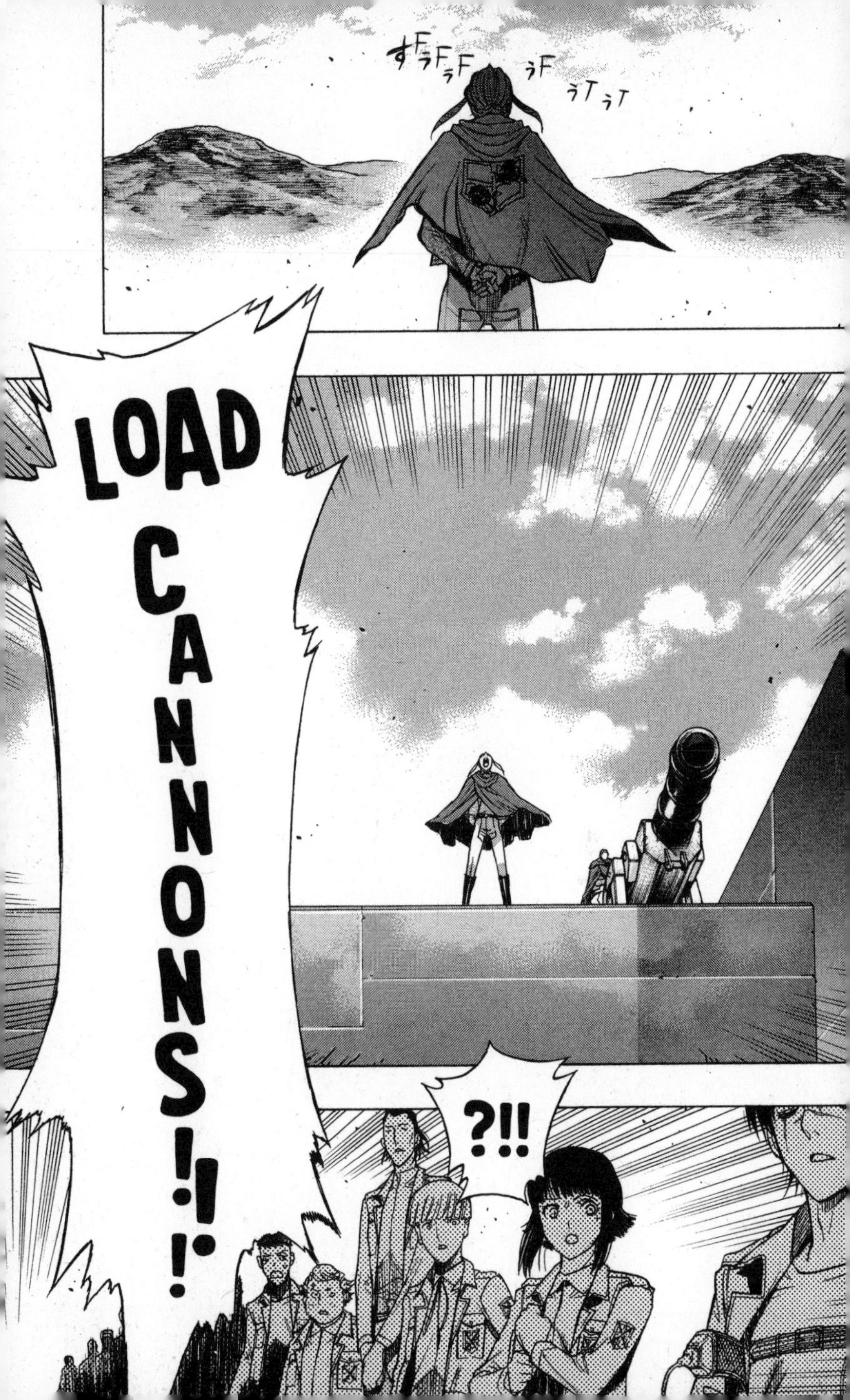
LOAD CANNONS!!!
?!!

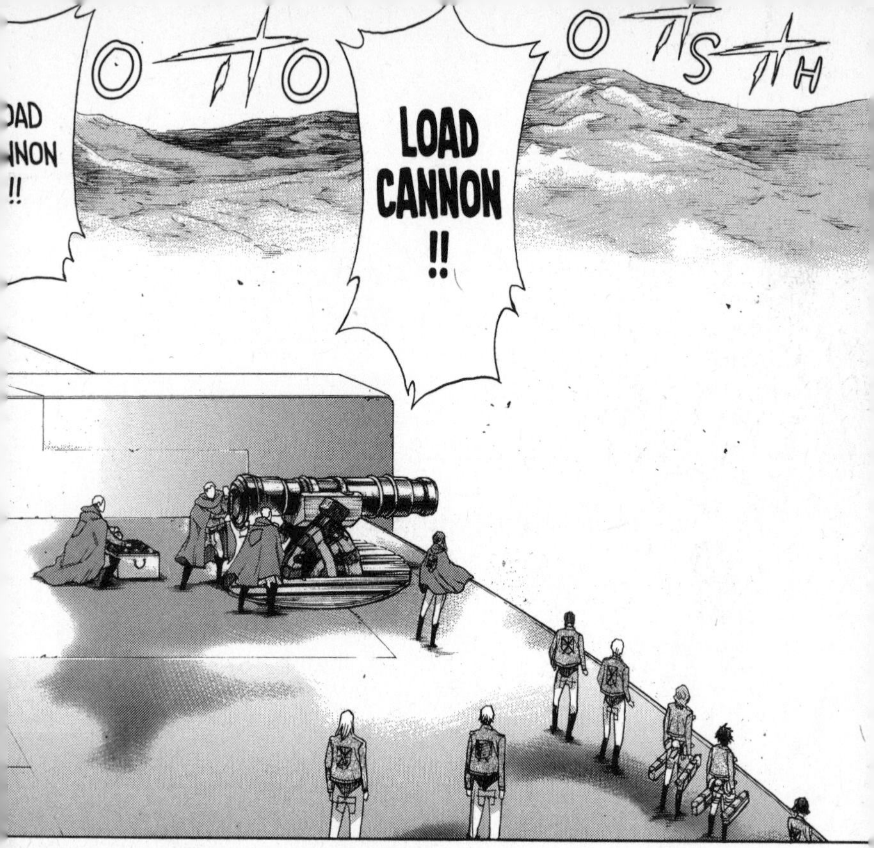
LOAD CANNON !!

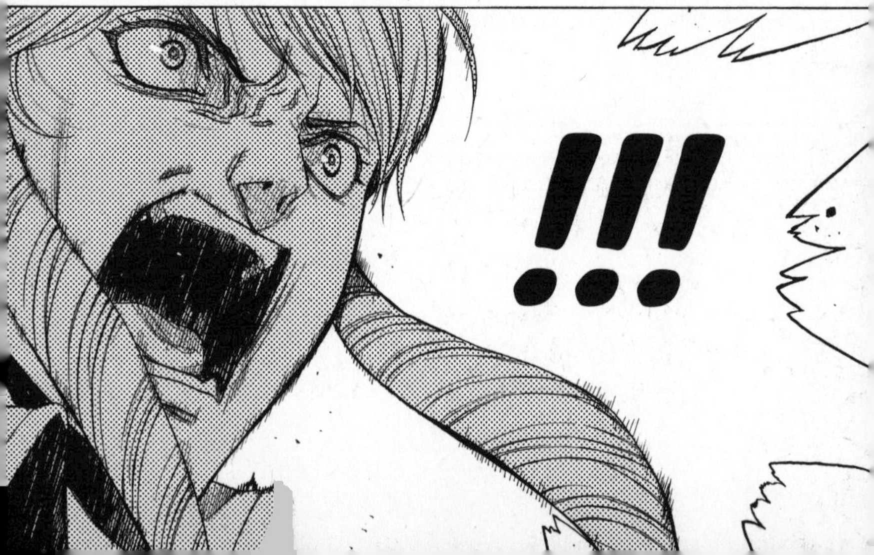
!!!

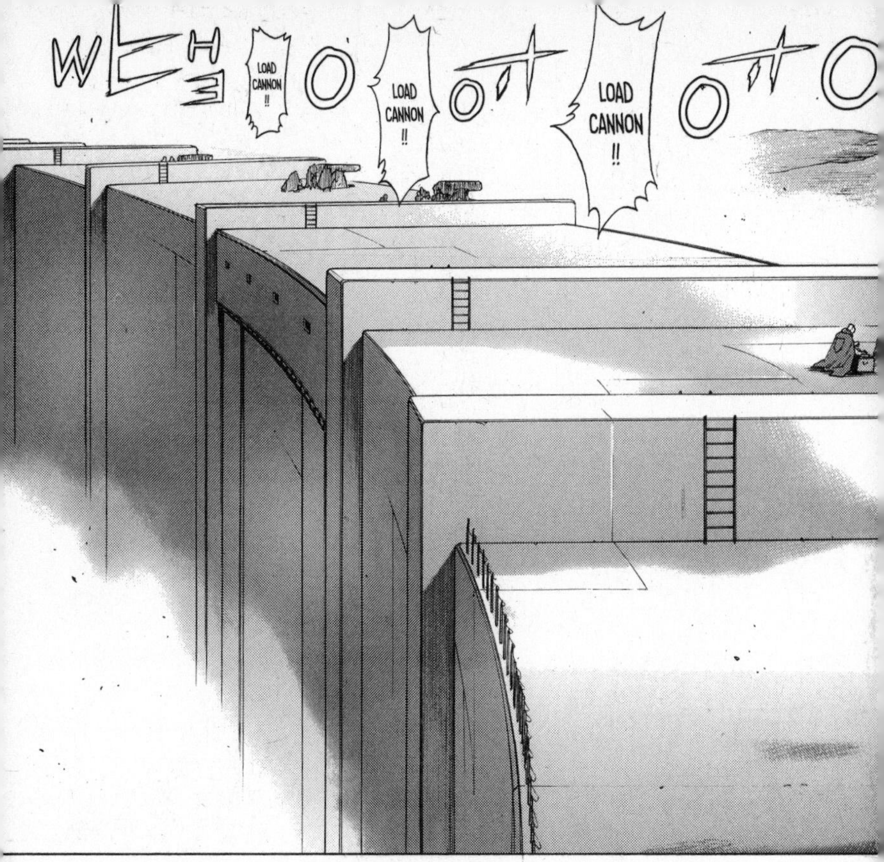
LOAD CANNON !!
LOAD CANNON !!
LOAD CANNON !!
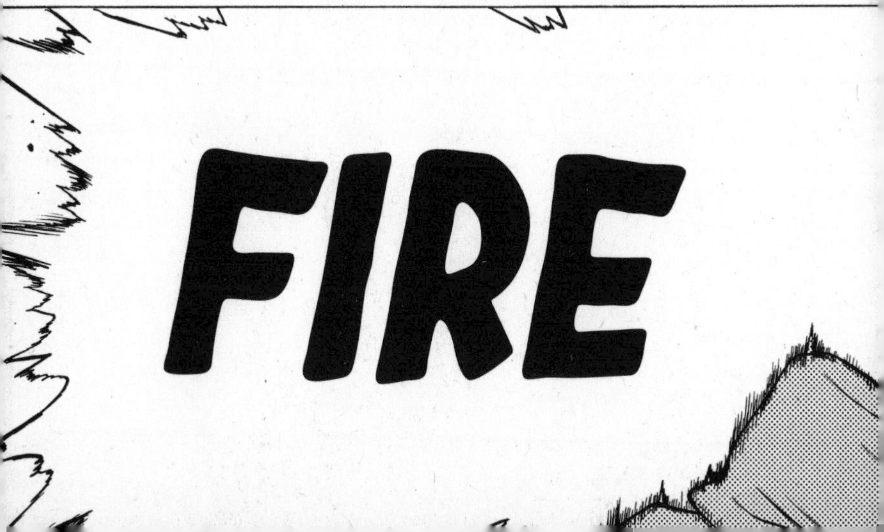
FIRE

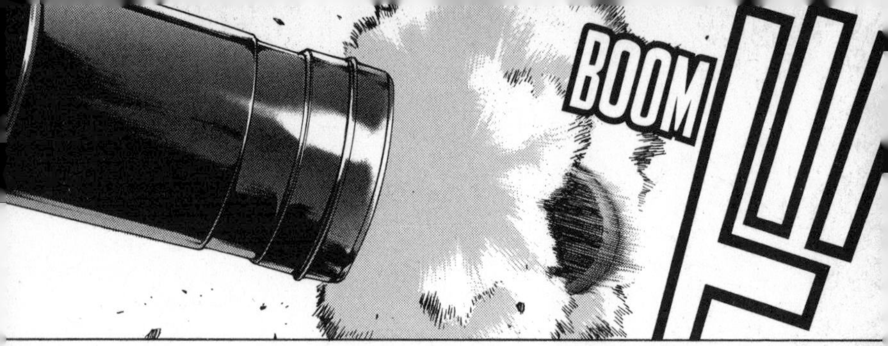
BOOM

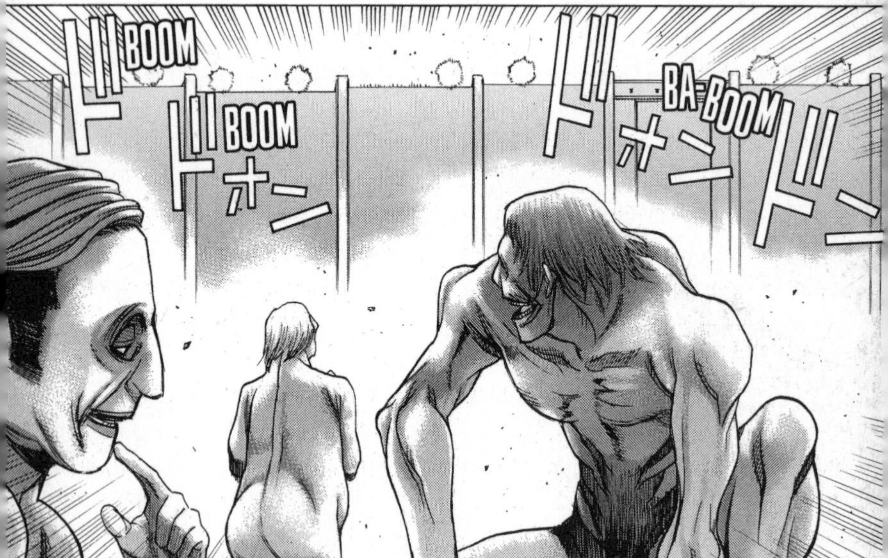
BA-BOOM
BOOM
BOOM

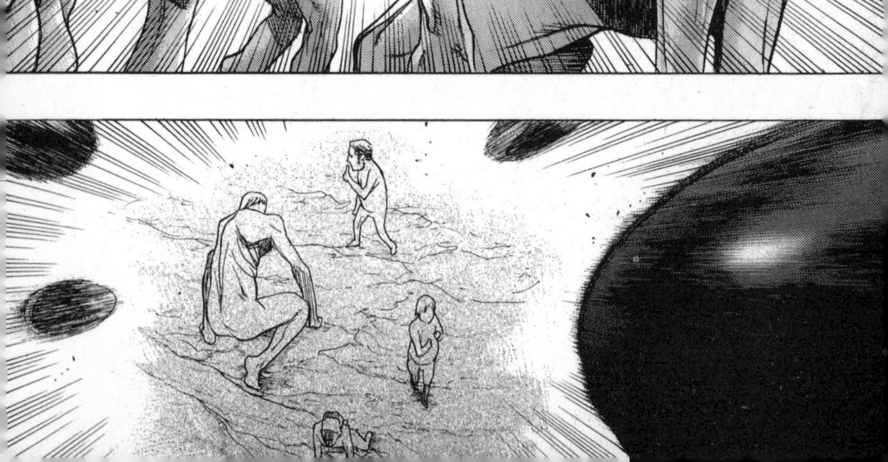

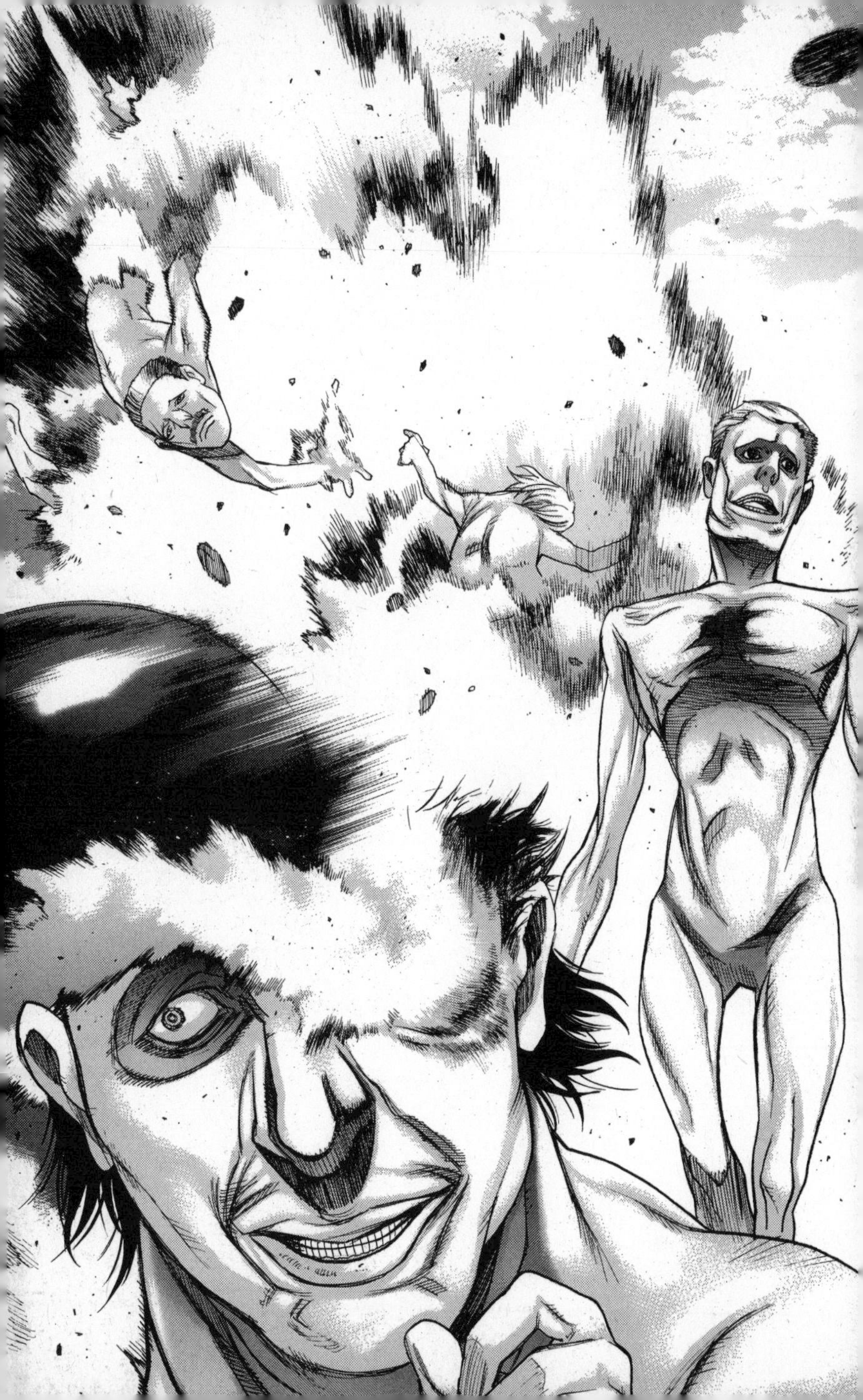

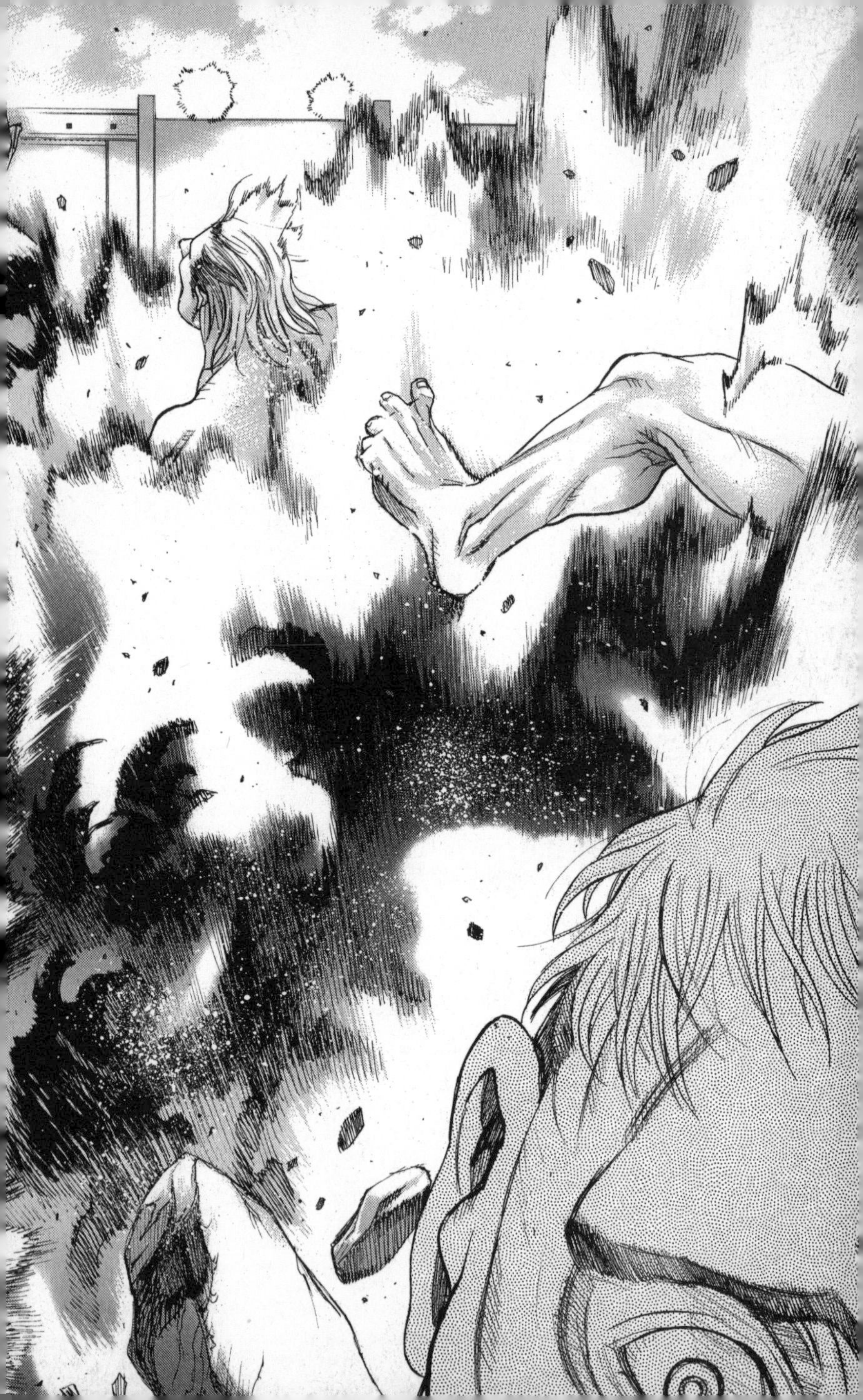

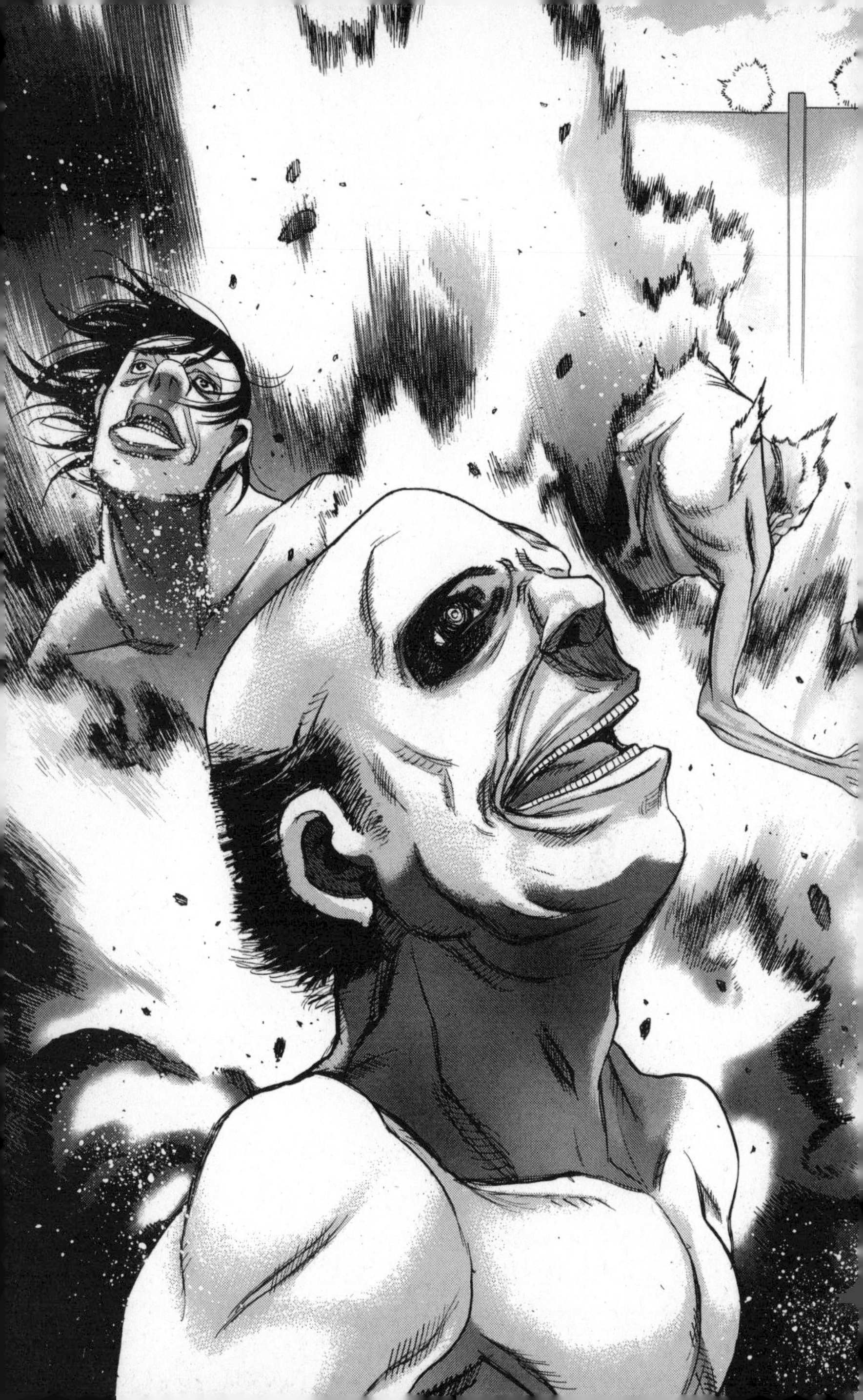

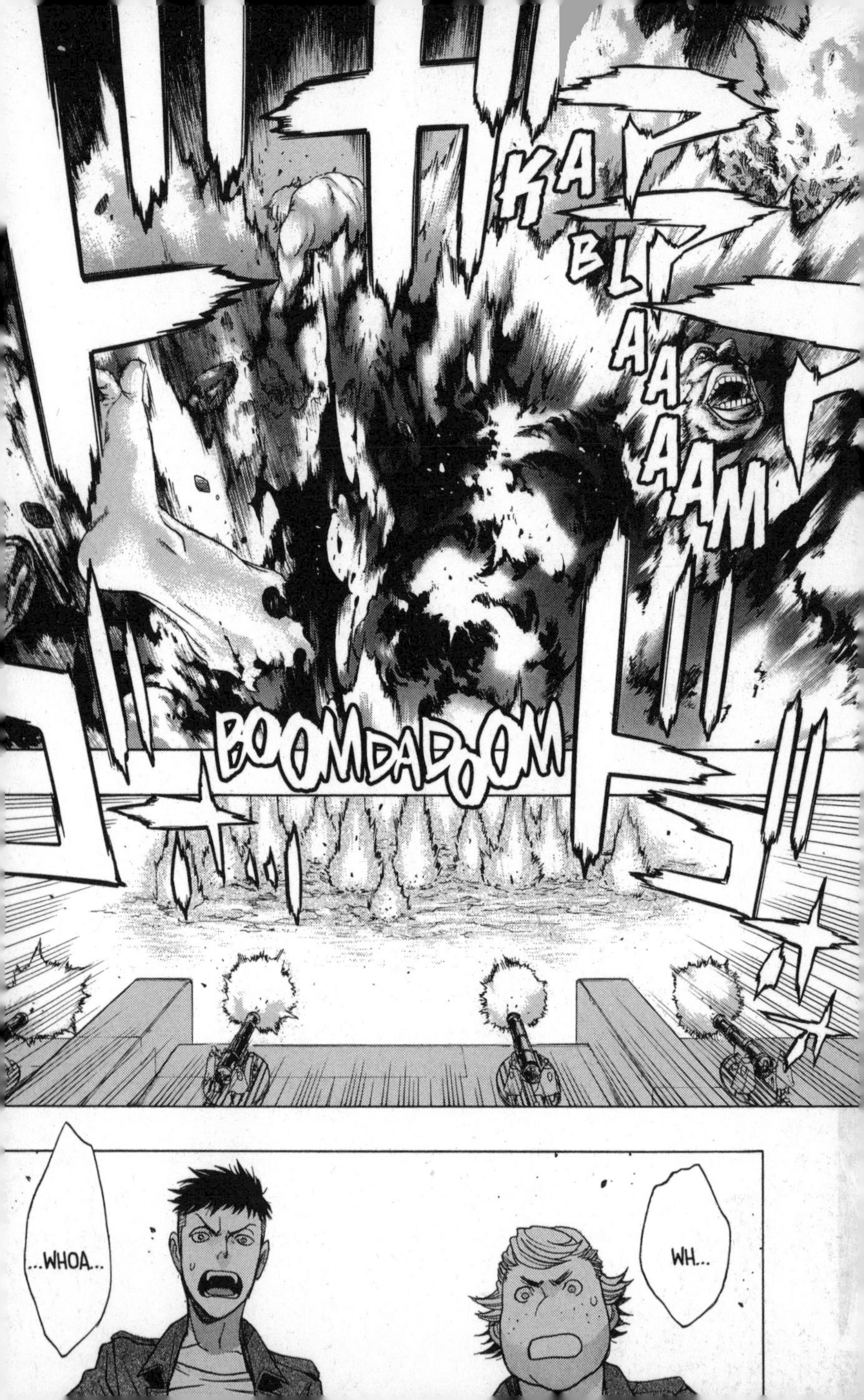
KABLAAAAM
BOOMDADOOM
WH...
...WHOA...

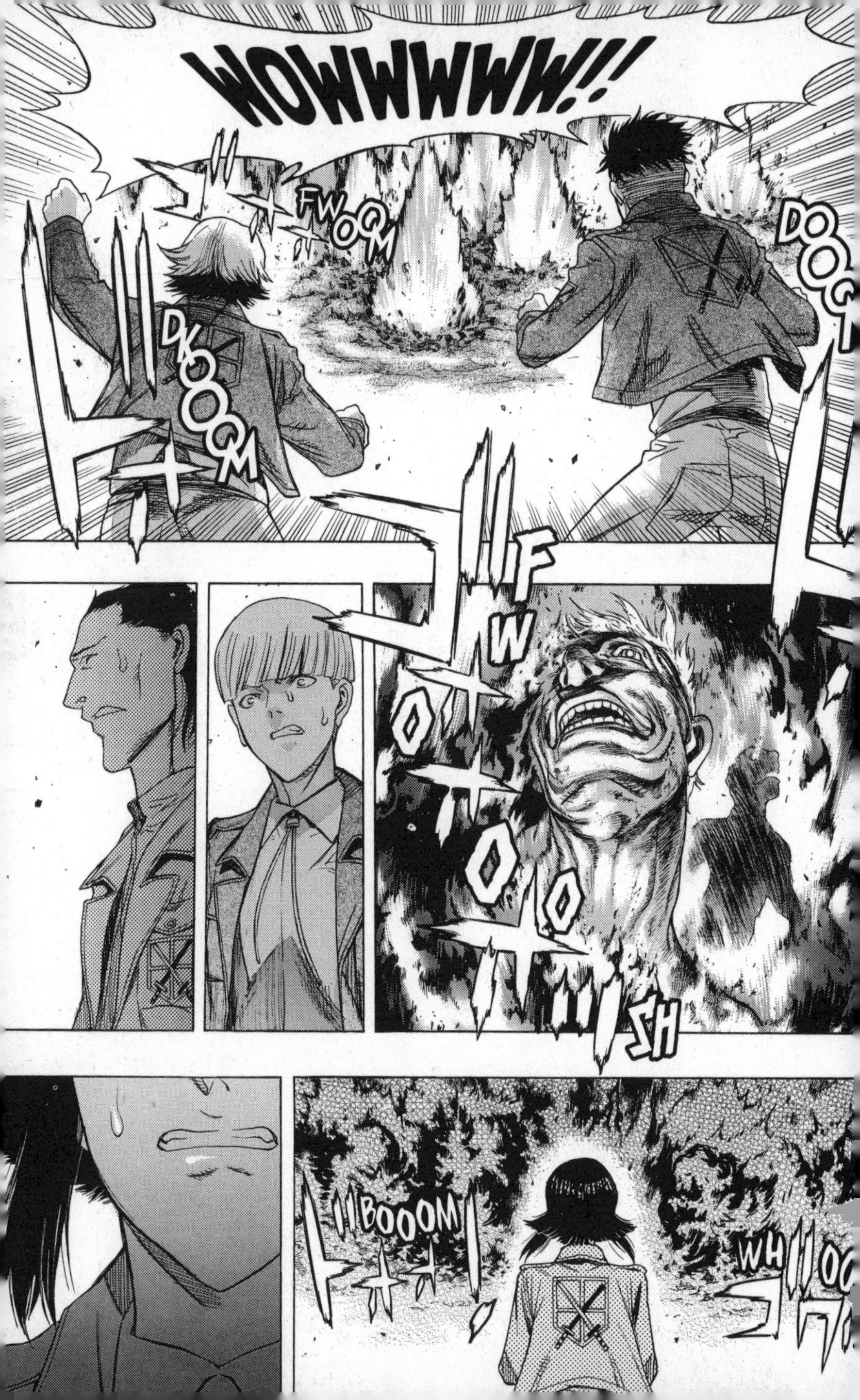
HOWWWWW!!
DOOG
FWOOM
DKOOOM
FWOOOOSH
WHOO
BOOOM

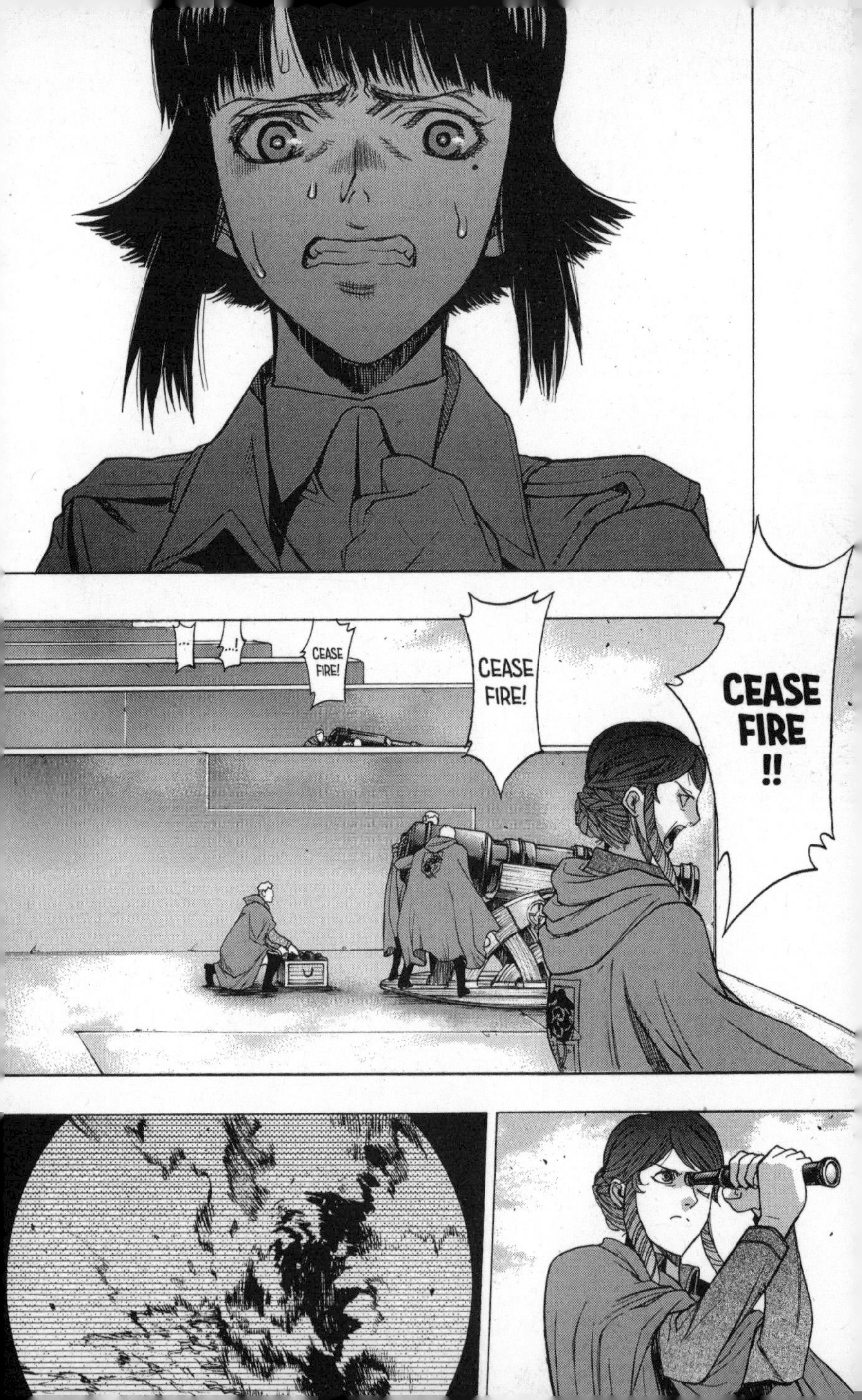
CEASE FIRE!!
CEASE FIRE!
CEASE FIRE!
...!
...

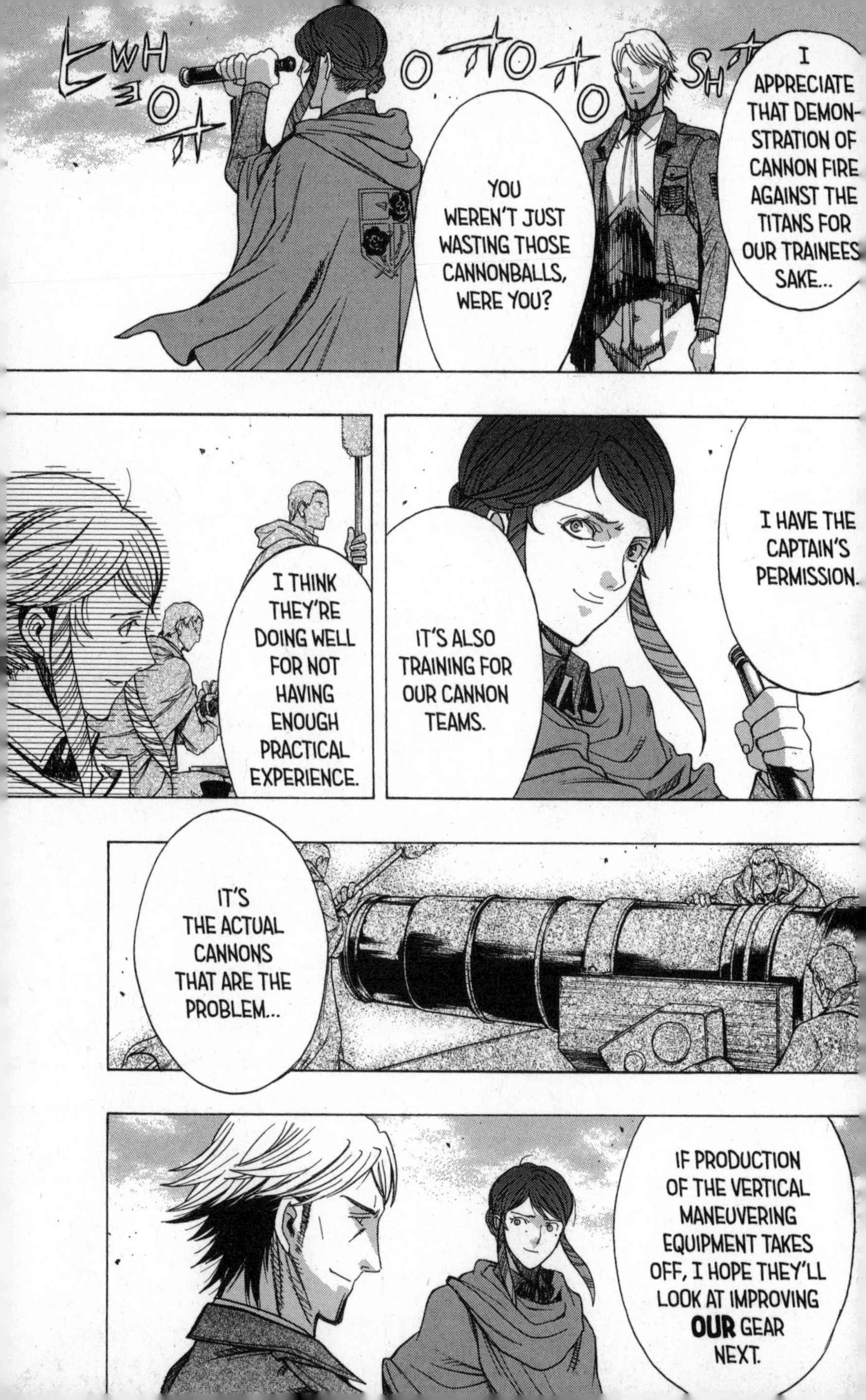
WHOOOOSH
I APPRECIATE THAT DEMONSTRATION OF CANNON FIRE AGAINST THE TITANS FOR OUR TRAINEES SAKE...
YOU WEREN'T JUST WASTING THOSE CANNONBALLS, WERE YOU?
I HAVE THE CAPTAIN'S PERMISSION.
IT'S ALSO TRAINING FOR OUR CANNON TEAMS.
I THINK THEY'RE DOING WELL FOR NOT HAVING ENOUGH PRACTICAL EXPERIENCE.
IT'S THE ACTUAL CANNONS THAT ARE THE PROBLEM...
IF PRODUCTION OF THE VERTICAL MANEUVERING EQUIPMENT TAKES OFF, I HOPE THEY'LL LOOK AT IMPROVING **OUR** GEAR NEXT.

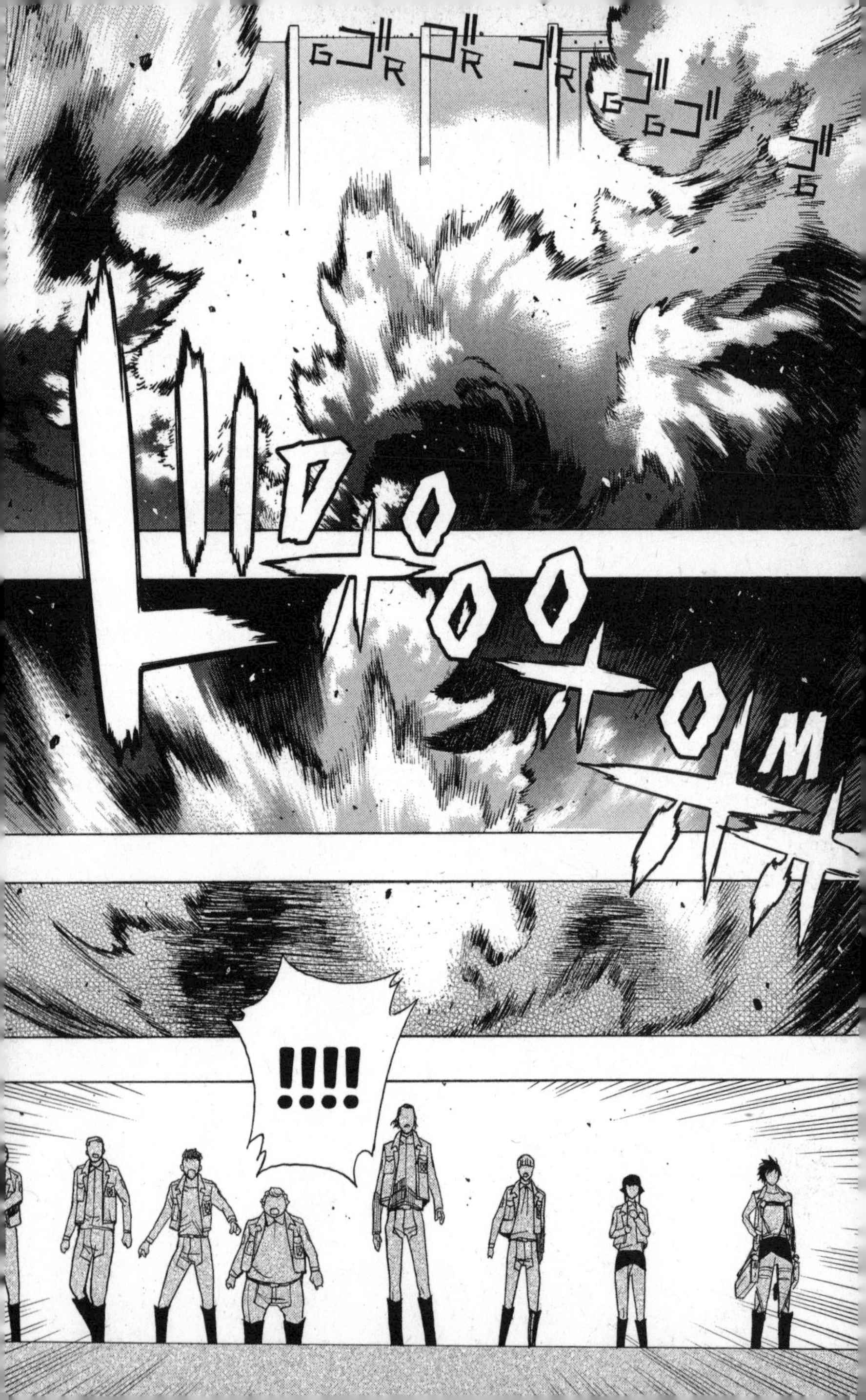
DOOOM
!!!!

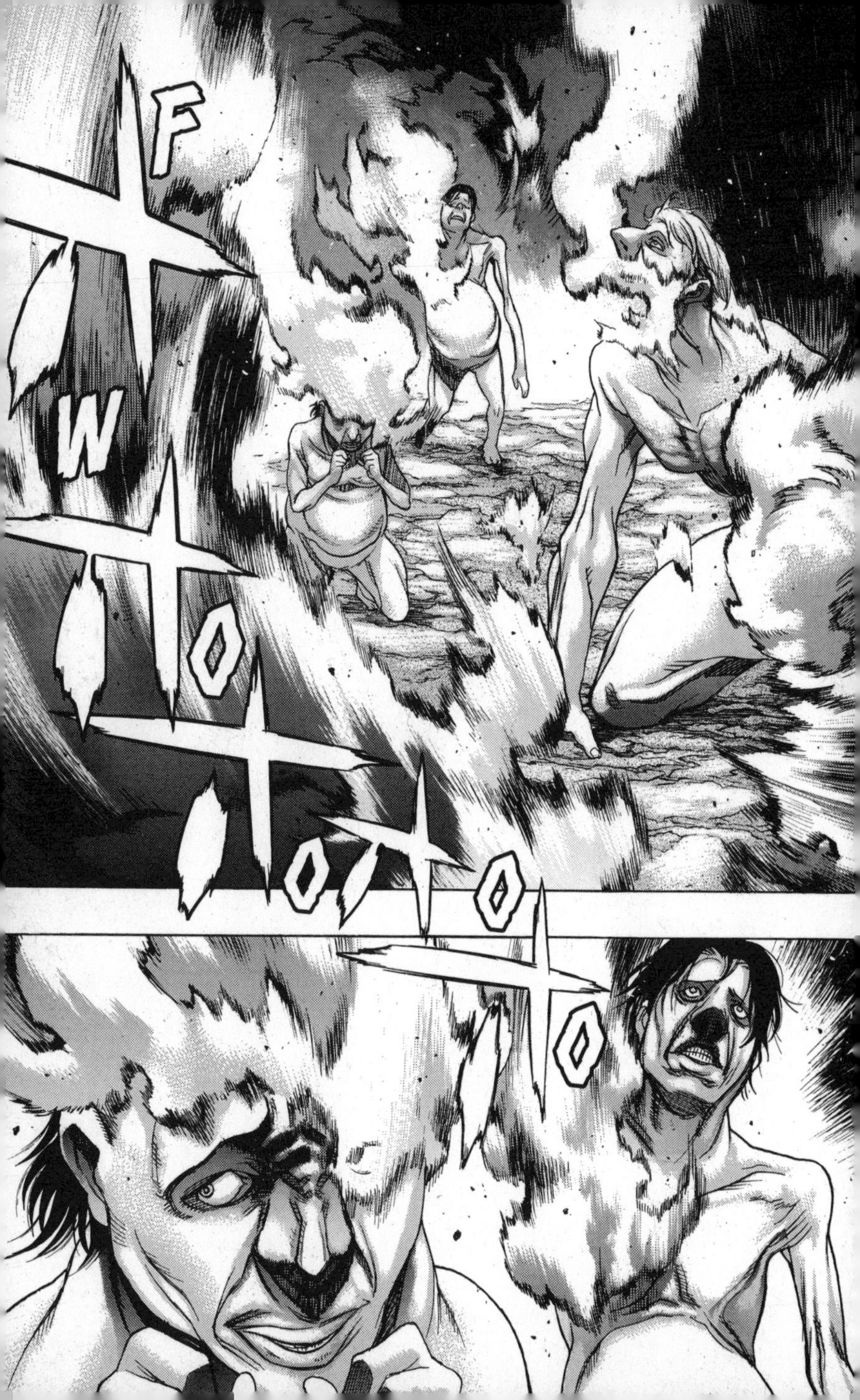
FWOOOOO

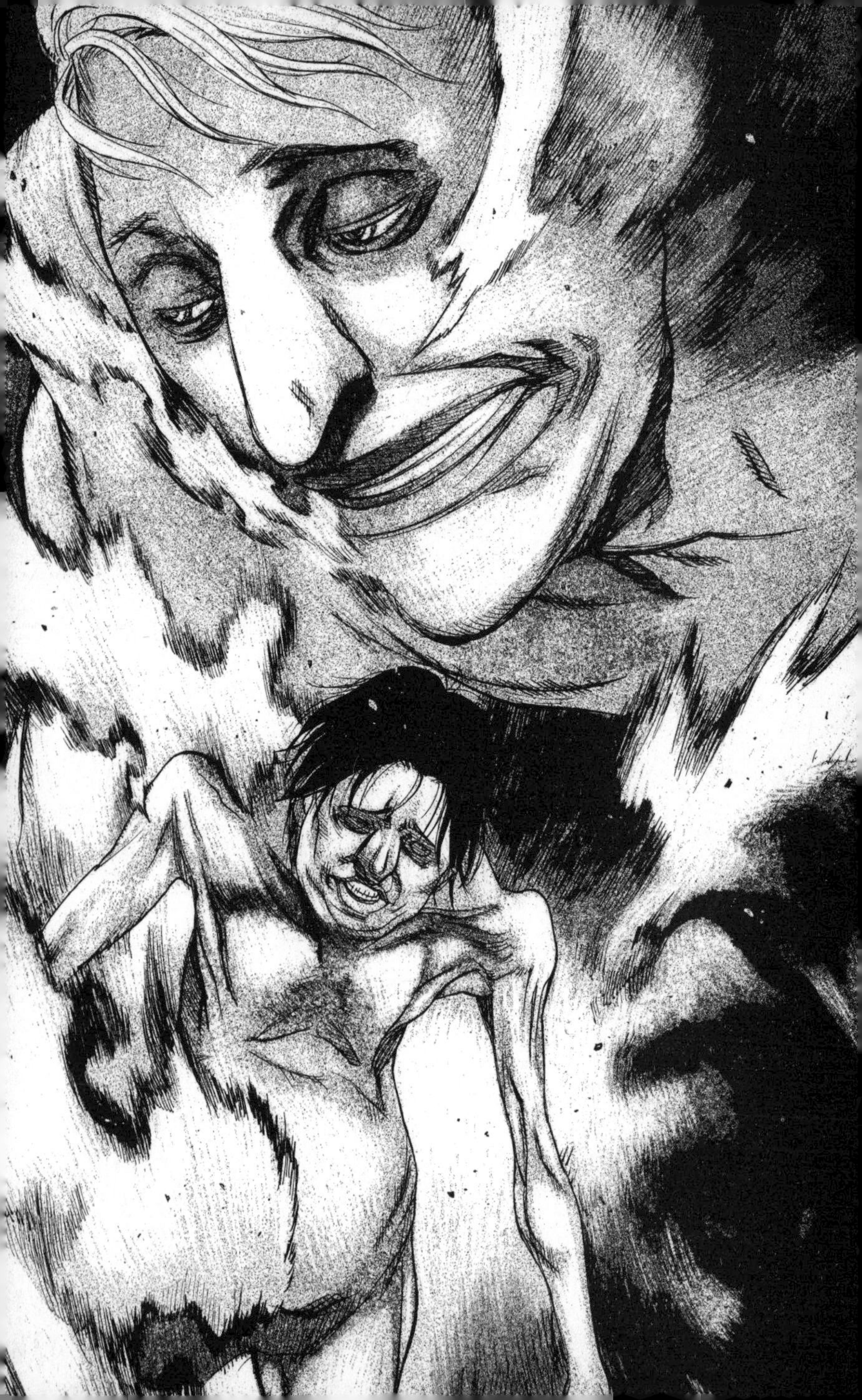

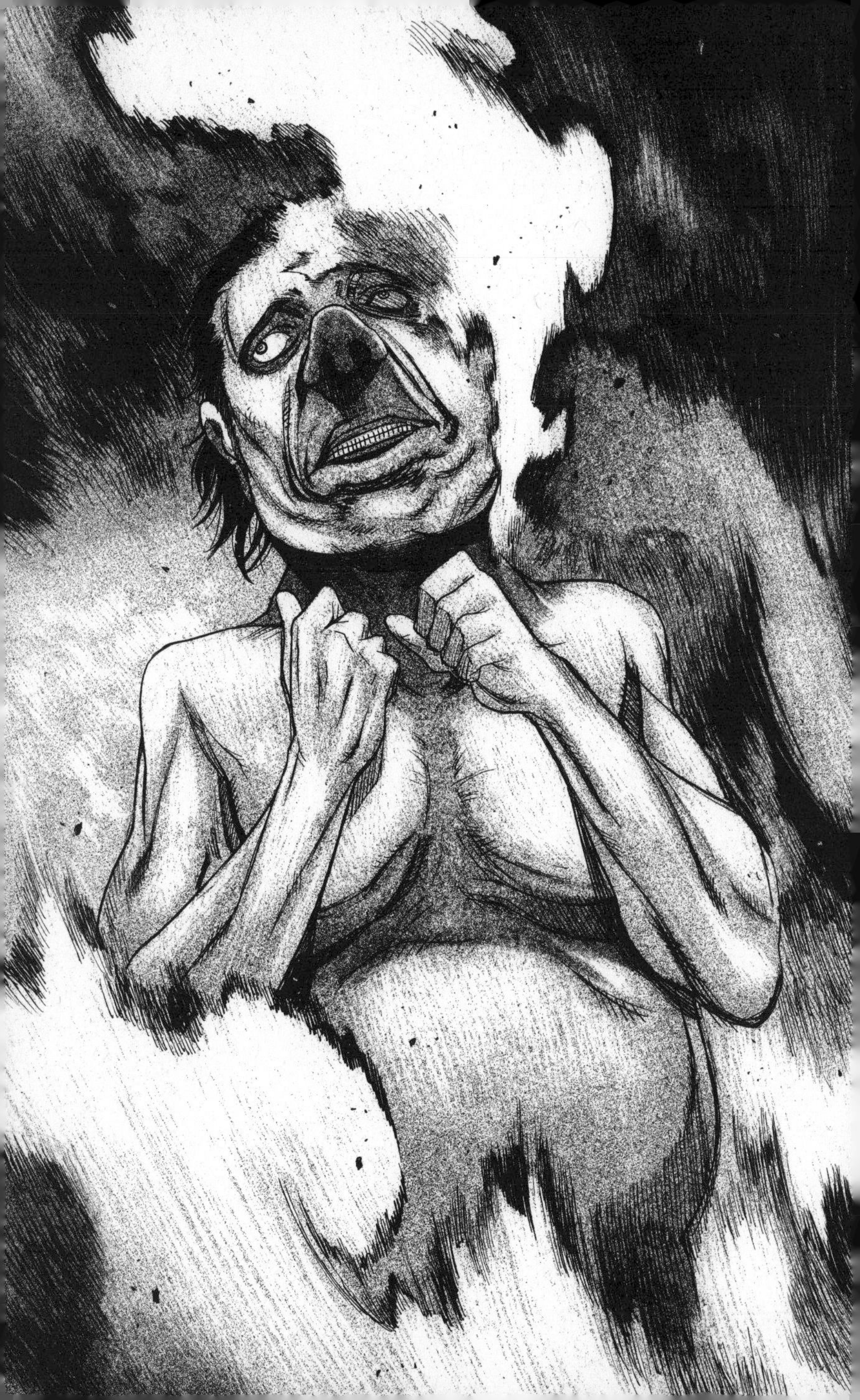

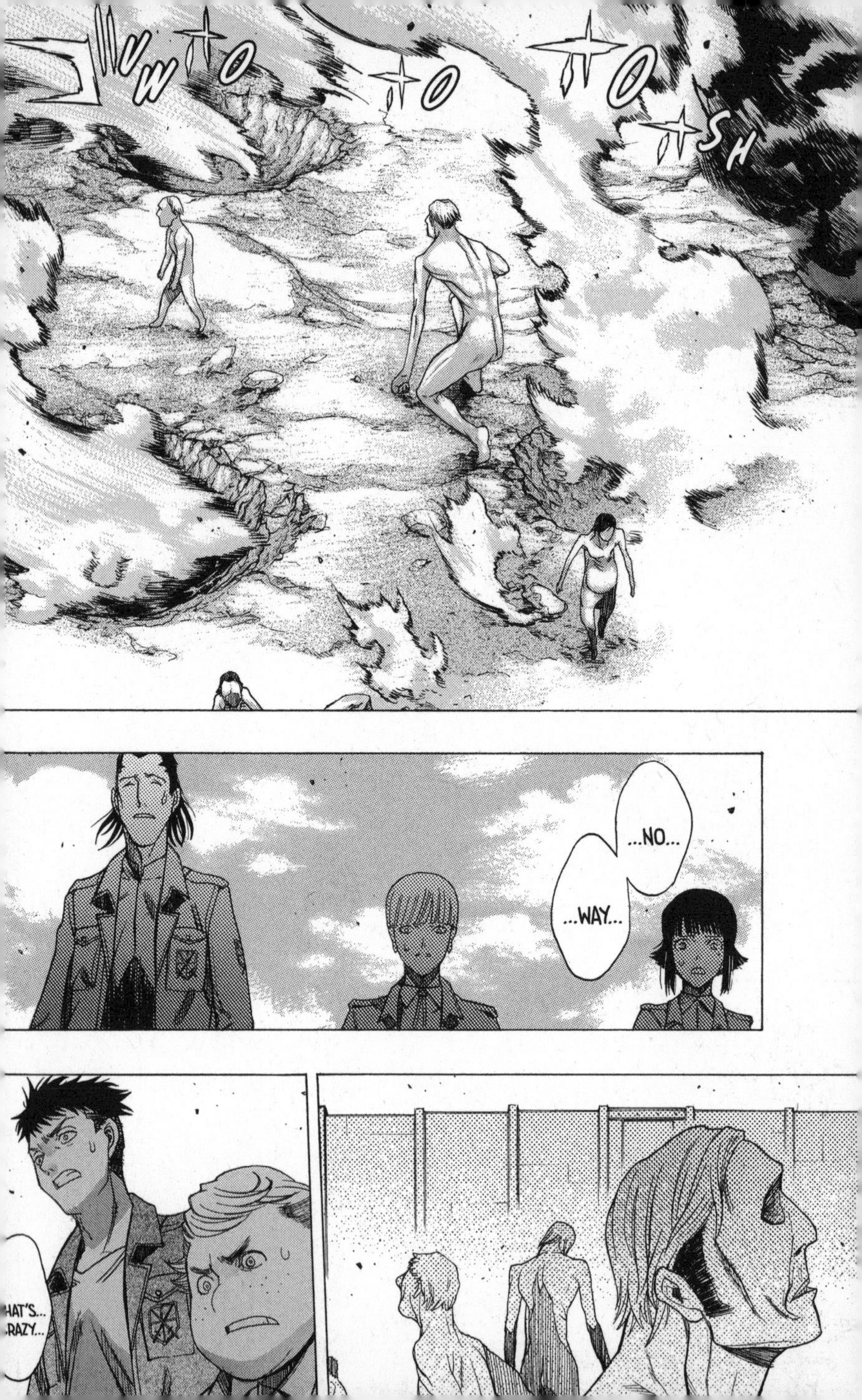
...NO...
...WAY...
HAT'S...
RAZY...

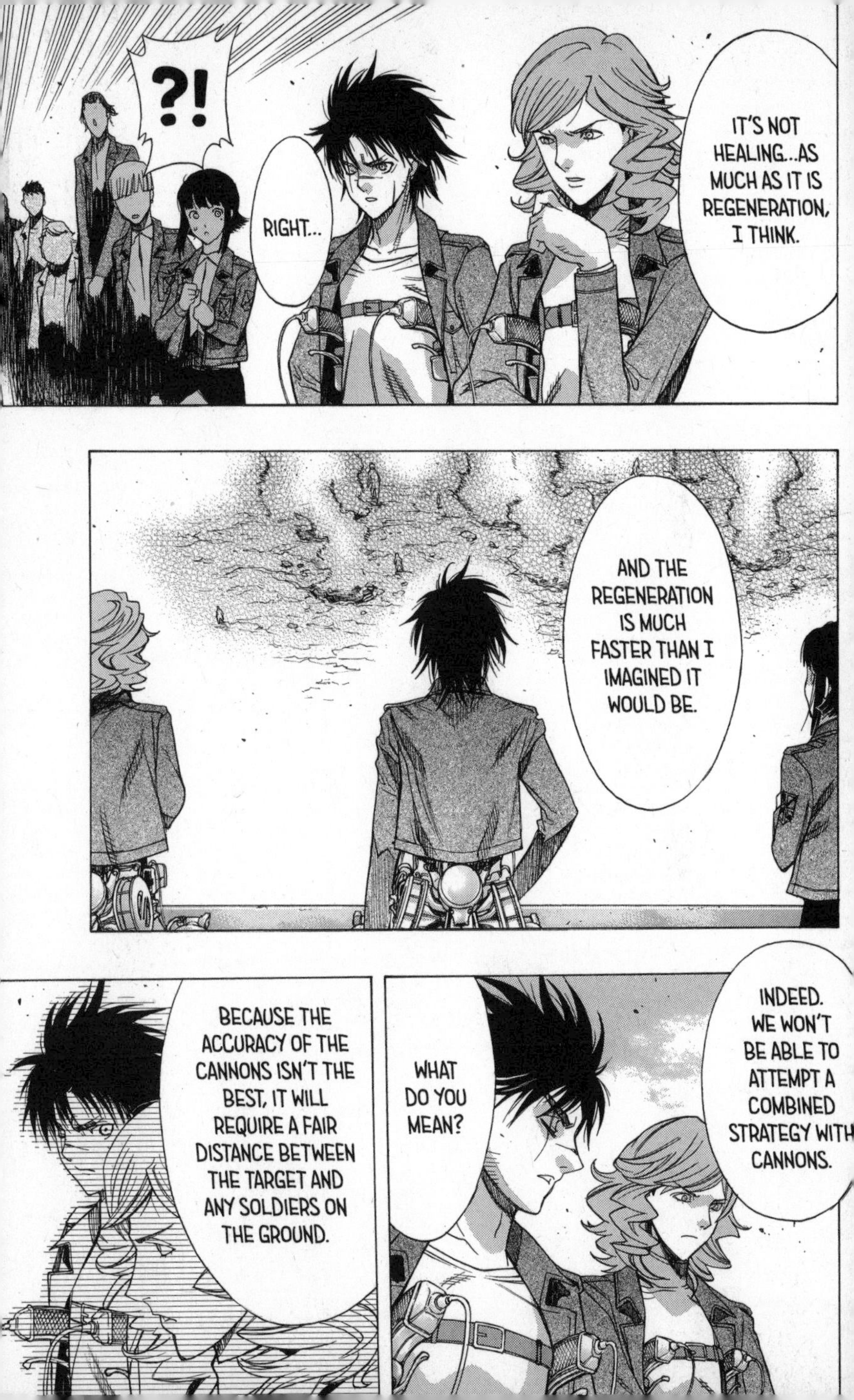
IT'S NOT HEALING...AS MUCH AS IT IS REGENERATION, I THINK.
RIGHT...
?!
AND THE REGENERATION IS MUCH FASTER THAN I IMAGINED IT WOULD BE.
INDEED. WE WON'T BE ABLE TO ATTEMPT A COMBINED STRATEGY WITH CANNONS.
WHAT DO YOU MEAN?
BECAUSE THE ACCURACY OF THE CANNONS ISN'T THE BEST, IT WILL REQUIRE A FAIR DISTANCE BETWEEN THE TARGET AND ANY SOLDIERS ON THE GROUND.

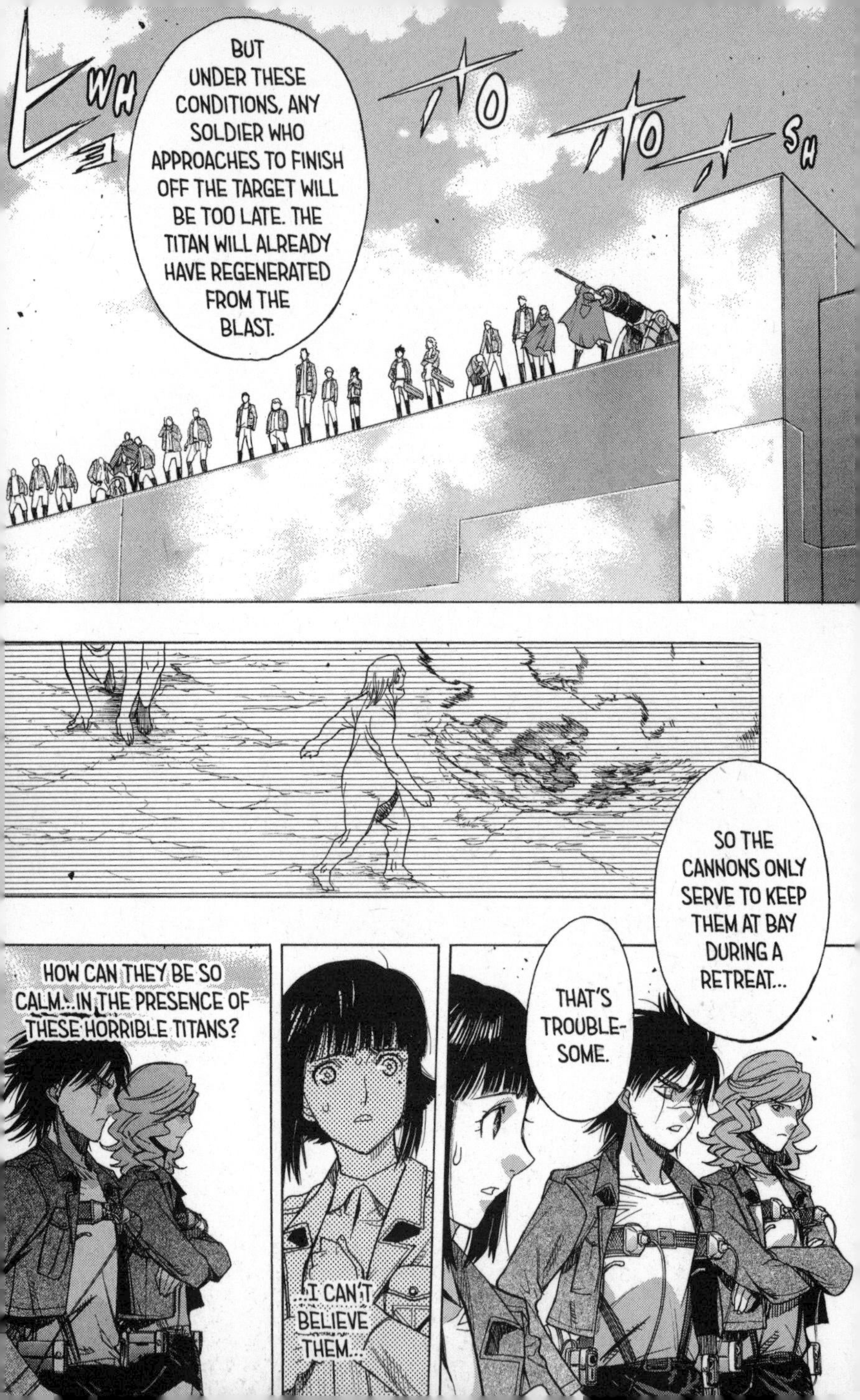
SH
WH
BUT UNDER THESE CONDITIONS, ANY SOLDIER WHO APPROACHES TO FINISH OFF THE TARGET WILL BE TOO LATE. THE TITAN WILL ALREADY HAVE REGENERATED FROM THE BLAST.
SO THE CANNONS ONLY SERVE TO KEEP THEM AT BAY DURING A RETREAT...
THAT'S TROUBLE-SOME.
...I CAN'T BELIEVE THEM...
HOW CAN THEY BE SO CALM...IN THE PRESENCE OF THESE HORRIBLE TITANS?

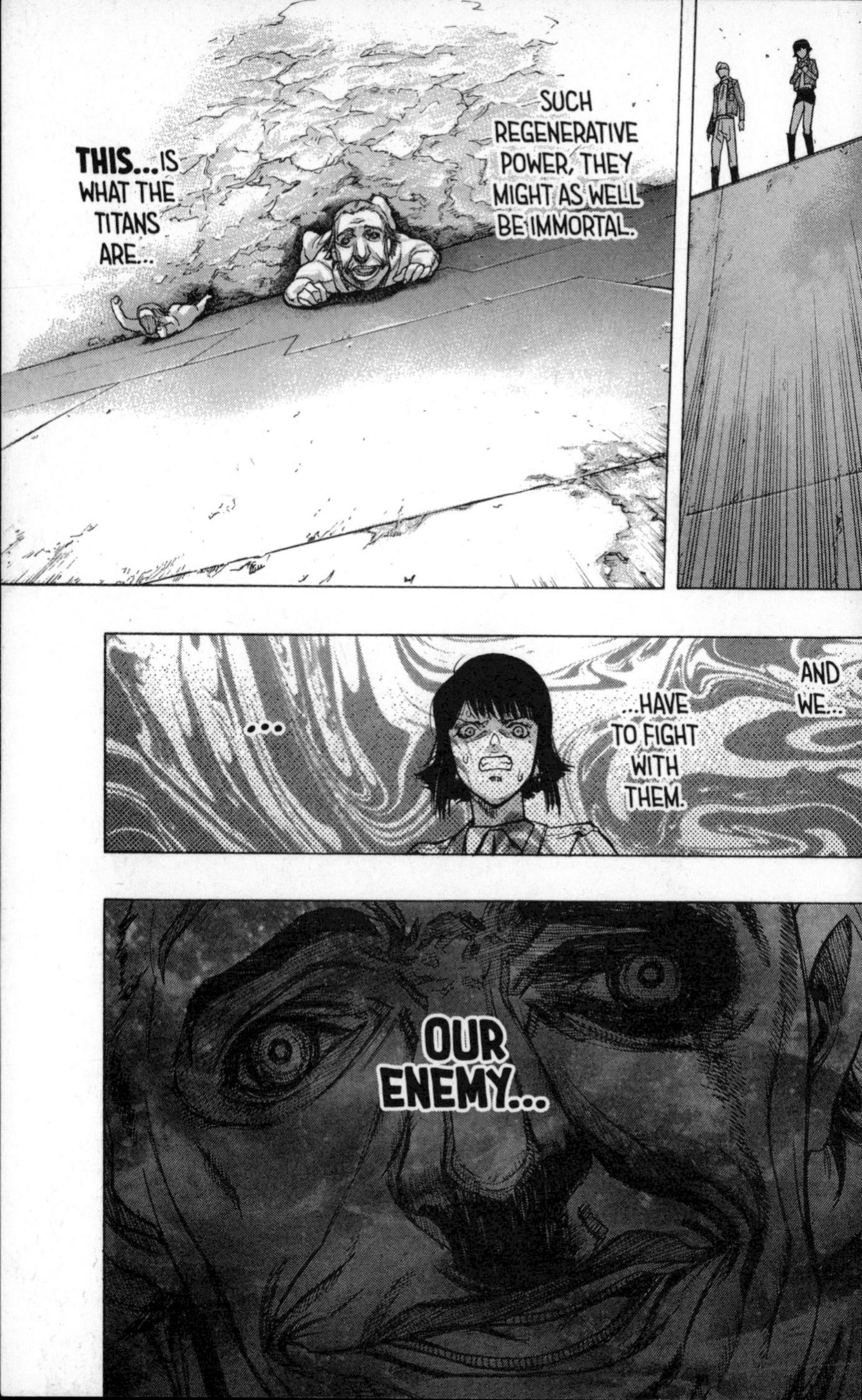
SUCH REGENERATIVE POWER, THEY MIGHT AS WELL BE IMMORTAL.
THIS... IS WHAT THE TITANS ARE...
AND WE...
...HAVE TO FIGHT WITH THEM.
...
OUR ENEMY...

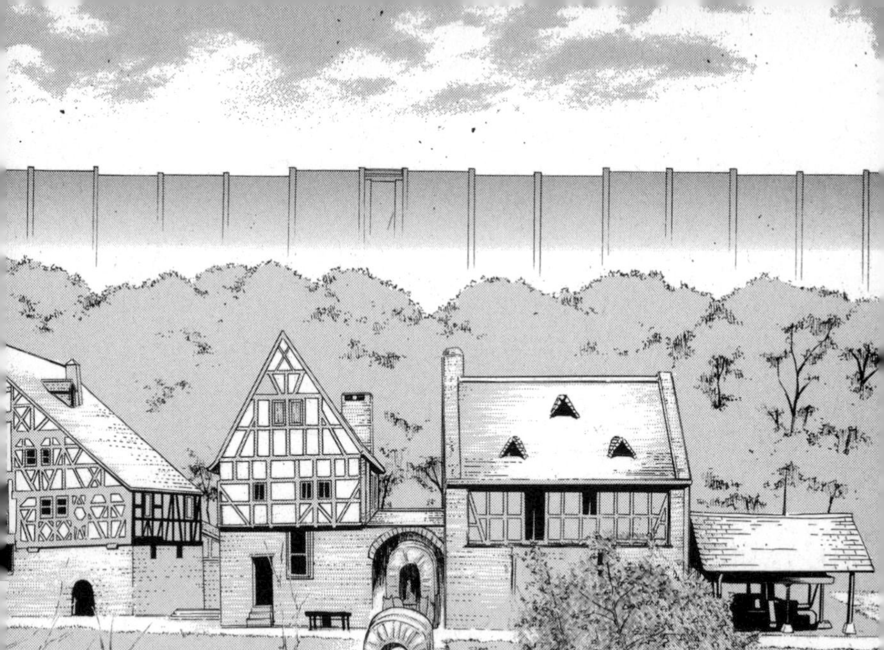

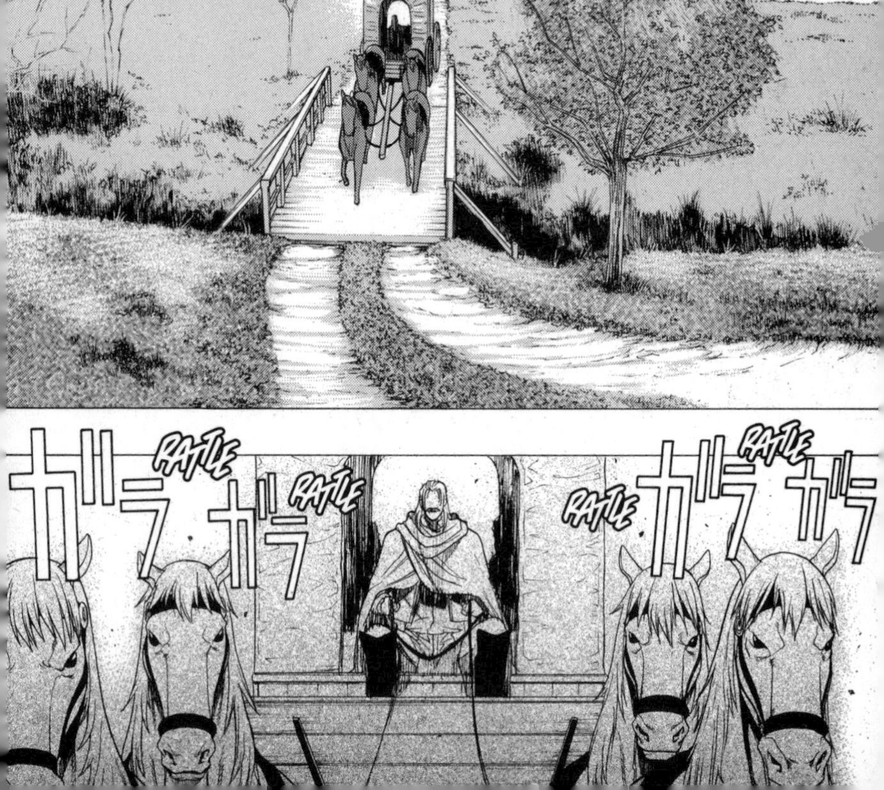
RATTLE
ガラ
RATTLE
ガラ
RATTLE
ガラ
RATTLE
ガラ

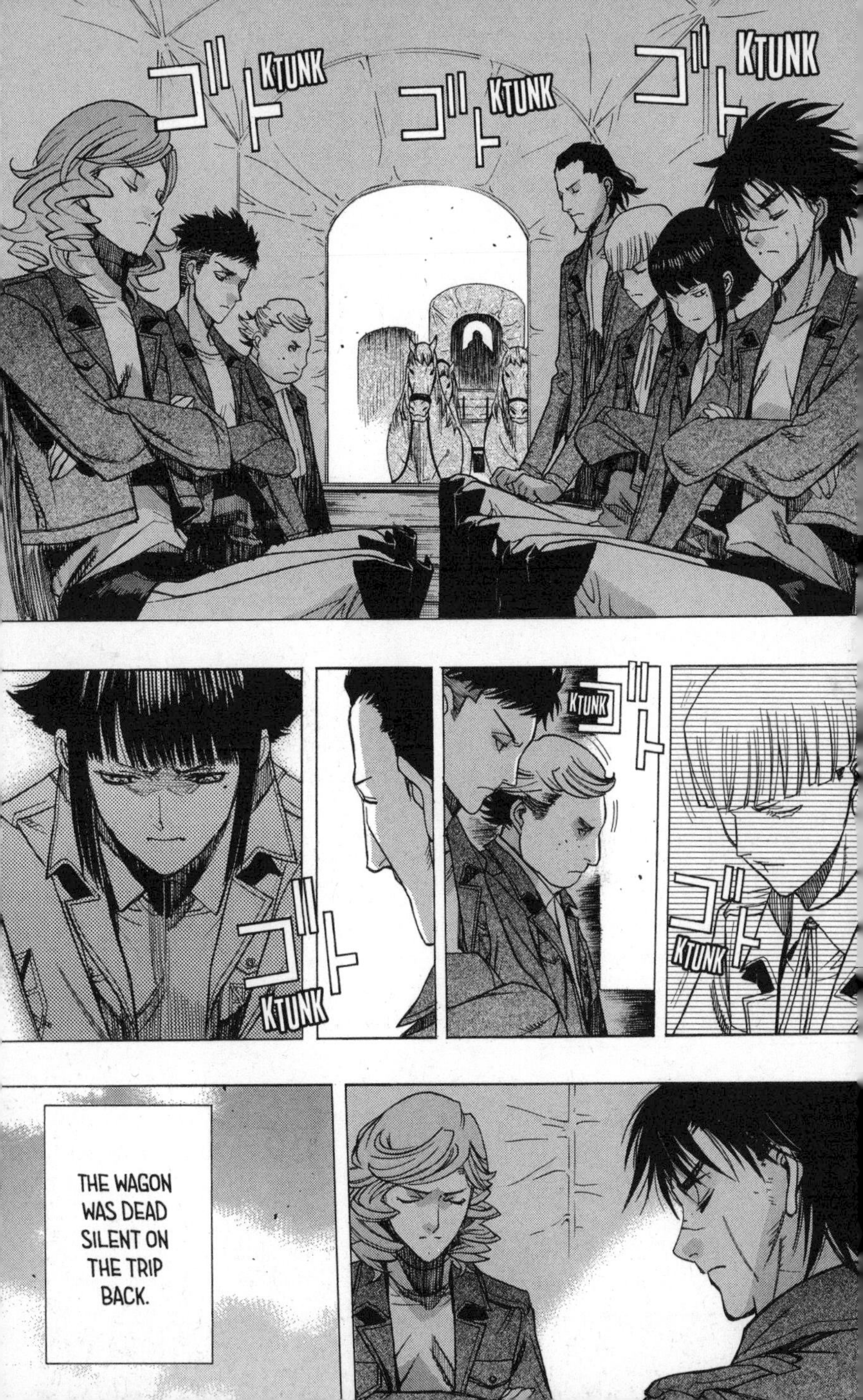
ゴト KTUNK
ゴト KTUNK
ゴト KTUNK
ゴト KTUNK
ゴト KTUNK
ゴト KTUNK
THE WAGON WAS DEAD SILENT ON THE TRIP BACK.

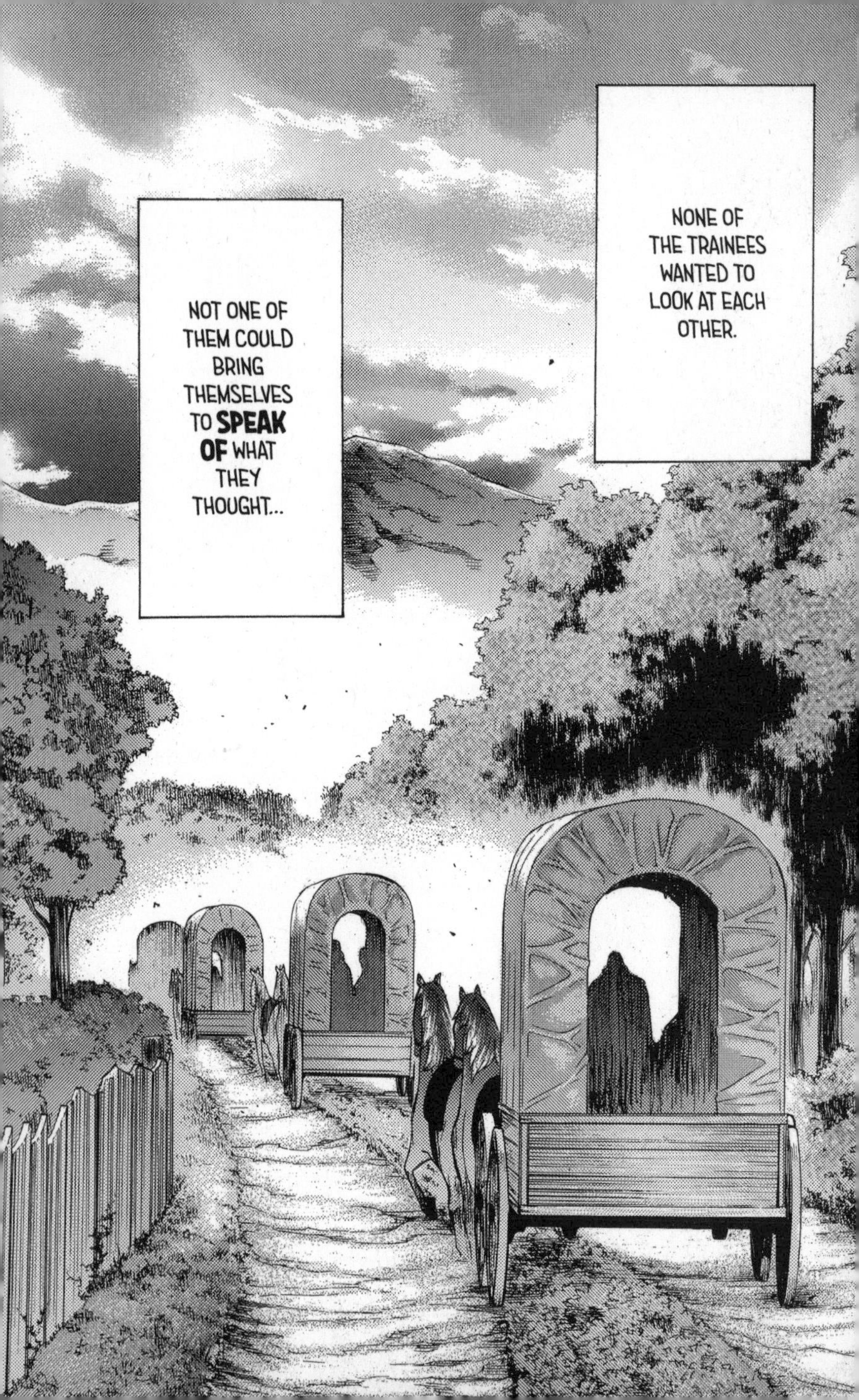
NONE OF THE TRAINEES WANTED TO LOOK AT EACH OTHER.
NOT ONE OF THEM COULD BRING THEMSELVES TO SPEAK OF WHAT THEY THOUGHT...

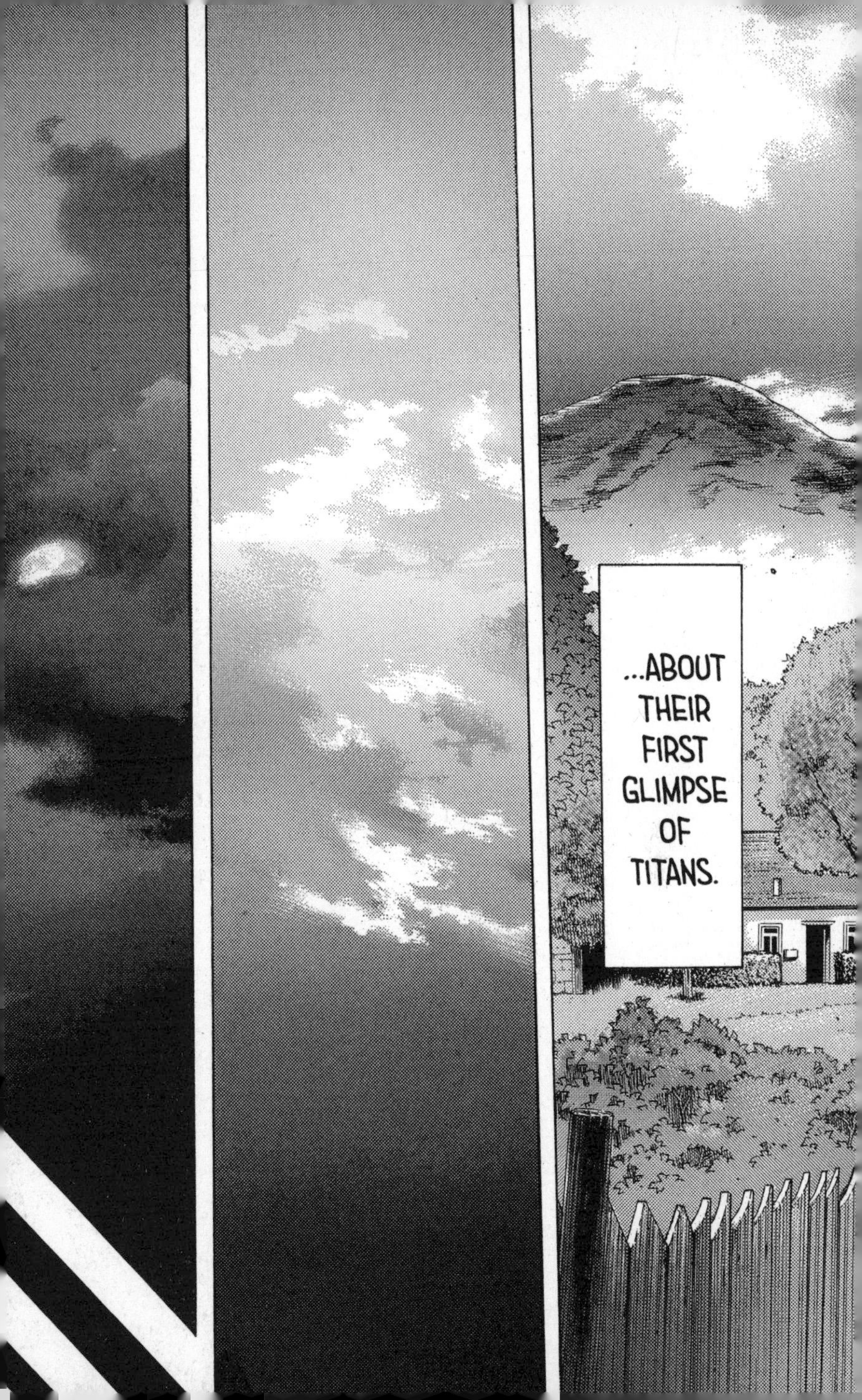
...ABOUT THEIR FIRST GLIMPSE OF TITANS.

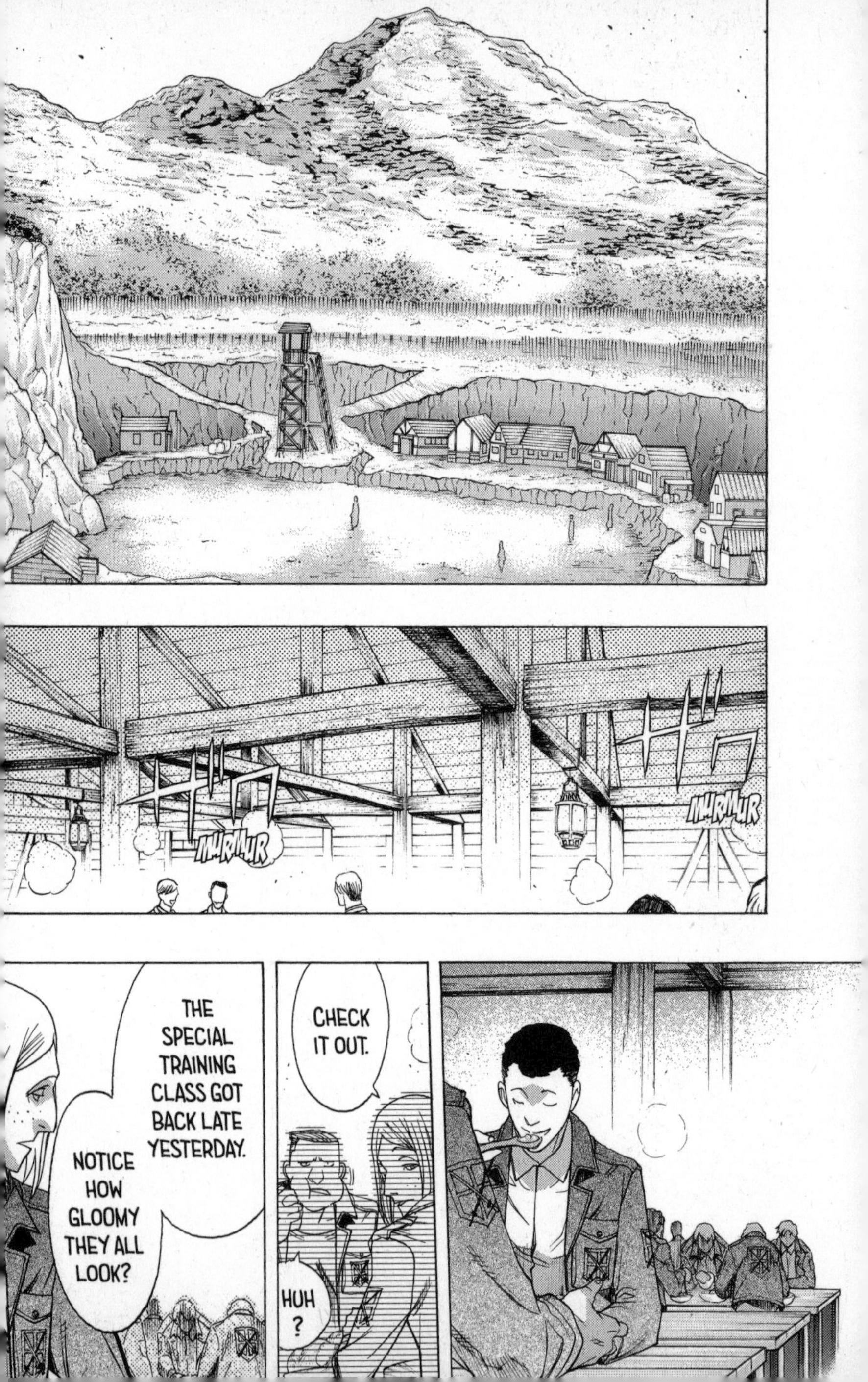
MURMUR
MURMUR
CHECK IT OUT.
HUH?
THE SPECIAL TRAINING CLASS GOT BACK LATE YESTERDAY.
NOTICE HOW GLOOMY THEY ALL LOOK?

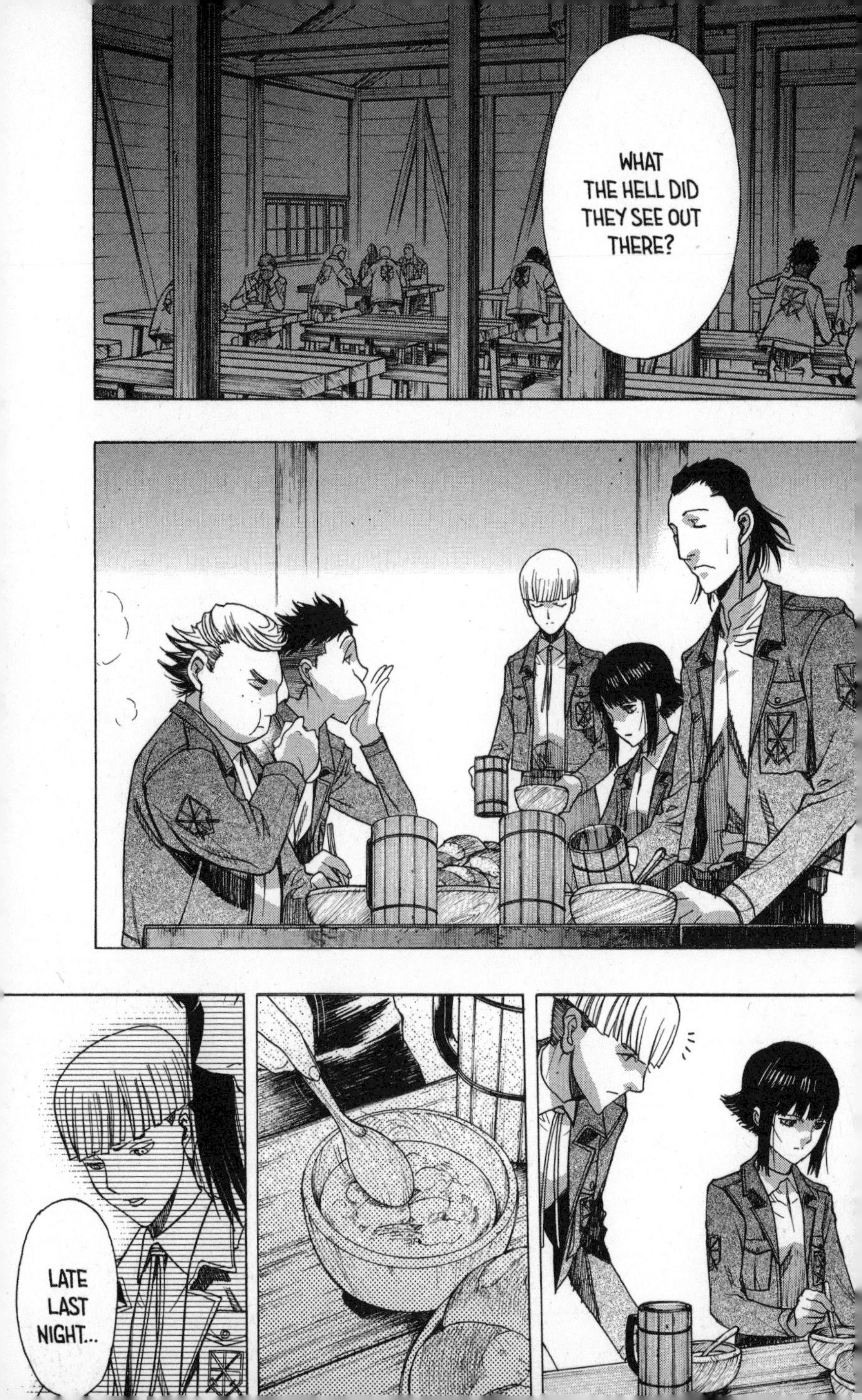
WHAT THE HELL DID THEY SEE OUT THERE?
LATE LAST NIGHT...

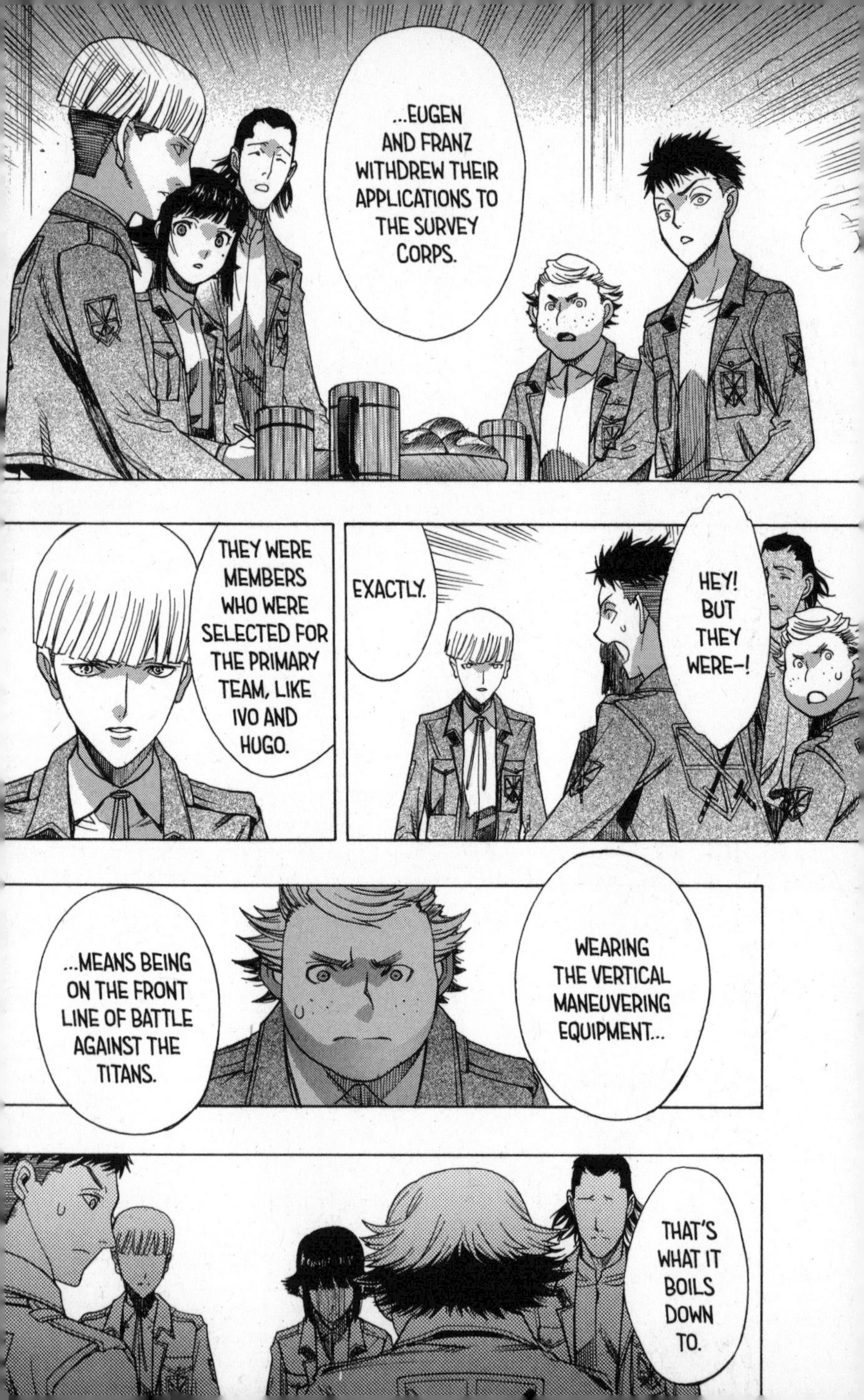
...EUGEN AND FRANZ WITHDREW THEIR APPLICATIONS TO THE SURVEY CORPS.
HEY! BUT THEY WERE-!
EXACTLY.
THEY WERE MEMBERS WHO WERE SELECTED FOR THE PRIMARY TEAM, LIKE IVO AND HUGO.
WEARING THE VERTICAL MANEUVERING EQUIPMENT...
...MEANS BEING ON THE FRONT LINE OF BATTLE AGAINST THE TITANS.
THAT'S WHAT IT BOILS DOWN TO.

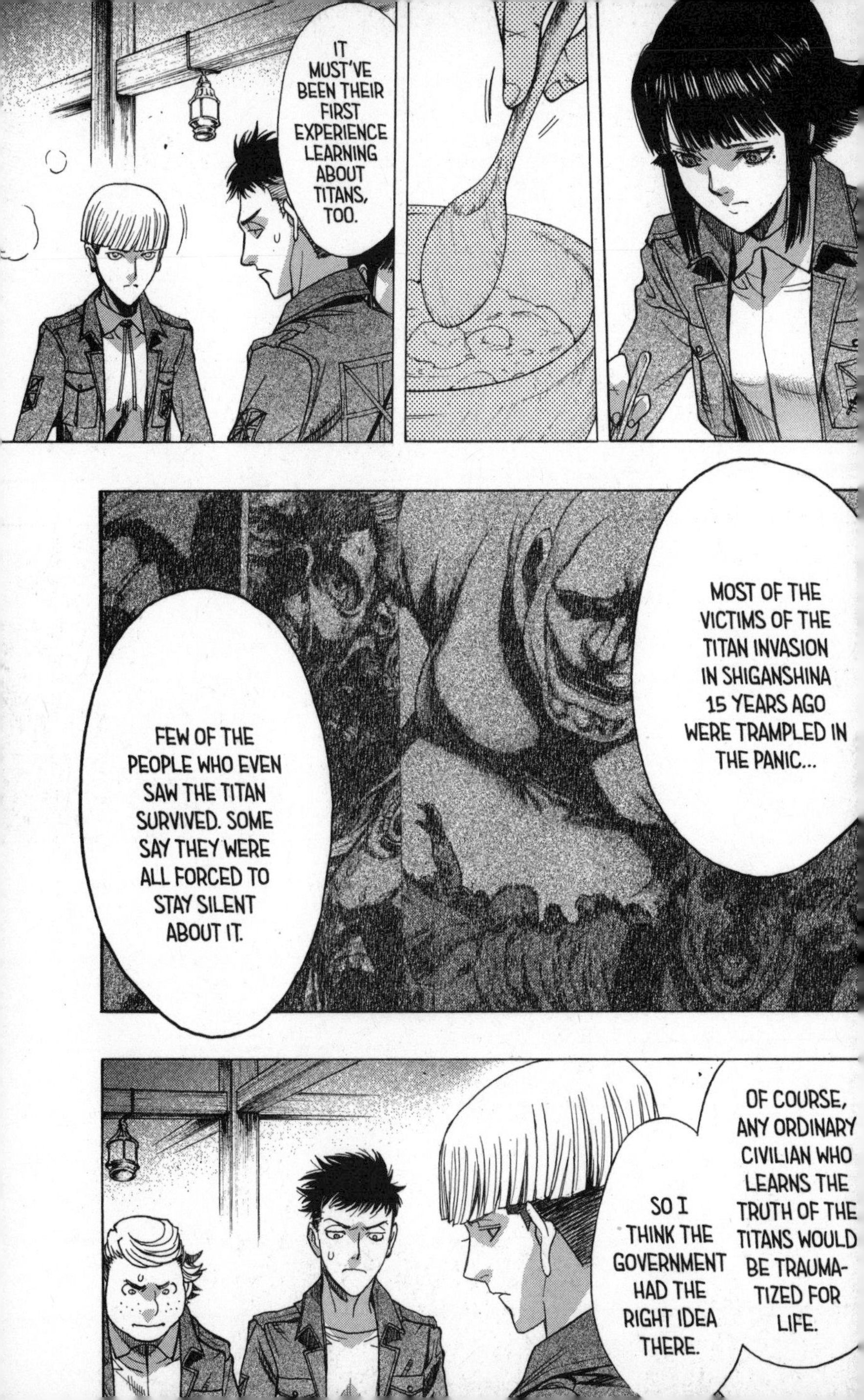
IT MUST'VE BEEN THEIR FIRST EXPERIENCE LEARNING ABOUT TITANS, TOO.
MOST OF THE VICTIMS OF THE TITAN INVASION IN SHIGANSHINA 15 YEARS AGO WERE TRAMPLED IN THE PANIC...
FEW OF THE PEOPLE WHO EVEN SAW THE TITAN SURVIVED. SOME SAY THEY WERE ALL FORCED TO STAY SILENT ABOUT IT.
OF COURSE, ANY ORDINARY CIVILIAN WHO LEARNS THE TRUTH OF THE TITANS WOULD BE TRAUMA-TIZED FOR LIFE.
SO I THINK THE GOVERNMENT HAD THE RIGHT IDEA THERE.

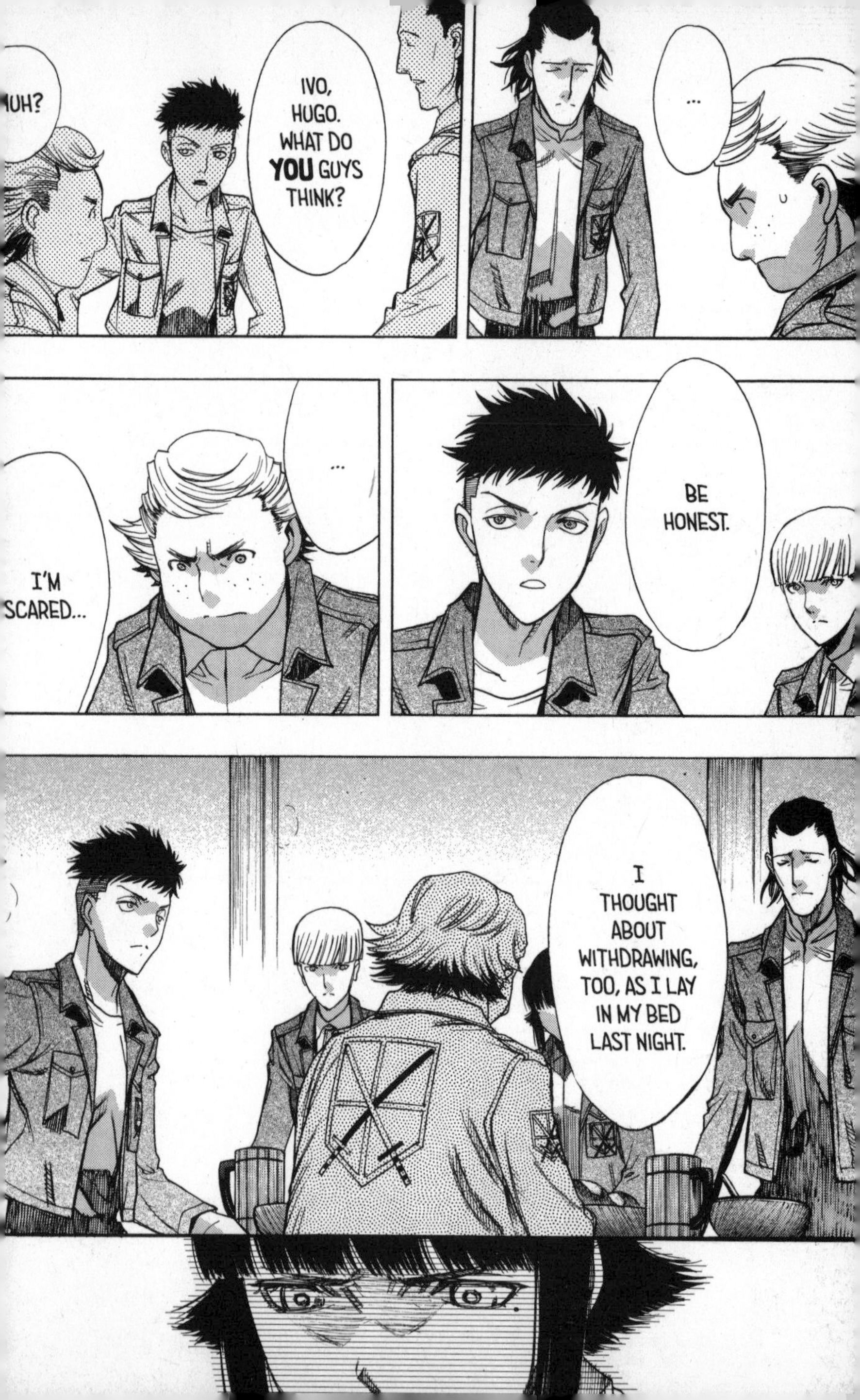
...
IVO, HUGO. WHAT DO **YOU** GUYS THINK?
HUH?
BE HONEST.
...
I'M SCARED...
I THOUGHT ABOUT WITHDRAWING, TOO, AS I LAY IN MY BED LAST NIGHT.

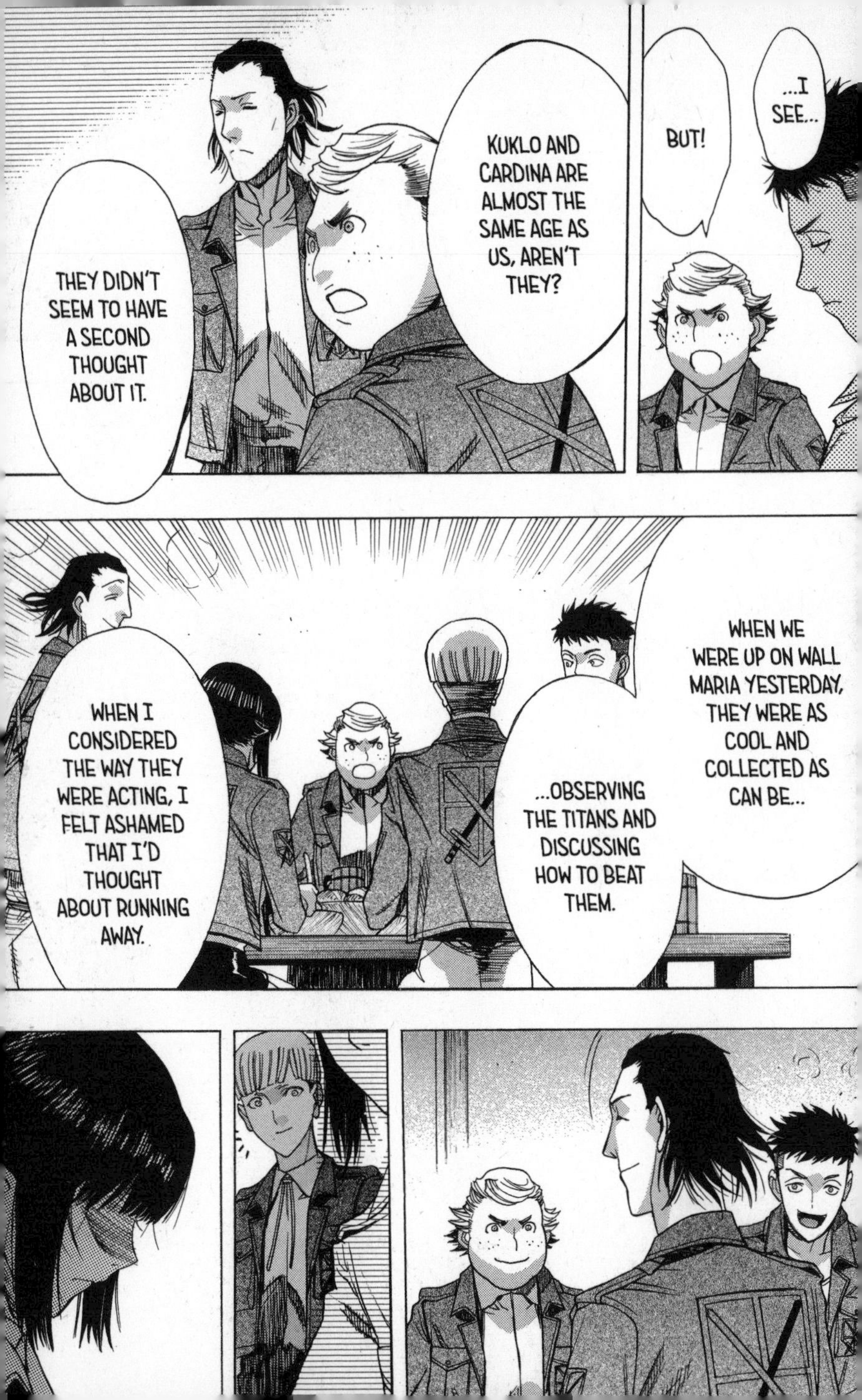
...I SEE...
BUT!
KUKLO AND CARDINA ARE ALMOST THE SAME AGE AS US, AREN'T THEY?
THEY DIDN'T SEEM TO HAVE A SECOND THOUGHT ABOUT IT.
WHEN WE WERE UP ON WALL MARIA YESTERDAY, THEY WERE AS COOL AND COLLECTED AS CAN BE...
...OBSERVING THE TITANS AND DISCUSSING HOW TO BEAT THEM.
WHEN I CONSIDERED THE WAY THEY WERE ACTING, I FELT ASHAMED THAT I'D THOUGHT ABOUT RUNNING AWAY.

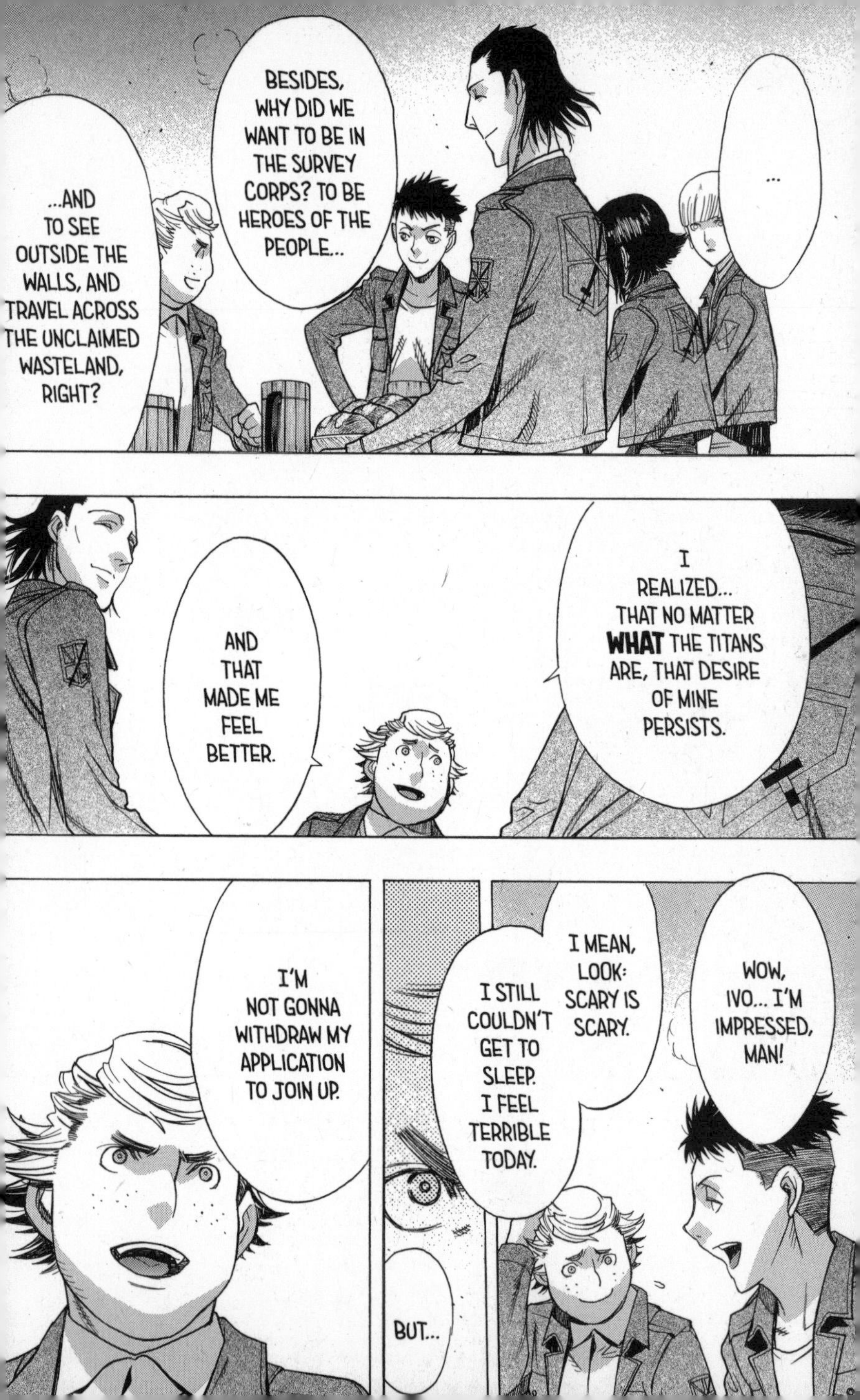
...
BESIDES, WHY DID WE WANT TO BE IN THE SURVEY CORPS? TO BE HEROES OF THE PEOPLE...
...AND TO SEE OUTSIDE THE WALLS, AND TRAVEL ACROSS THE UNCLAIMED WASTELAND, RIGHT?
I REALIZED... THAT NO MATTER WHAT THE TITANS ARE, THAT DESIRE OF MINE PERSISTS.
AND THAT MADE ME FEEL BETTER.
WOW, IVO... I'M IMPRESSED, MAN!
I MEAN, LOOK: SCARY IS SCARY.
I STILL COULDN'T GET TO SLEEP. I FEEL TERRIBLE TODAY.
BUT...
I'M NOT GONNA WITHDRAW MY APPLICATION TO JOIN UP.

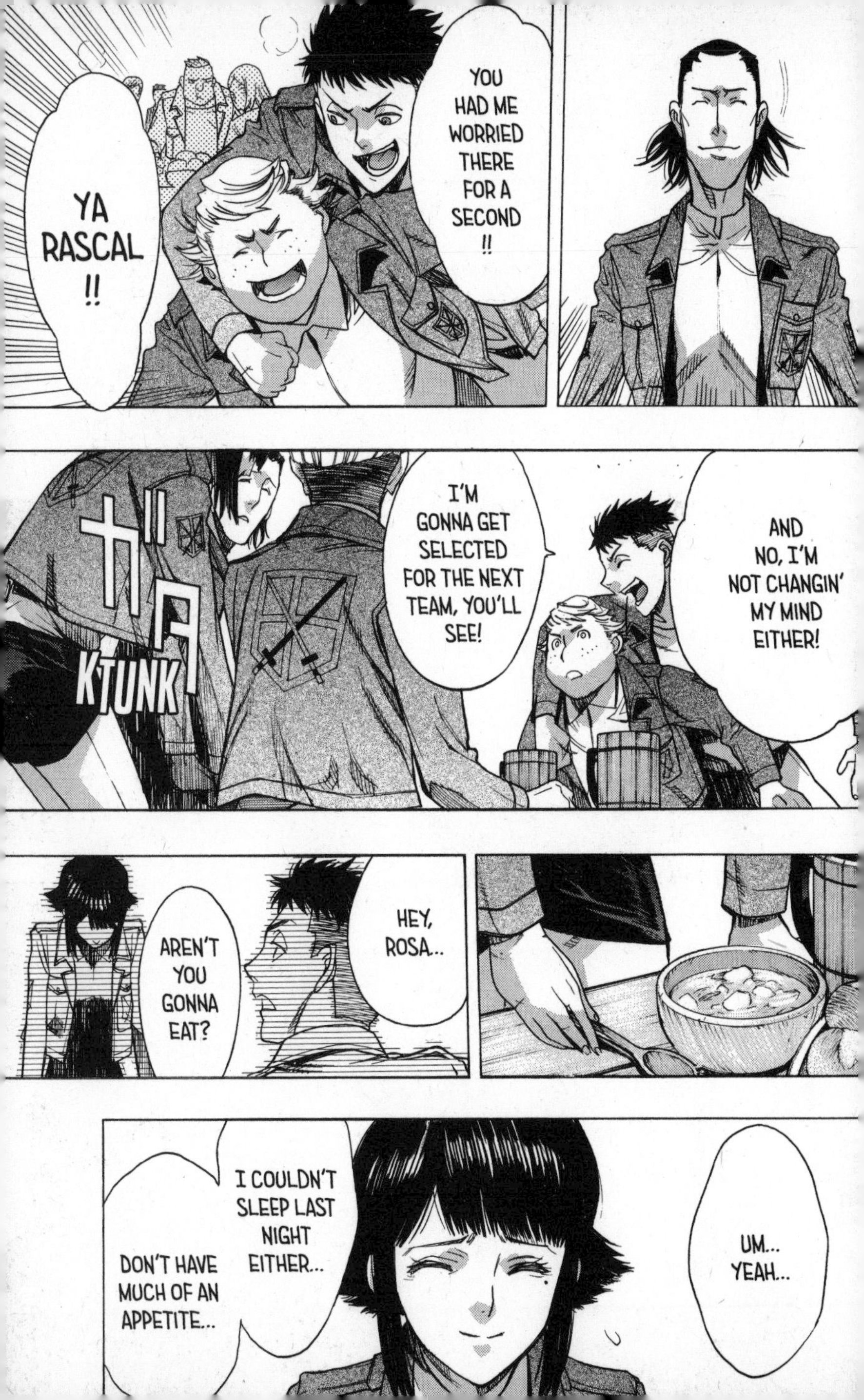
YOU HAD ME WORRIED THERE FOR A SECOND !!
YA RASCAL !!
AND NO, I'M NOT CHANGIN' MY MIND EITHER!
I'M GONNA GET SELECTED FOR THE NEXT TEAM, YOU'LL SEE!
ガタ
KTUNK
HEY, ROSA...
AREN'T YOU GONNA EAT?
UM... YEAH...
I COULDN'T SLEEP LAST NIGHT EITHER...
DON'T HAVE MUCH OF AN APPETITE...

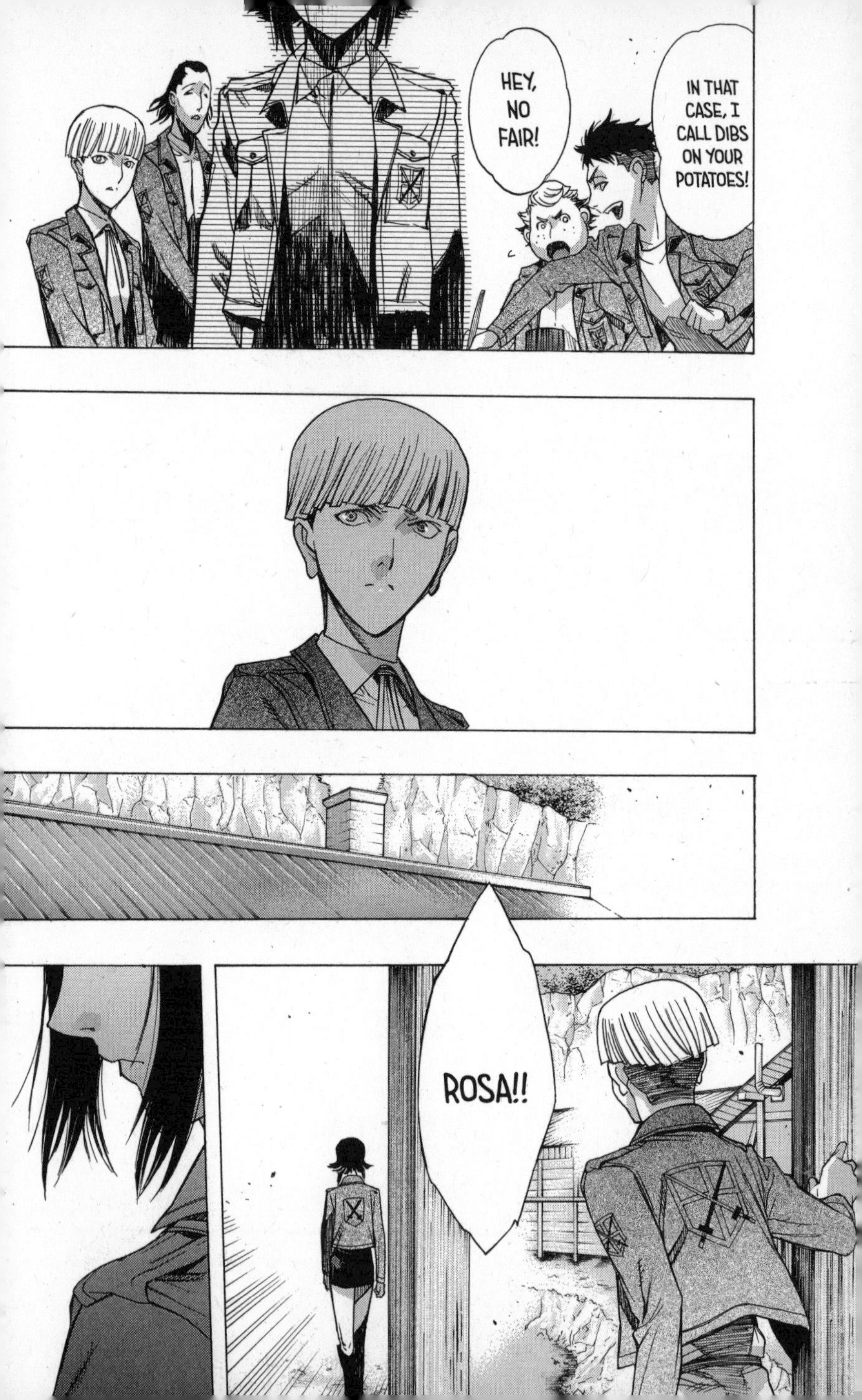
IN THAT CASE, I CALL DIBS ON YOUR POTATOES!
HEY, NO FAIR!
ROSA!!

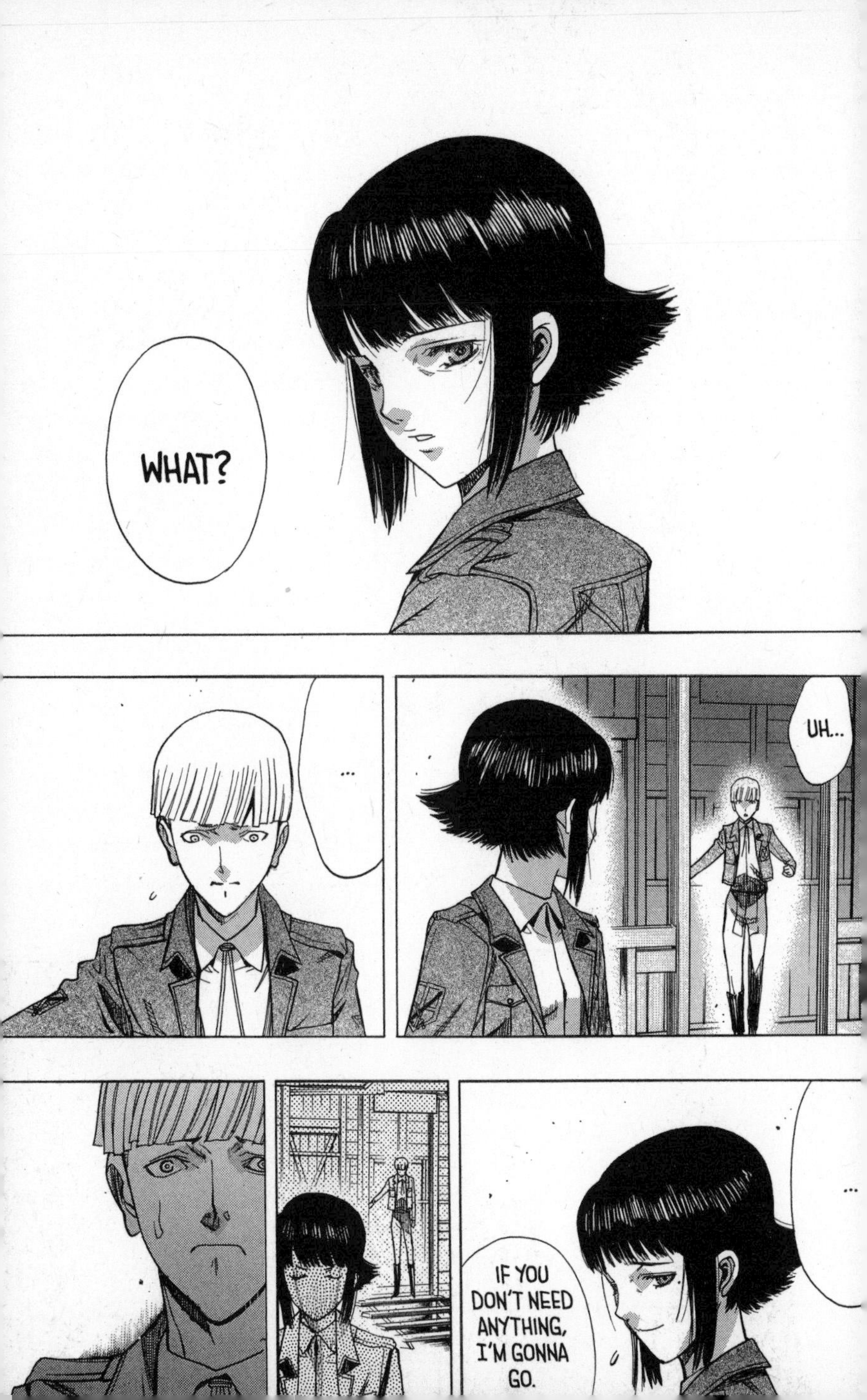
WHAT?
UH...
...
...
IF YOU DON'T NEED ANYTHING, I'M GONNA GO.

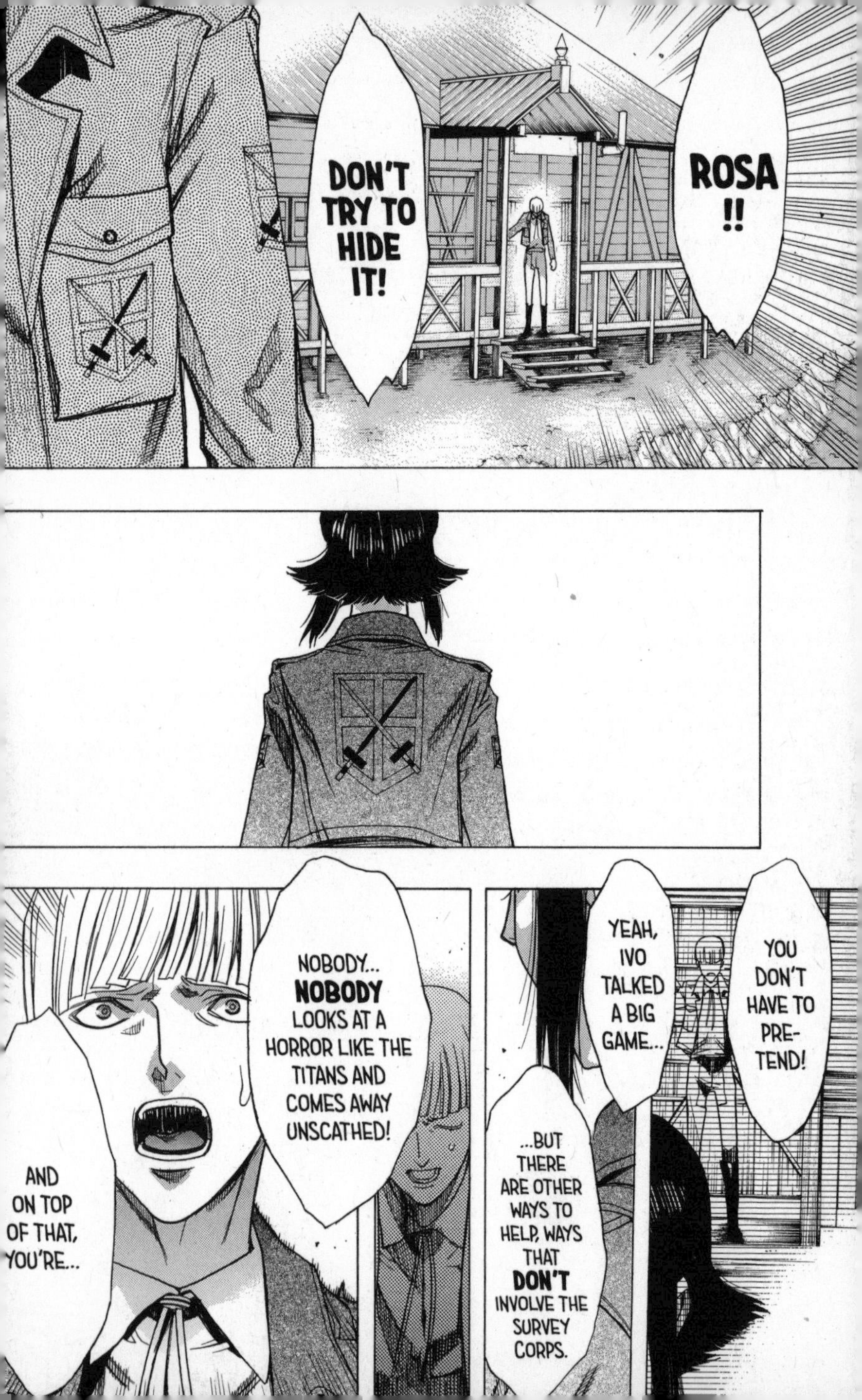
ROSA!!
DON'T TRY TO HIDE IT!
YOU DON'T HAVE TO PRE-TEND!
YEAH, IVO TALKED A BIG GAME...
...BUT THERE ARE OTHER WAYS TO HELP, WAYS THAT **DON'T** INVOLVE THE SURVEY CORPS.
NOBODY... **NOBODY** LOOKS AT A HORROR LIKE THE TITANS AND COMES AWAY UNSCATHED!
AND ON TOP OF THAT, YOU'RE...

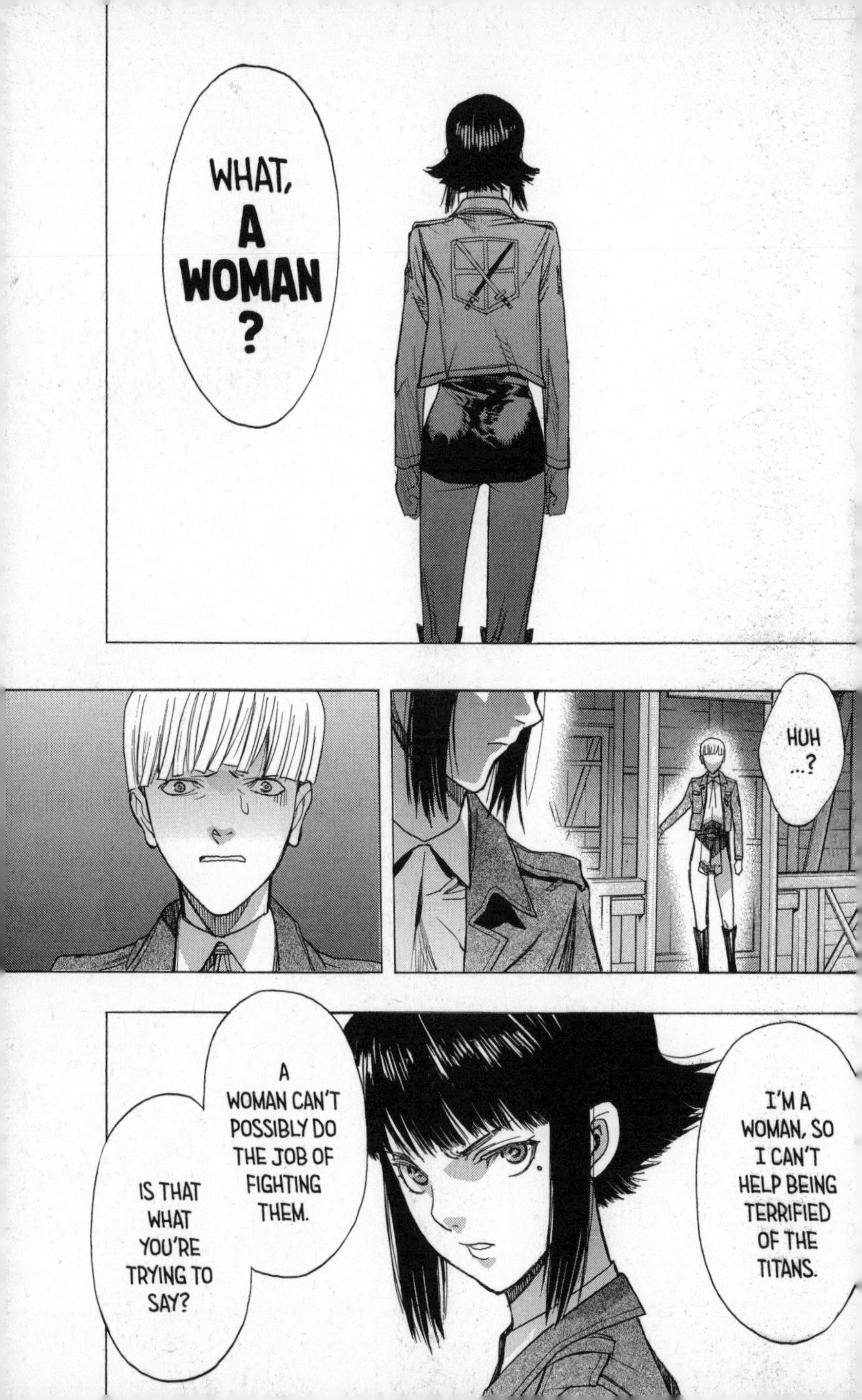
WHAT, A WOMAN ?
HUH ...?
I'M A WOMAN, SO I CAN'T HELP BEING TERRIFIED OF THE TITANS.
A WOMAN CAN'T POSSIBLY DO THE JOB OF FIGHTING THEM.
IS THAT WHAT YOU'RE TRYING TO SAY?

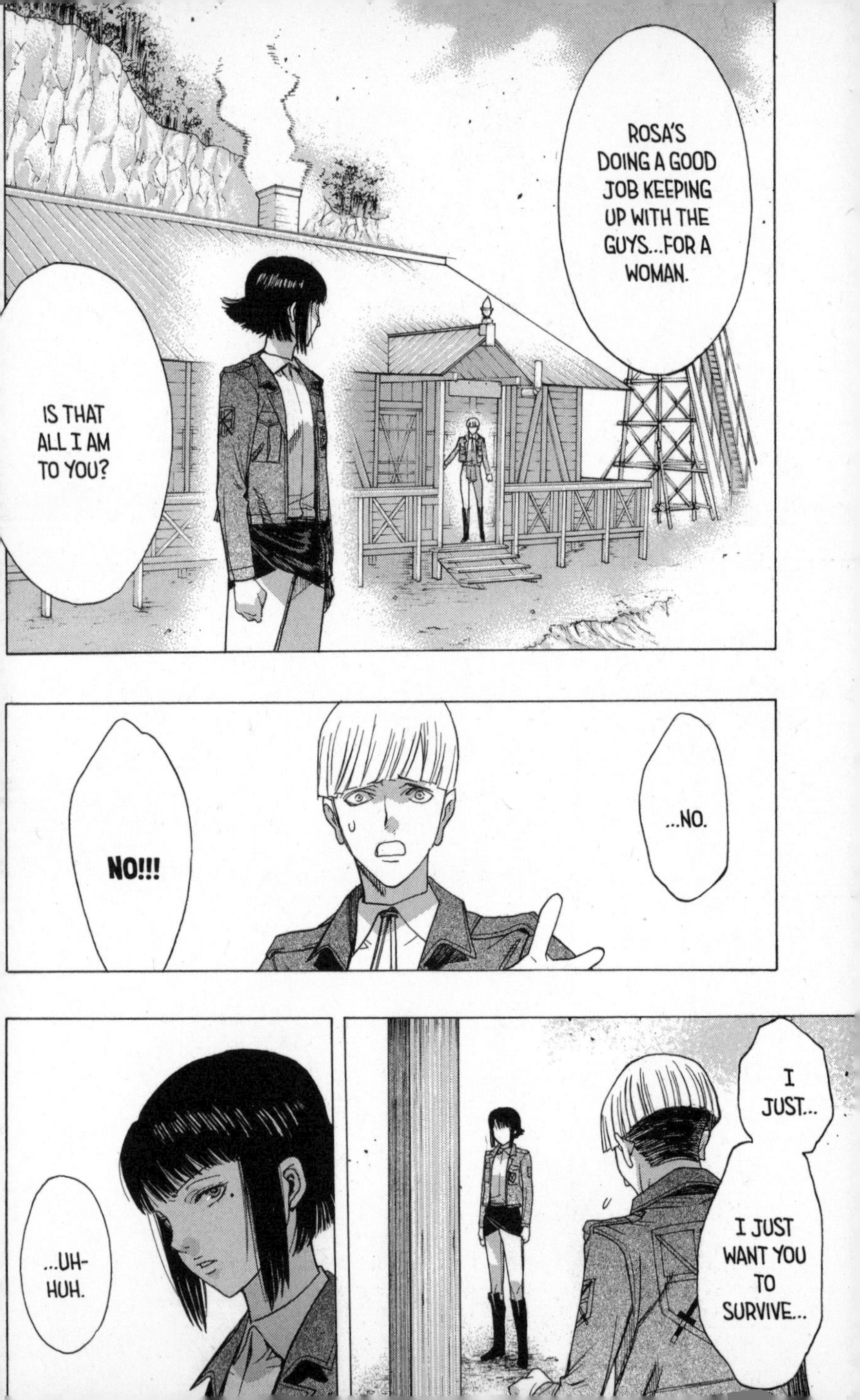
ROSA'S DOING A GOOD JOB KEEPING UP WITH THE GUYS...FOR A WOMAN.
IS THAT ALL I AM TO YOU?
...NO.
NO!!!
I JUST...
I JUST WANT YOU TO SURVIVE...
...UH-HUH.

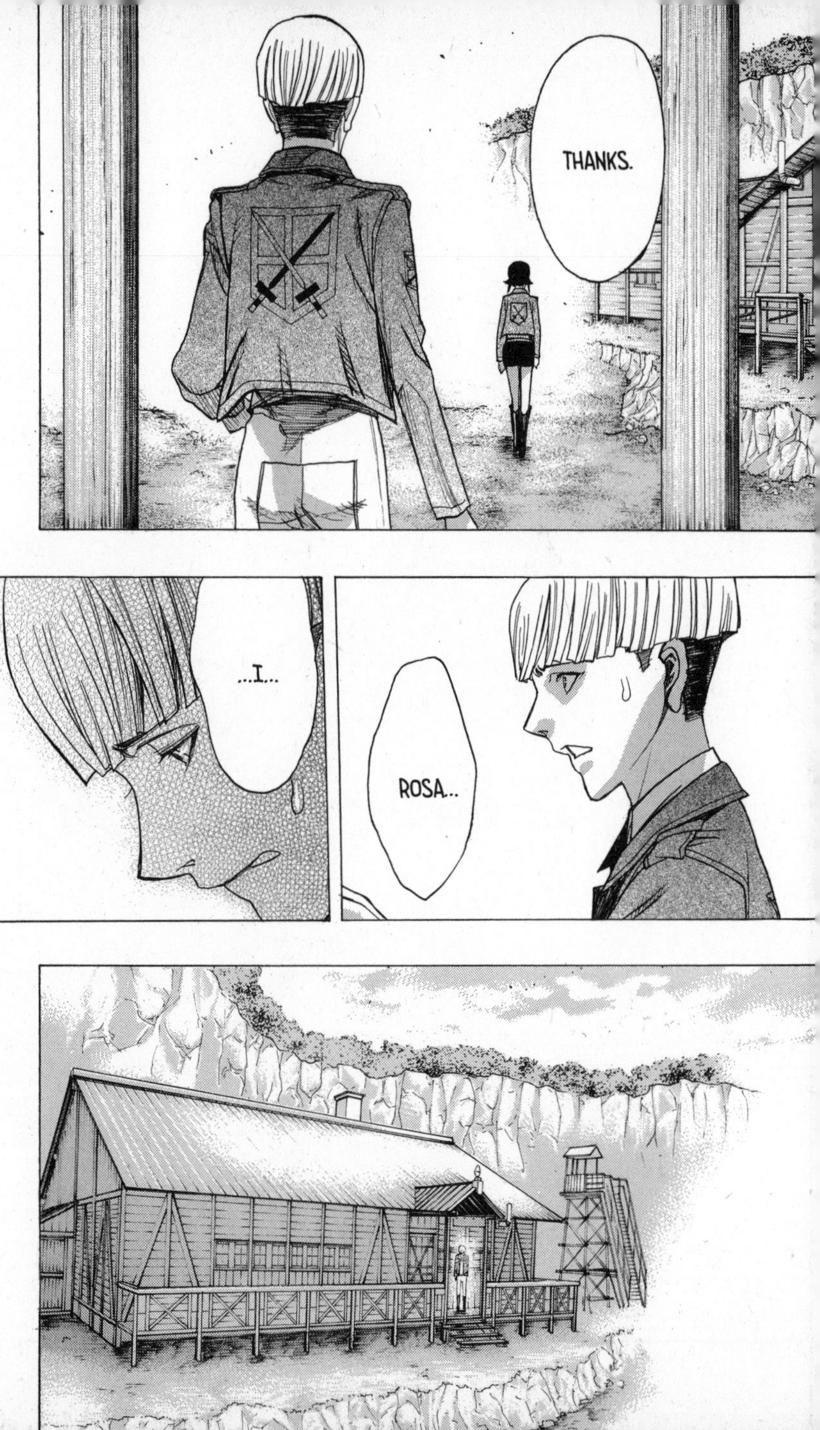
THANKS.
ROSA...
...I...

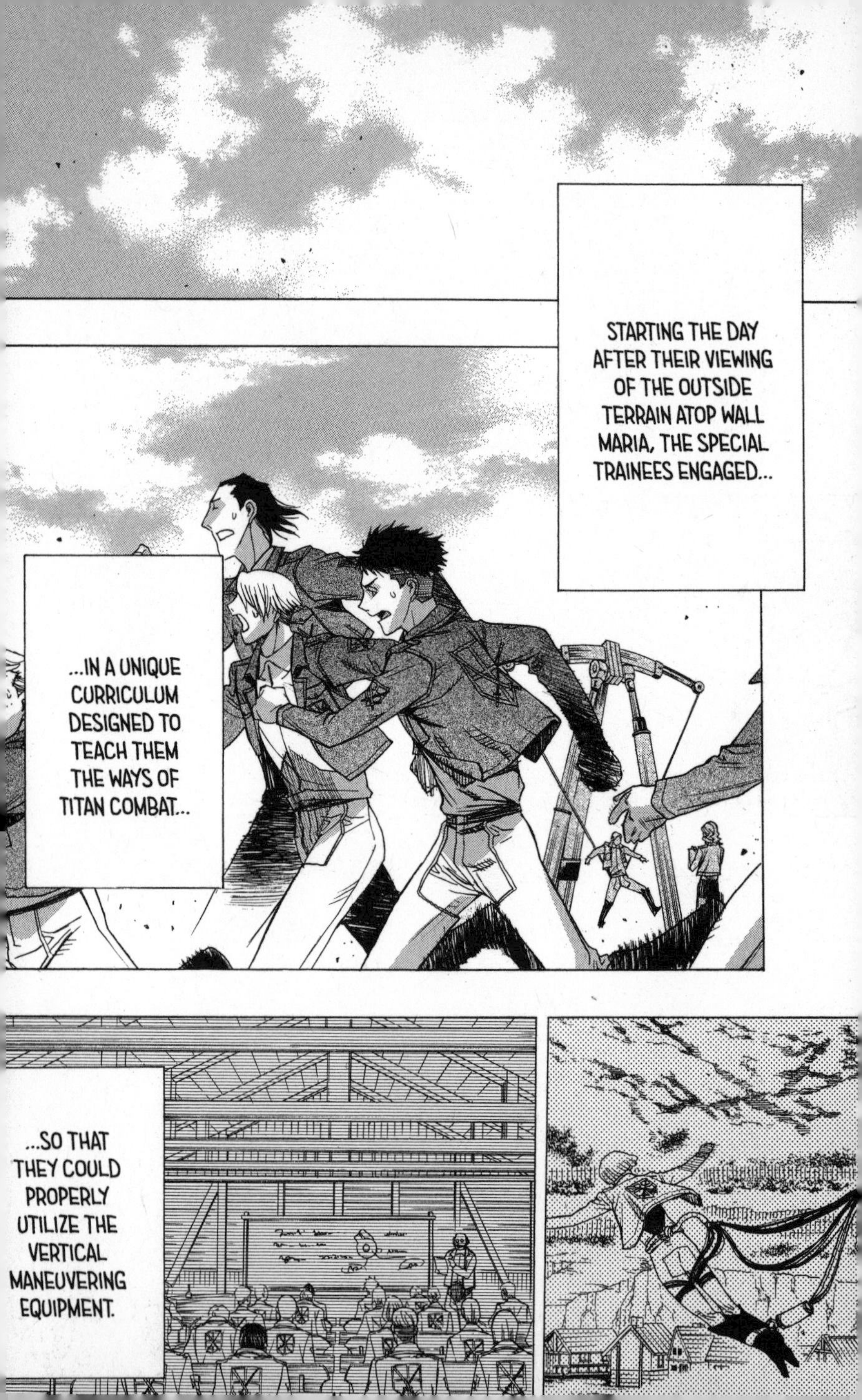
STARTING THE DAY AFTER THEIR VIEWING OF THE OUTSIDE TERRAIN ATOP WALL MARIA, THE SPECIAL TRAINEES ENGAGED...
...IN A UNIQUE CURRICULUM DESIGNED TO TEACH THEM THE WAYS OF TITAN COMBAT...
...SO THAT THEY COULD PROPERLY UTILIZE THE VERTICAL MANEUVERING EQUIPMENT.

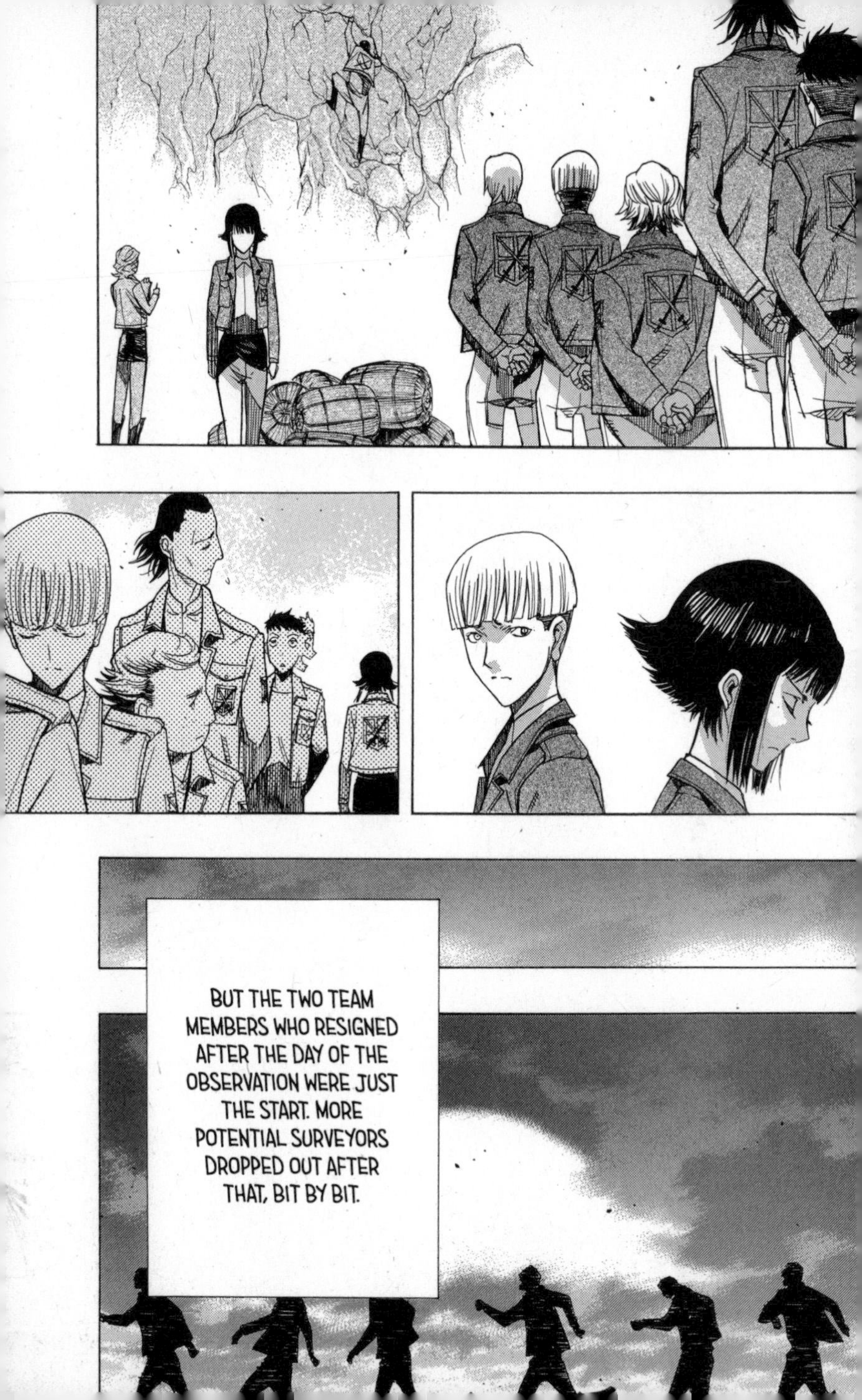
BUT THE TWO TEAM MEMBERS WHO RESIGNED AFTER THE DAY OF THE OBSERVATION WERE JUST THE START. MORE POTENTIAL SURVEYORS DROPPED OUT AFTER THAT, BIT BY BIT.

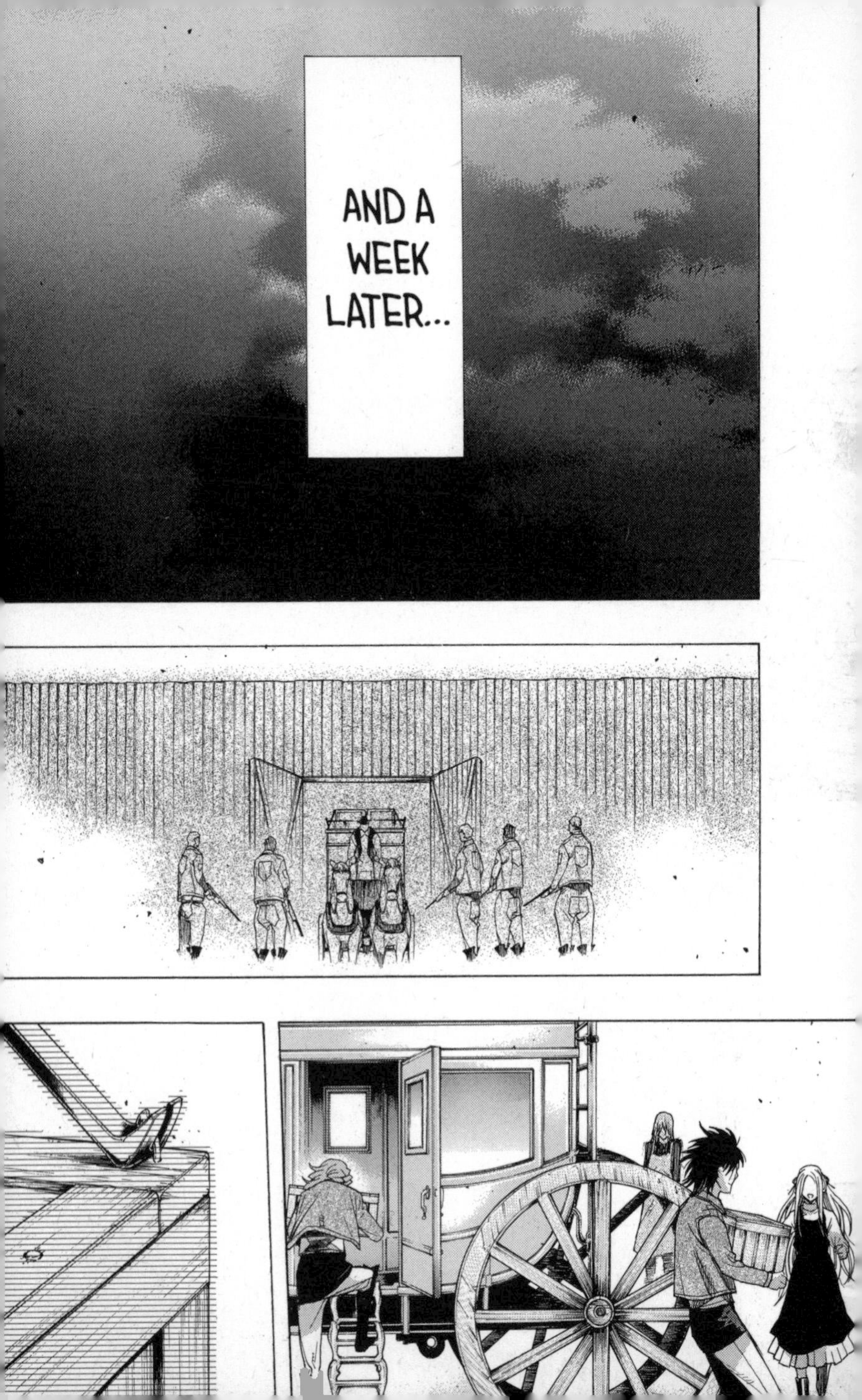
AND A WEEK LATER...

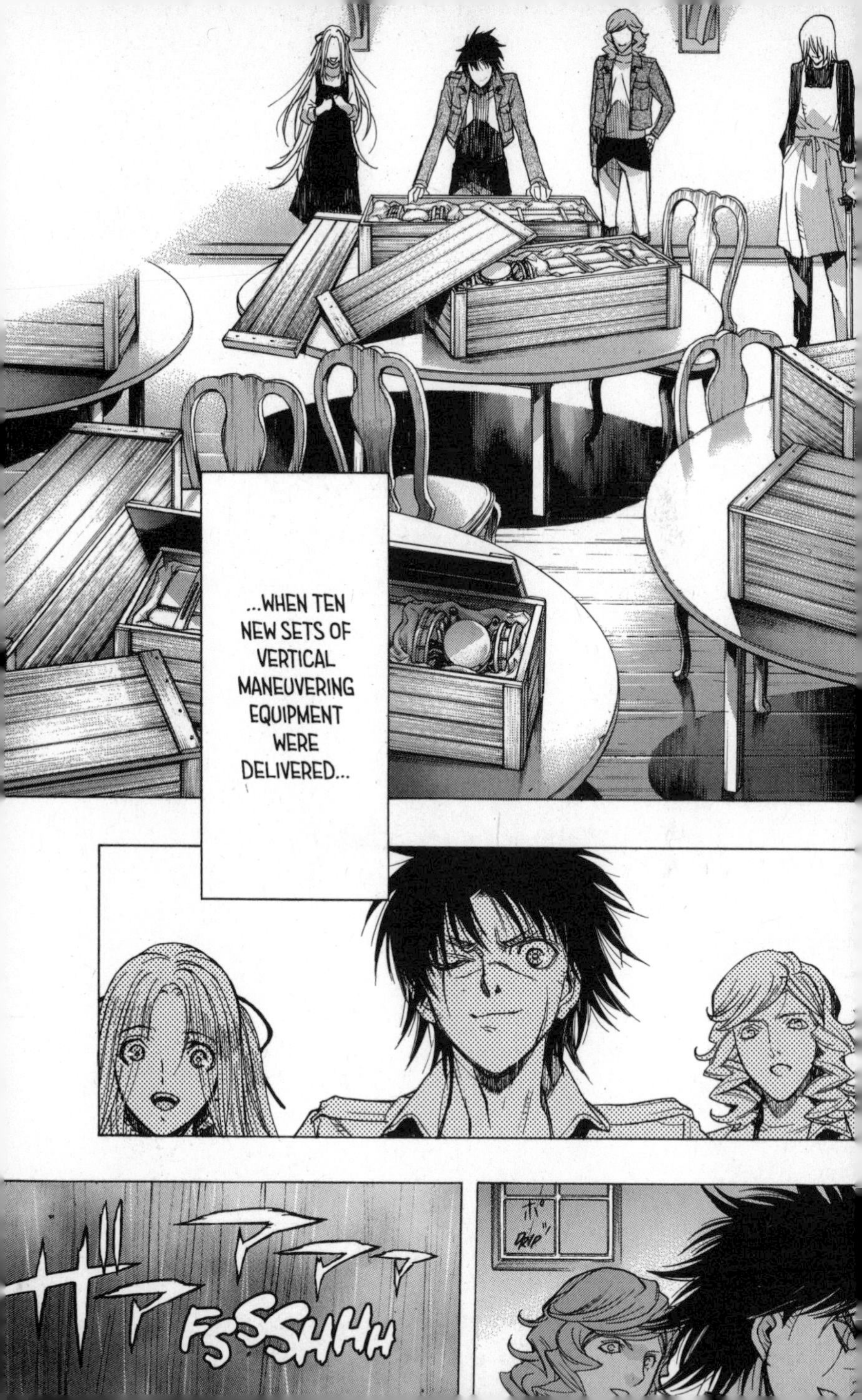
...WHEN TEN NEW SETS OF VERTICAL MANEUVERING EQUIPMENT WERE DELIVERED...
DRIP
FSSSHHH

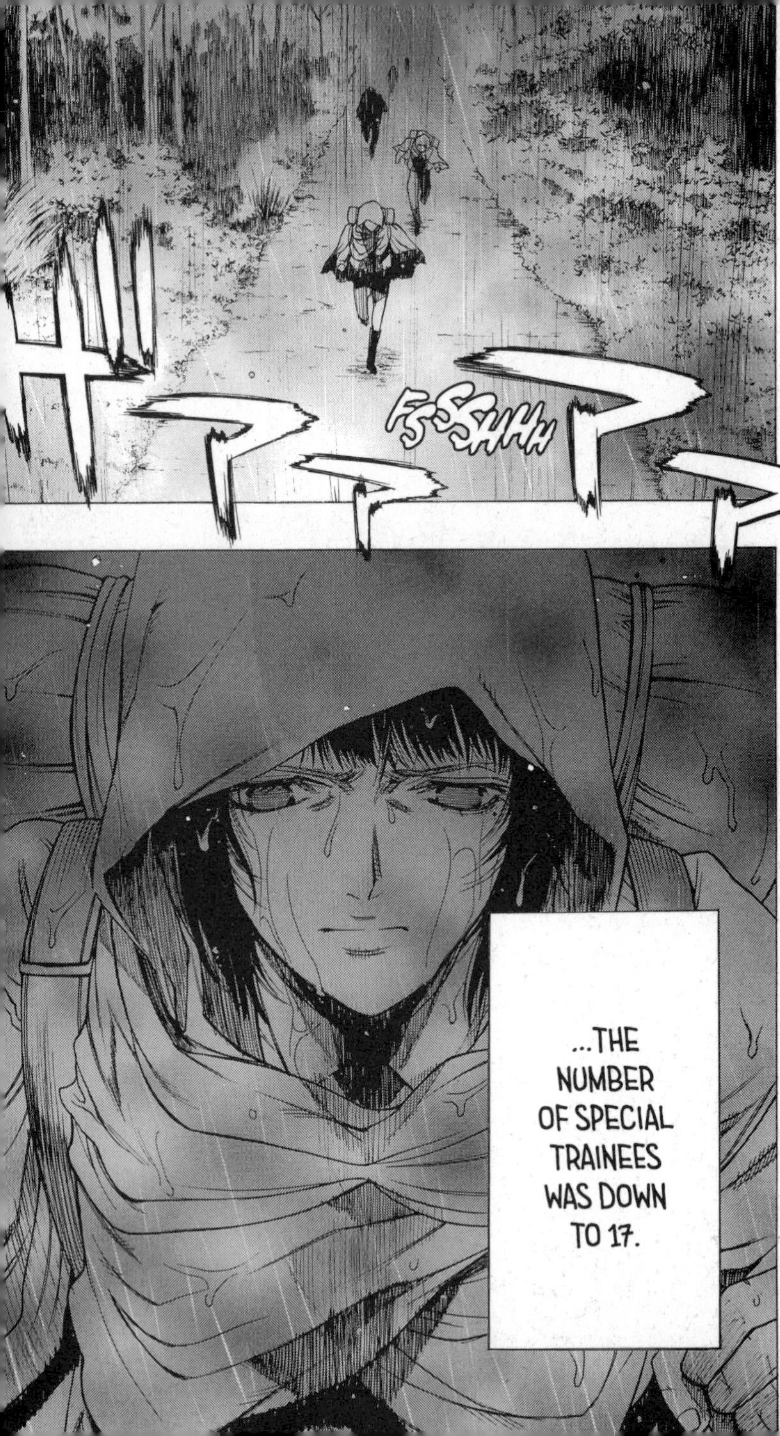
ザアアアア
FSSSHHH
...THE NUMBER OF SPECIAL TRAINEES WAS DOWN TO 17.

Chapter 50: Labyrinth of the Demon's Womb · En

ATTACK on TITAN
BEFORE THE FALL

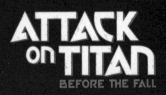

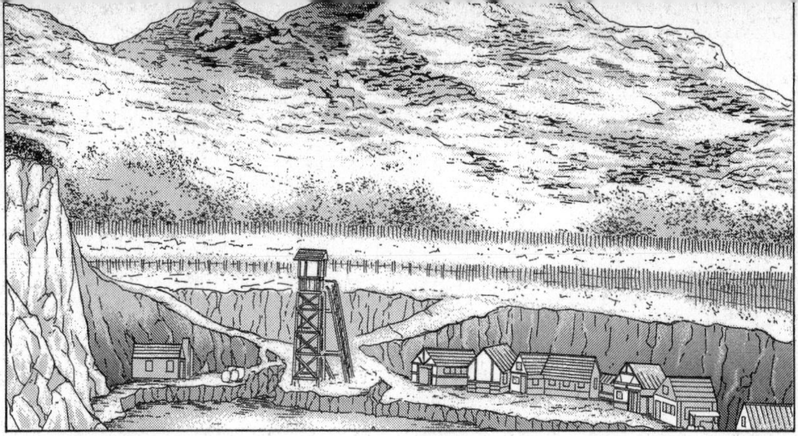
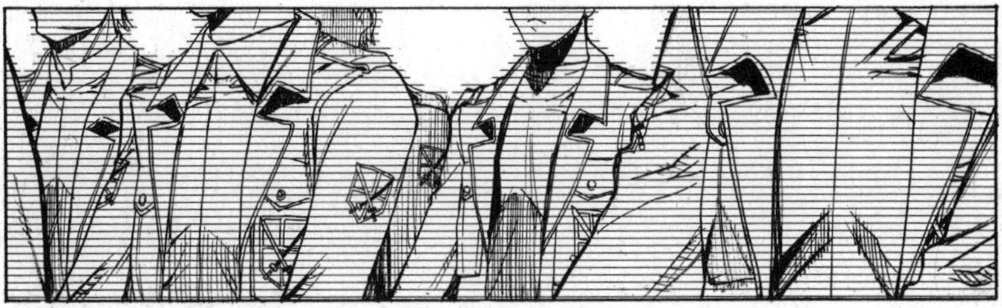
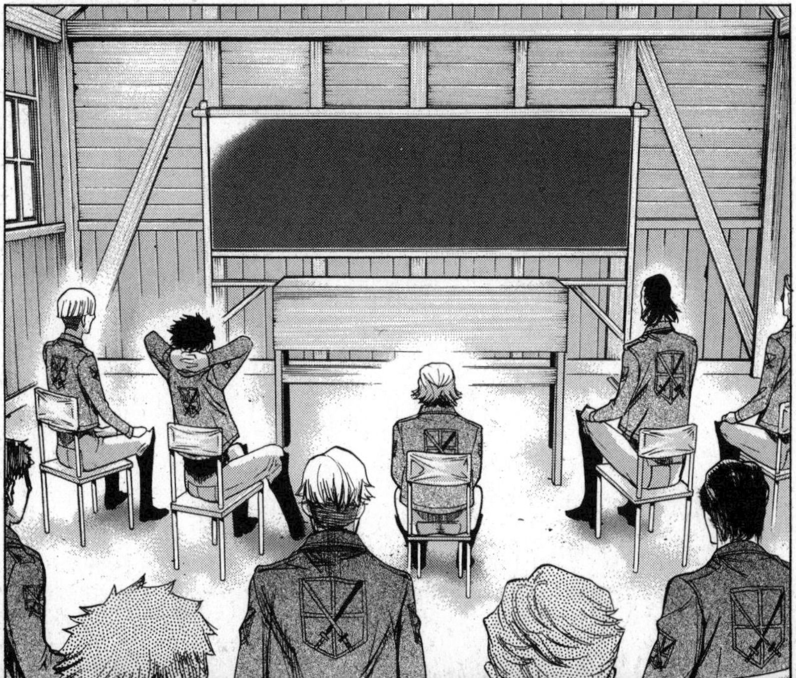

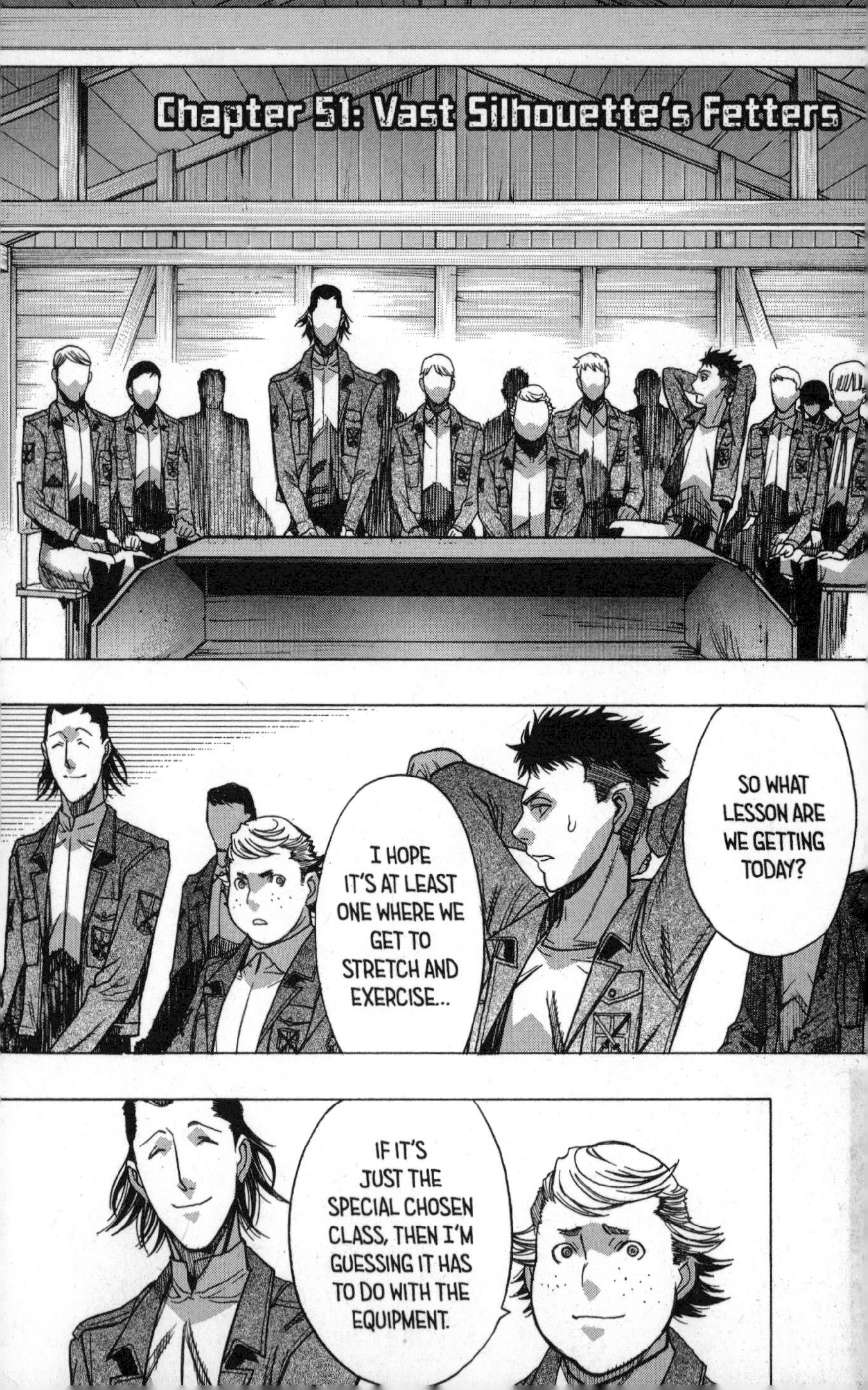
Chapter 51: Vast Silhouette's Fetters
SO WHAT LESSON ARE WE GETTING TODAY?
I HOPE IT'S AT LEAST ONE WHERE WE GET TO STRETCH AND EXERCISE...
IF IT'S JUST THE SPECIAL CHOSEN CLASS, THEN I'M GUESSING IT HAS TO DO WITH THE EQUIPMENT.

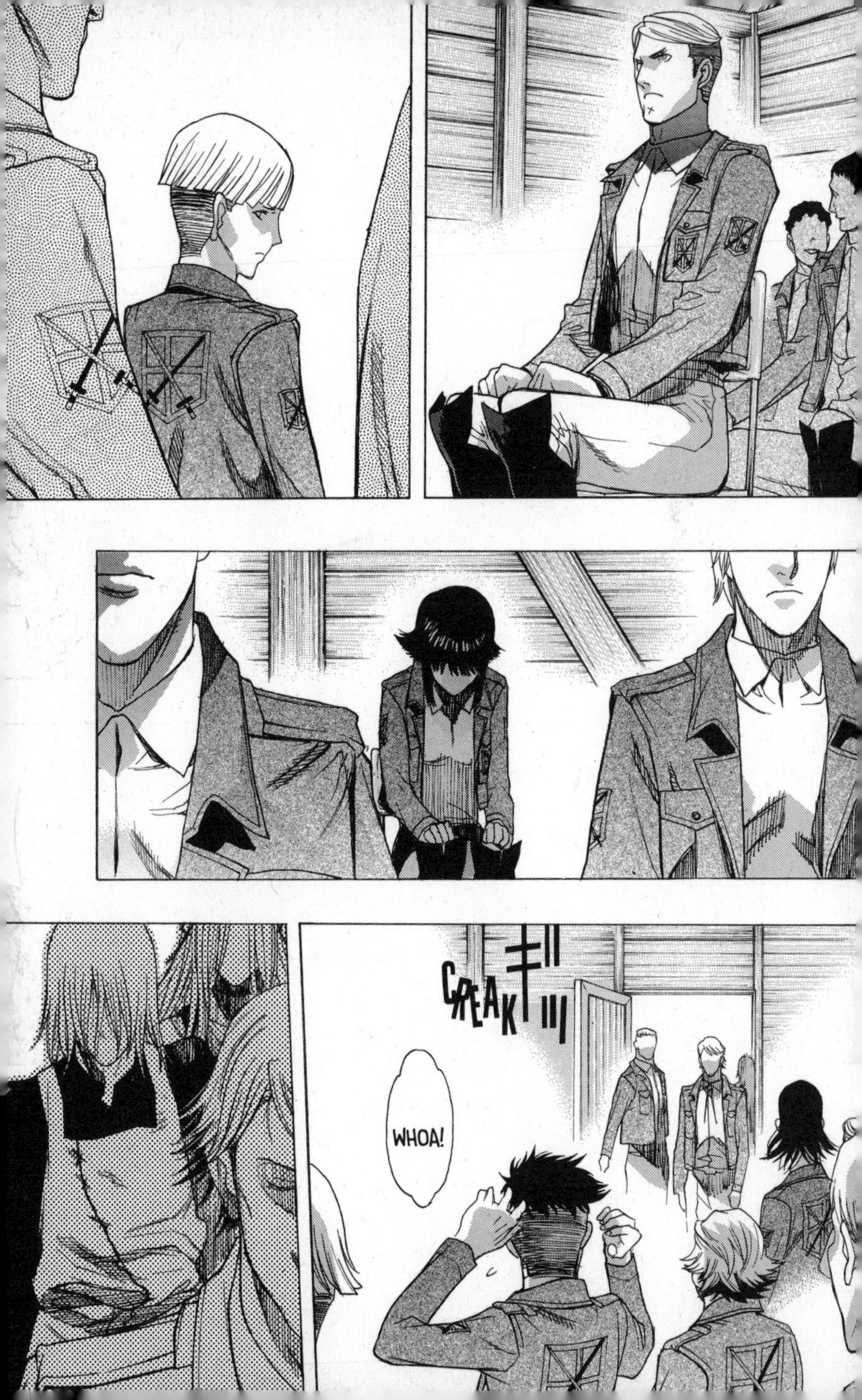
CREAK
WHOA!

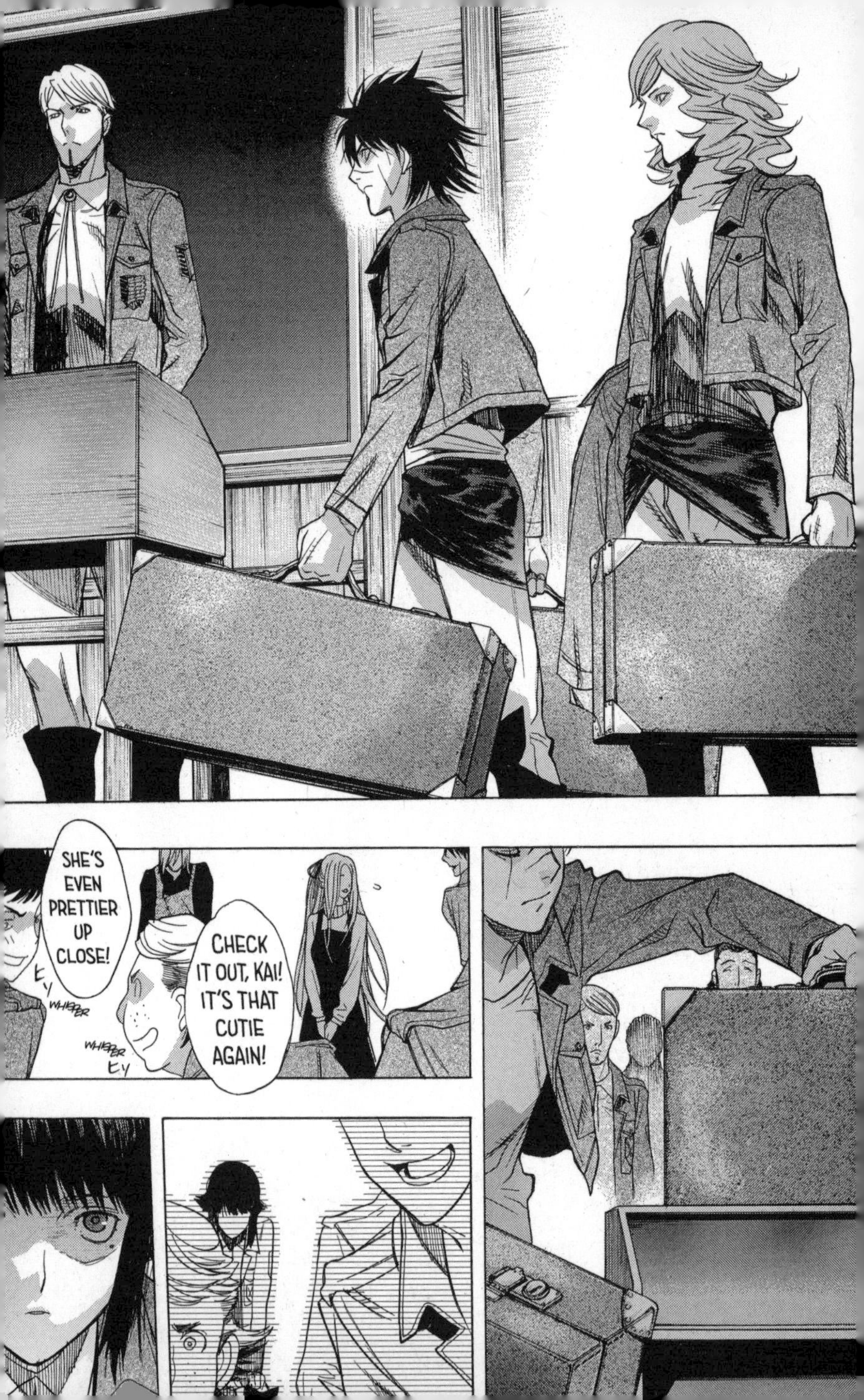
CHECK IT OUT, KAI! IT'S THAT CUTIE AGAIN!
WHISPER
SHE'S EVEN PRETTIER UP CLOSE!
WHISPER

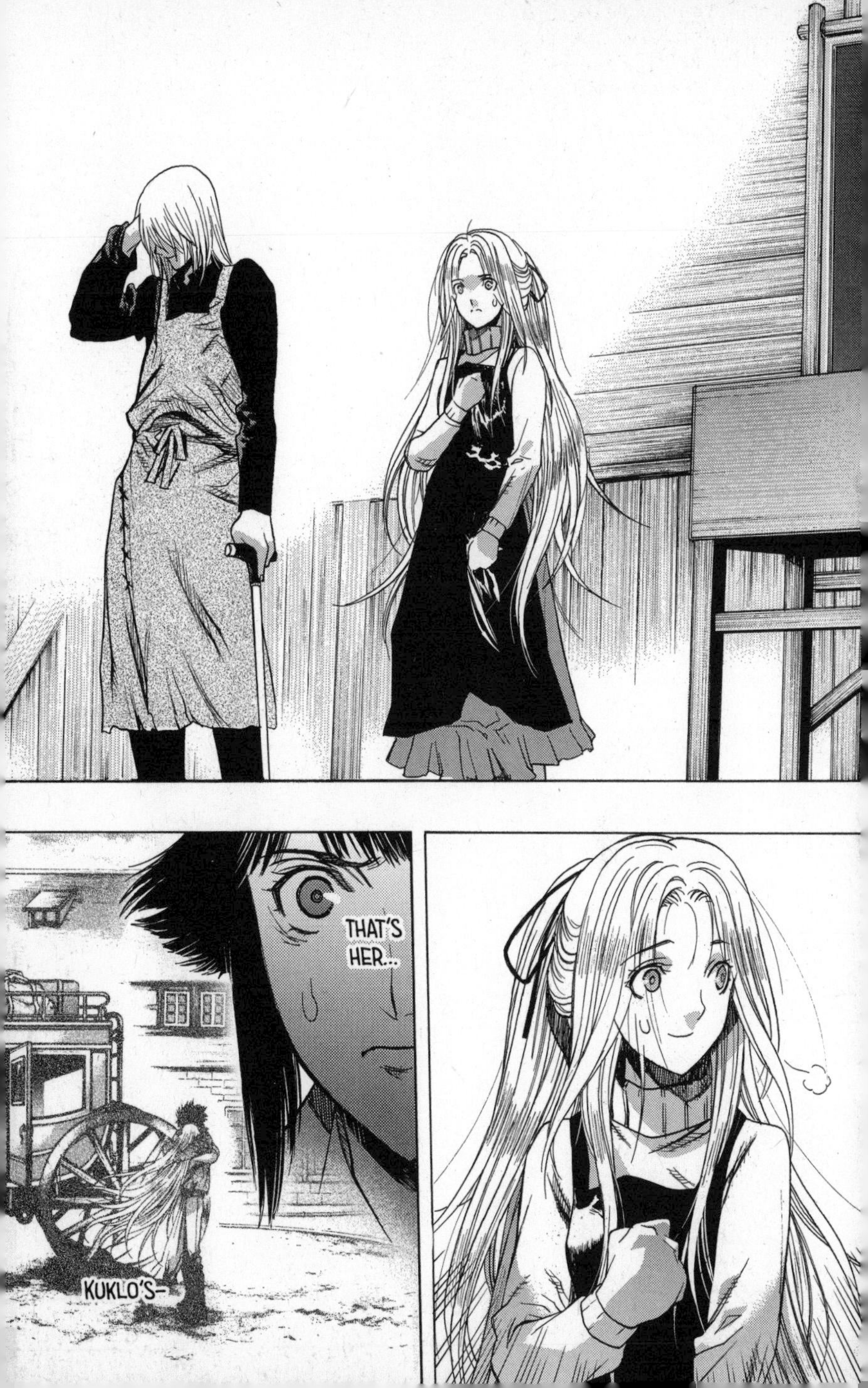
THAT'S HER...
KUKLO'S-

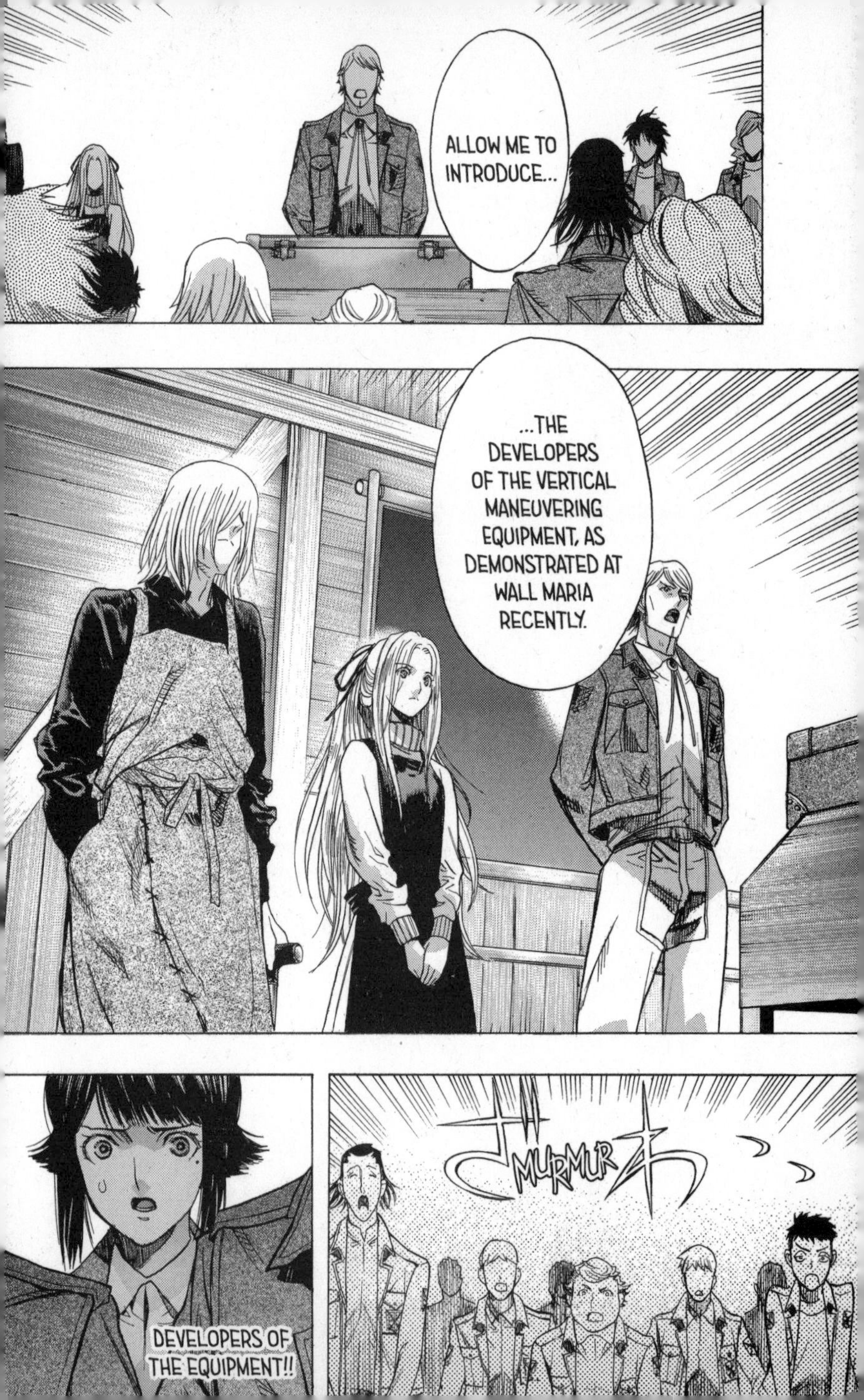
ALLOW ME TO INTRODUCE...
...THE DEVELOPERS OF THE VERTICAL MANEUVERING EQUIPMENT, AS DEMONSTRATED AT WALL MARIA RECENTLY.
MURMUR
DEVELOPERS OF THE EQUIPMENT!!

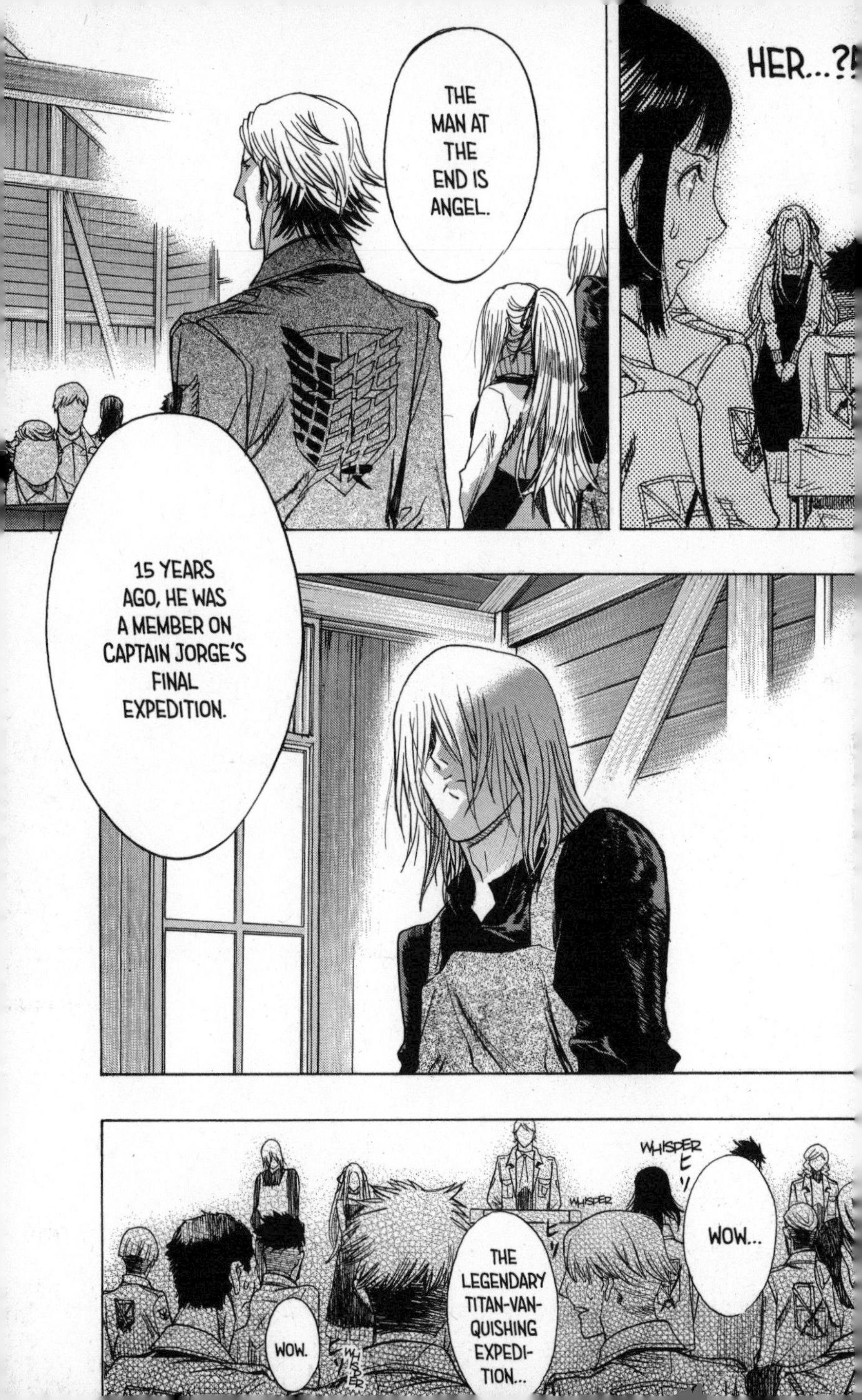
THE MAN AT THE END IS ANGEL.
HER...?!
15 YEARS AGO, HE WAS A MEMBER ON CAPTAIN JORGE'S FINAL EXPEDITION.
WHISPER
WOW...
WHISPER
THE LEGENDARY TITAN-VANQUISHING EXPEDITION...
WHISPER
WOW.

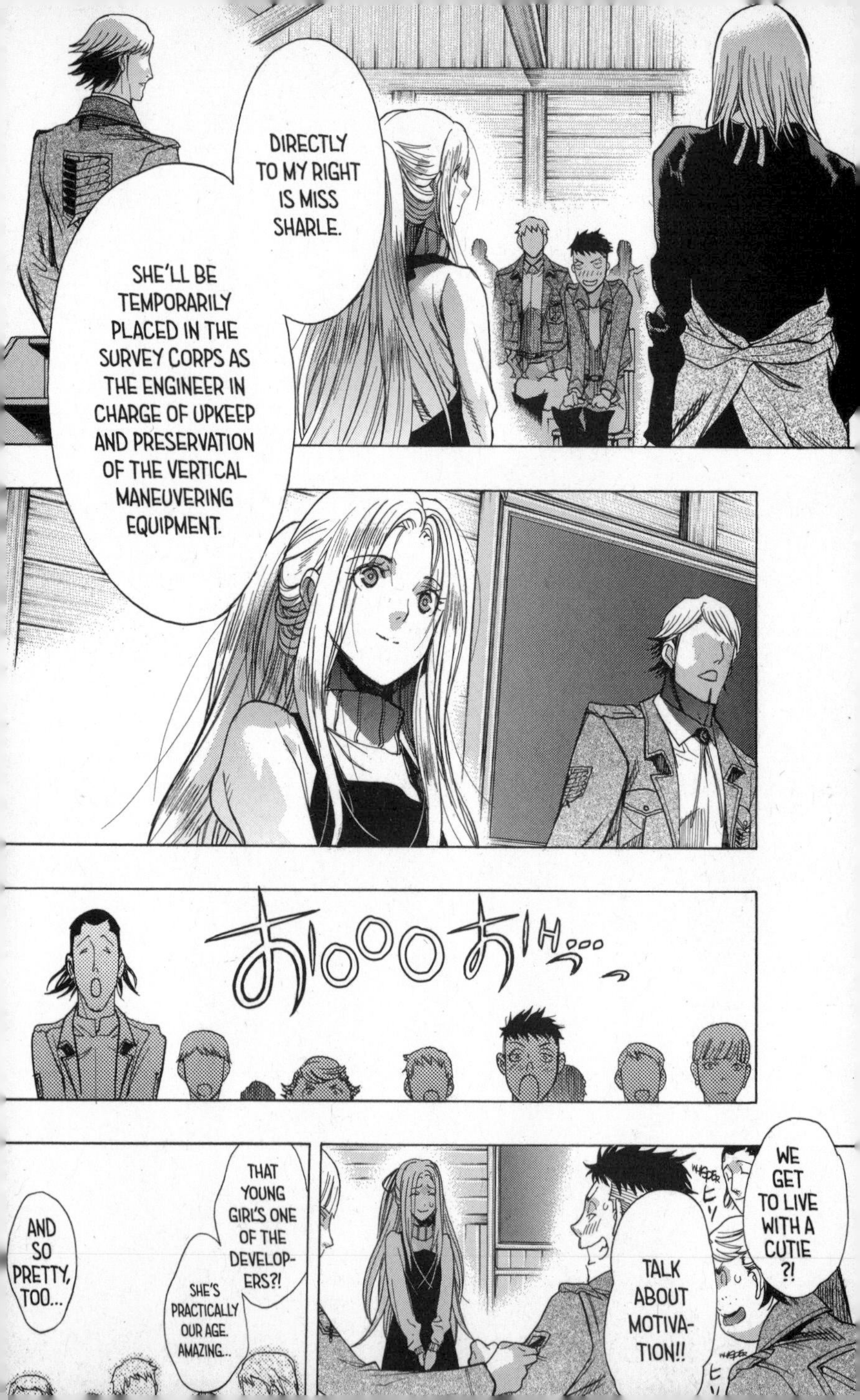
DIRECTLY TO MY RIGHT IS MISS SHARLE.
SHE'LL BE TEMPORARILY PLACED IN THE SURVEY CORPS AS THE ENGINEER IN CHARGE OF UPKEEP AND PRESERVATION OF THE VERTICAL MANEUVERING EQUIPMENT.
WE GET TO LIVE WITH A CUTIE?!
TALK ABOUT MOTIVATION!!
THAT YOUNG GIRL'S ONE OF THE DEVELOPERS?!
SHE'S PRACTICALLY OUR AGE. AMAZING...
AND SO PRETTY, TOO...

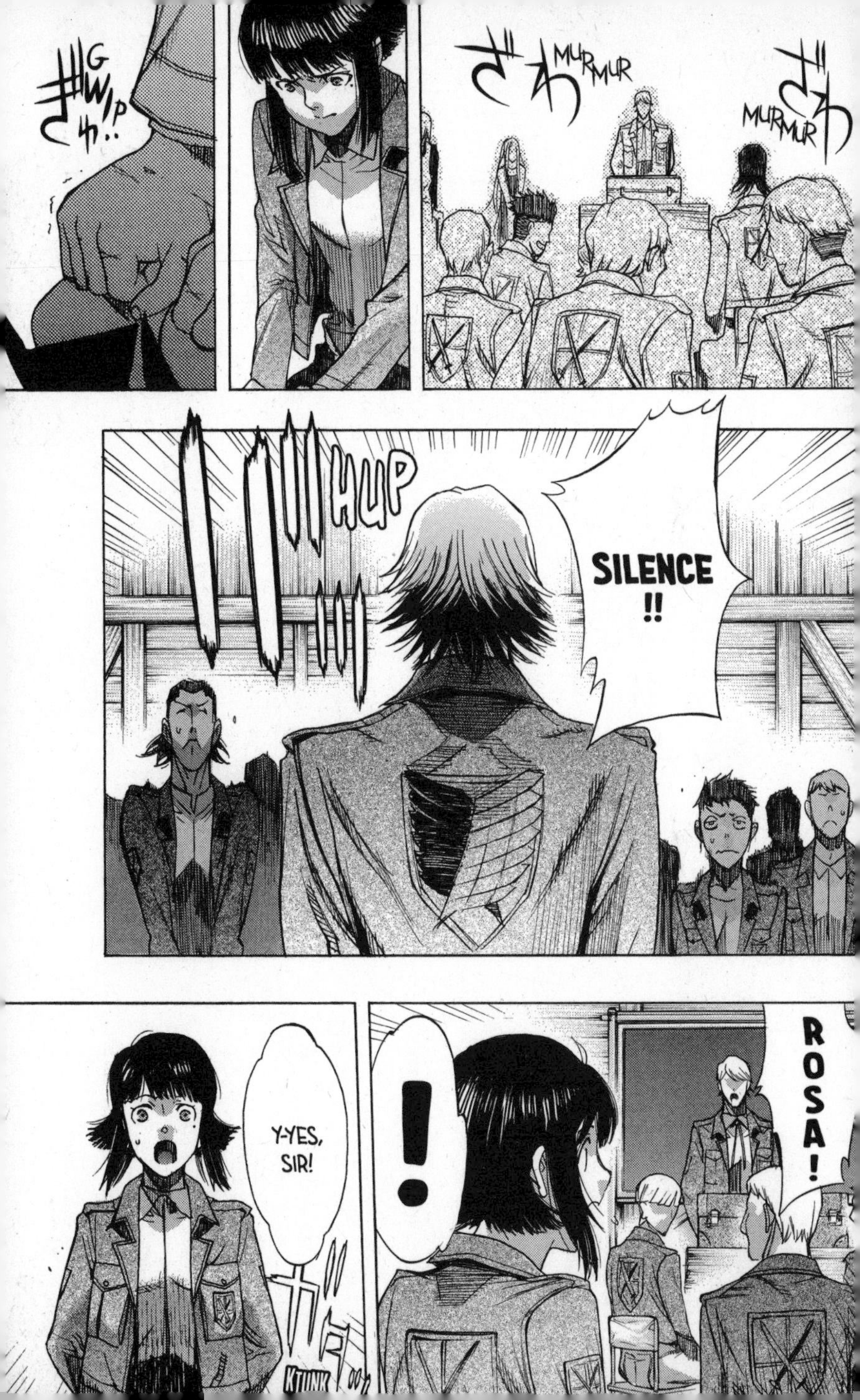

ざわ MURMUR
ざわ MURMUR
ぎゅ.. GWIP..
SILENCE!!
HUP
ROSA!
!
Y-YES, SIR!
KTUNK

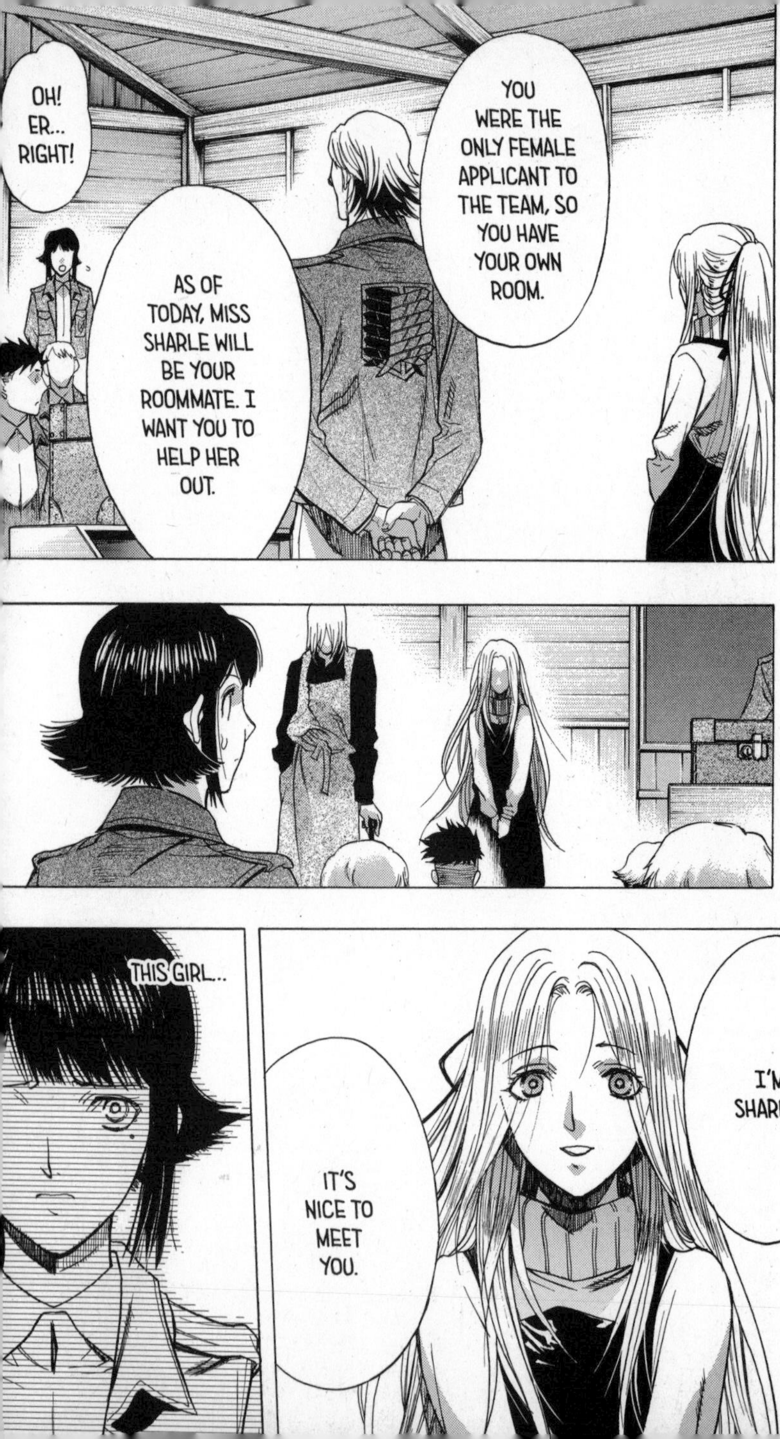
YOU WERE THE ONLY FEMALE APPLICANT TO THE TEAM, SO YOU HAVE YOUR OWN ROOM.
AS OF TODAY, MISS SHARLE WILL BE YOUR ROOMMATE. I WANT YOU TO HELP HER OUT.
OH! ER... RIGHT!
I'M SHARLE.
IT'S NICE TO MEET YOU.
THIS GIRL...

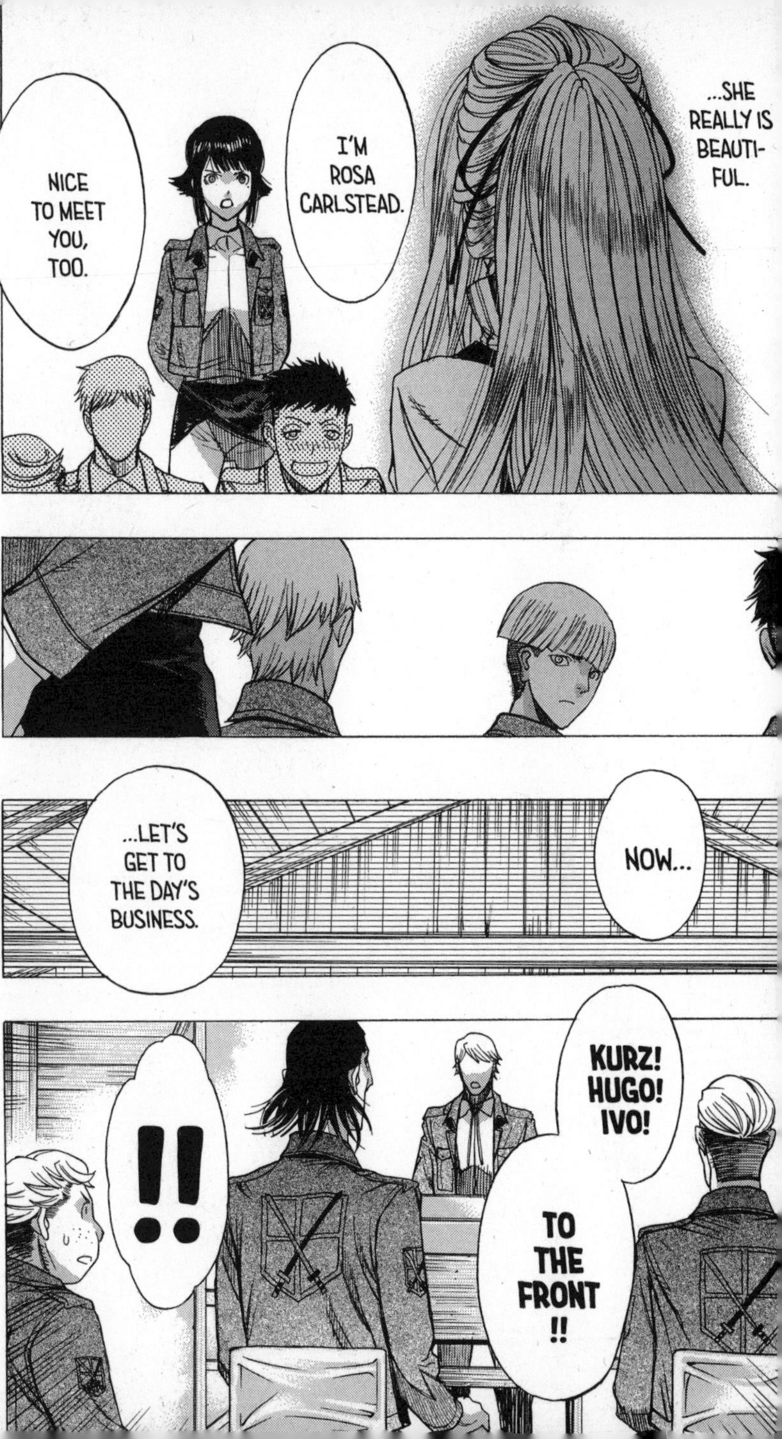
...SHE REALLY IS BEAUTI-FUL.
I'M ROSA CARLSTEAD.
NICE TO MEET YOU, TOO.
NOW...
...LET'S GET TO THE DAY'S BUSINESS.
KURZ! HUGO! IVO!
TO THE FRONT !!
!!

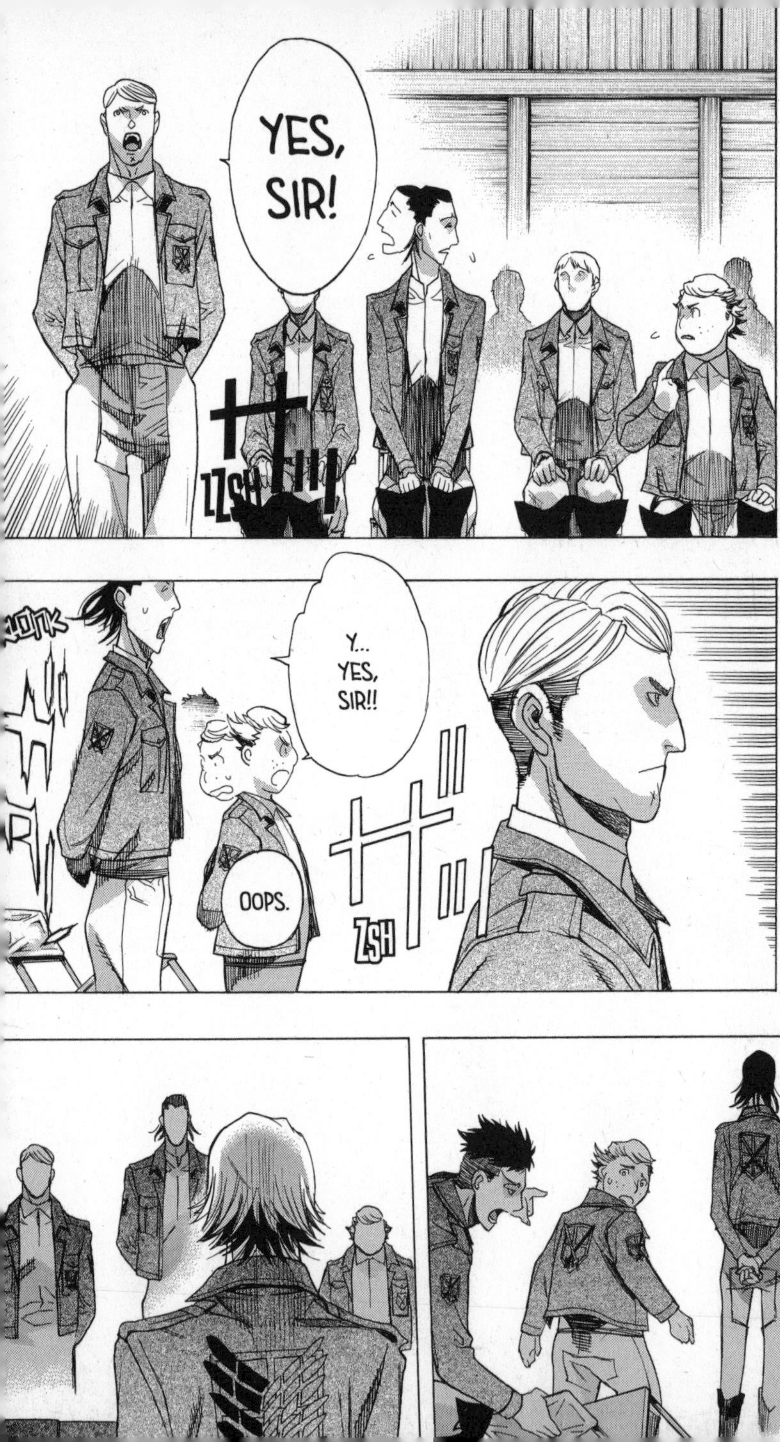
YES, SIR!
ZZSH
Y... YES, SIR!!
ZSH
OOPS.

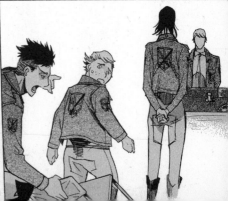

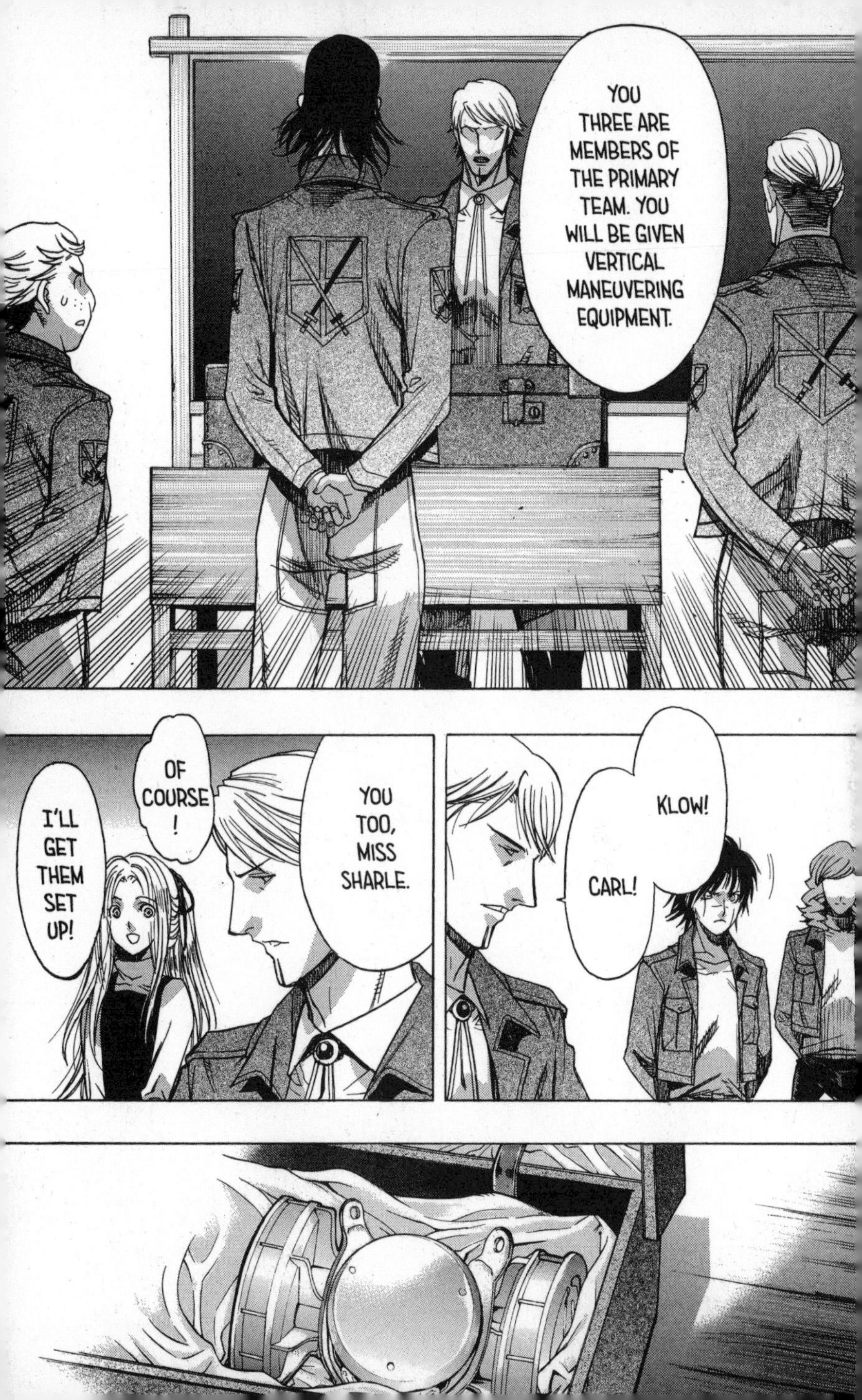
YOU THREE ARE MEMBERS OF THE PRIMARY TEAM. YOU WILL BE GIVEN VERTICAL MANEUVERING EQUIPMENT.
KLOW! CARL!
YOU TOO, MISS SHARLE.
OF COURSE!
I'LL GET THEM SET UP!

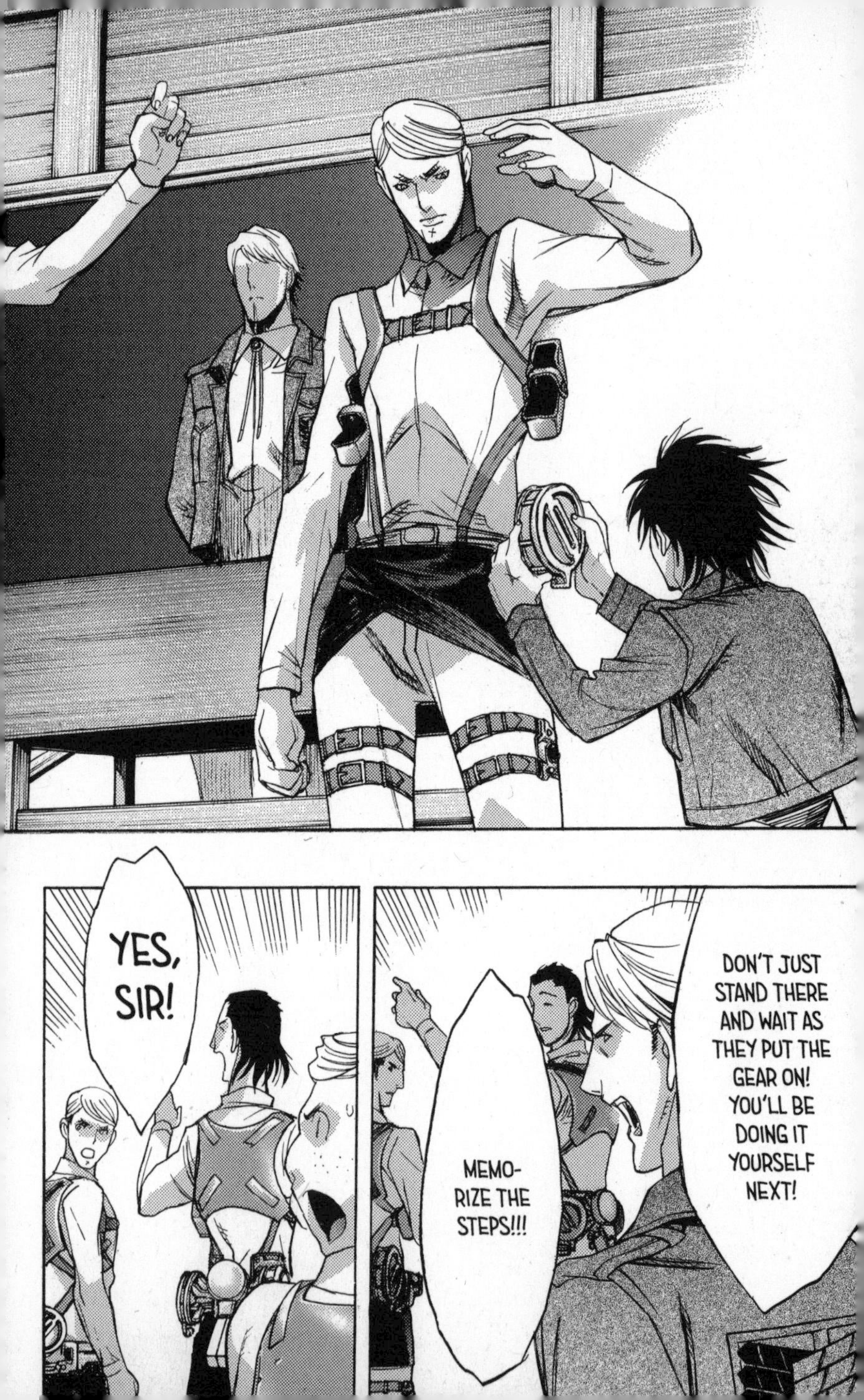
DON'T JUST STAND THERE AND WAIT AS THEY PUT THE GEAR ON! YOU'LL BE DOING IT YOURSELF NEXT!
MEMO-RIZE THE STEPS!!!
YES, SIR!

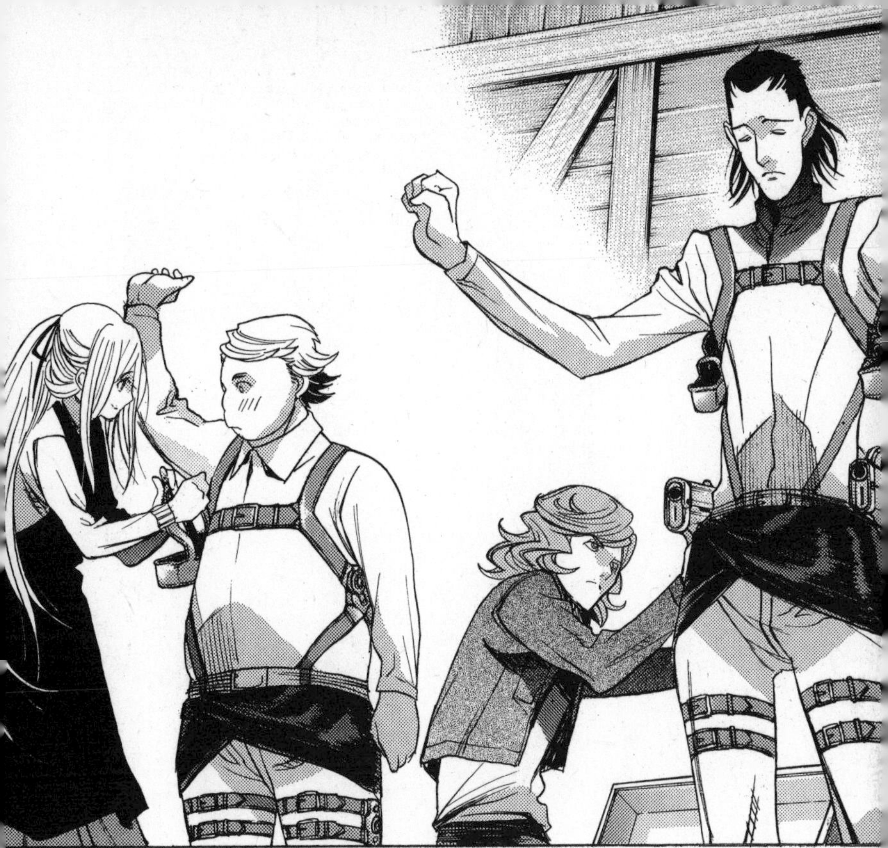

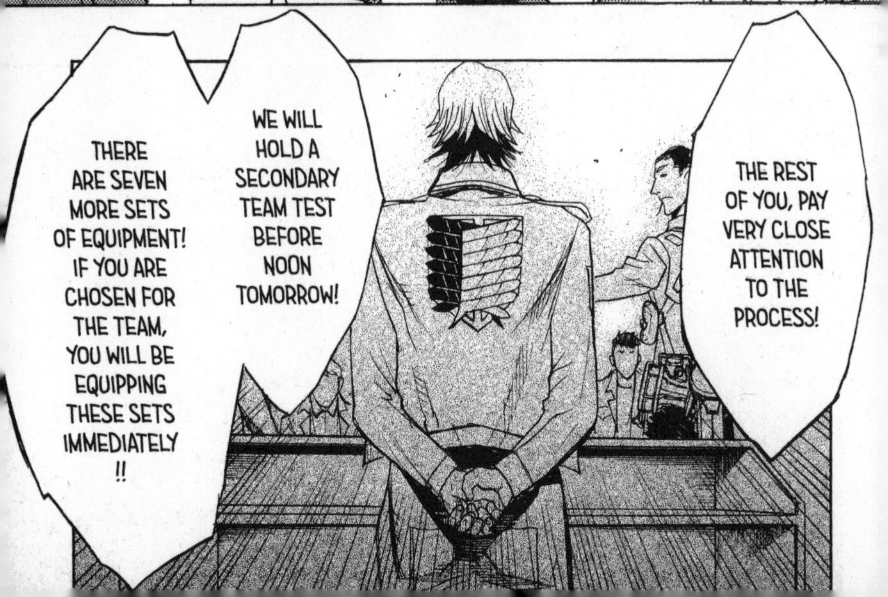
THE REST OF YOU, PAY VERY CLOSE ATTENTION TO THE PROCESS!
WE WILL HOLD A SECONDARY TEAM TEST BEFORE NOON TOMORROW!
THERE ARE SEVEN MORE SETS OF EQUIPMENT! IF YOU ARE CHOSEN FOR THE TEAM, YOU WILL BE EQUIPPING THESE SETS IMMEDIATELY !!

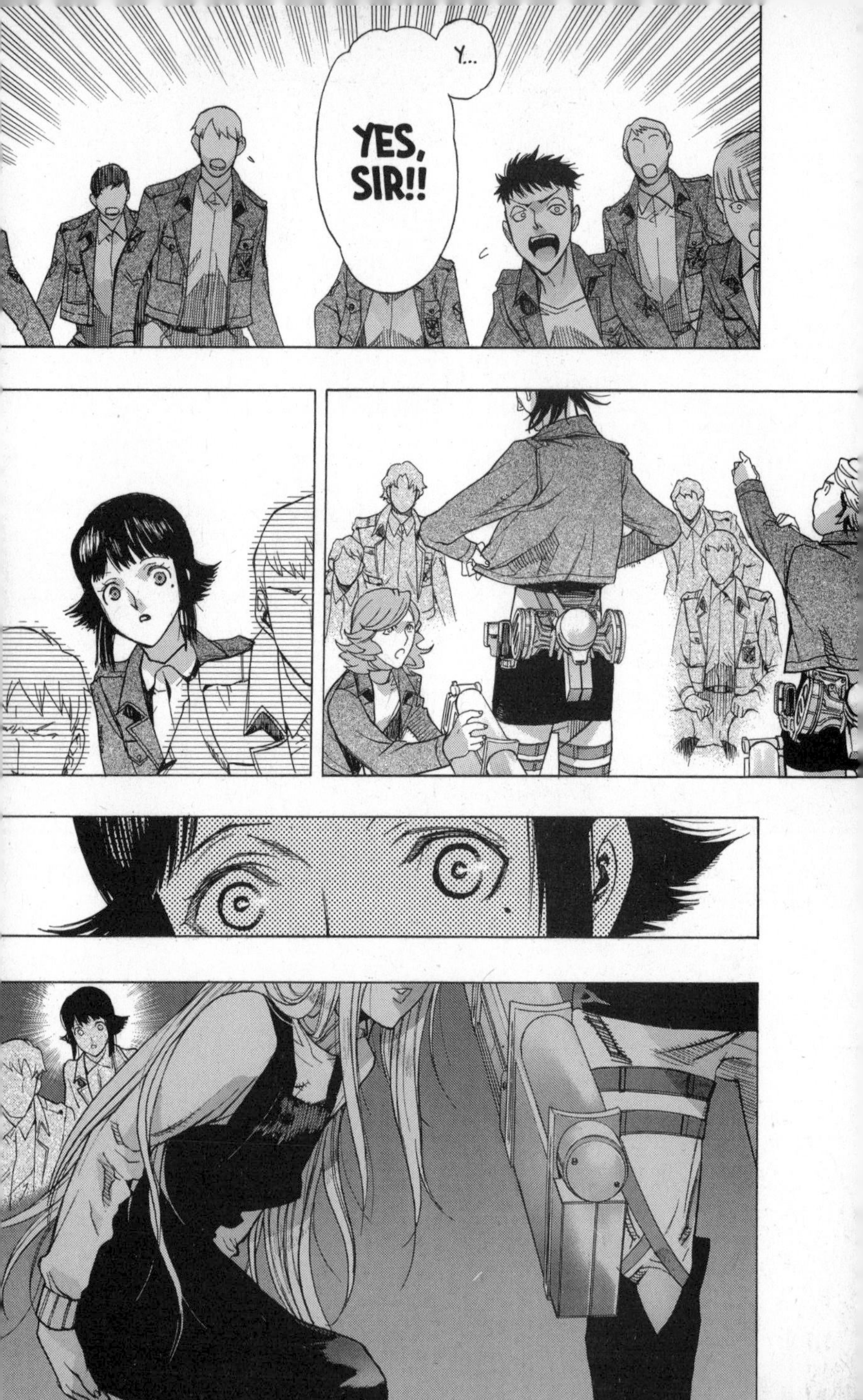
Y...
YES, SIR!!

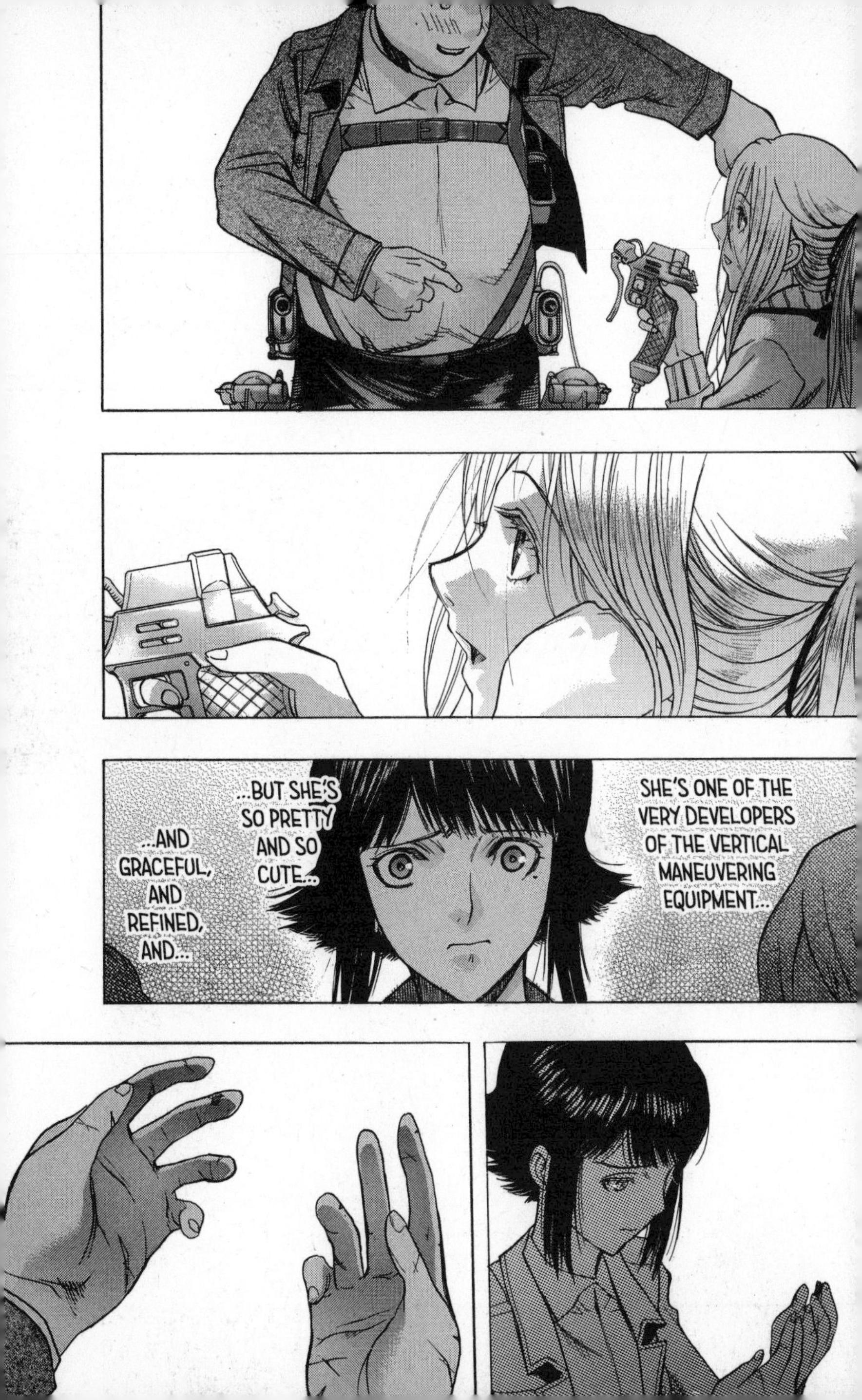
SHE'S ONE OF THE VERY DEVELOPERS OF THE VERTICAL MANEUVERING EQUIPMENT...
...BUT SHE'S SO PRETTY AND SO CUTE...
...AND GRACEFUL, AND REFINED, AND...

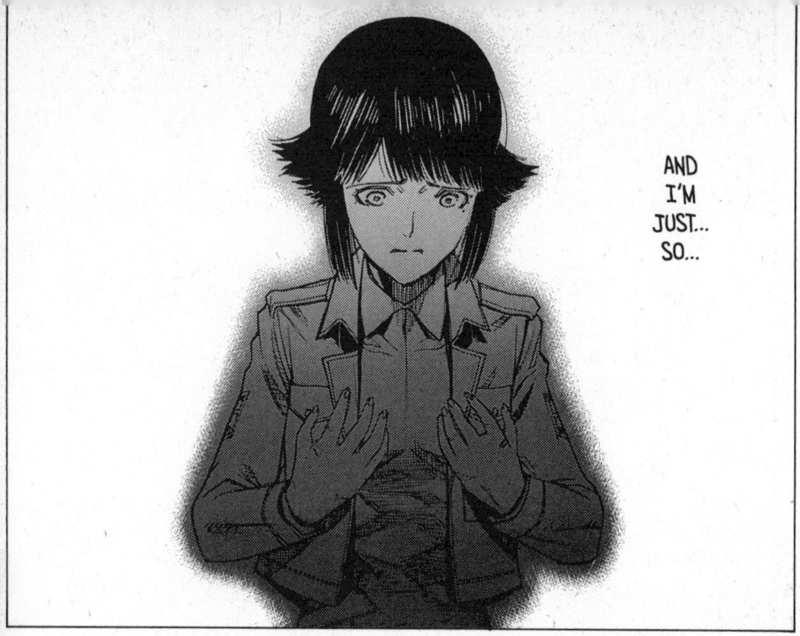
AND I'M JUST... SO...
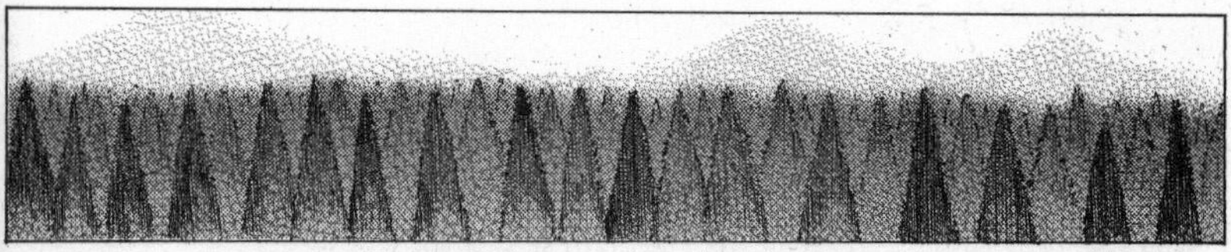
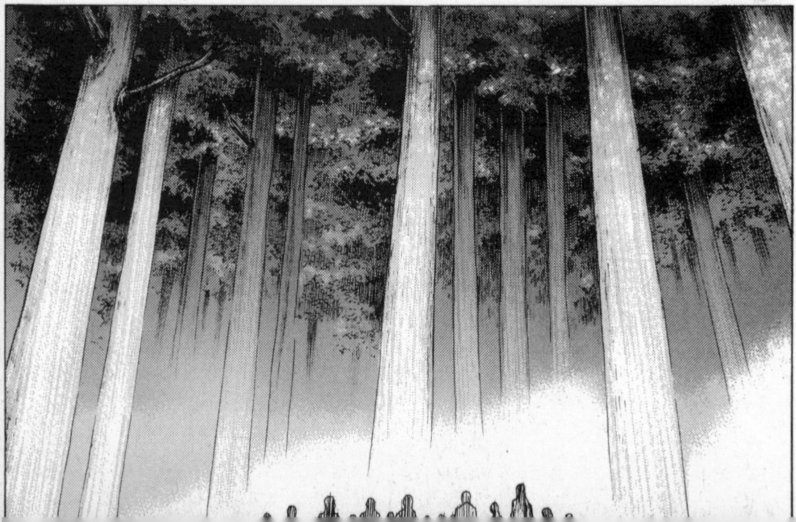

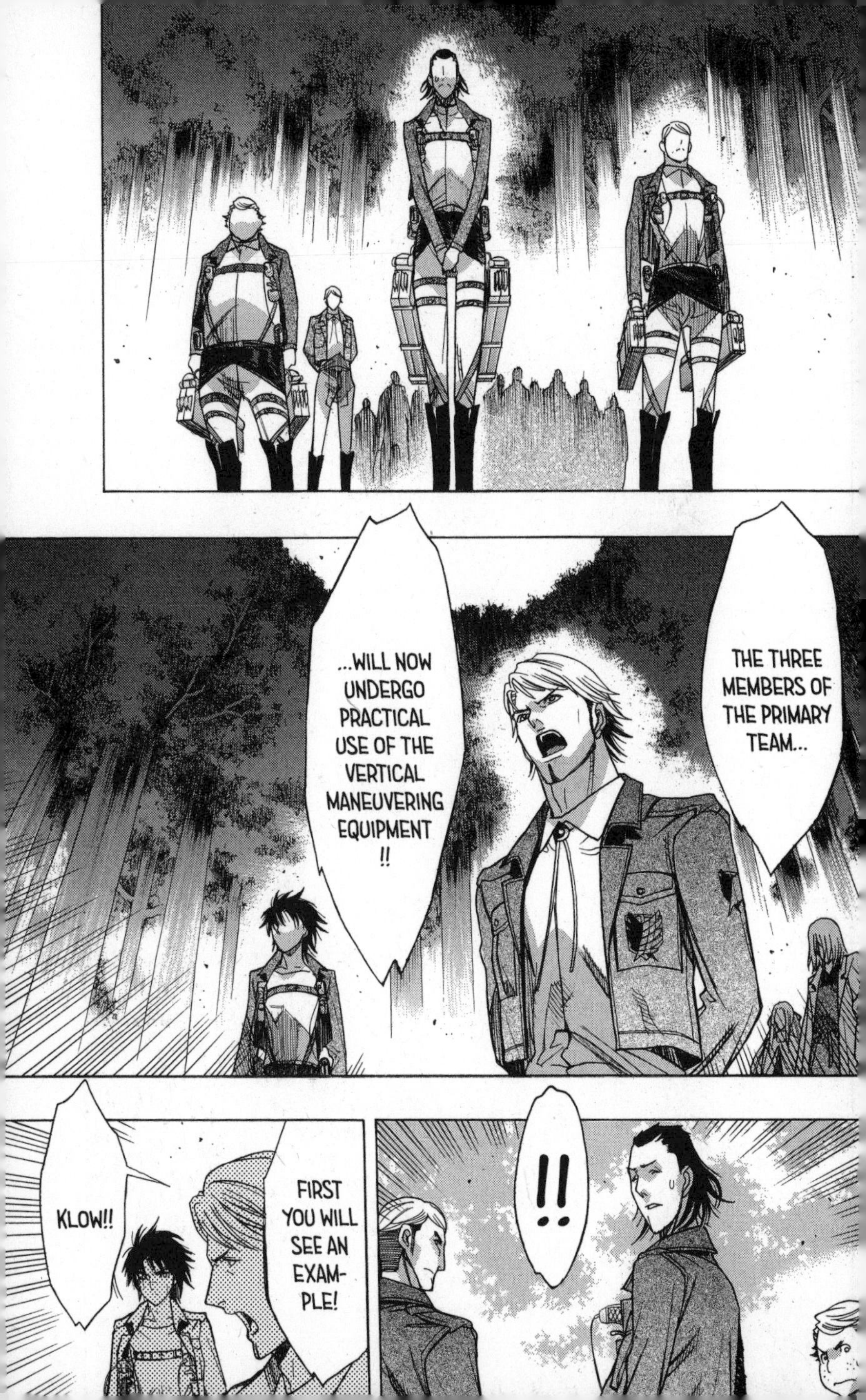
THE THREE MEMBERS OF THE PRIMARY TEAM...
...WILL NOW UNDERGO PRACTICAL USE OF THE VERTICAL MANEUVERING EQUIPMENT !!
!!
FIRST YOU WILL SEE AN EXAM-PLE!
KLOW!!

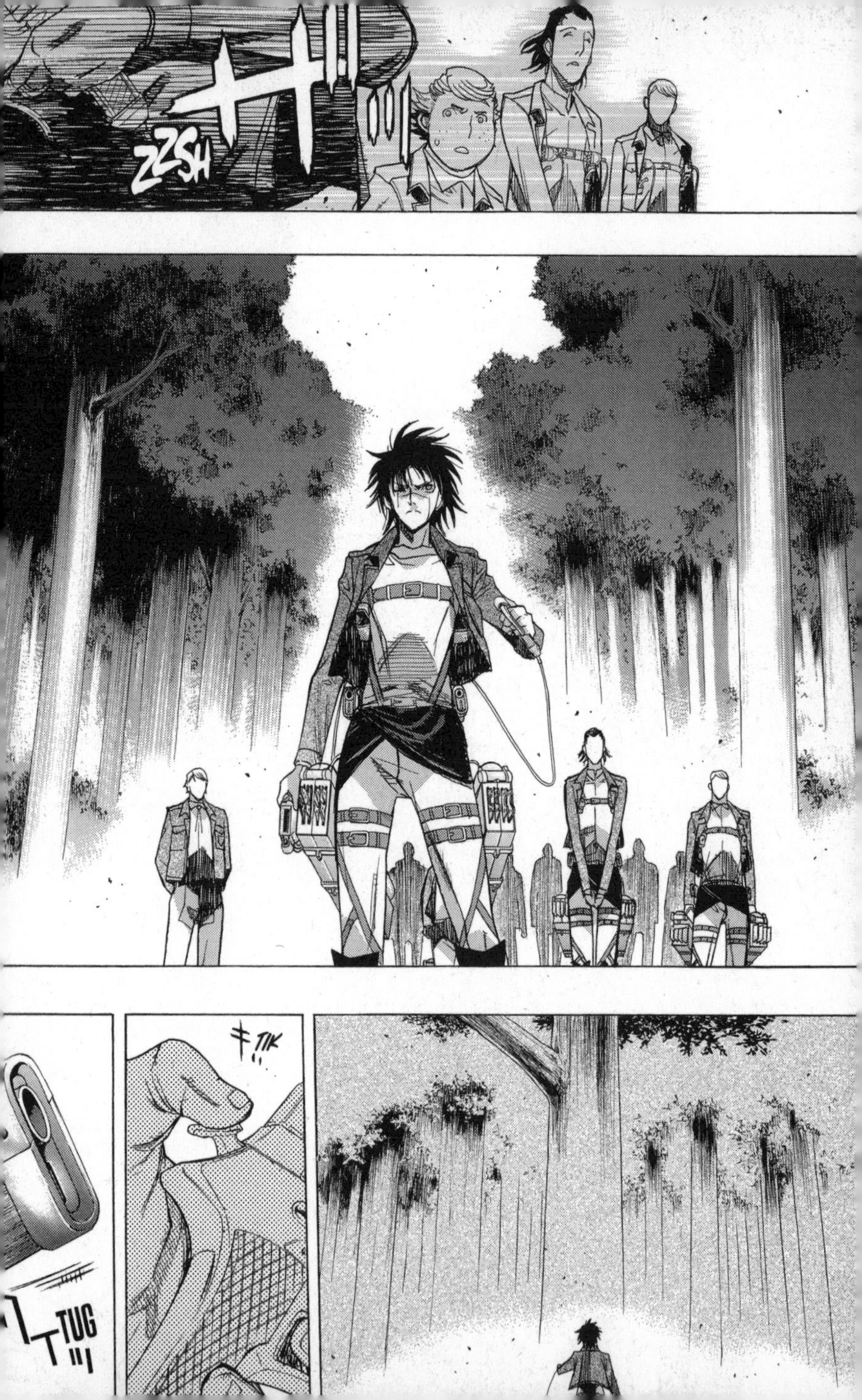
ZZSH
TIK
TUG

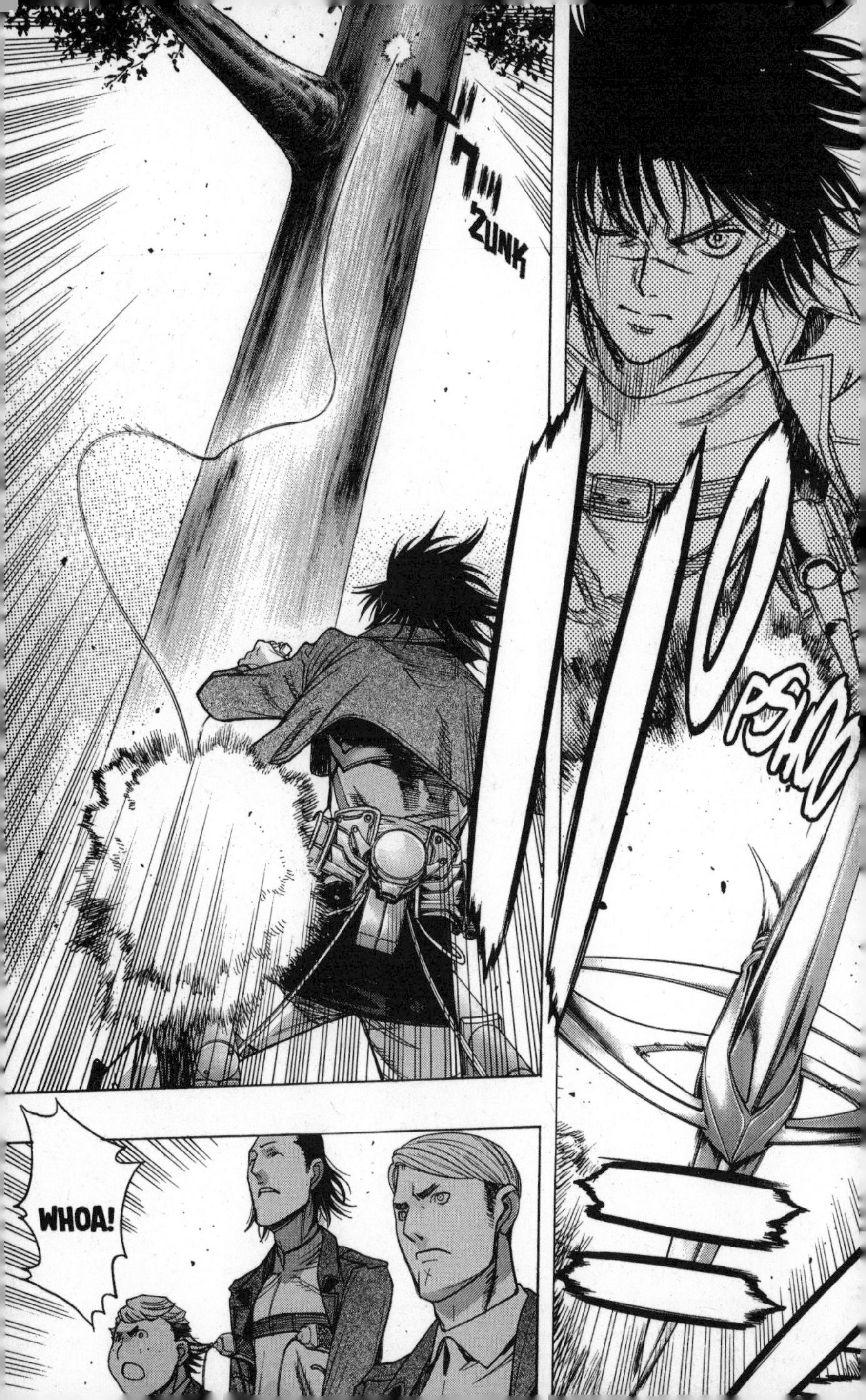
PSHOO
ZUNK
WHOA!

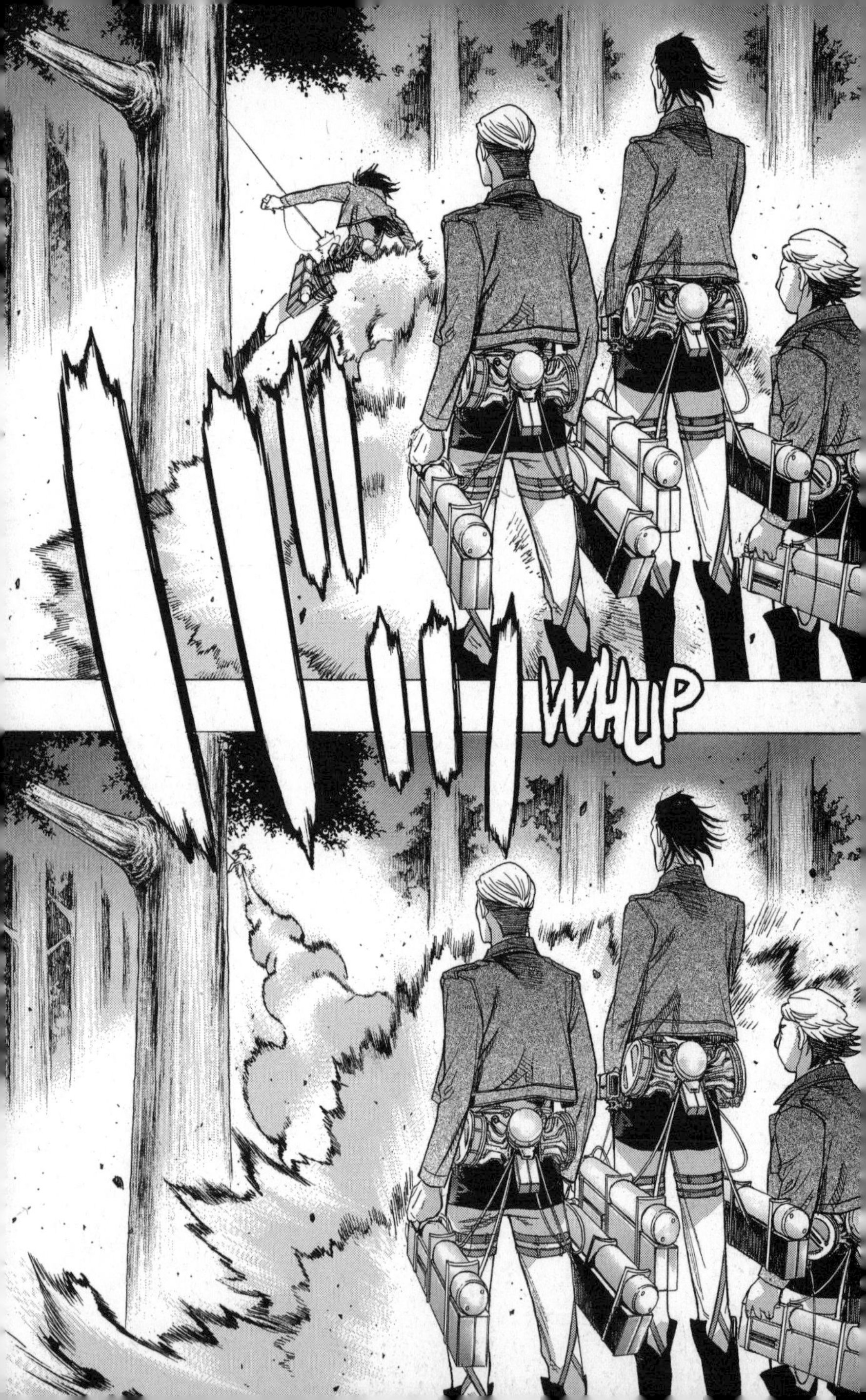
WHUP

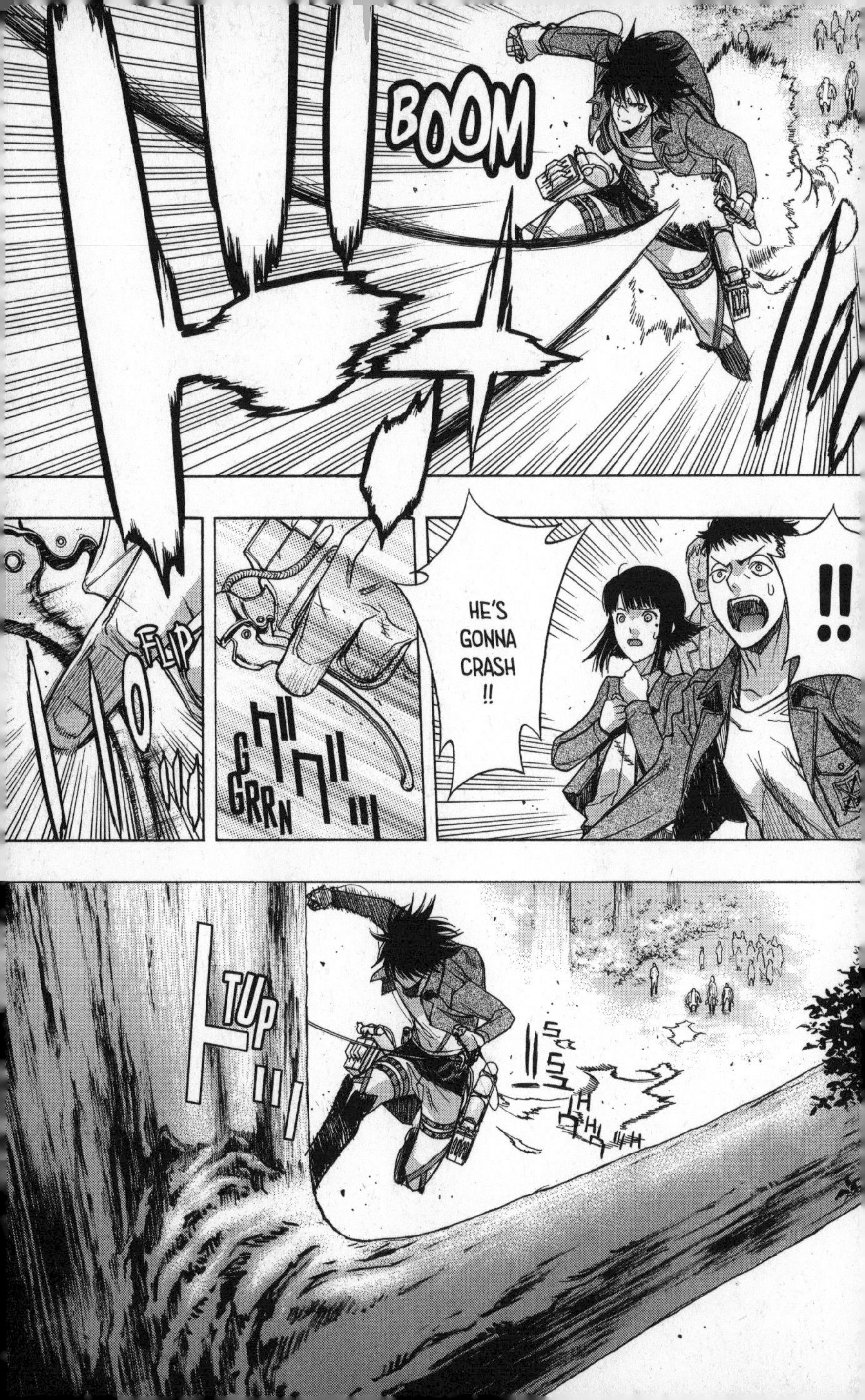
BOOM
!!
HE'S GONNA CRASH !!
GRRN
FLIP
TUP
SHHH

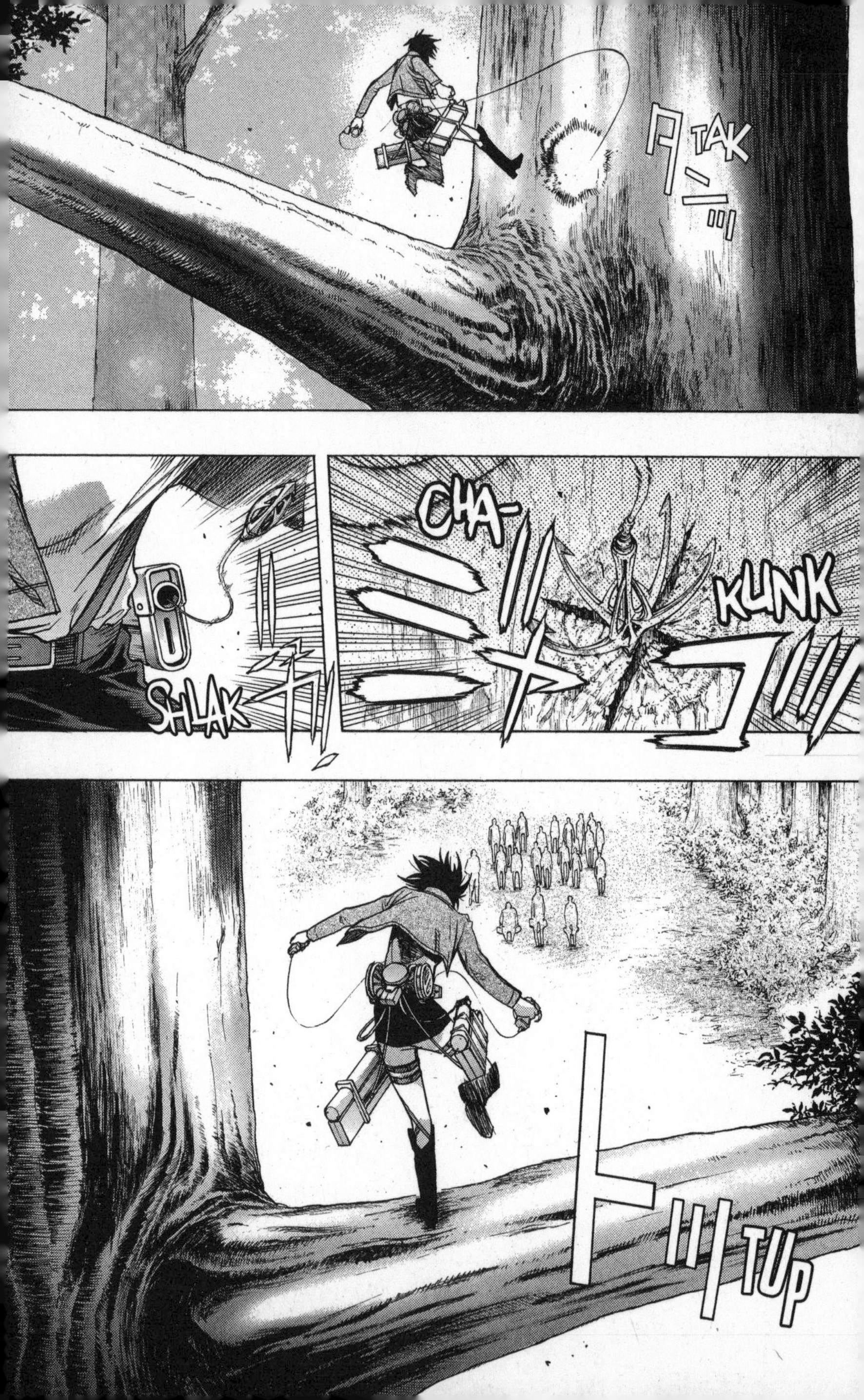
TAK
KUNK
CHA-
SHLAK
TUP

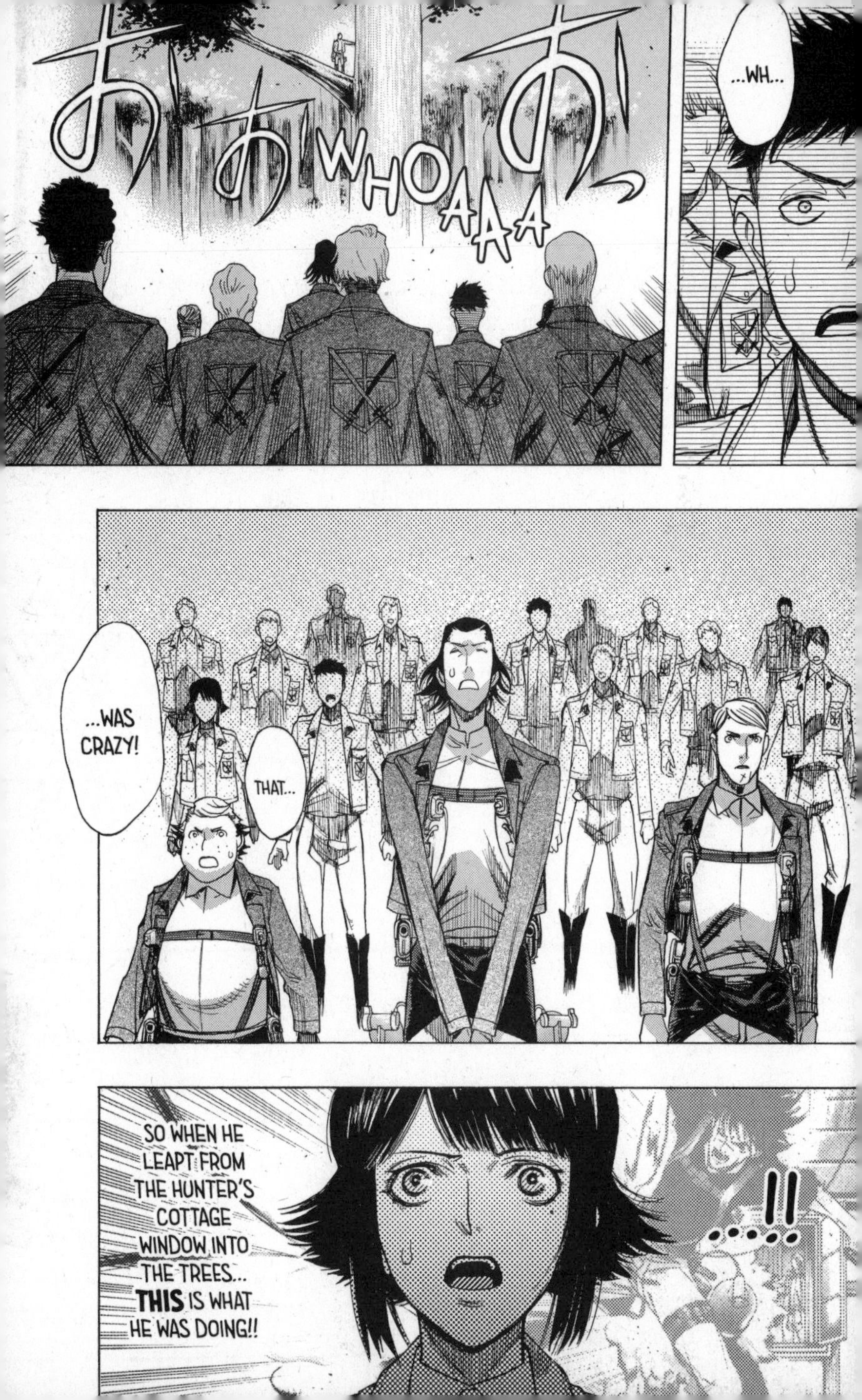
...WH...
おおお
WHOAAA
THAT...
...WAS CRAZY!
....!!
SO WHEN HE LEAPT FROM THE HUNTER'S COTTAGE WINDOW INTO THE TREES... **THIS** IS WHAT HE WAS DOING!!

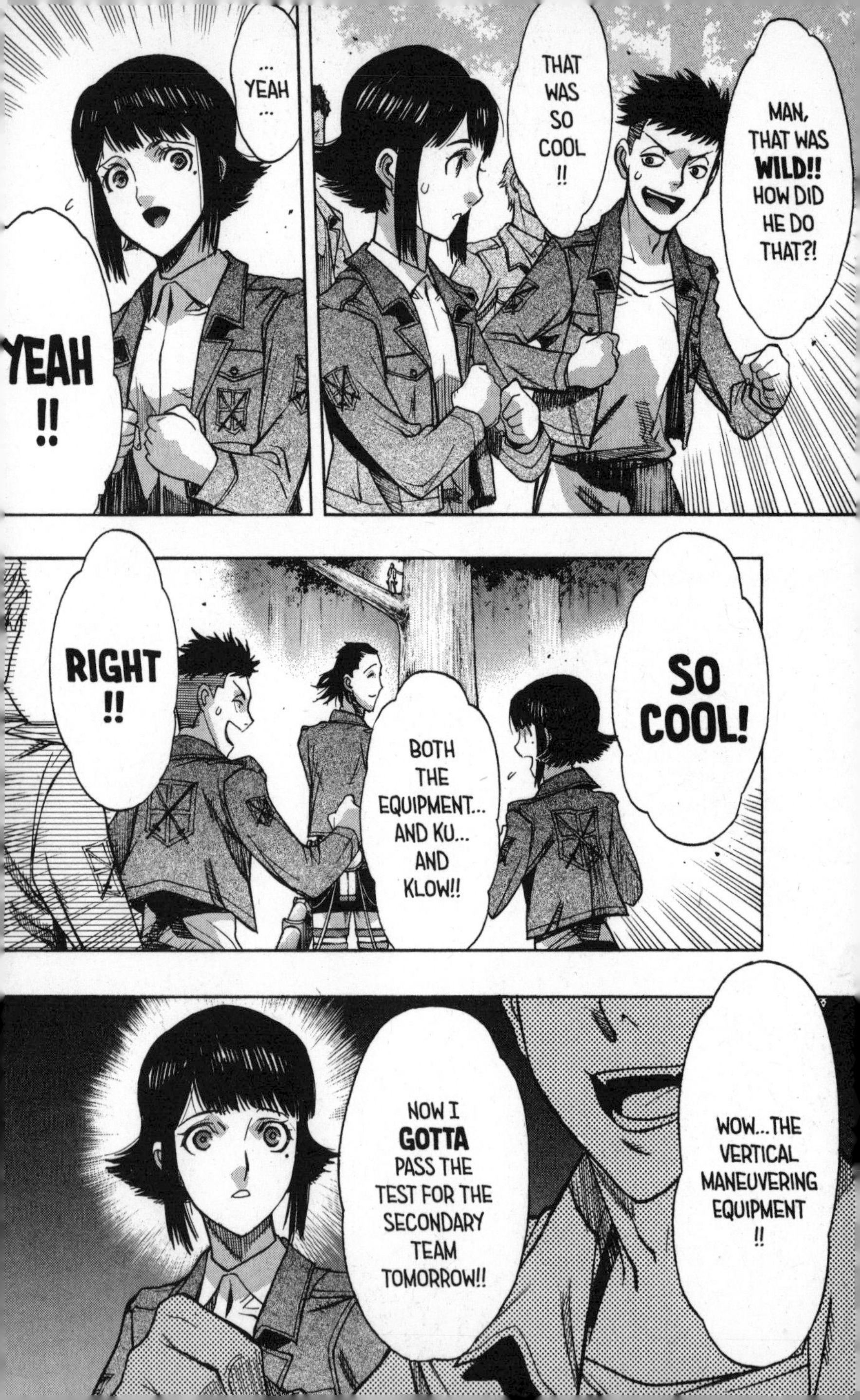
MAN, THAT WAS **WILD!!** HOW DID HE DO THAT?!
THAT WAS SO COOL !!
... YEAH ...
YEAH !!
SO COOL!
BOTH THE EQUIPMENT... AND KU... AND KLOW!!
RIGHT !!
WOW...THE VERTICAL MANEUVERING EQUIPMENT !!
NOW I **GOTTA** PASS THE TEST FOR THE SECONDARY TEAM TOMORROW!!

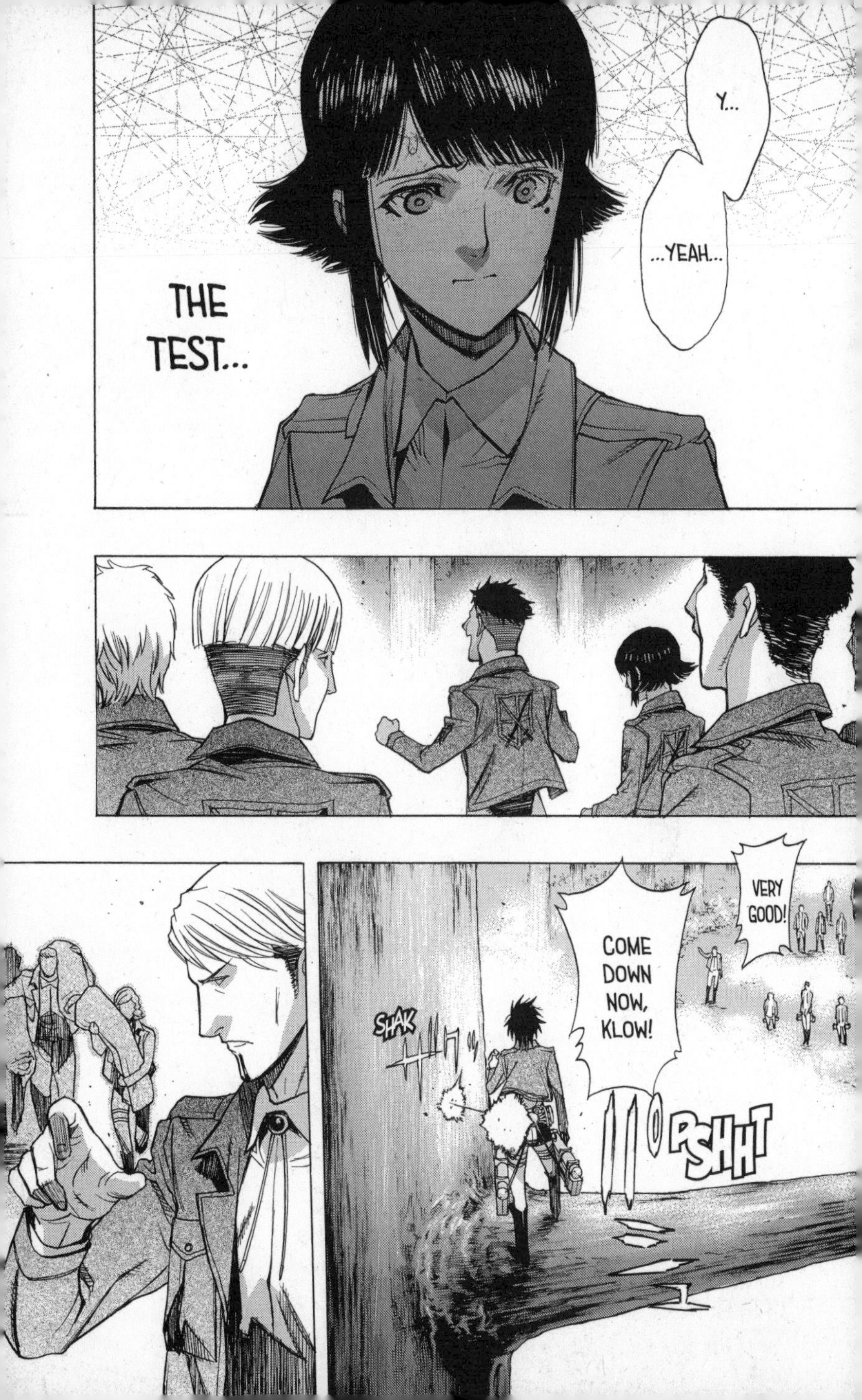
Y...
...YEAH...
THE TEST...
VERY GOOD!
COME DOWN NOW, KLOW!
PSHHT
SHAK

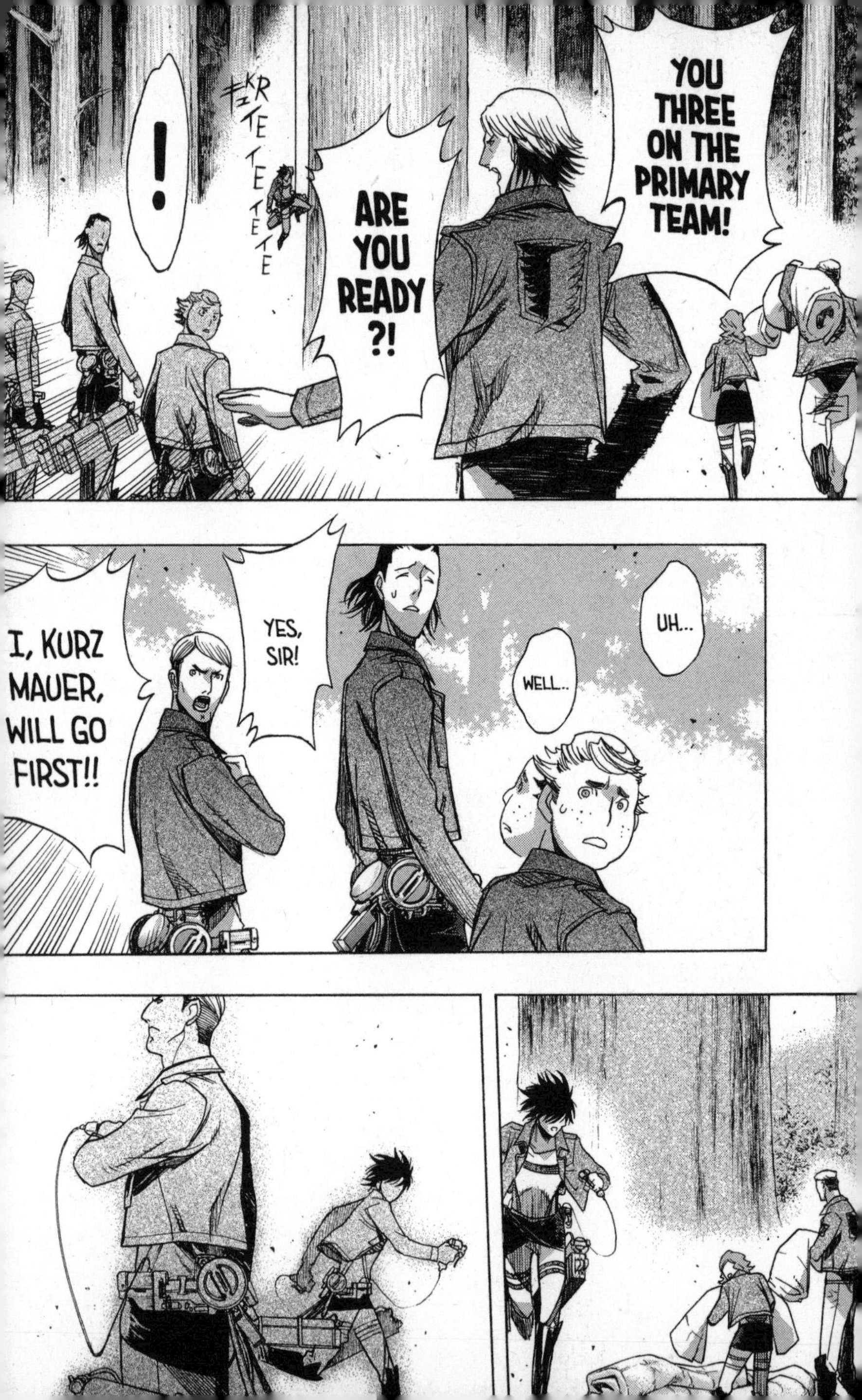
YOU THREE ON THE PRIMARY TEAM!
ARE YOU READY?!
KR TE TE TE TE
!
UH...
WELL...
YES, SIR!
I, KURZ MAUER, WILL GO FIRST!!

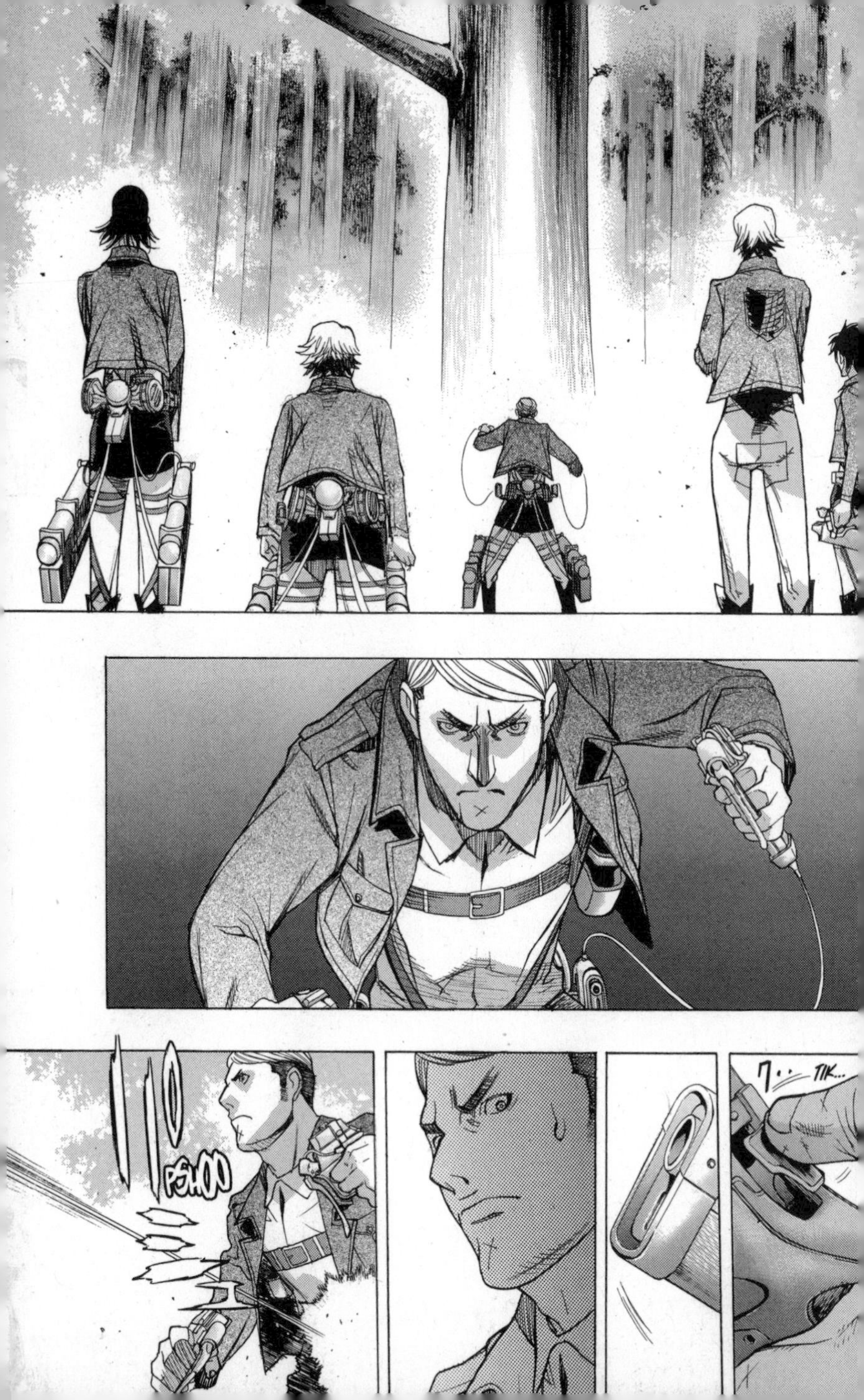
TIK...
PSHOO

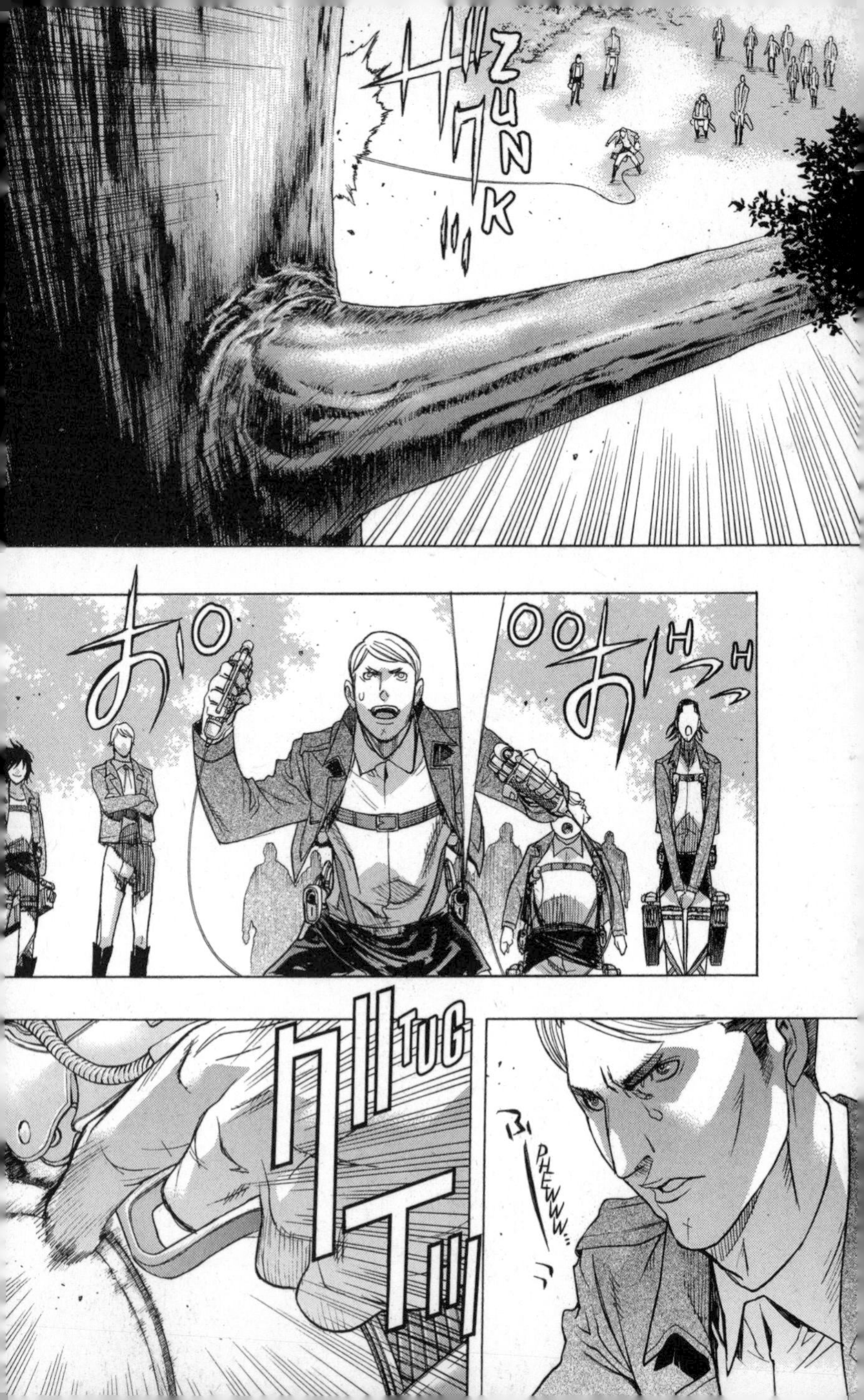
ZUNK
OOHH
O
PHEWWW...
TUG

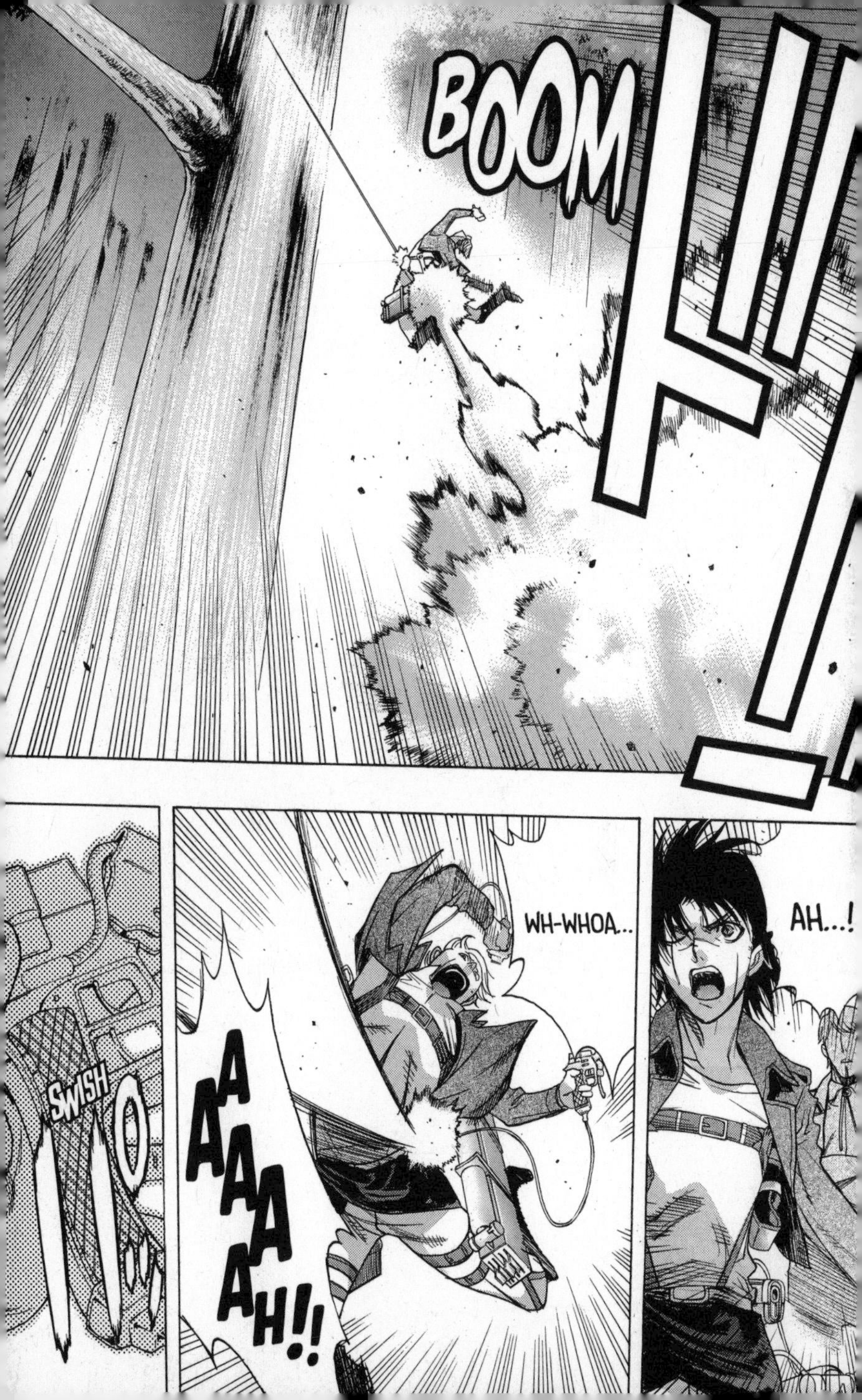
BOOM!!!
AH...!
WH-WHOA...
AAAAAAH!!!
SWISH

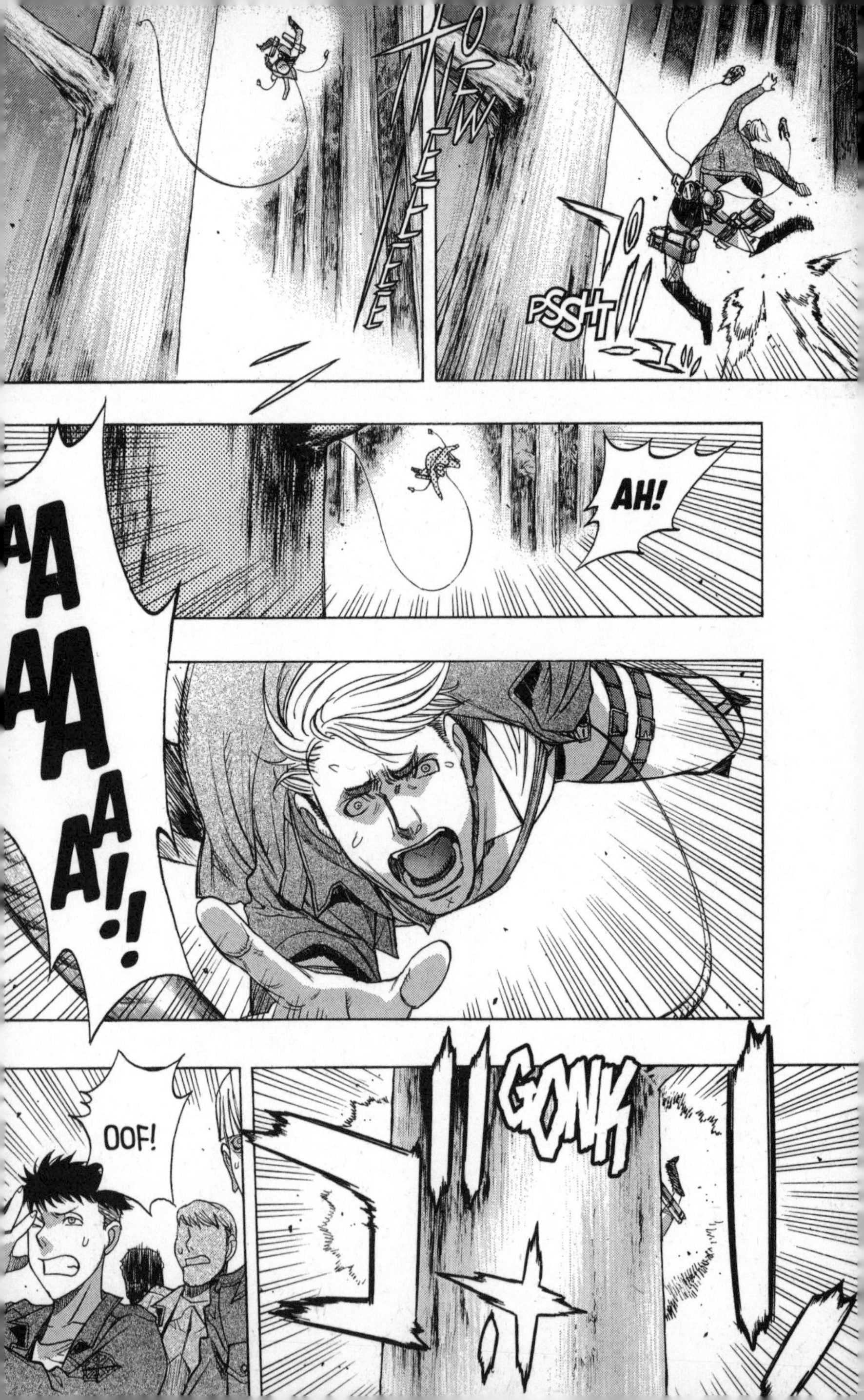
PSSHT
FWEEEEEE
AH!
AAAAAAA!!
GONK
OOF!

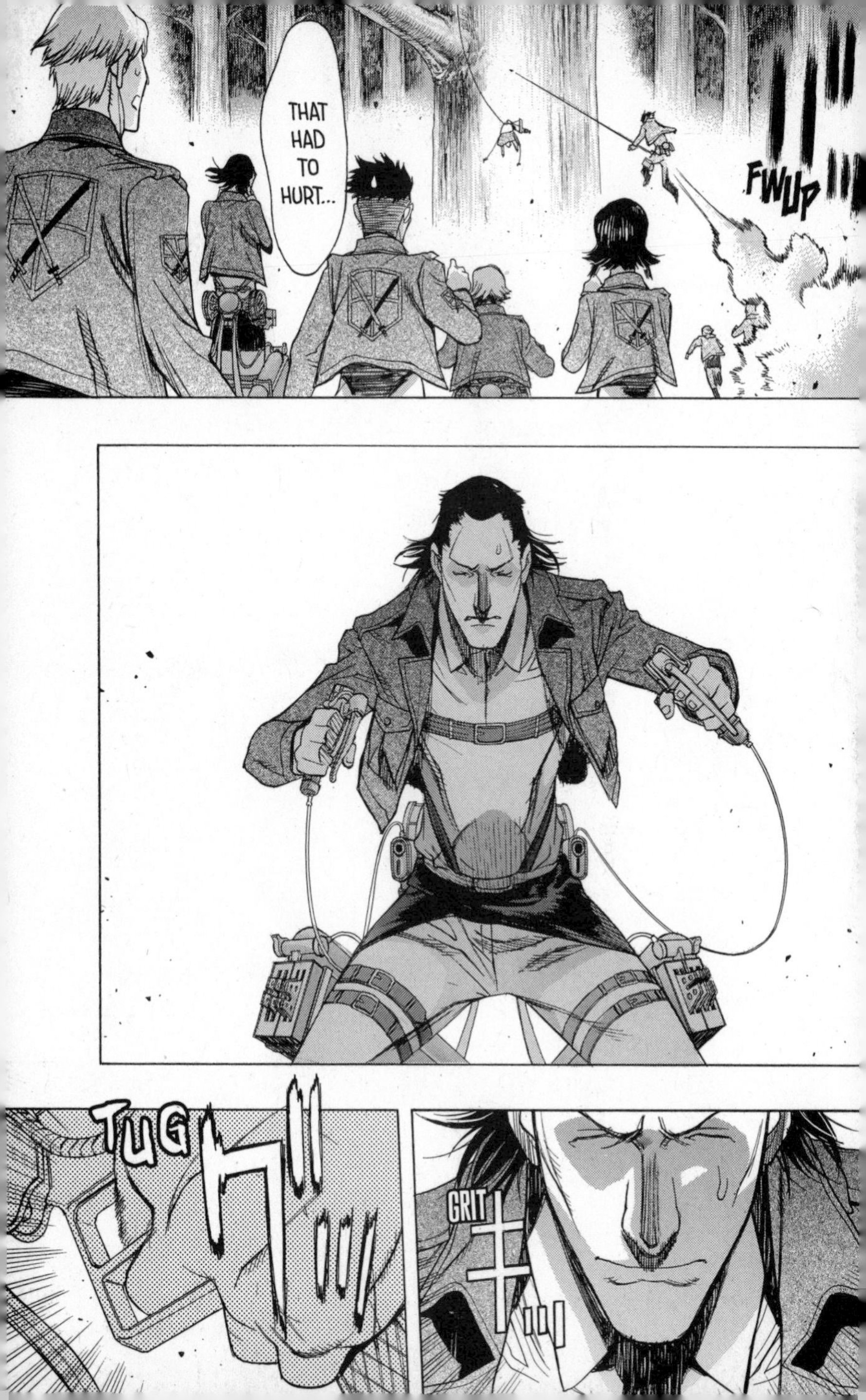
FWUP
THAT HAD TO HURT...
GRIT
TUG

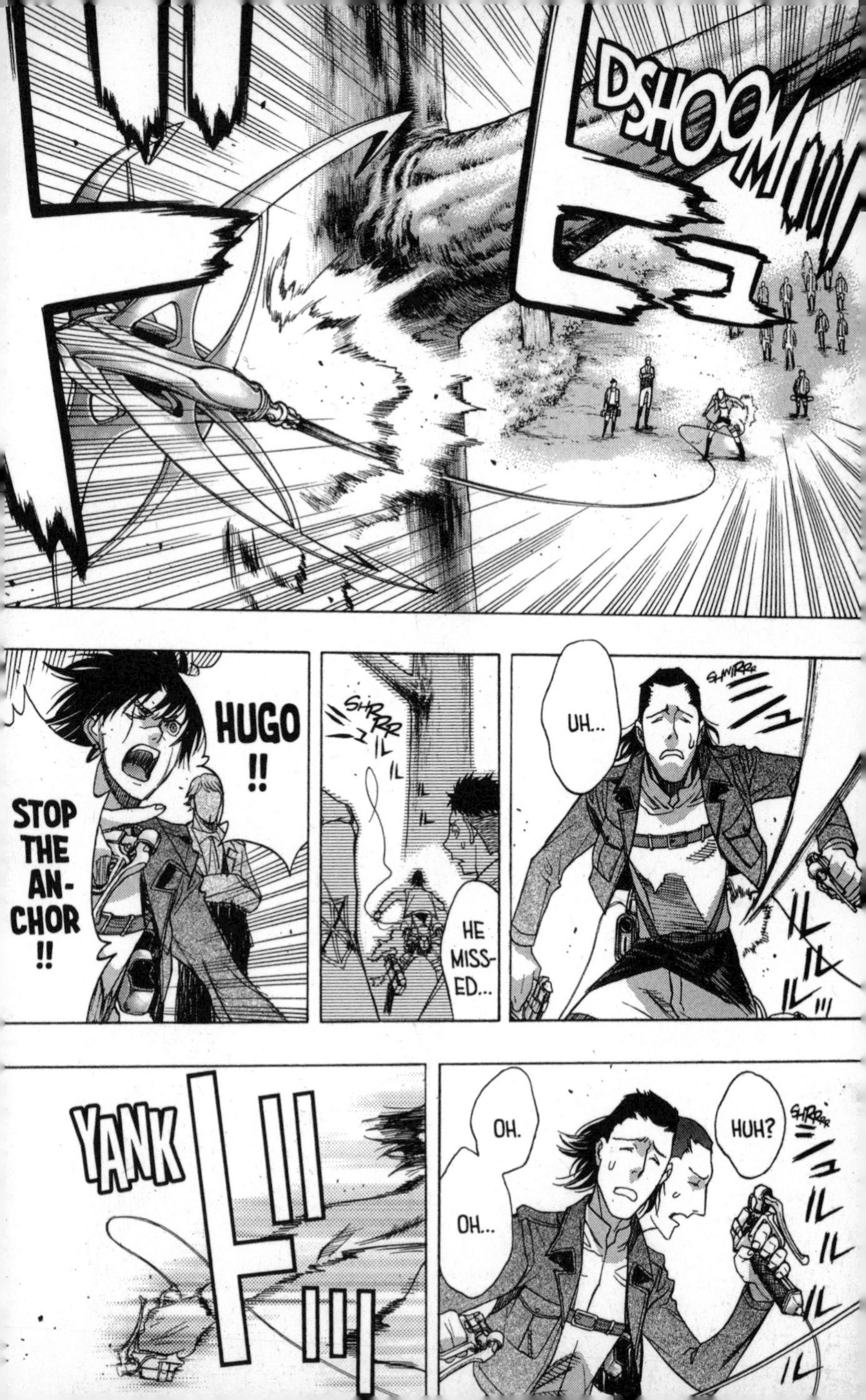
DSHOOM
UH...
HE MISSED...
HUGO!!
STOP THE ANCHOR!!
HUH?
OH.
OH...
YANK

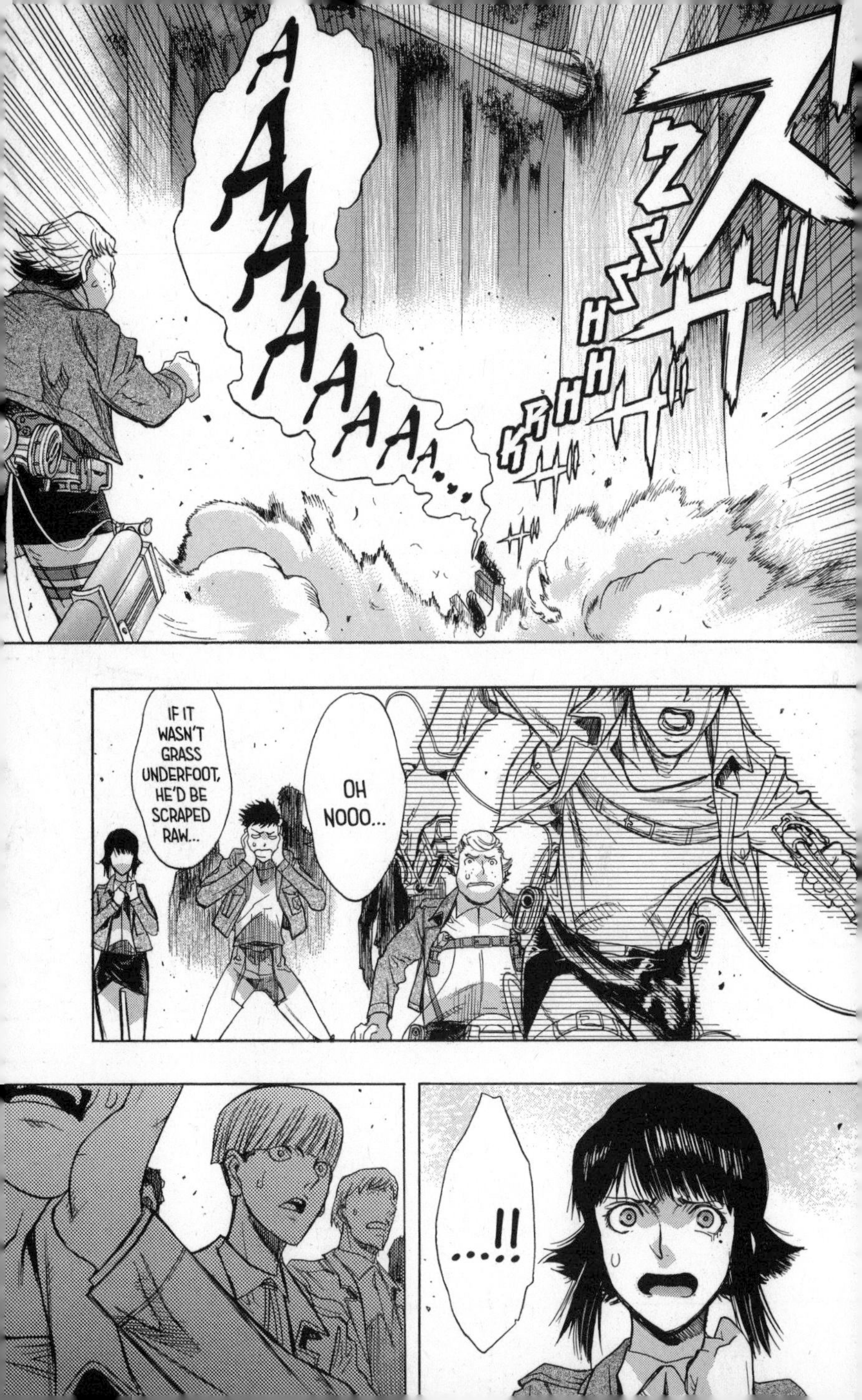

AAAAAAAAA...
KRHHHSSZ
OH NOOO...
IF IT WASN'T GRASS UNDERFOOT, HE'D BE SCRAPED RAW...
...!!

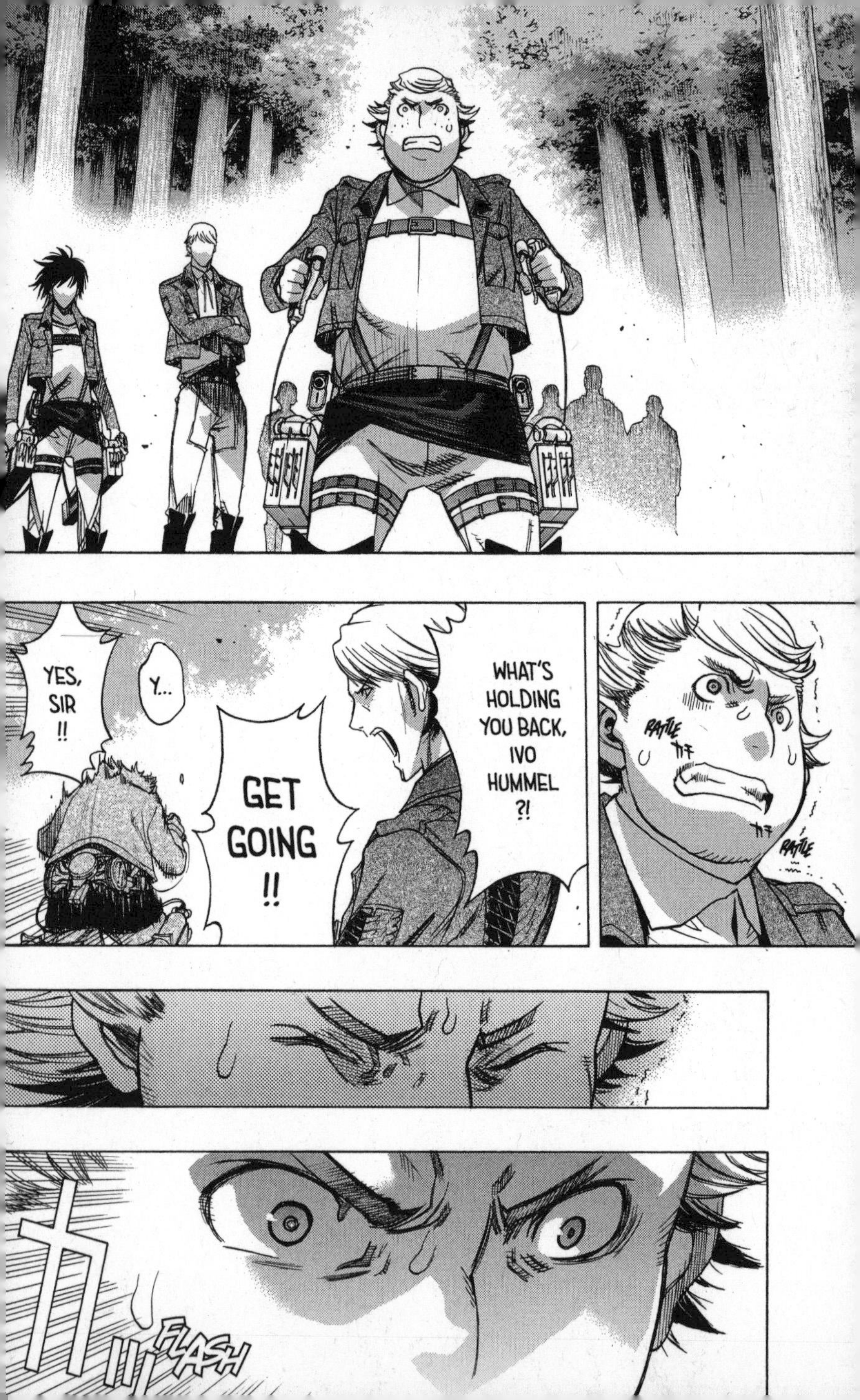
RATTLE
RATTLE
WHAT'S HOLDING YOU BACK, IVO HUMMEL ?!
GET GOING !!
Y...
YES, SIR !!
FLASH

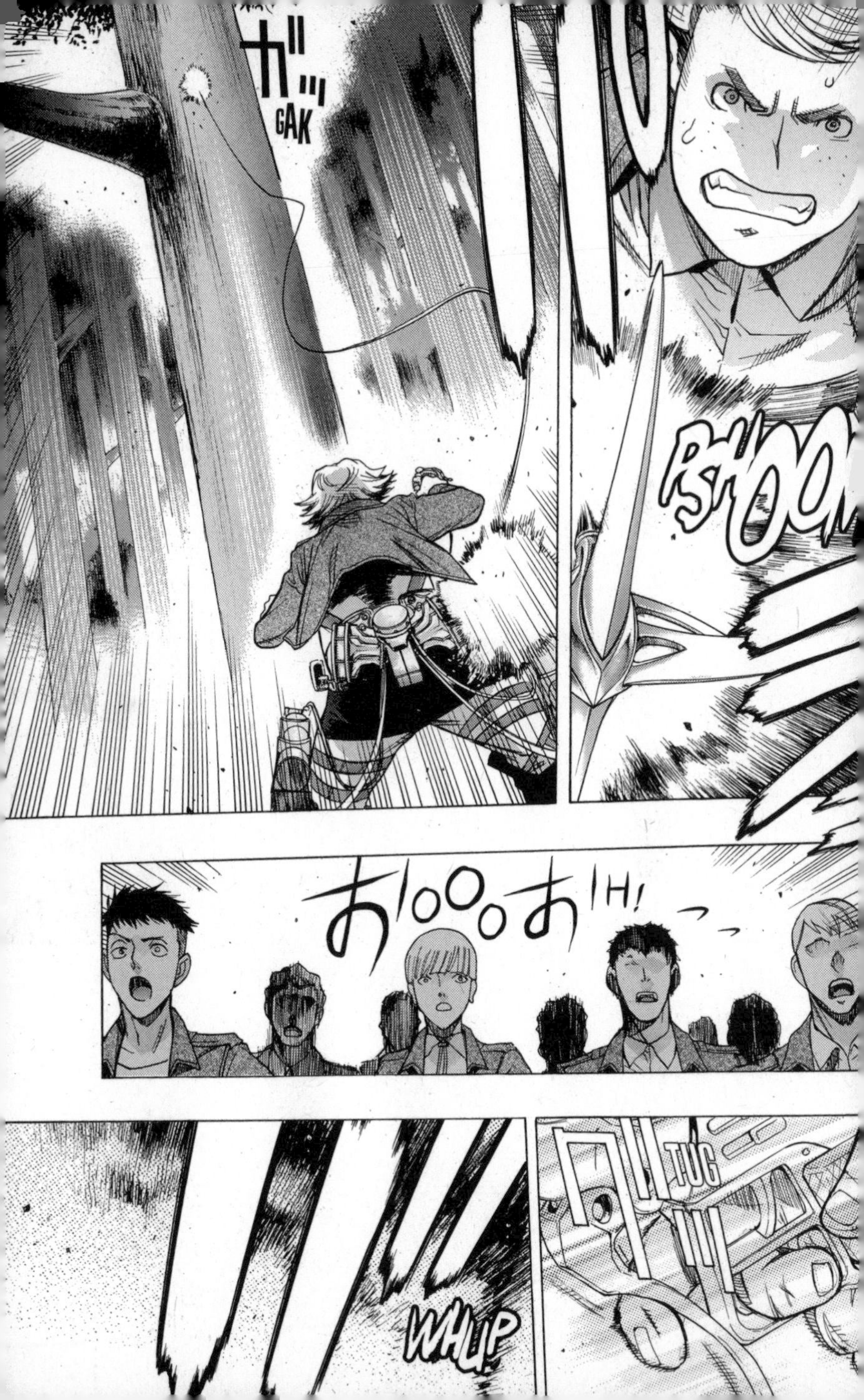
PSHOOM
GAK
OOOOOH!
TUG
WHUP

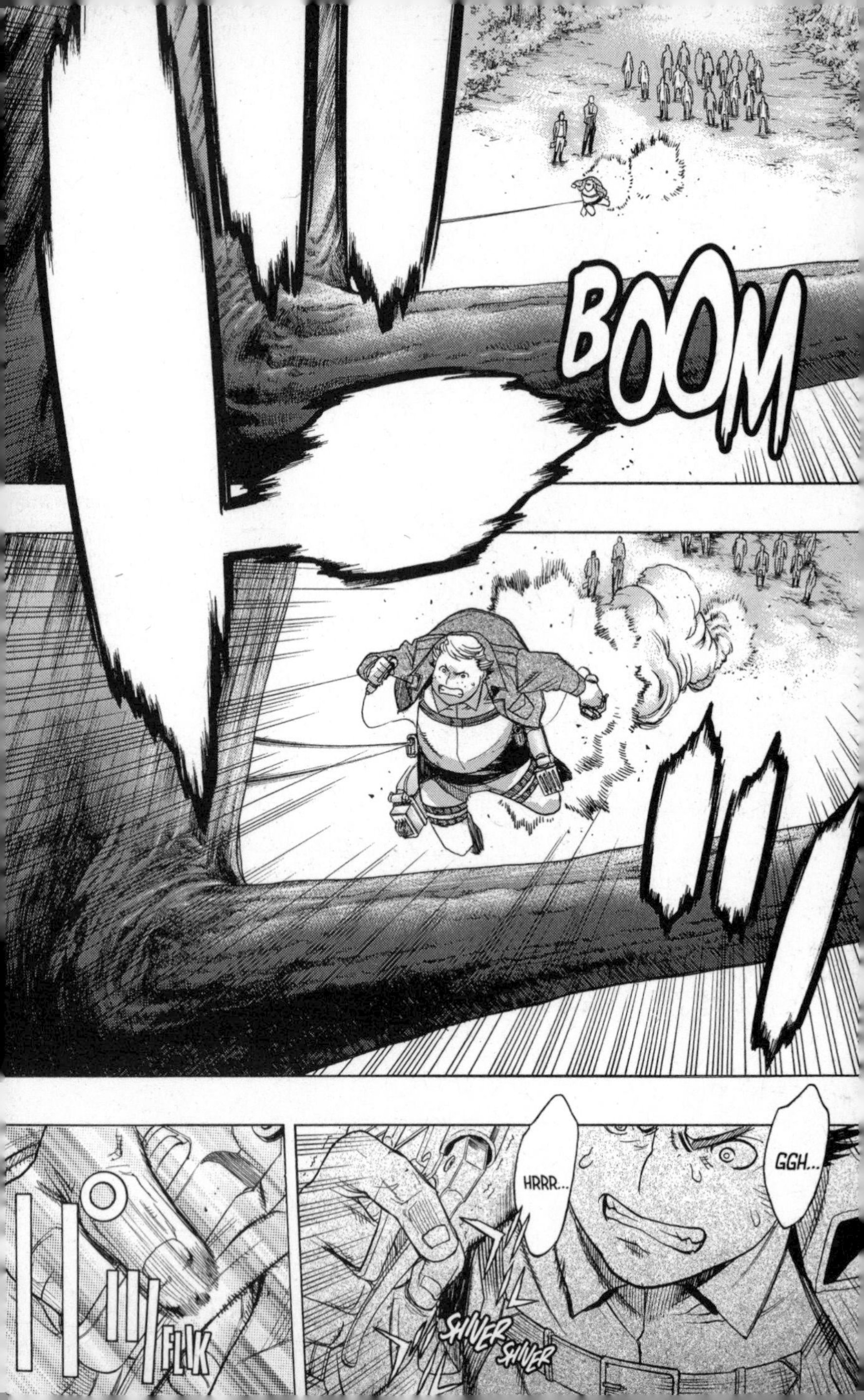
BOOM
GGH...
HRRR...
SHIVER SHIVER
FLIK

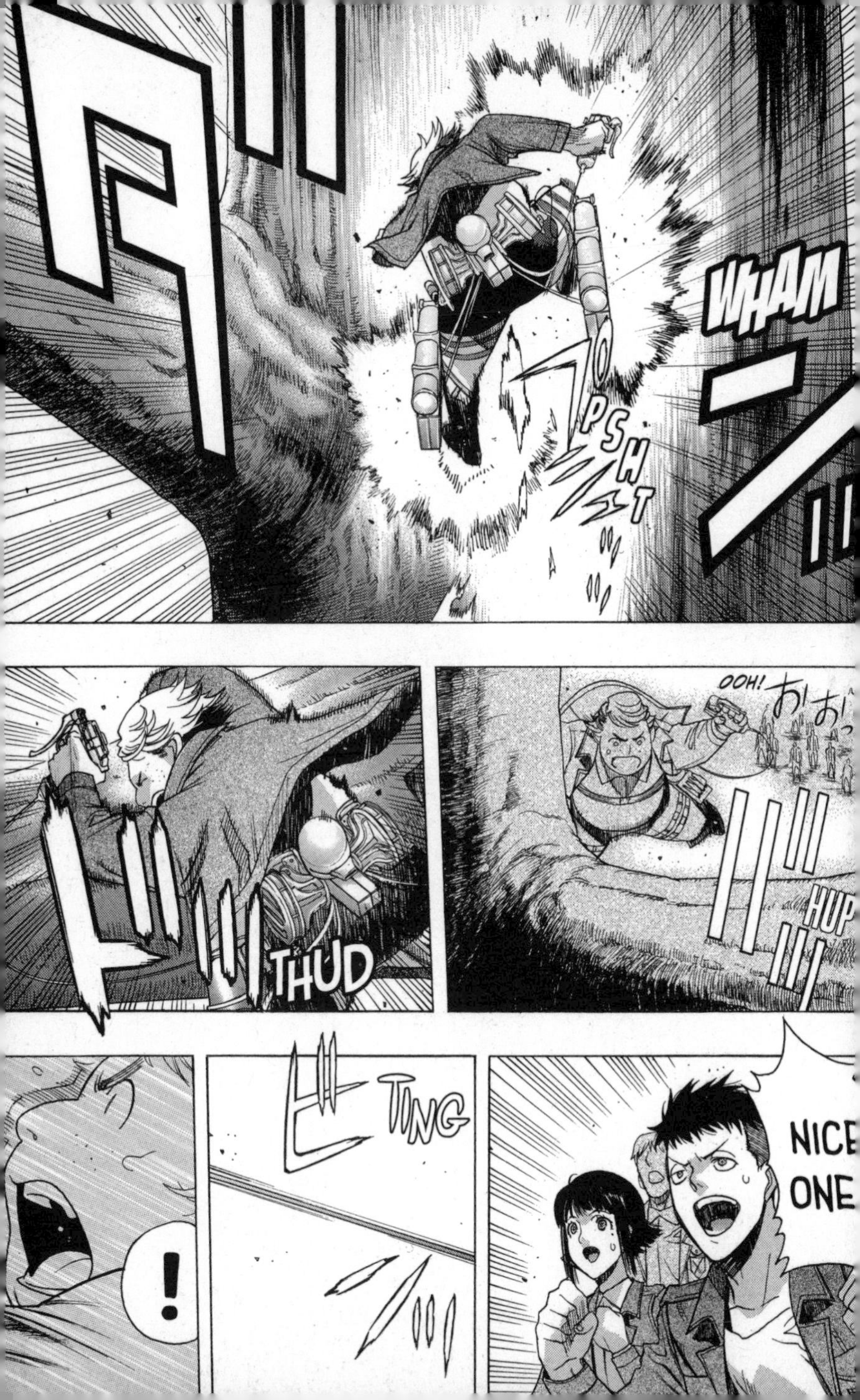
WHAM
PSHT
OOH!
HUP
THUD
NICE ONE
TING
!

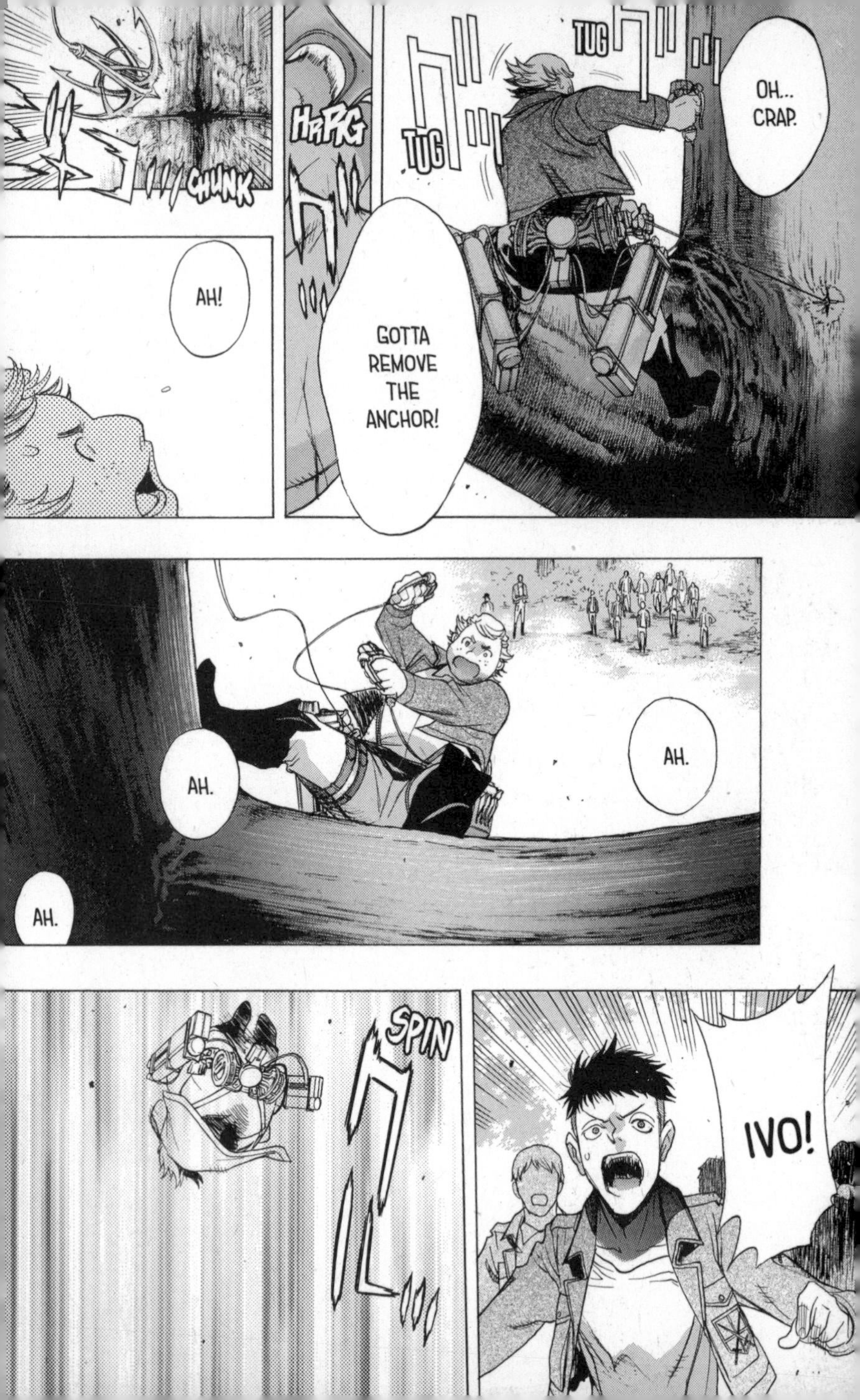
TUG
OH... CRAP.
TUG
HRPG
GOTTA REMOVE THE ANCHOR!
CHUNK
AH!
AH.
AH.
AH.
IVO!
SPIN

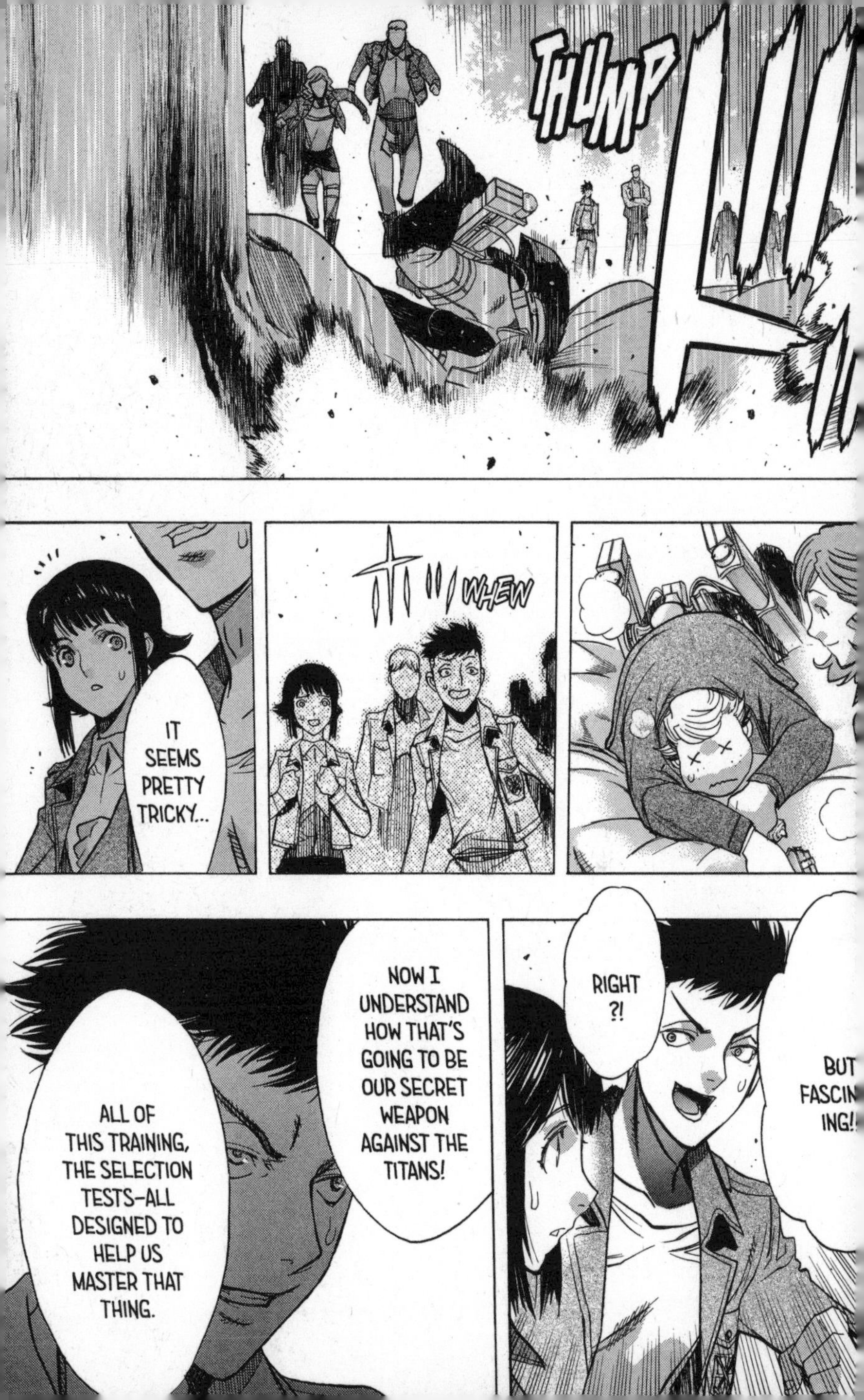
THUMP
WHEW
IT SEEMS PRETTY TRICKY...
RIGHT?!
BUT FASCIN ING!!
NOW I UNDERSTAND HOW THAT'S GOING TO BE OUR SECRET WEAPON AGAINST THE TITANS!
ALL OF THIS TRAINING, THE SELECTION TESTS—ALL DESIGNED TO HELP US MASTER THAT THING.

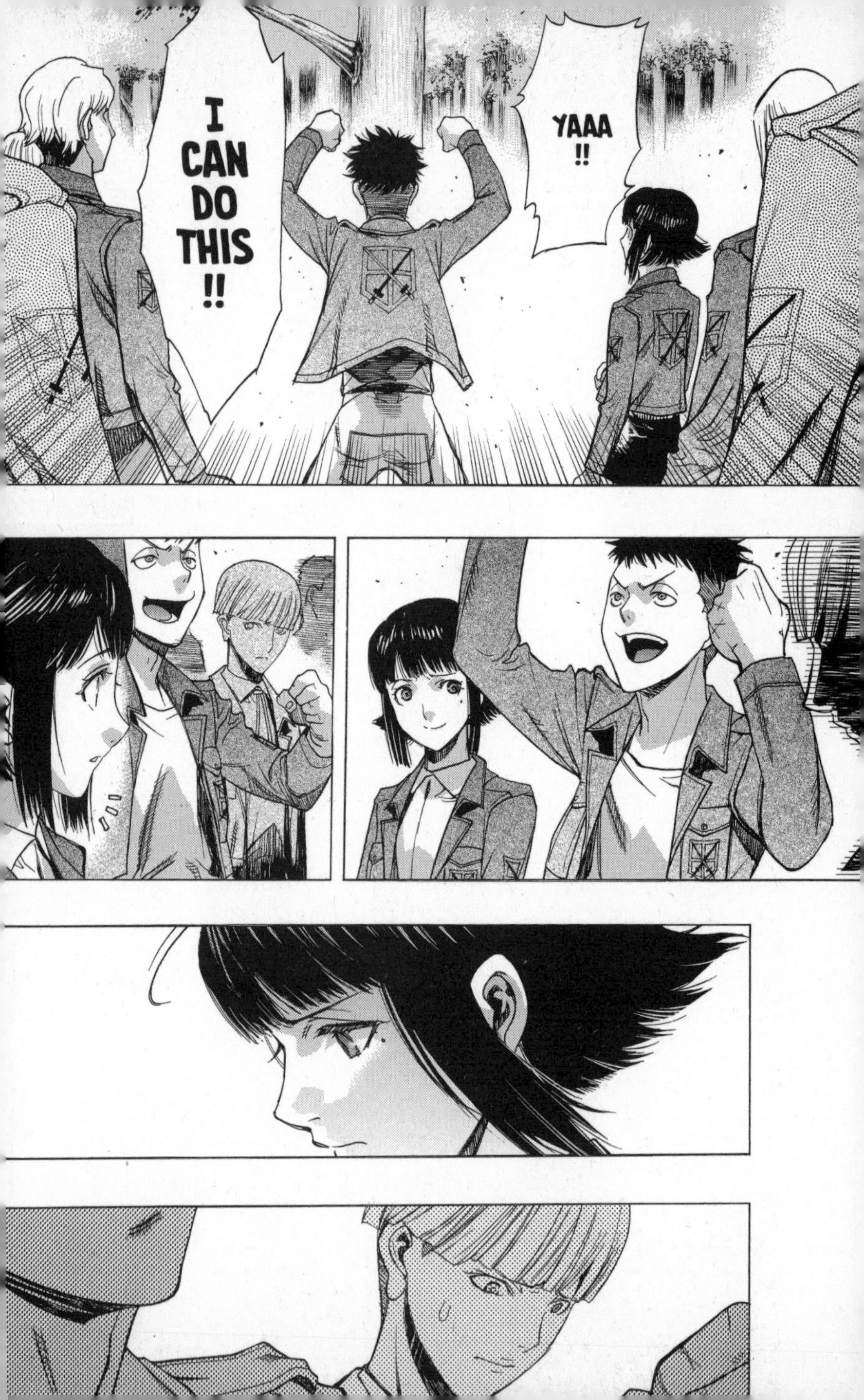
YAAA !!
I CAN DO THIS !!

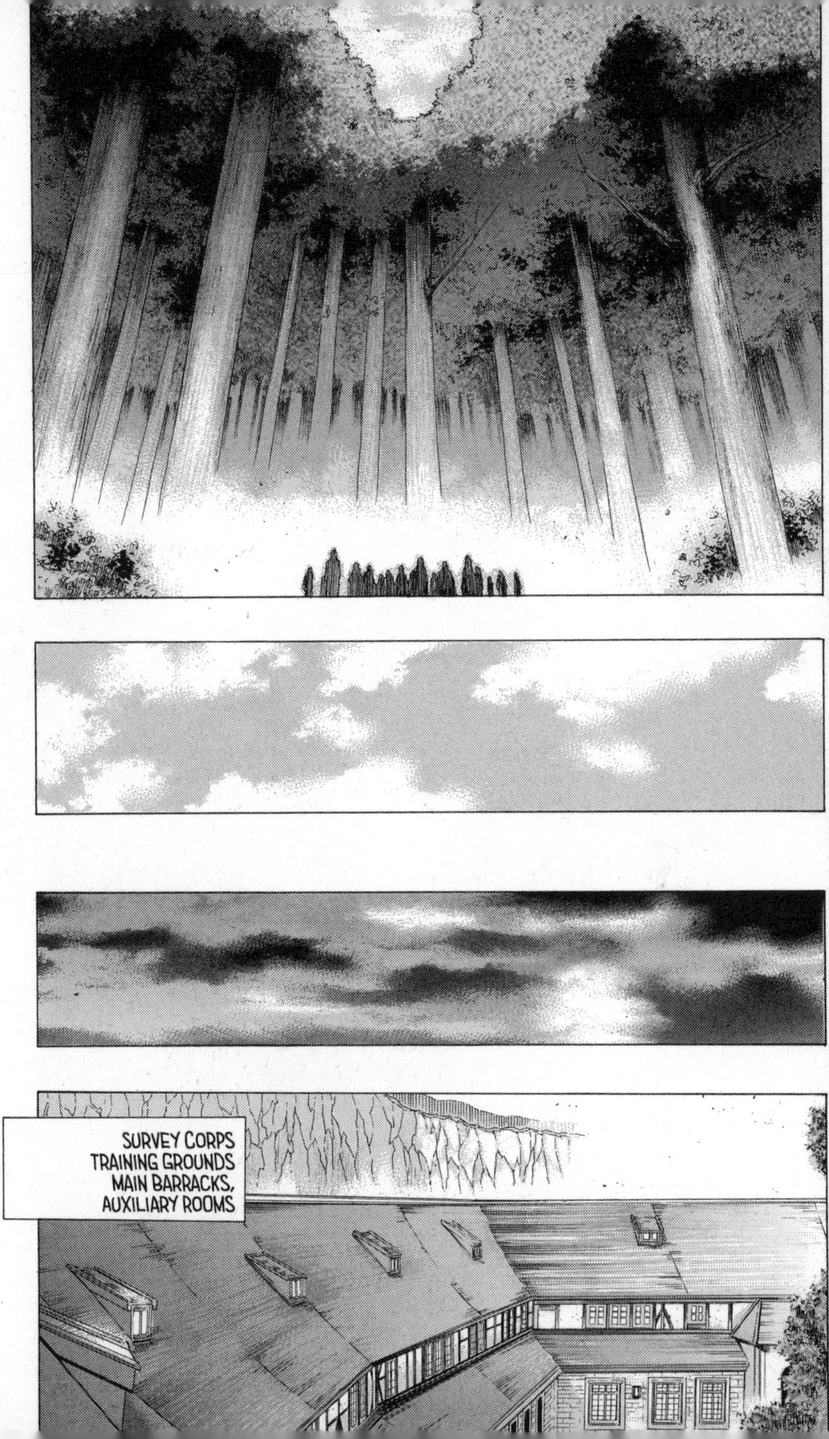
SURVEY CORPS
TRAINING GROUNDS
MAIN BARRACKS,
AUXILIARY ROOMS

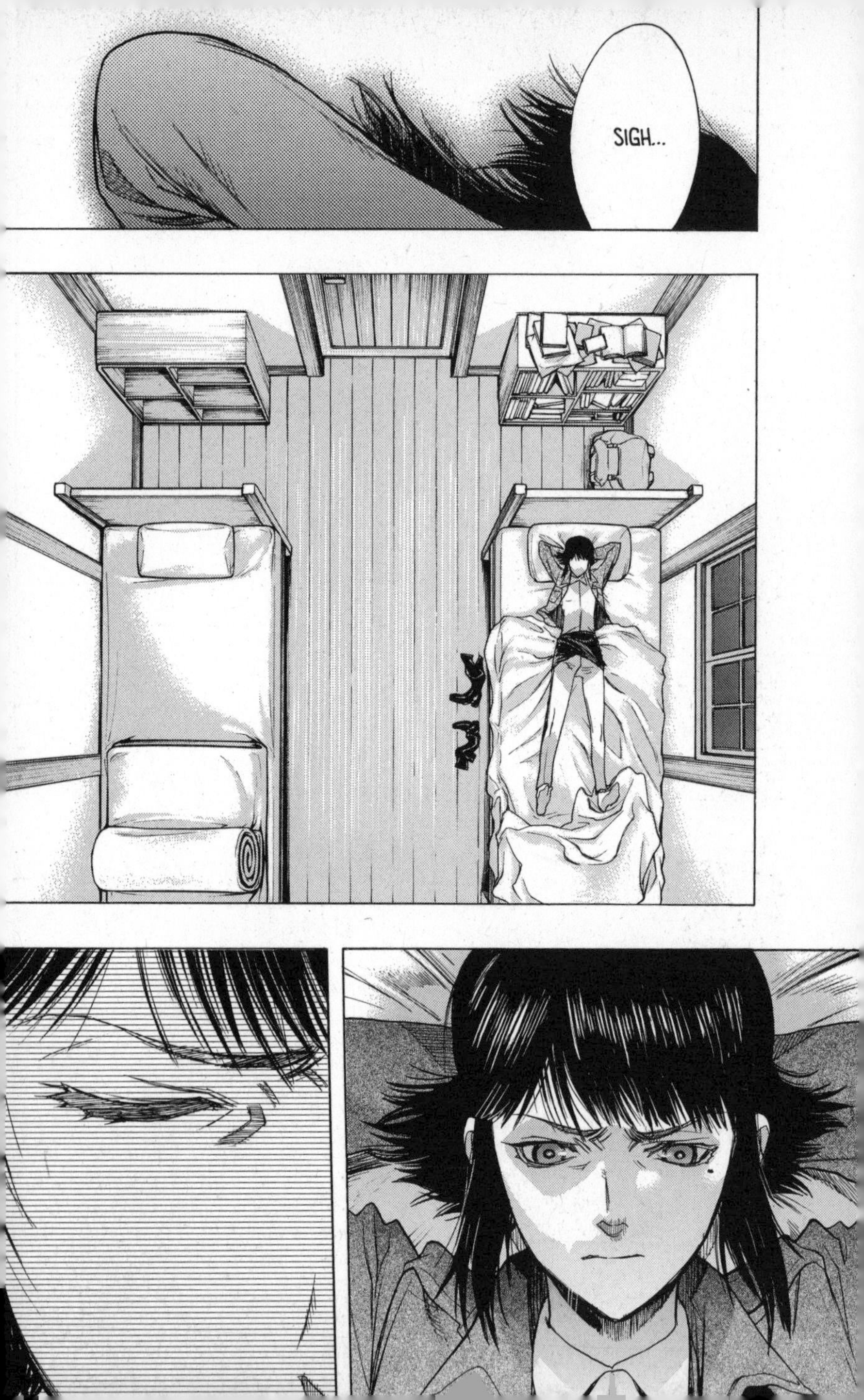
SIGH...

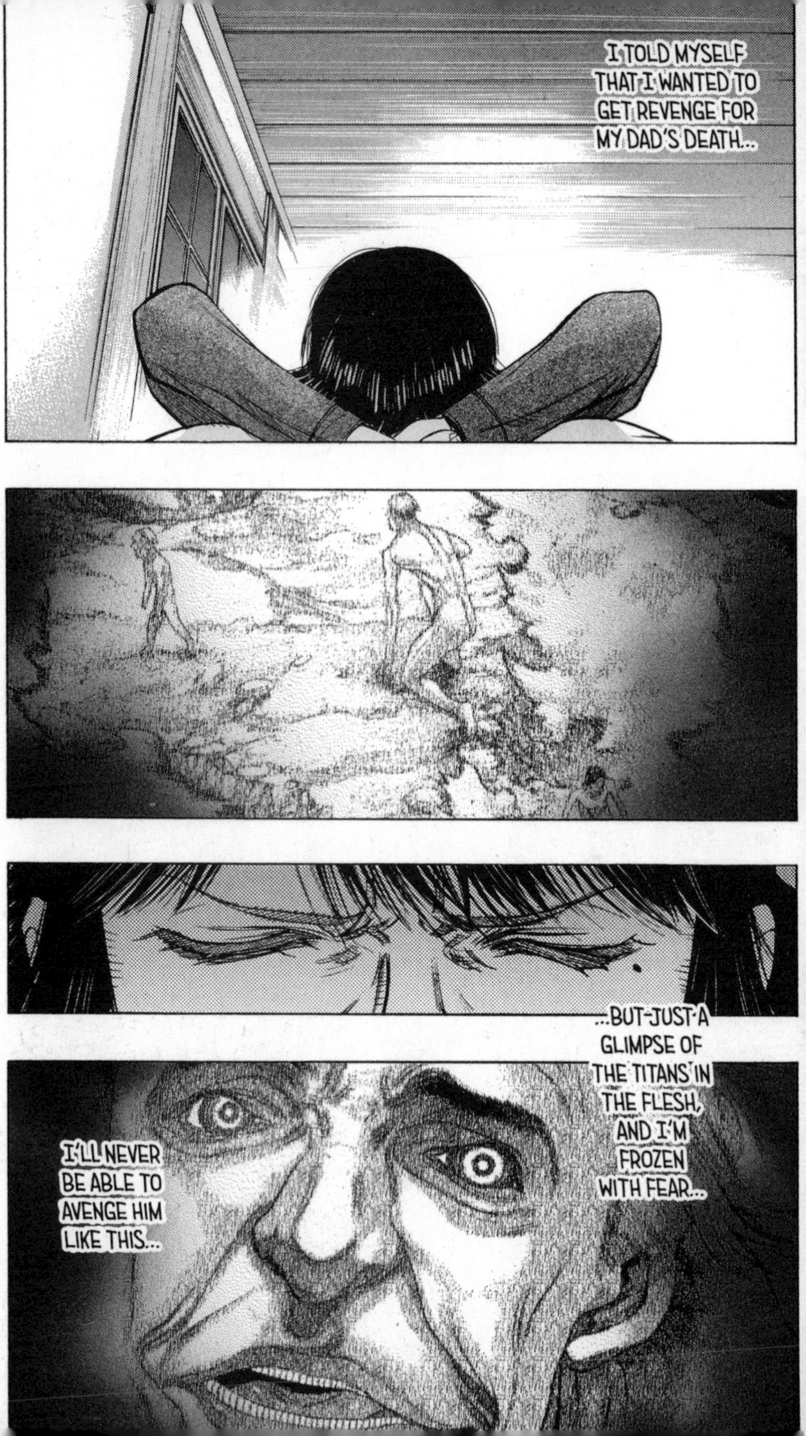
I TOLD MYSELF THAT I WANTED TO GET REVENGE FOR MY DAD'S DEATH...
...BUT JUST A GLIMPSE OF THE TITANS IN THE FLESH, AND I'M FROZEN WITH FEAR...
I'LL NEVER BE ABLE TO AVENGE HIM LIKE THIS...

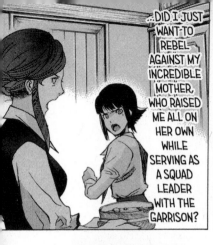

DID I JUST WANT TO SHOW UP THOSE BULLIES WHO TAUNTED ME FOR BEING A GIRL WITH ONLY ONE PARENT?
OR...
...DID I JUST WANT TO REBEL AGAINST MY INCREDIBLE MOTHER, WHO RAISED ME ALL ON HER OWN WHILE SERVING AS A SQUAD LEADER WITH THE GARRISON?
BUT...
...I JUST WANT TO BE WITH MY FRIENDS...
...MORE THAN VENGEANCE RIGHT NOW...
AND...
I WANT TO USE THE VERTICAL MANEUVERING EQUIPMENT...

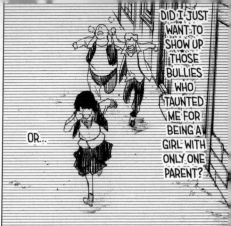

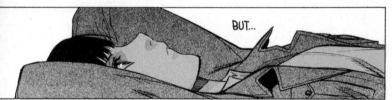

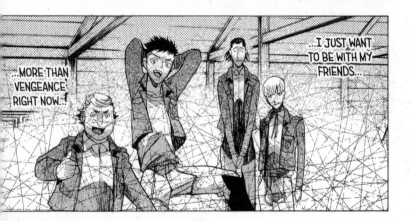

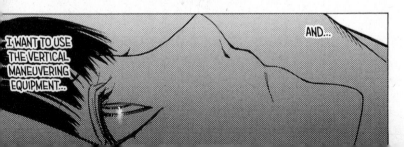

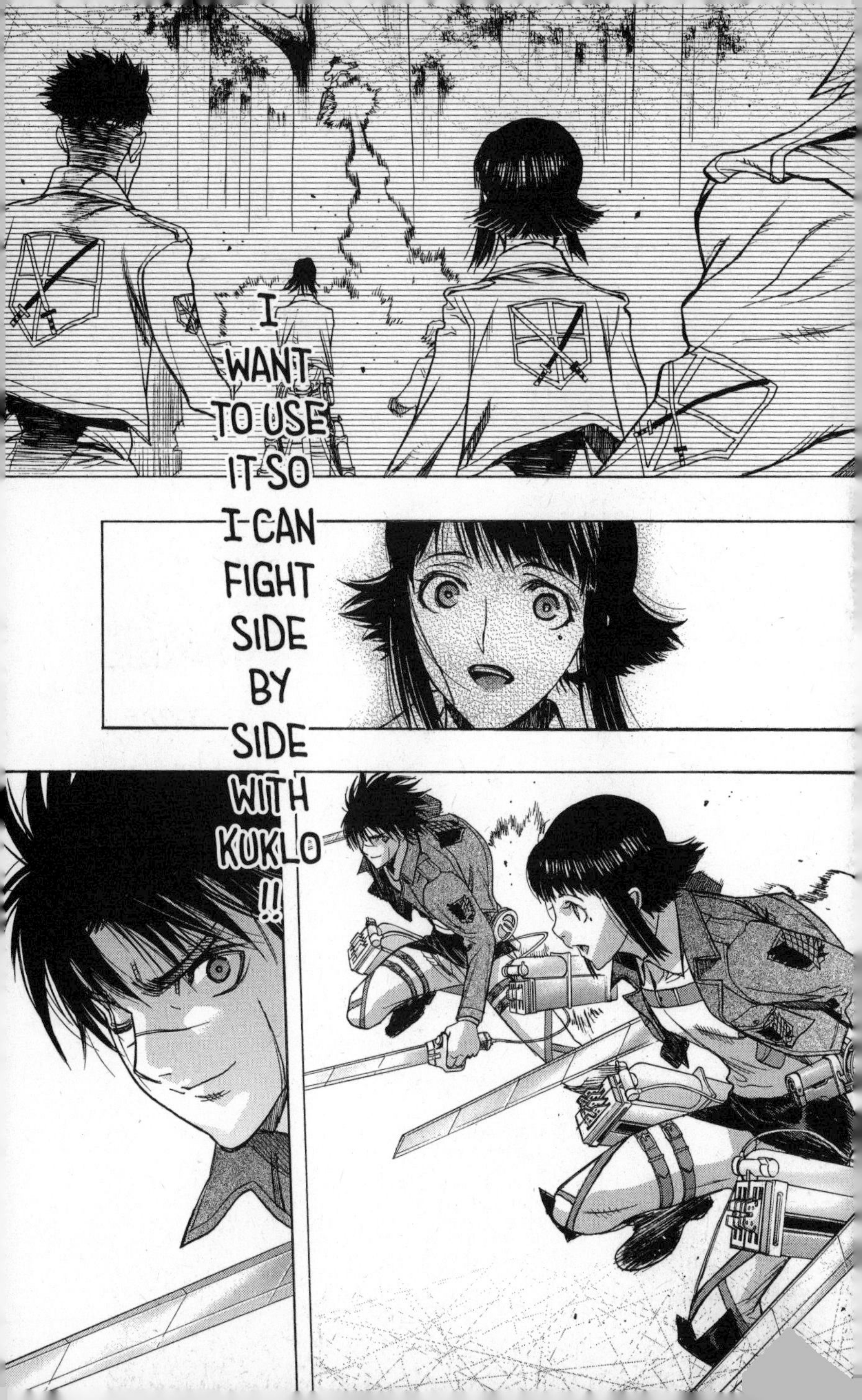
I WANT TO USE IT SO I CAN FIGHT SIDE BY SIDE WITH KUKLO!!

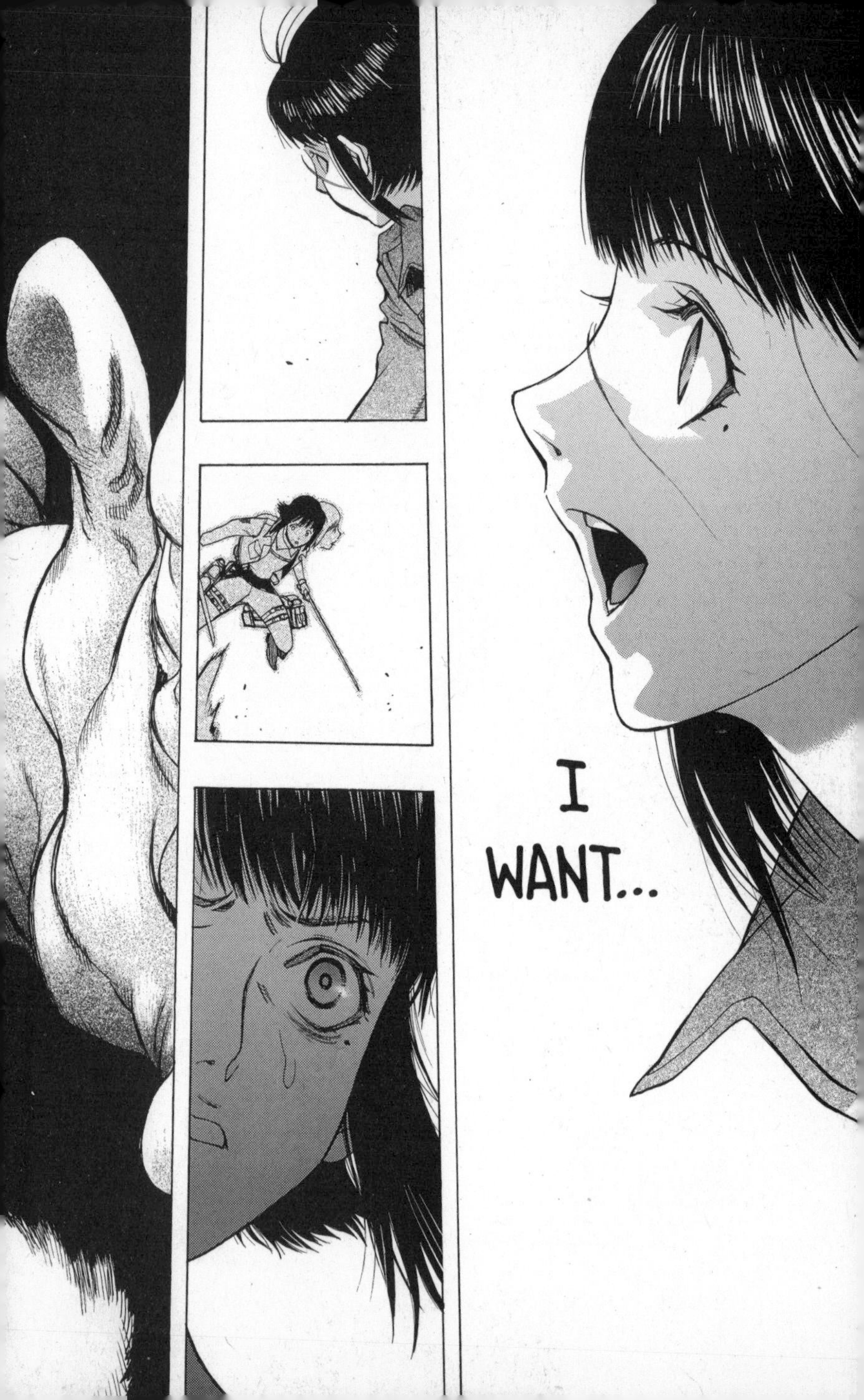
I WANT...

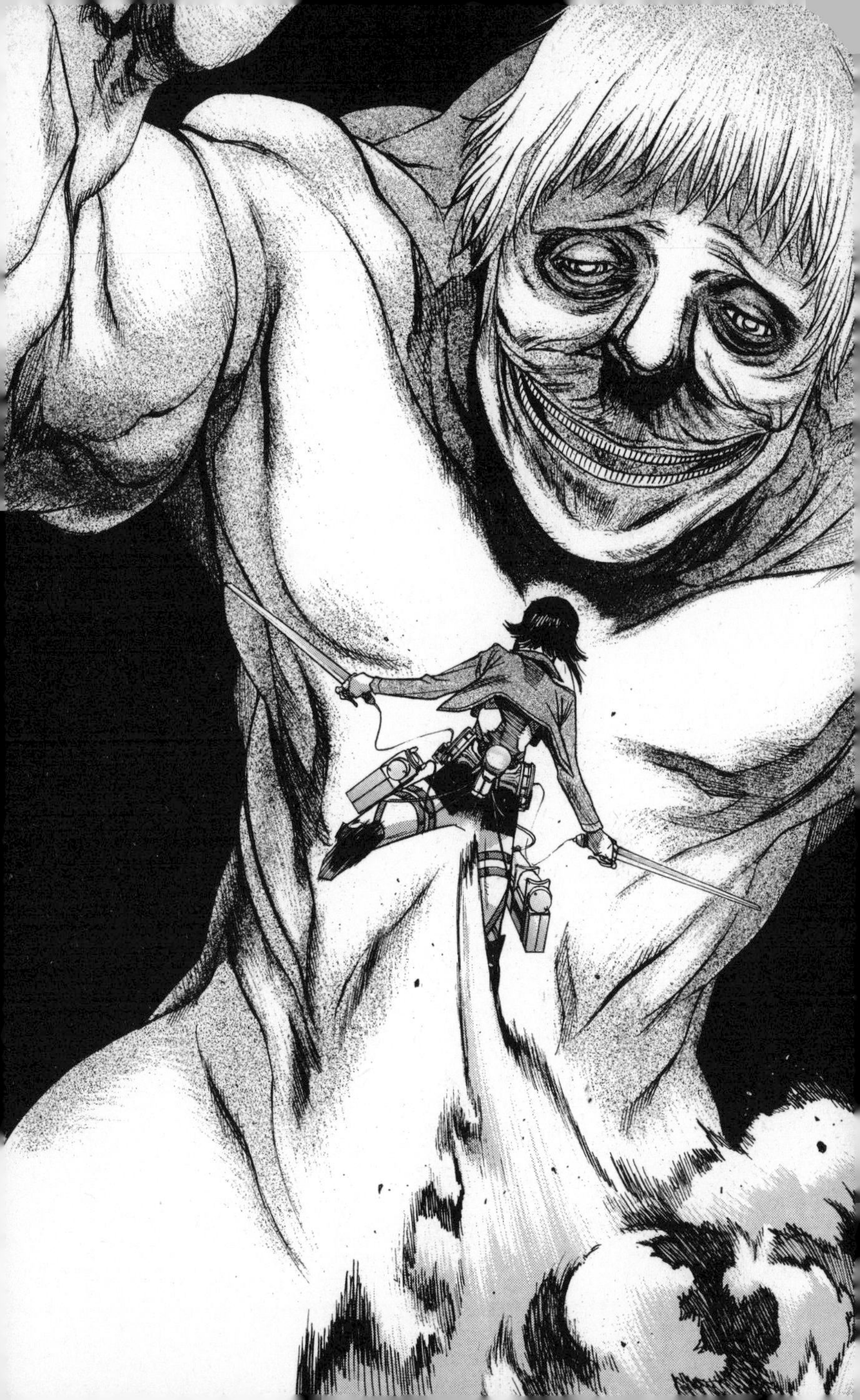

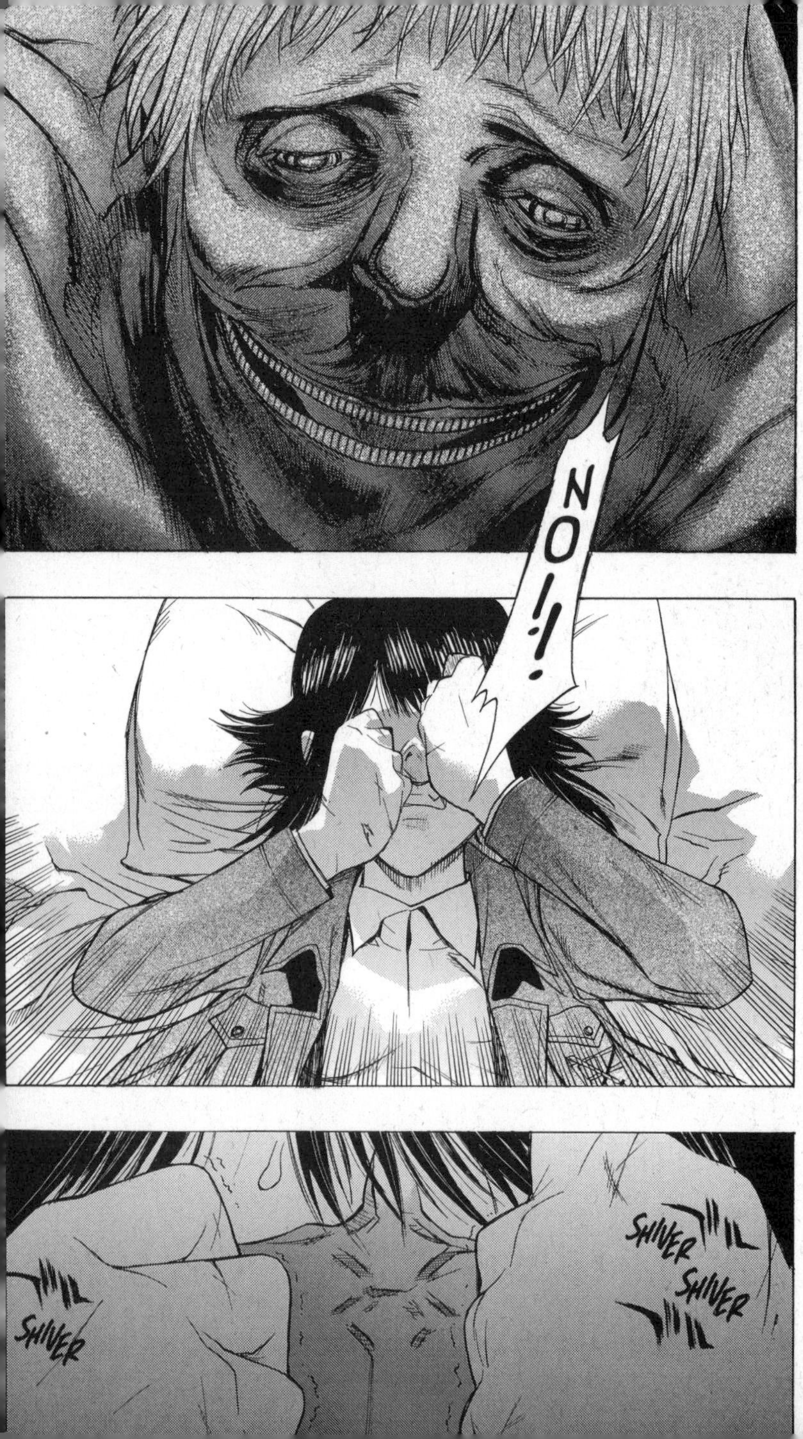
NO!!!
SHIVER
SHIVER
SHIVER

Chapter 51: Vast Silhouette's Fetters · End

ATTACK ON TITAN
BEFORE THE FALL

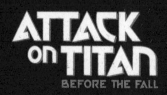

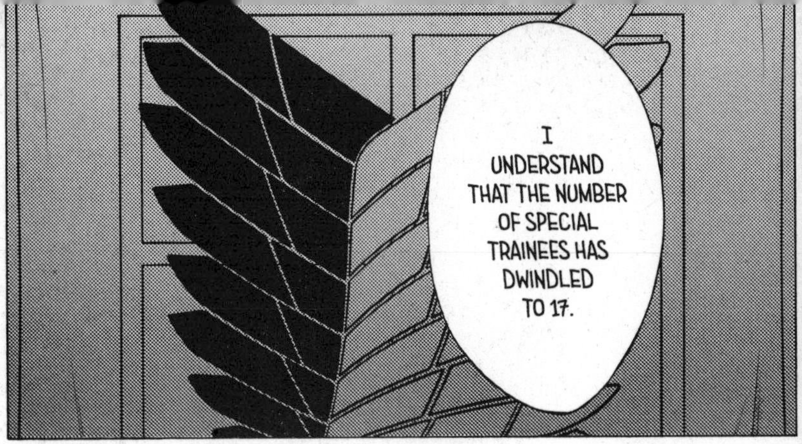
I UNDERSTAND THAT THE NUMBER OF SPECIAL TRAINEES HAS DWINDLED TO 17.
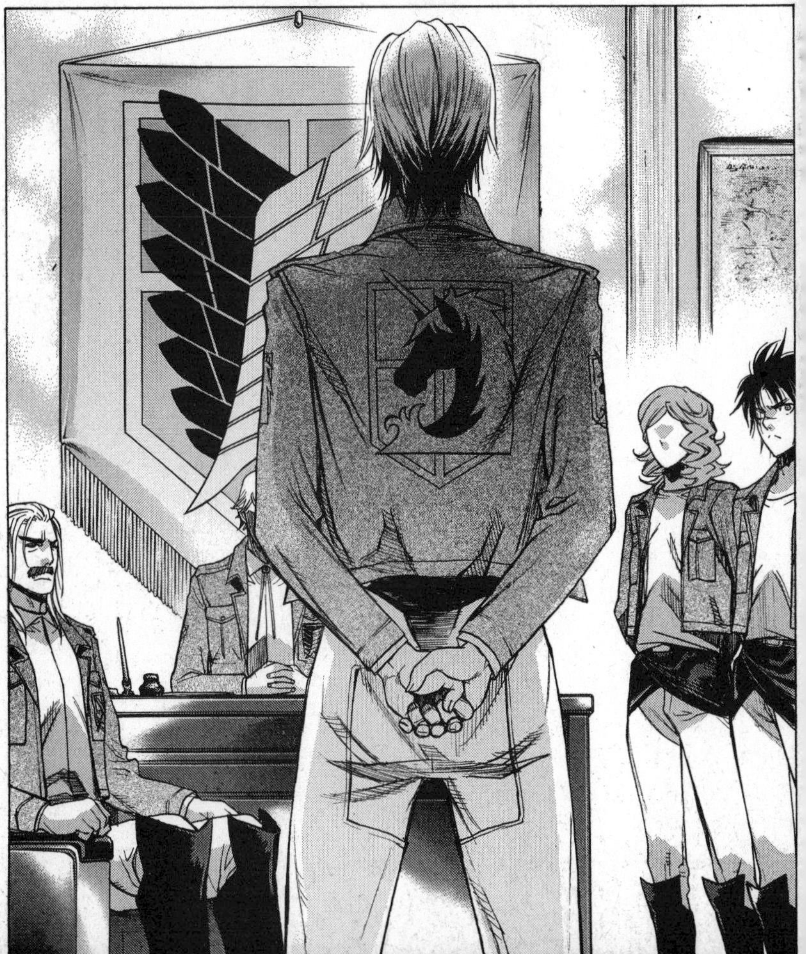

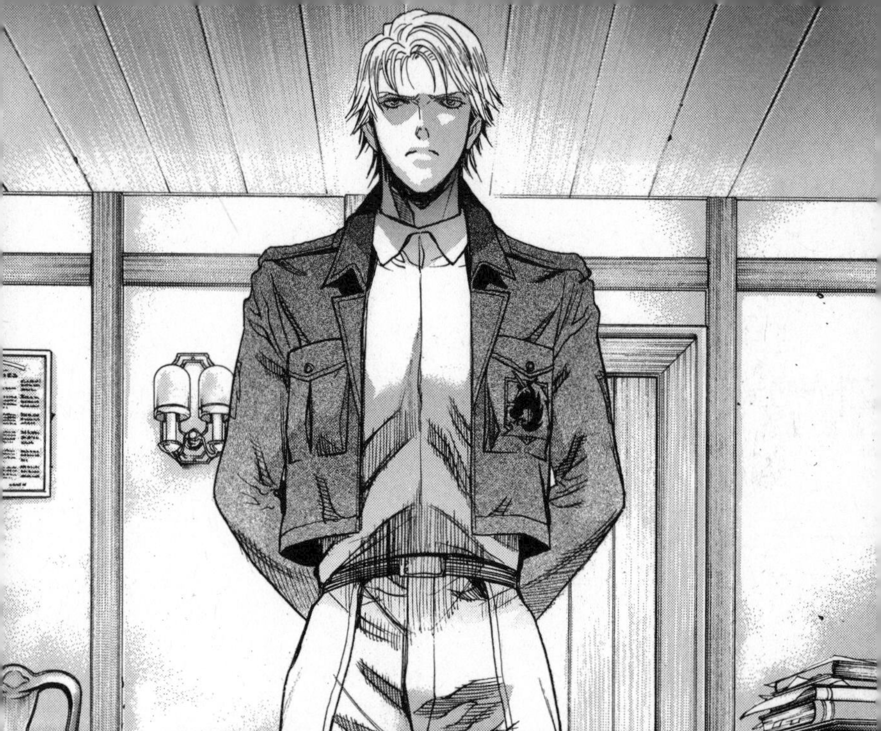
Chapter 52: Genesis of the Wings of Hope

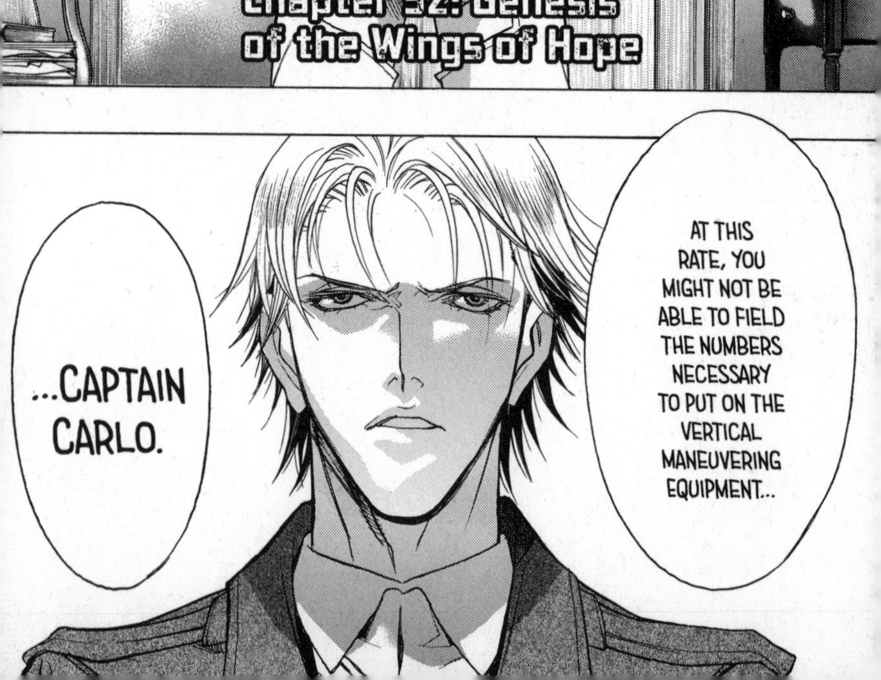
AT THIS RATE, YOU MIGHT NOT BE ABLE TO FIELD THE NUMBERS NECESSARY TO PUT ON THE VERTICAL MANEUVERING EQUIPMENT...
...CAPTAIN CARLO.

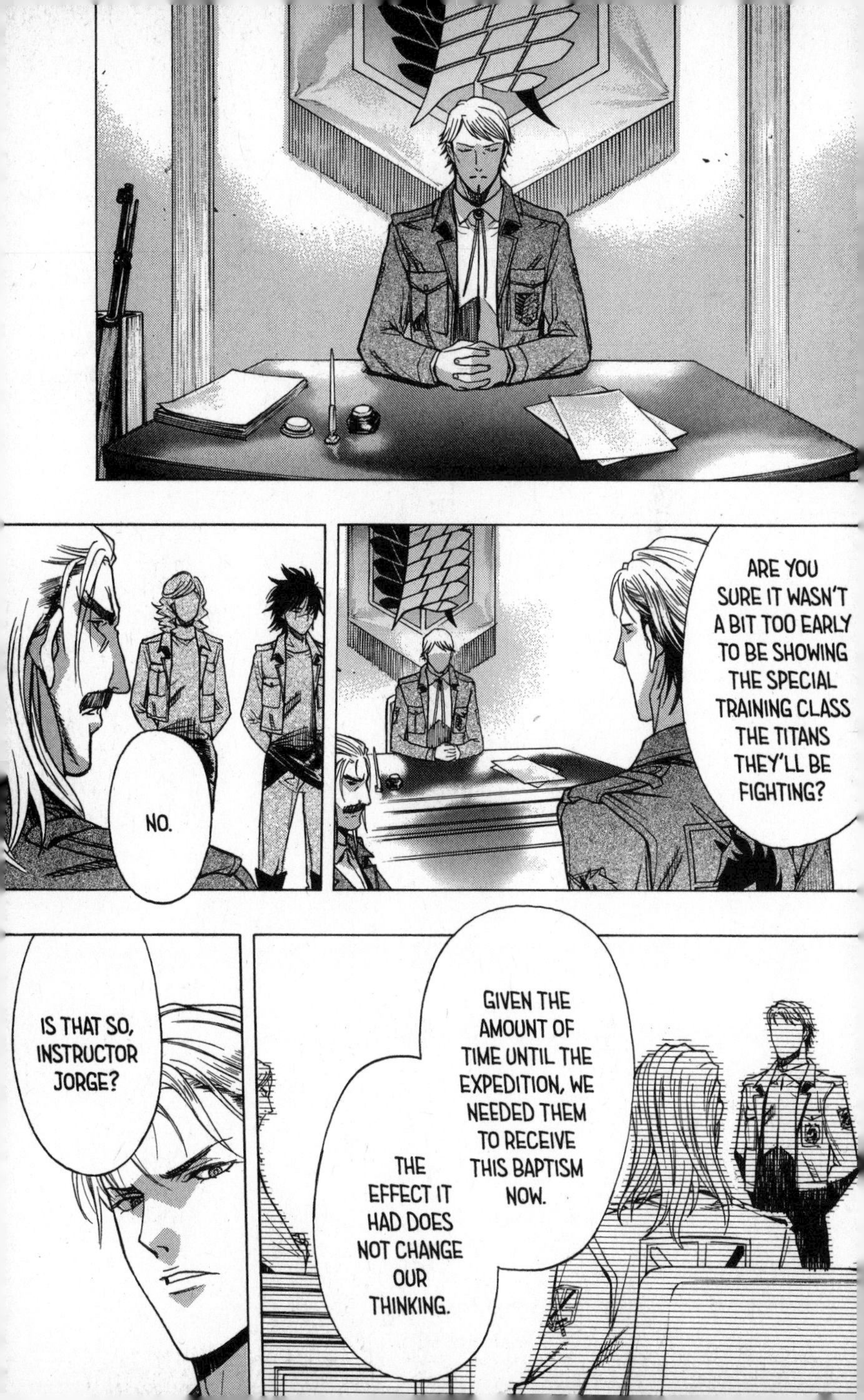
ARE YOU SURE IT WASN'T A BIT TOO EARLY TO BE SHOWING THE SPECIAL TRAINING CLASS THE TITANS THEY'LL BE FIGHTING?
NO.
GIVEN THE AMOUNT OF TIME UNTIL THE EXPEDITION, WE NEEDED THEM TO RECEIVE THIS BAPTISM NOW.
THE EFFECT IT HAD DOES NOT CHANGE OUR THINKING.
IS THAT SO, INSTRUCTOR JORGE?

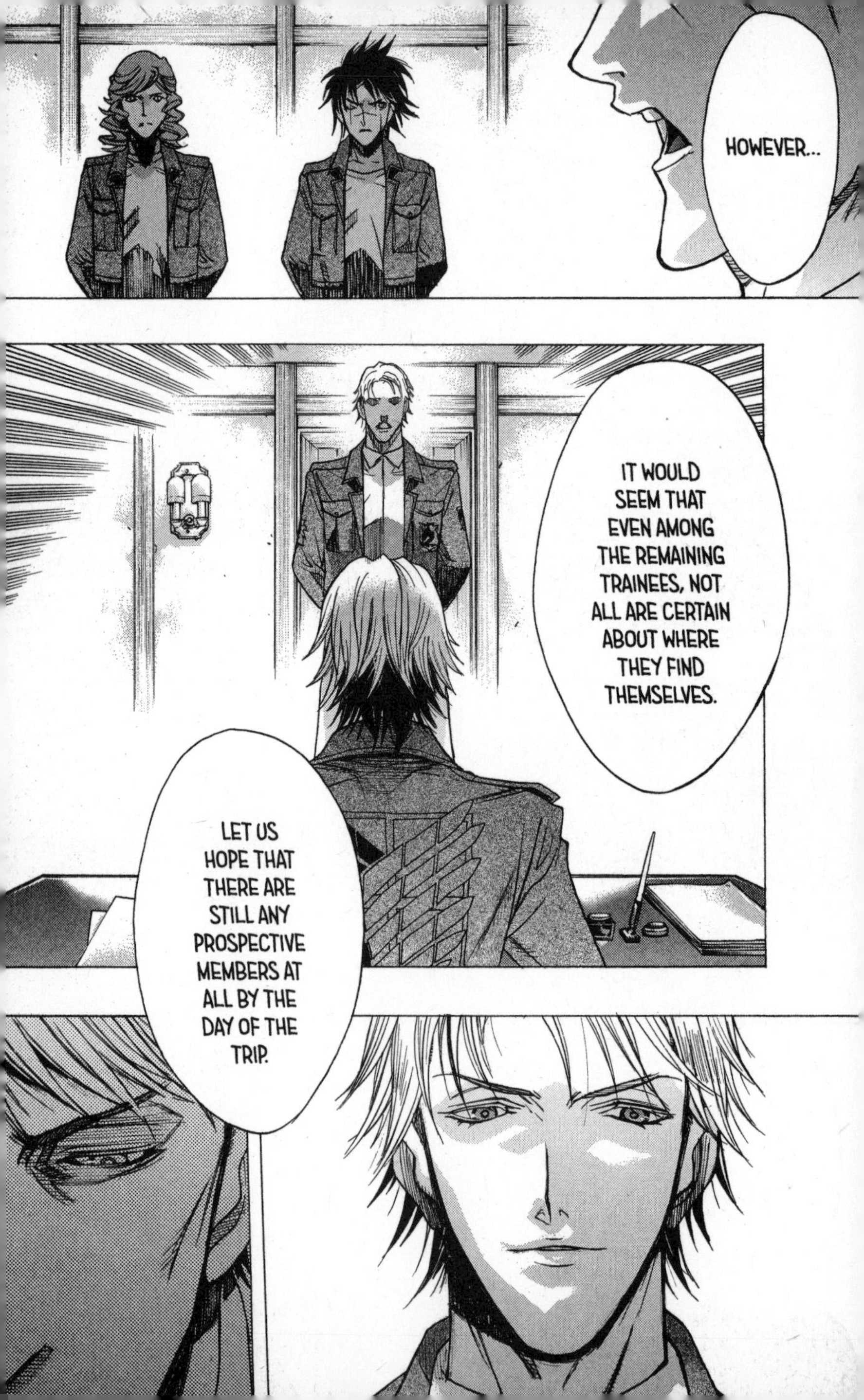
HOWEVER...
IT WOULD SEEM THAT EVEN AMONG THE REMAINING TRAINEES, NOT ALL ARE CERTAIN ABOUT WHERE THEY FIND THEMSELVES.
LET US HOPE THAT THERE ARE STILL ANY PROSPECTIVE MEMBERS AT ALL BY THE DAY OF THE TRIP.

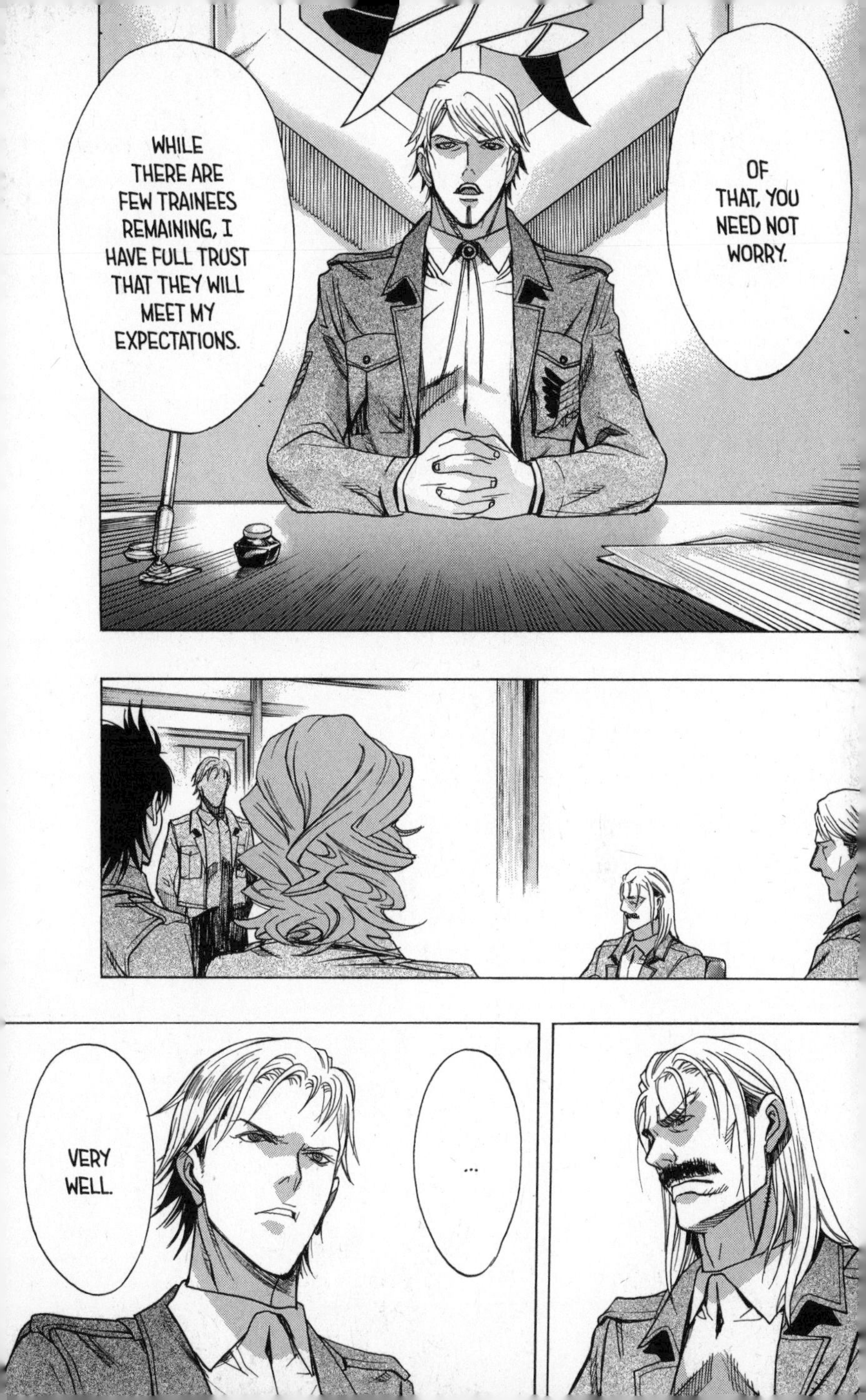
OF THAT, YOU NEED NOT WORRY.
WHILE THERE ARE FEW TRAINEES REMAINING, I HAVE FULL TRUST THAT THEY WILL MEET MY EXPECTATIONS.
...
VERY WELL.

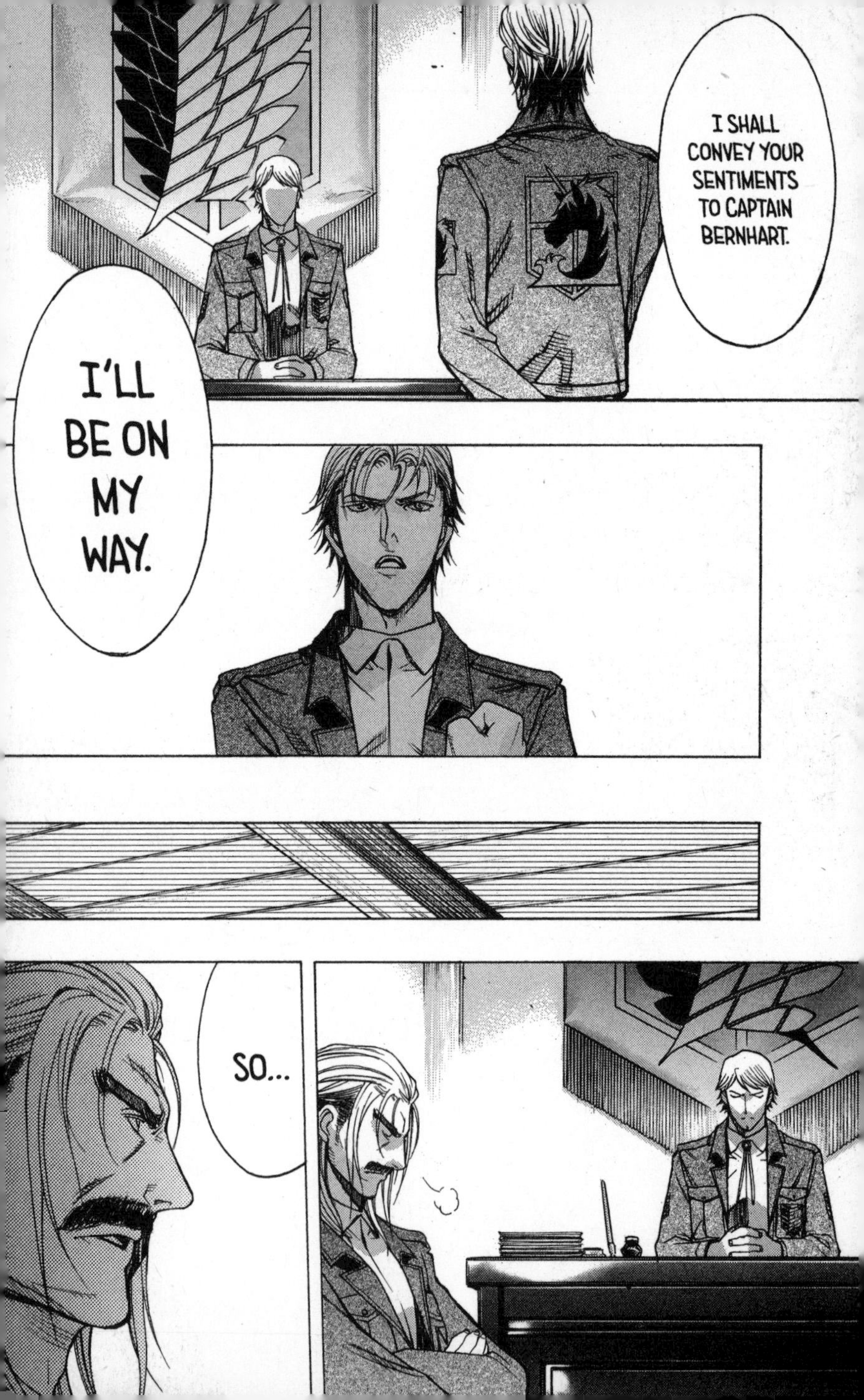
I SHALL CONVEY YOUR SENTIMENTS TO CAPTAIN BERNHART.
I'LL BE ON MY WAY.
SO...

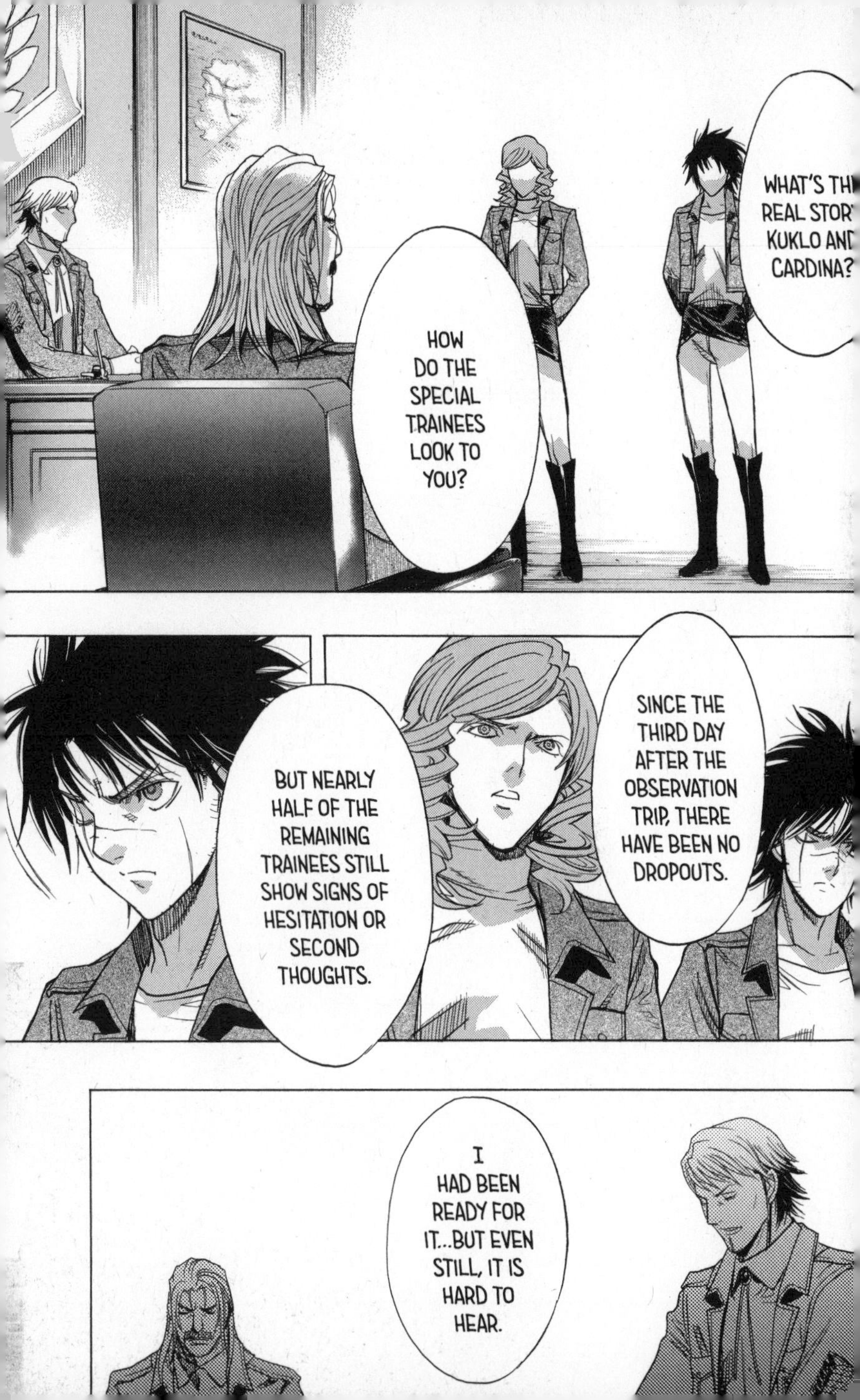
WHAT'S TH REAL STOR KUKLO AN CARDINA?
HOW DO THE SPECIAL TRAINEES LOOK TO YOU?
SINCE THE THIRD DAY AFTER THE OBSERVATION TRIP, THERE HAVE BEEN NO DROPOUTS.
BUT NEARLY HALF OF THE REMAINING TRAINEES STILL SHOW SIGNS OF HESITATION OR SECOND THOUGHTS.
I HAD BEEN READY FOR IT...BUT EVEN STILL, IT IS HARD TO HEAR.

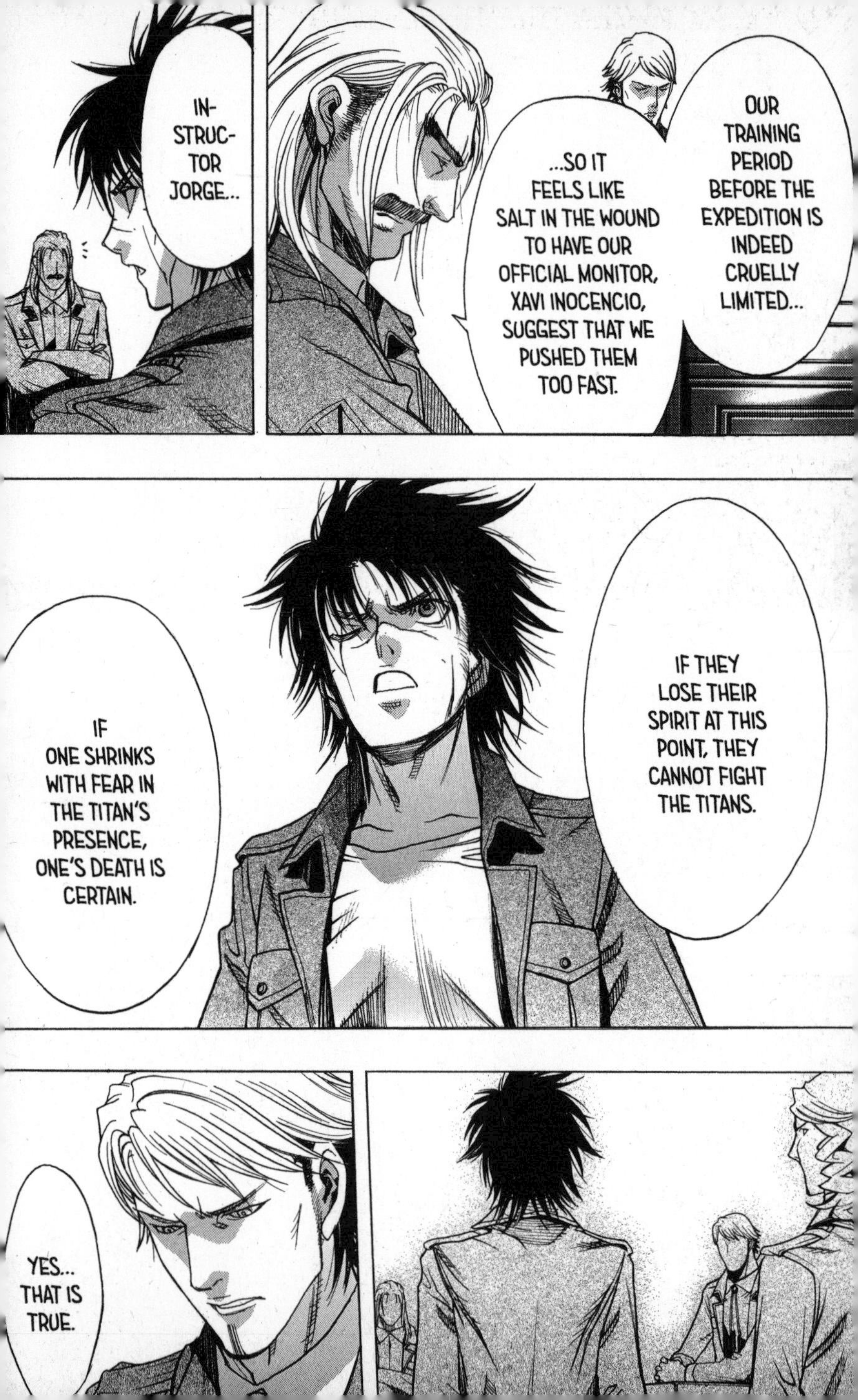
OUR TRAINING PERIOD BEFORE THE EXPEDITION IS INDEED CRUELLY LIMITED...
...SO IT FEELS LIKE SALT IN THE WOUND TO HAVE OUR OFFICIAL MONITOR, XAVI INOCENCIO, SUGGEST THAT WE PUSHED THEM TOO FAST.
IN-STRUC-TOR JORGE...
IF THEY LOSE THEIR SPIRIT AT THIS POINT, THEY CANNOT FIGHT THE TITANS.
IF ONE SHRINKS WITH FEAR IN THE TITAN'S PRESENCE, ONE'S DEATH IS CERTAIN.
YES... THAT IS TRUE.

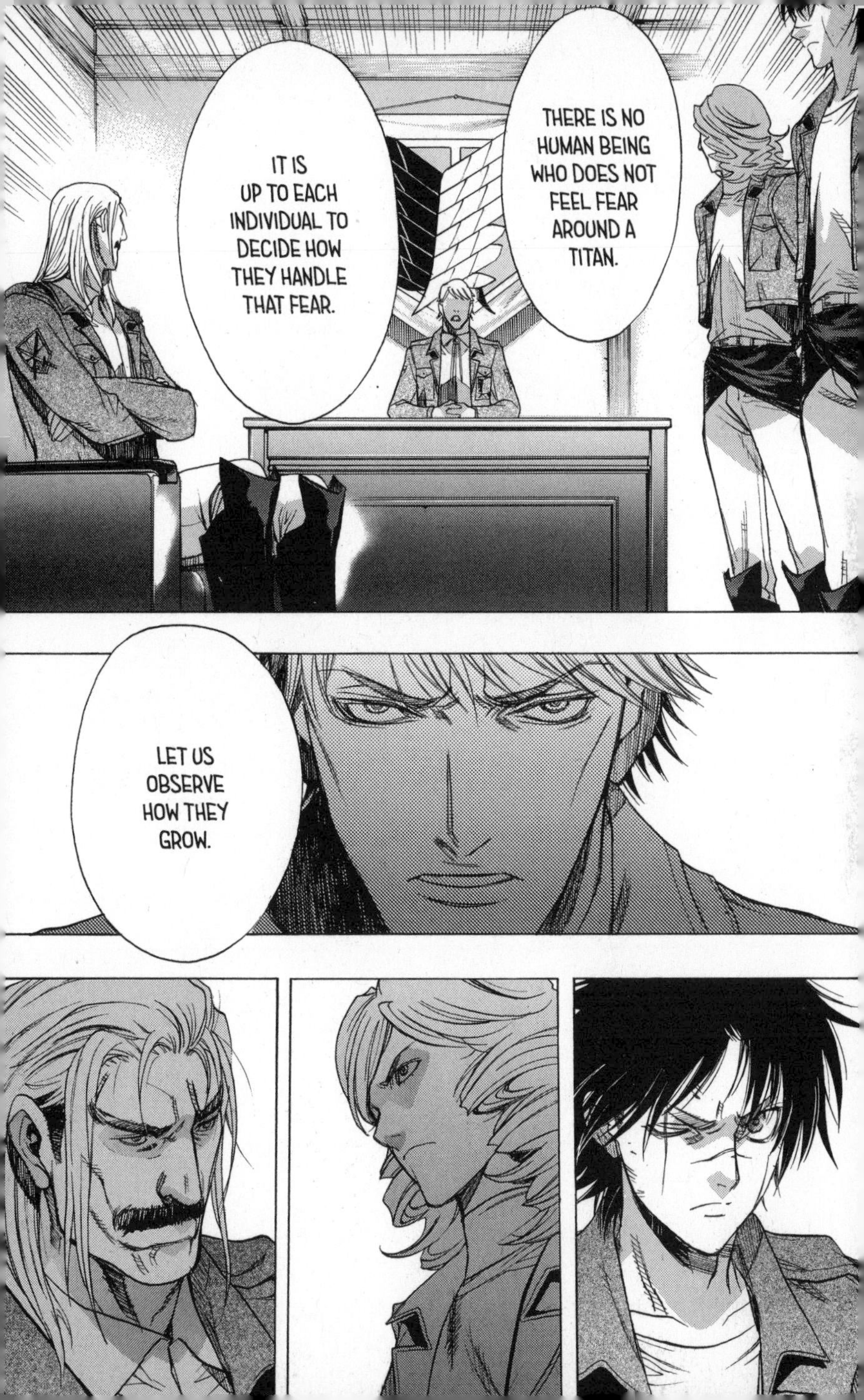
THERE IS NO HUMAN BEING WHO DOES NOT FEEL FEAR AROUND A TITAN.
IT IS UP TO EACH INDIVIDUAL TO DECIDE HOW THEY HANDLE THAT FEAR.
LET US OBSERVE HOW THEY GROW.

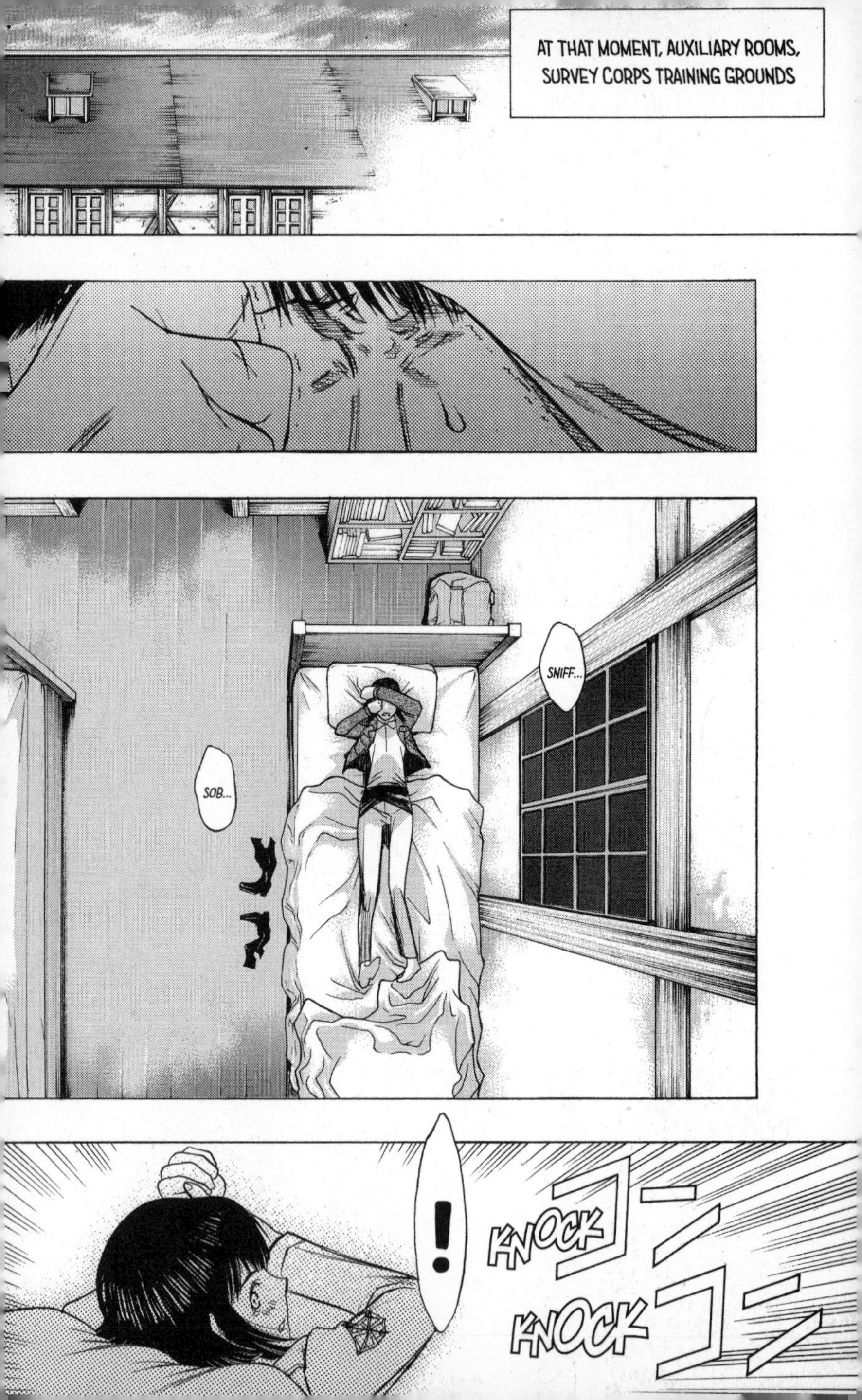
AT THAT MOMENT, AUXILIARY ROOMS, SURVEY CORPS TRAINING GROUNDS
SNIFF...
SOB...
!
KNOCK
KNOCK

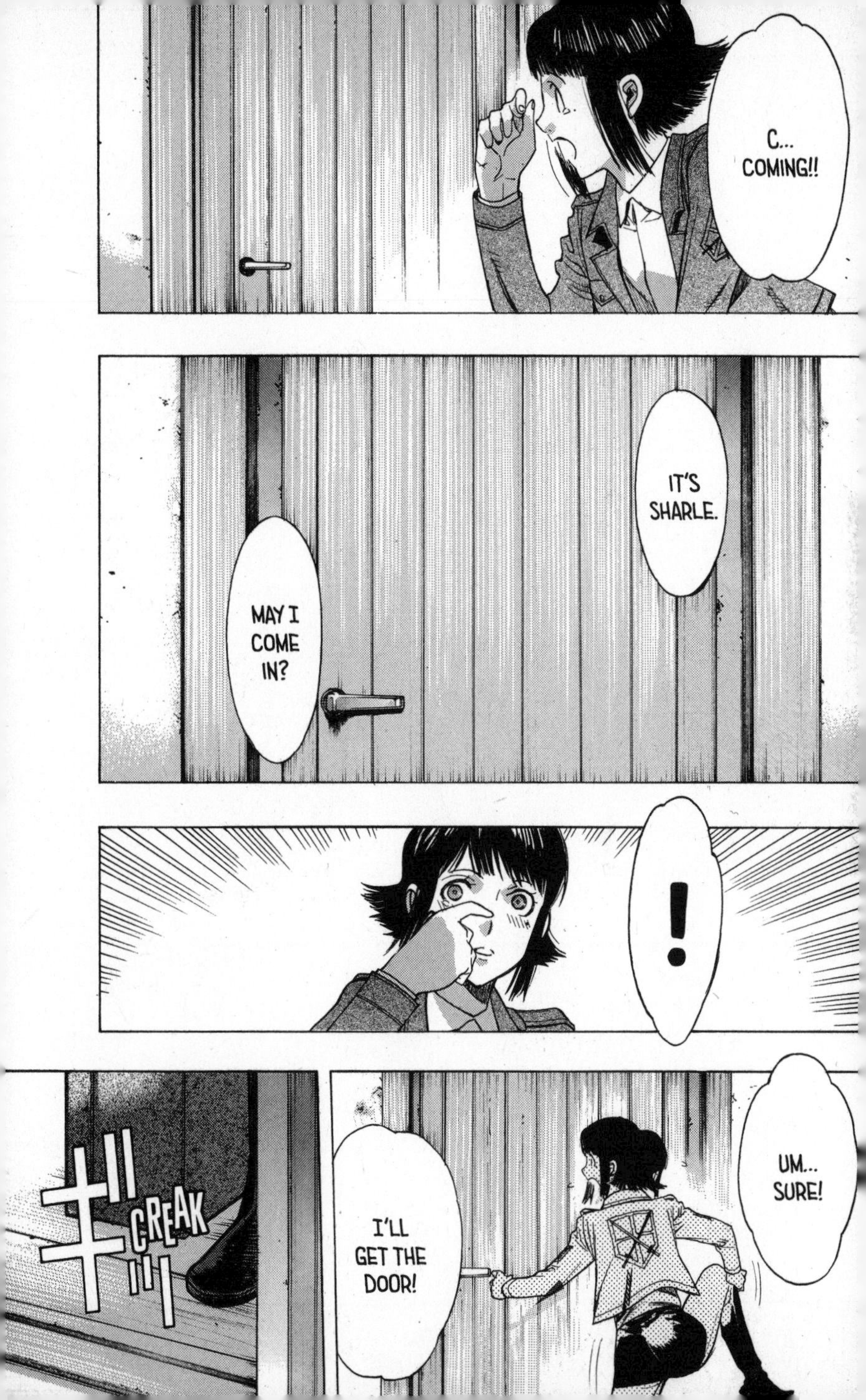
C... COMING!!
IT'S SHARLE.
MAY I COME IN?
!
UM... SURE!
I'LL GET THE DOOR!
CREAK

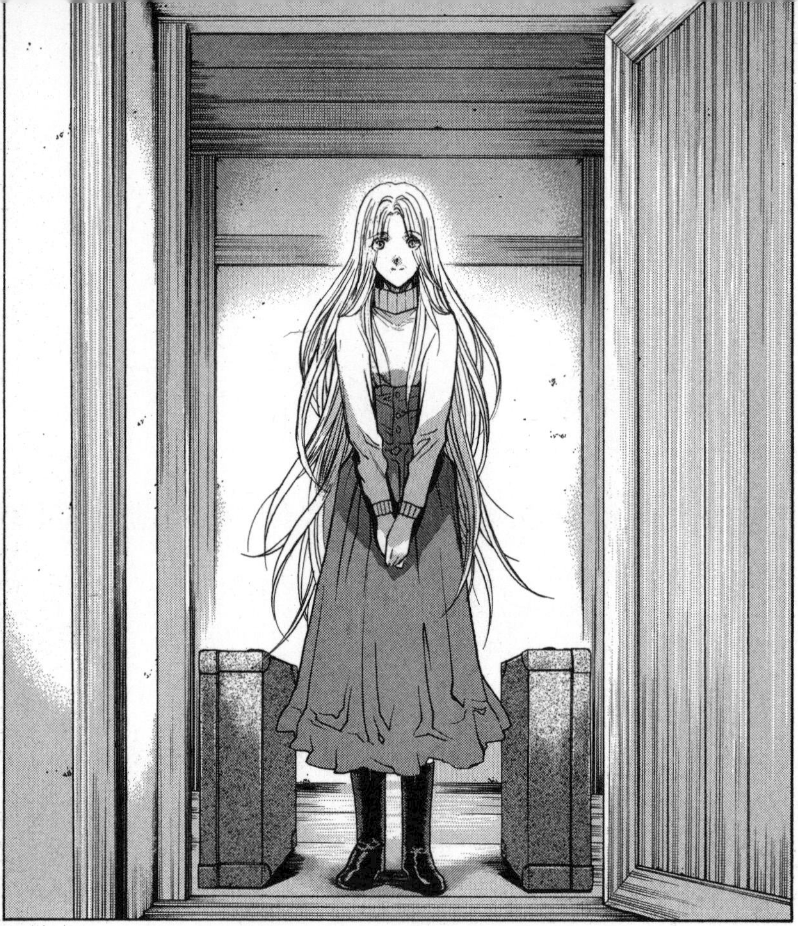

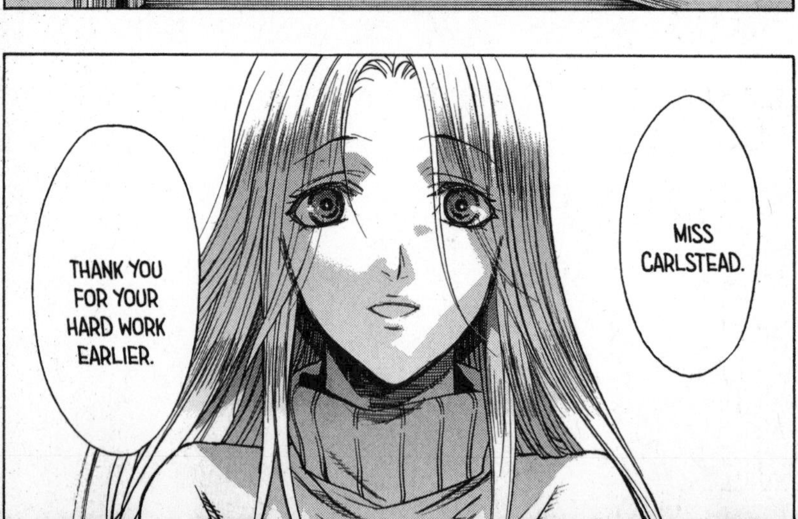
MISS CARLSTEAD.
THANK YOU FOR YOUR HARD WORK EARLIER.

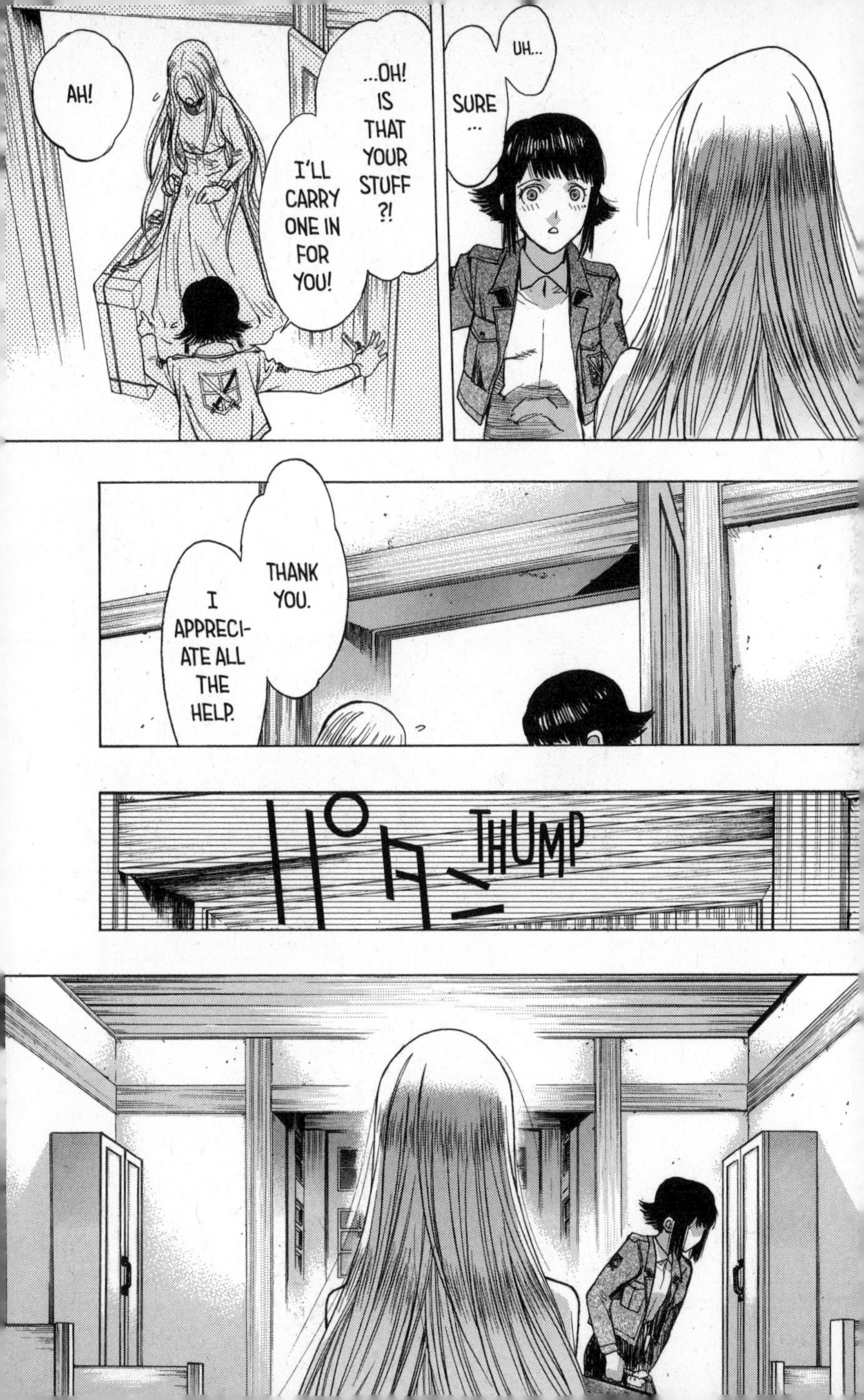
AH!
...OH! IS THAT YOUR STUFF ?!
I'LL CARRY ONE IN FOR YOU!
UH... SURE ...
THANK YOU.
I APPRECI-ATE ALL THE HELP.
THUMP

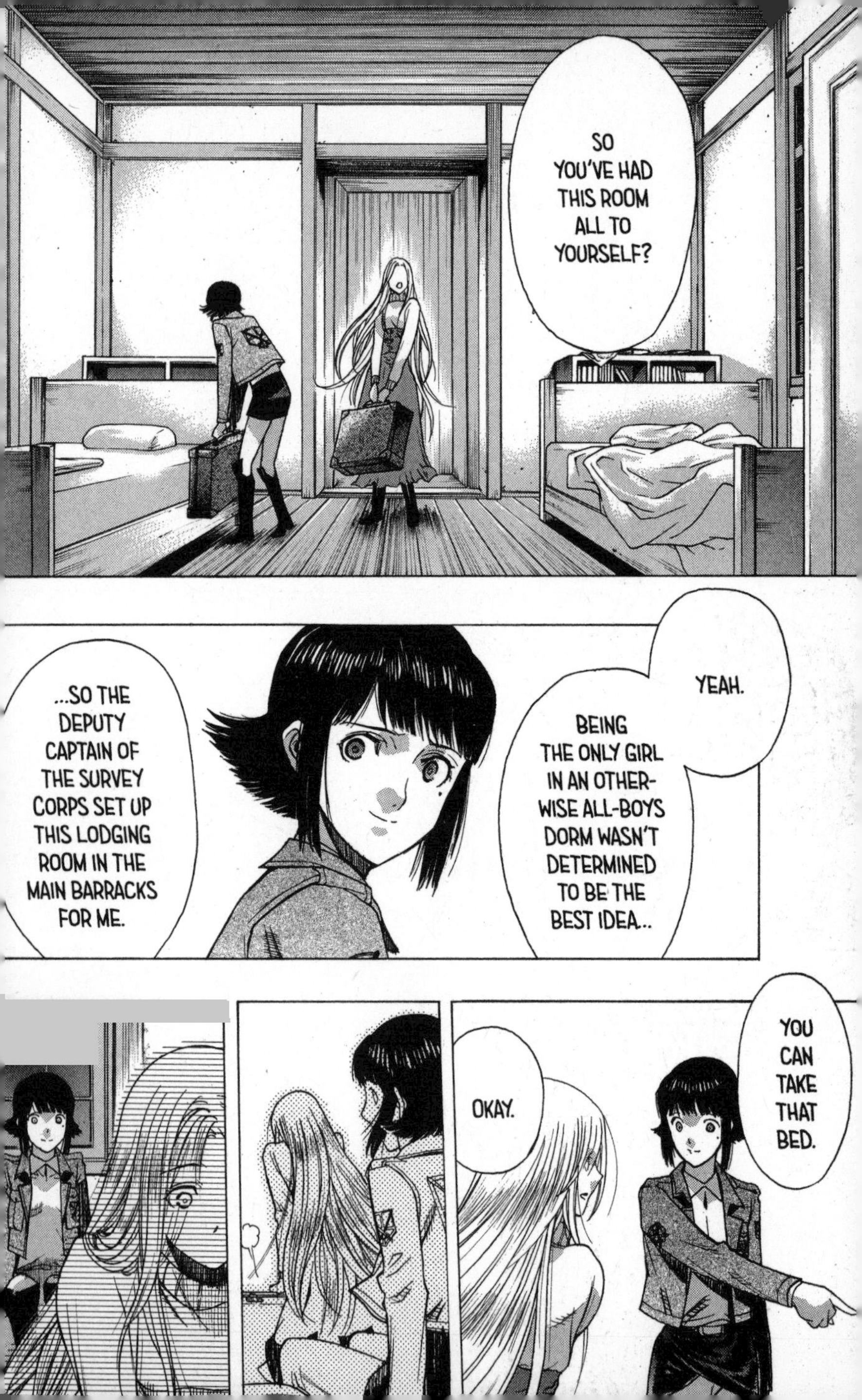
SO YOU'VE HAD THIS ROOM ALL TO YOURSELF?
YEAH.
BEING THE ONLY GIRL IN AN OTHER-WISE ALL-BOYS DORM WASN'T DETERMINED TO BE THE BEST IDEA..
...SO THE DEPUTY CAPTAIN OF THE SURVEY CORPS SET UP THIS LODGING ROOM IN THE MAIN BARRACKS FOR ME.
YOU CAN TAKE THAT BED.
OKAY.

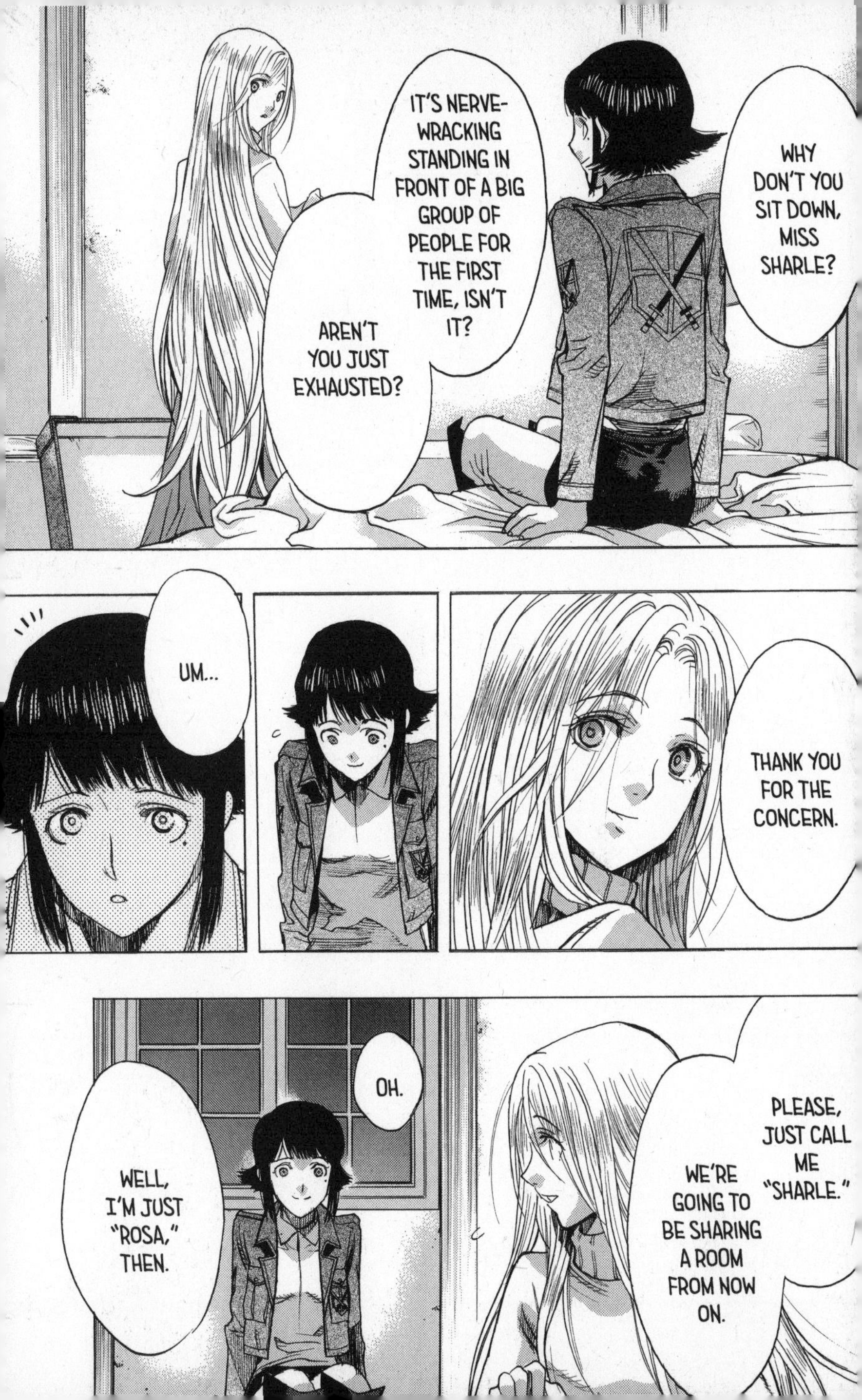
WHY DON'T YOU SIT DOWN, MISS SHARLE?
IT'S NERVE-WRACKING STANDING IN FRONT OF A BIG GROUP OF PEOPLE FOR THE FIRST TIME, ISN'T IT?
AREN'T YOU JUST EXHAUSTED?
THANK YOU FOR THE CONCERN.
UM...
PLEASE, JUST CALL ME "SHARLE."
WE'RE GOING TO BE SHARING A ROOM FROM NOW ON.
OH.
WELL, I'M JUST "ROSA," THEN.

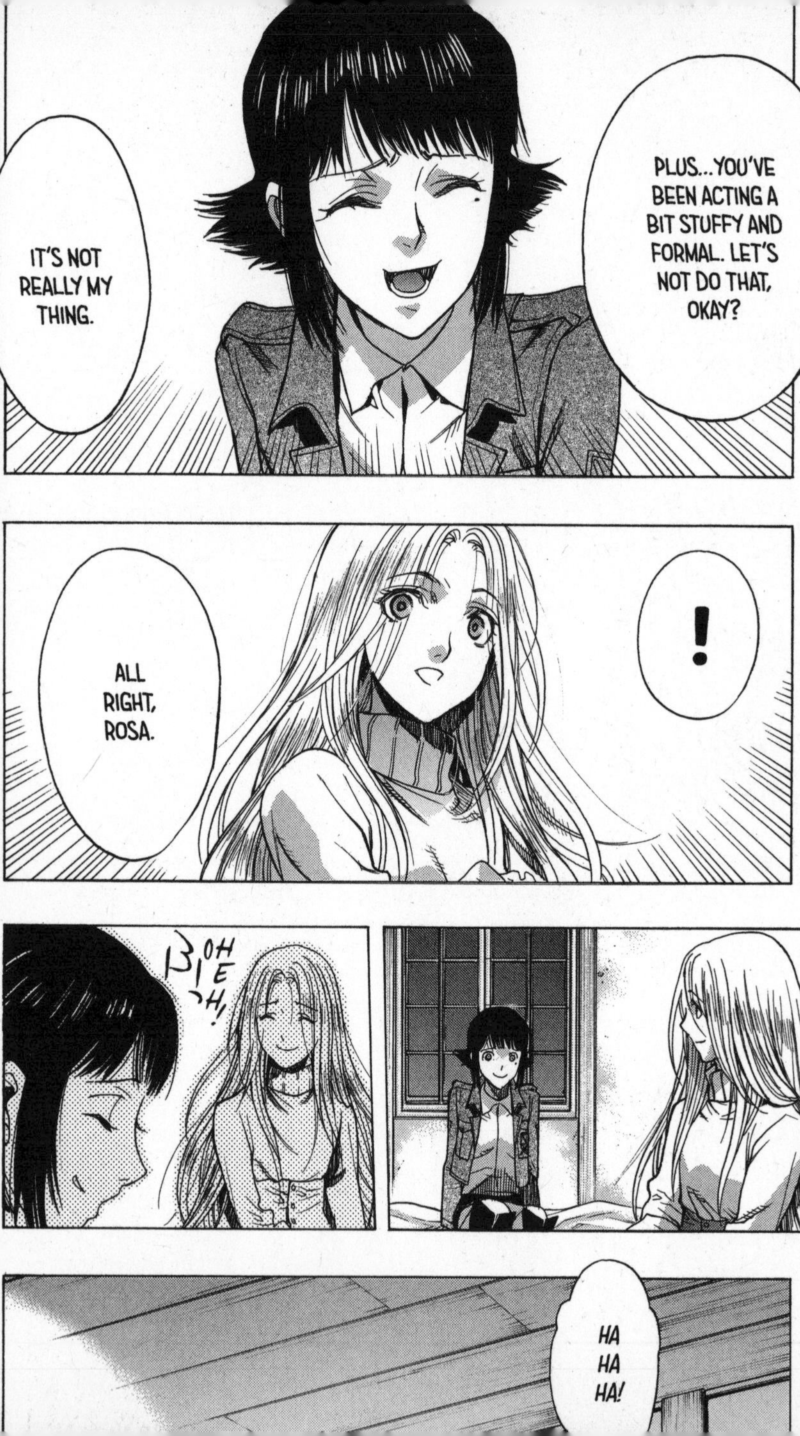
PLUS...YOU'VE BEEN ACTING A BIT STUFFY AND FORMAL. LET'S NOT DO THAT, OKAY?
IT'S NOT REALLY MY THING.
!
ALL RIGHT, ROSA.
HA HA HA!

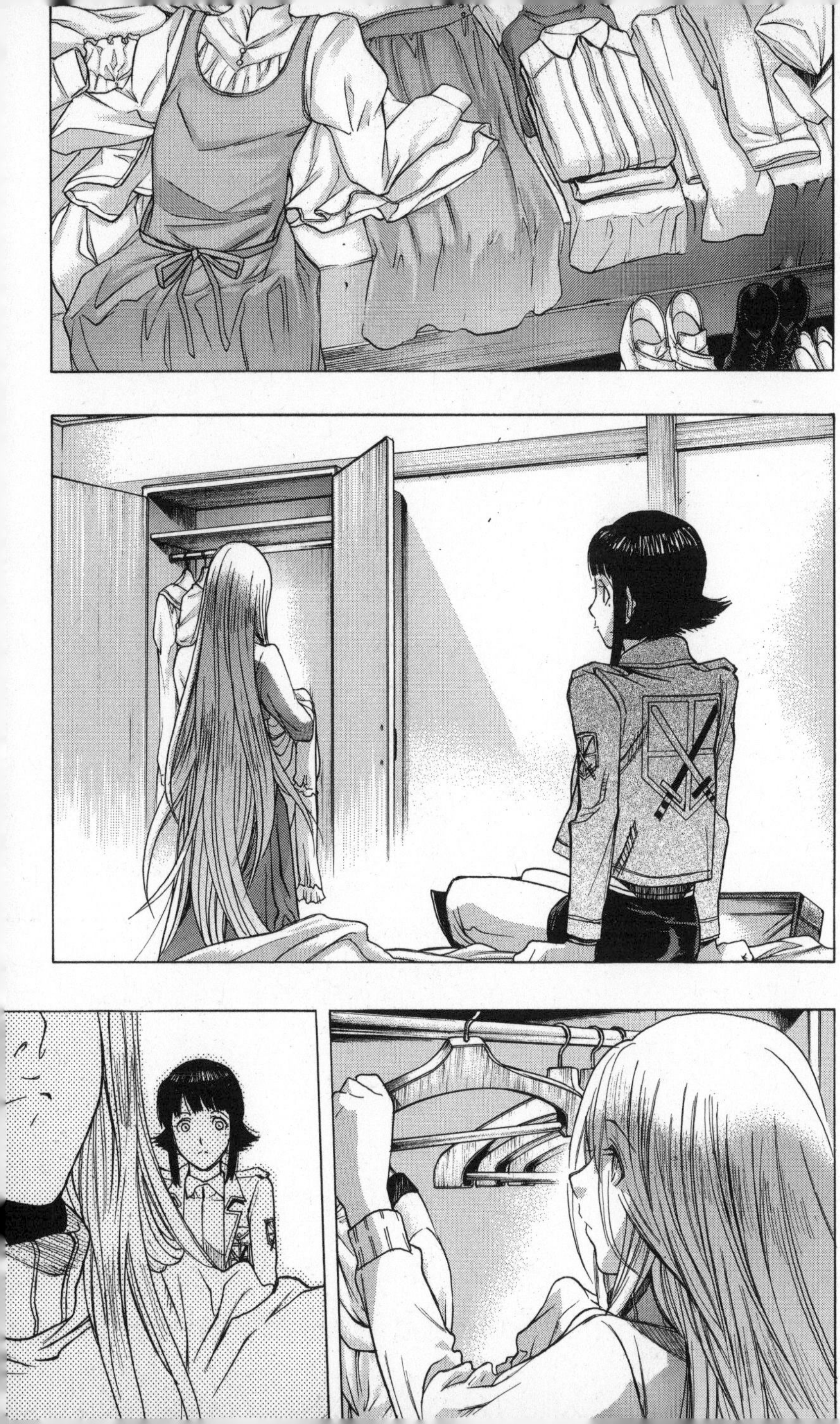

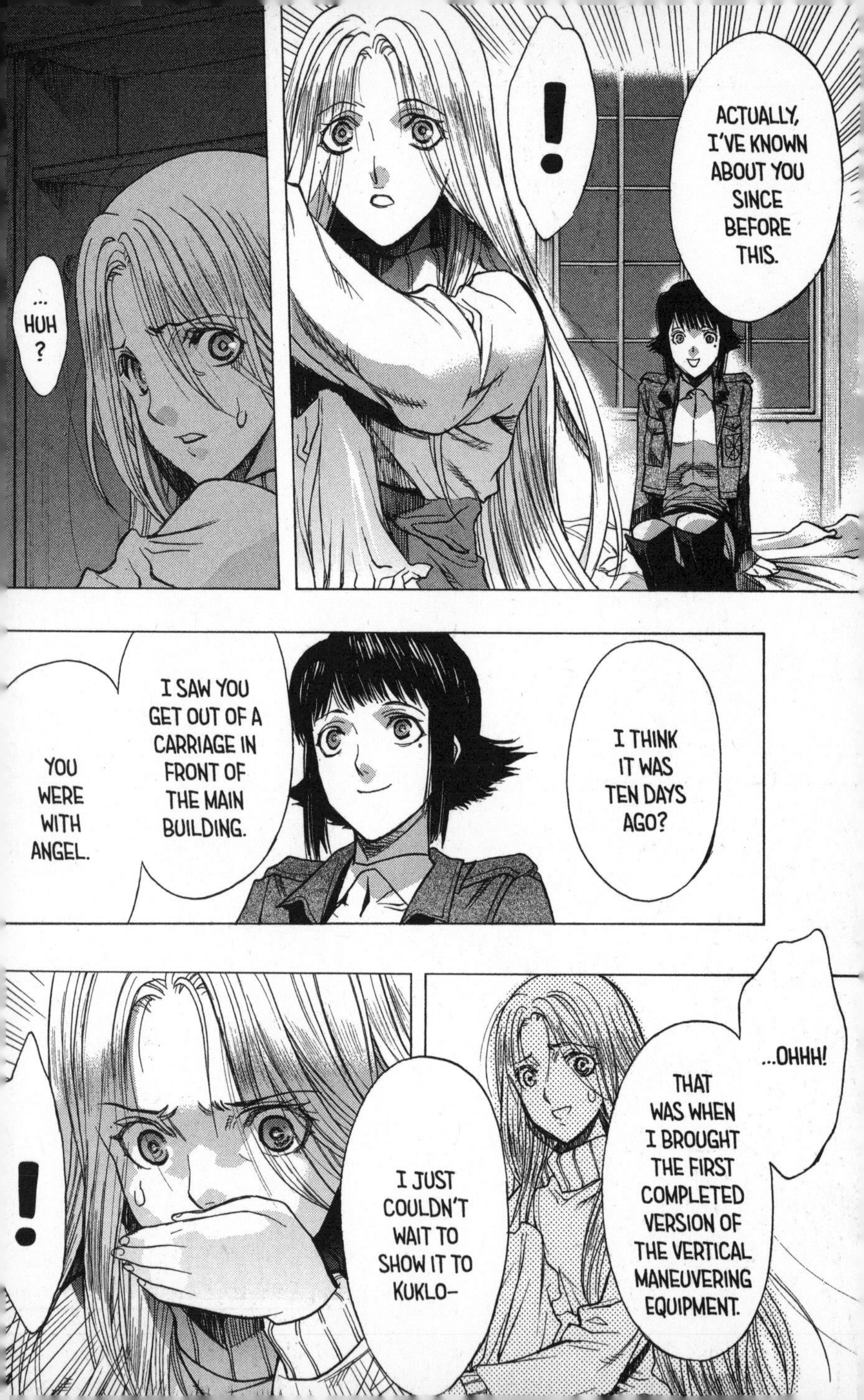
ACTUALLY, I'VE KNOWN ABOUT YOU SINCE BEFORE THIS.
!
... HUH ?
I THINK IT WAS TEN DAYS AGO?
I SAW YOU GET OUT OF A CARRIAGE IN FRONT OF THE MAIN BUILDING.
YOU WERE WITH ANGEL.
...OHHH!
THAT WAS WHEN I BROUGHT THE FIRST COMPLETED VERSION OF THE VERTICAL MANEUVERING EQUIPMENT.
I JUST COULDN'T WAIT TO SHOW IT TO KUKLO-
!

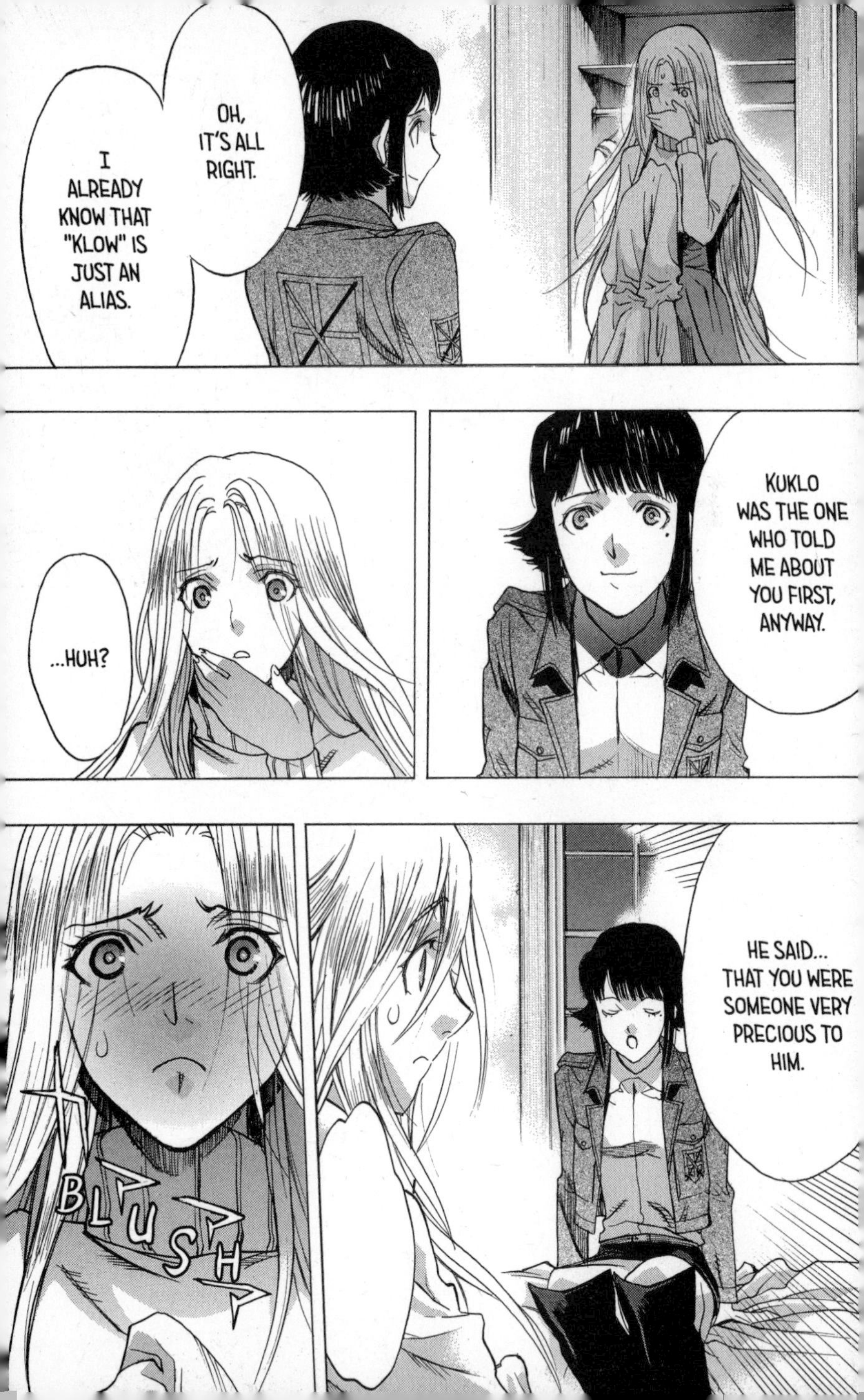
OH, IT'S ALL RIGHT.
I ALREADY KNOW THAT "KLOW" IS JUST AN ALIAS.
KUKLO WAS THE ONE WHO TOLD ME ABOUT YOU FIRST, ANYWAY.
...HUH?
HE SAID... THAT YOU WERE SOMEONE VERY PRECIOUS TO HIM.
BLUSH

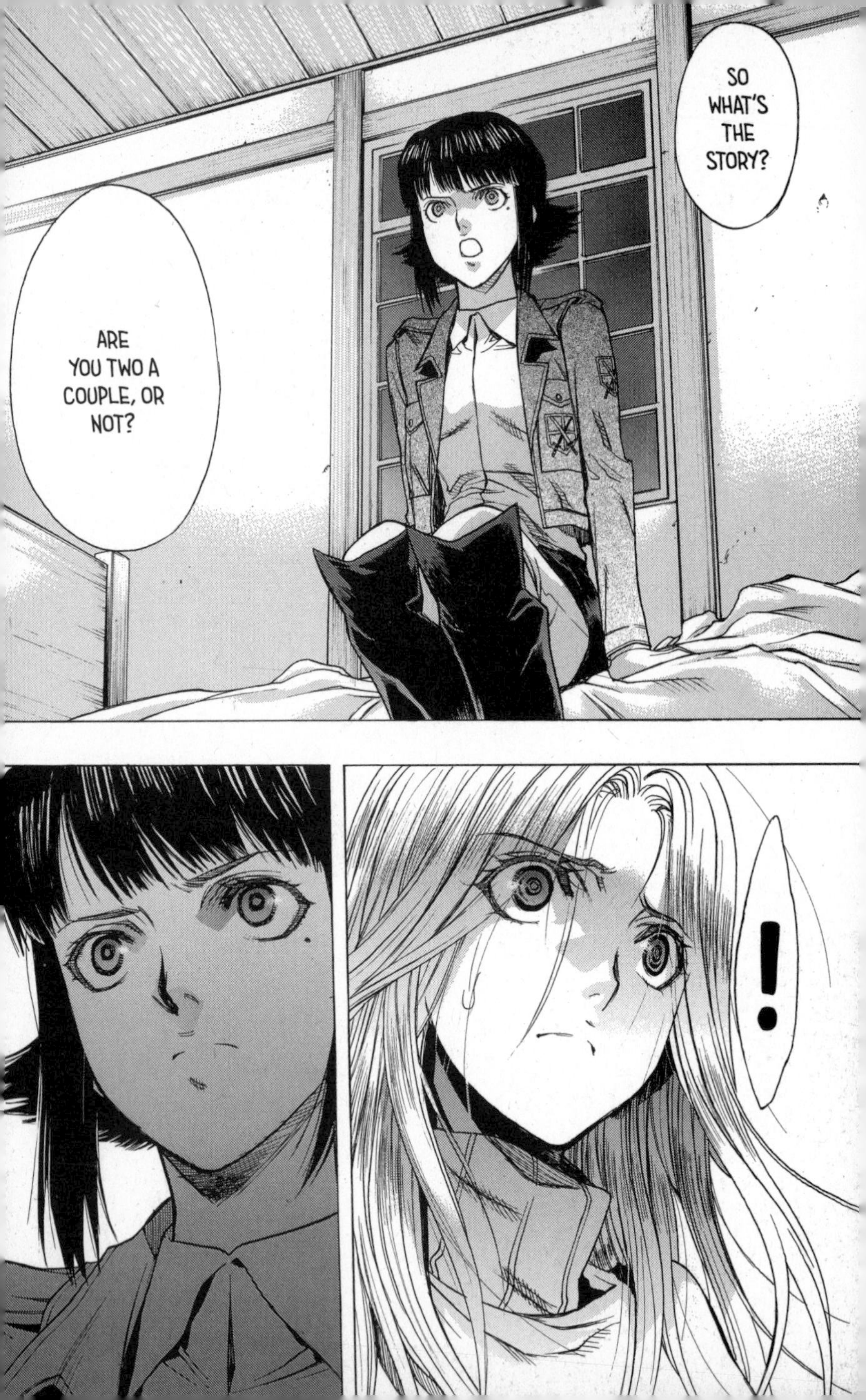
SO WHAT'S THE STORY?
ARE YOU TWO A COUPLE, OR NOT?
!

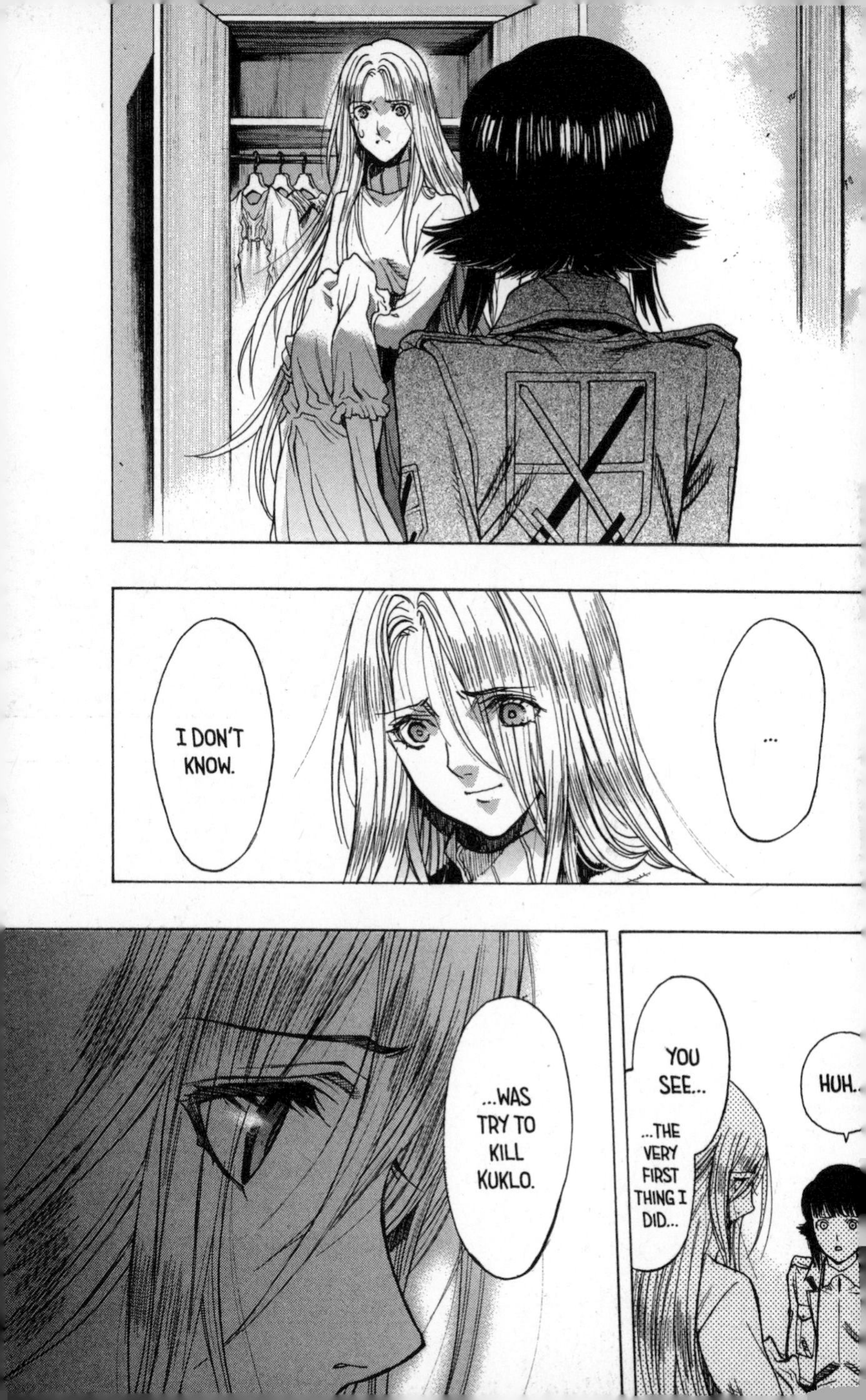
...
I DON'T KNOW.
HUH...
YOU SEE...
...THE VERY FIRST THING I DID...
...WAS TRY TO KILL KUKLO.

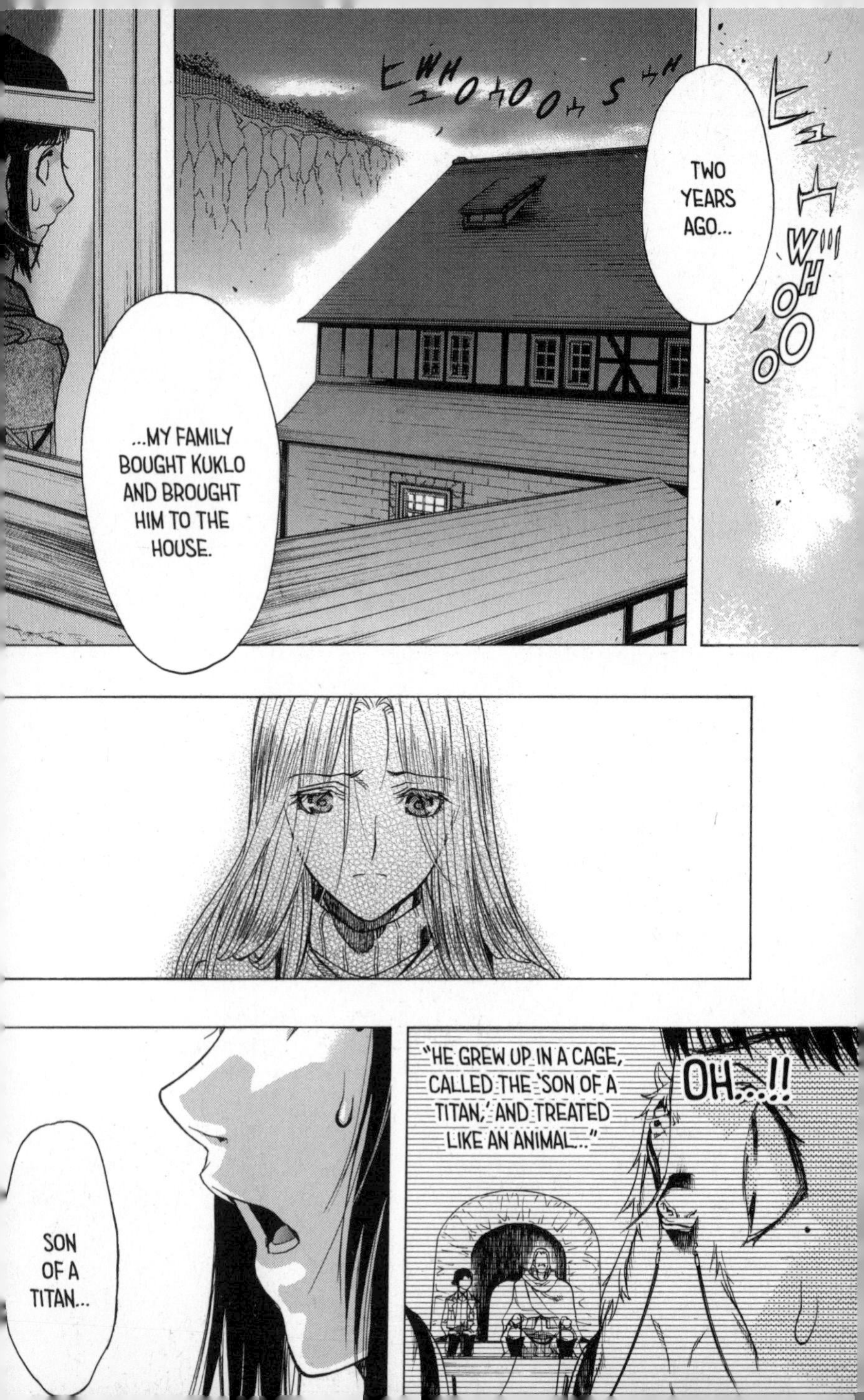
WHOOO
TWO YEARS AGO...
...MY FAMILY BOUGHT KUKLO AND BROUGHT HIM TO THE HOUSE.
"HE GREW UP IN A CAGE, CALLED THE 'SON OF A TITAN,' AND TREATED LIKE AN ANIMAL..."
OH...!!
SON OF A TITAN...

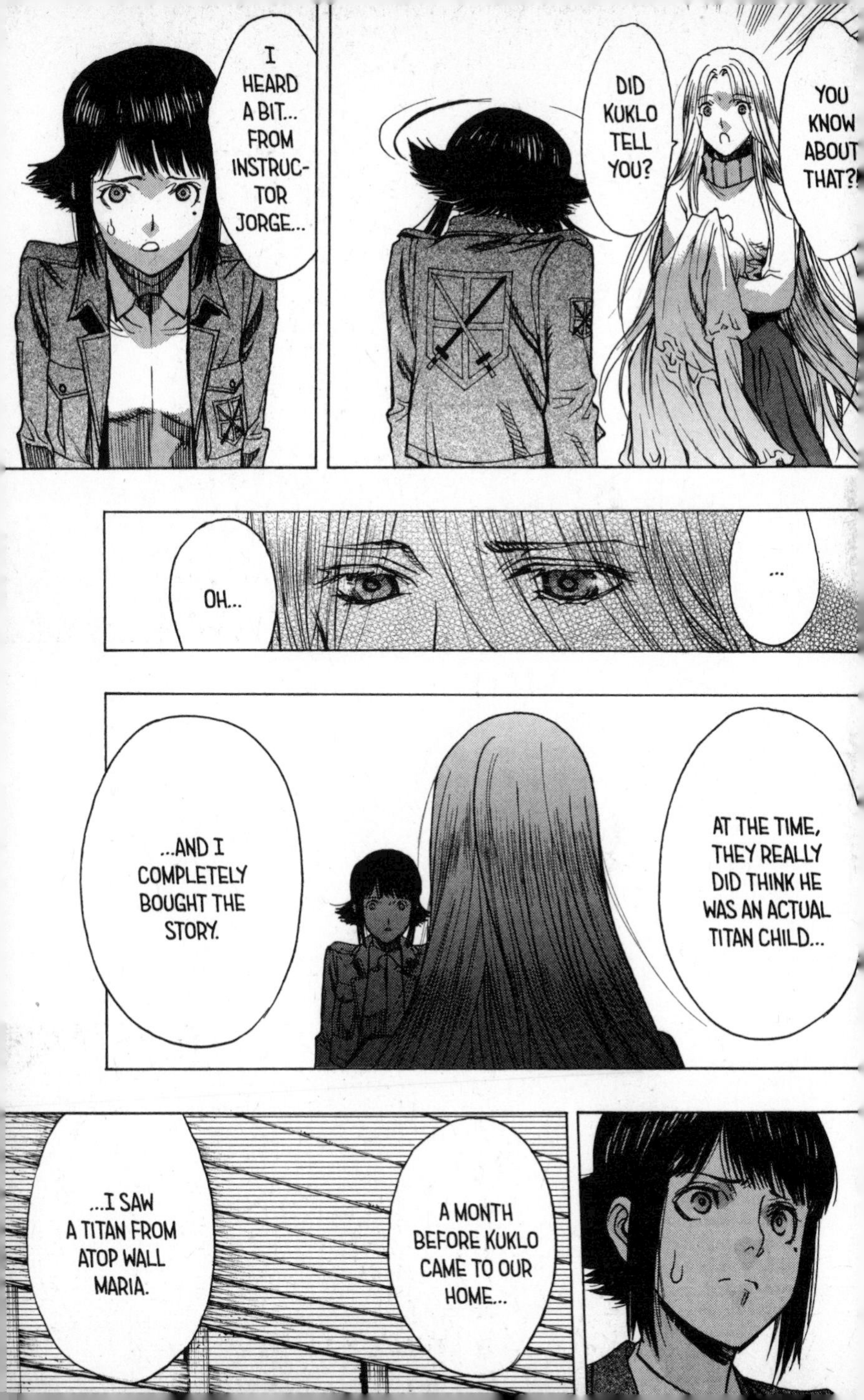
YOU KNOW ABOUT THAT?!
DID KUKLO TELL YOU?
I HEARD A BIT... FROM INSTRUCTOR JORGE...
...
OH...
AT THE TIME, THEY REALLY DID THINK HE WAS AN ACTUAL TITAN CHILD...
...AND I COMPLETELY BOUGHT THE STORY.
A MONTH BEFORE KUKLO CAME TO OUR HOME...
...I SAW A TITAN FROM ATOP WALL MARIA.

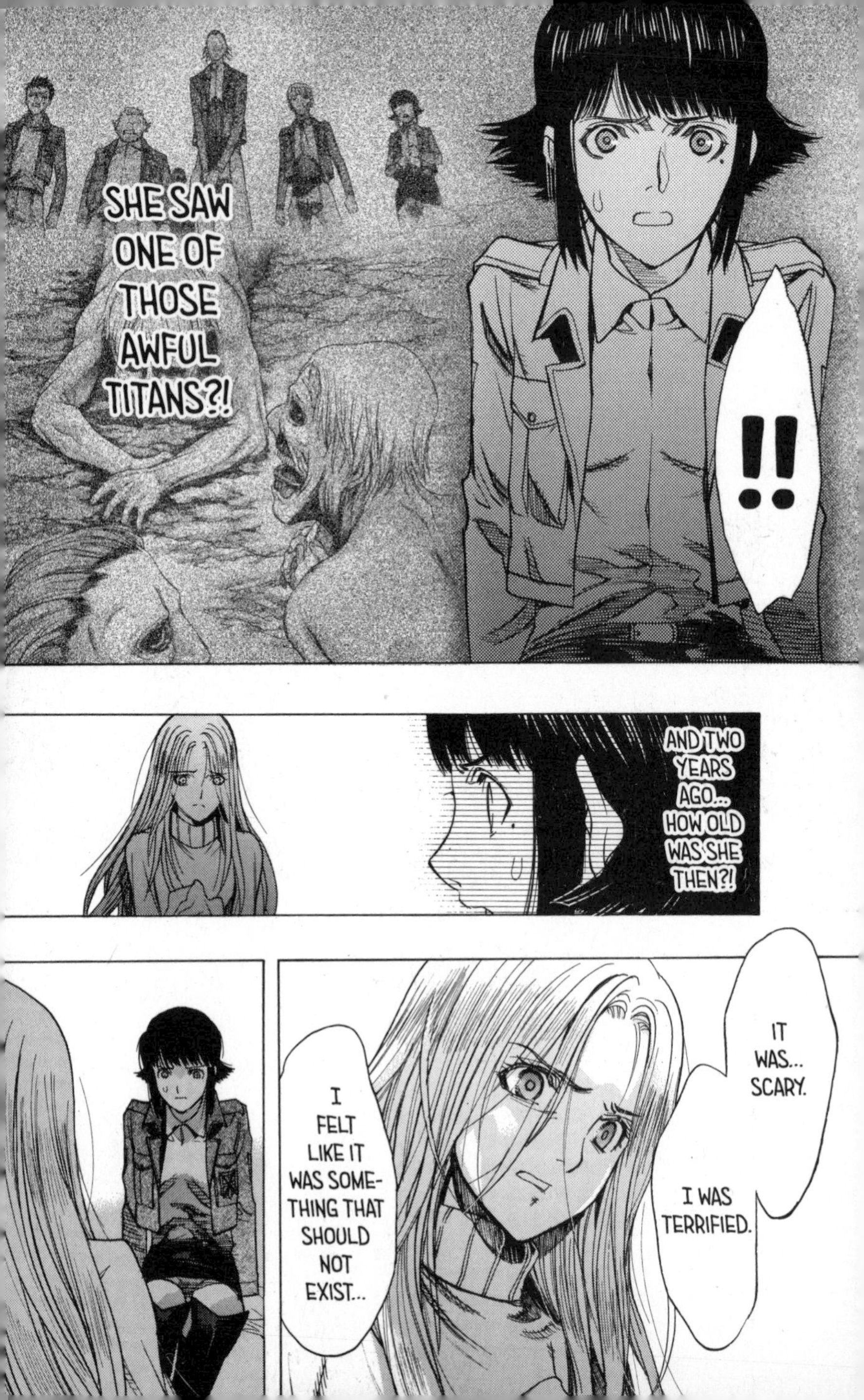
!!
SHE SAW ONE OF THOSE AWFUL TITANS?!
AND TWO YEARS AGO... HOW OLD WAS SHE THEN?!
IT WAS... SCARY.
I WAS TERRIFIED.
I FELT LIKE IT WAS SOME-THING THAT SHOULD NOT EXIST...

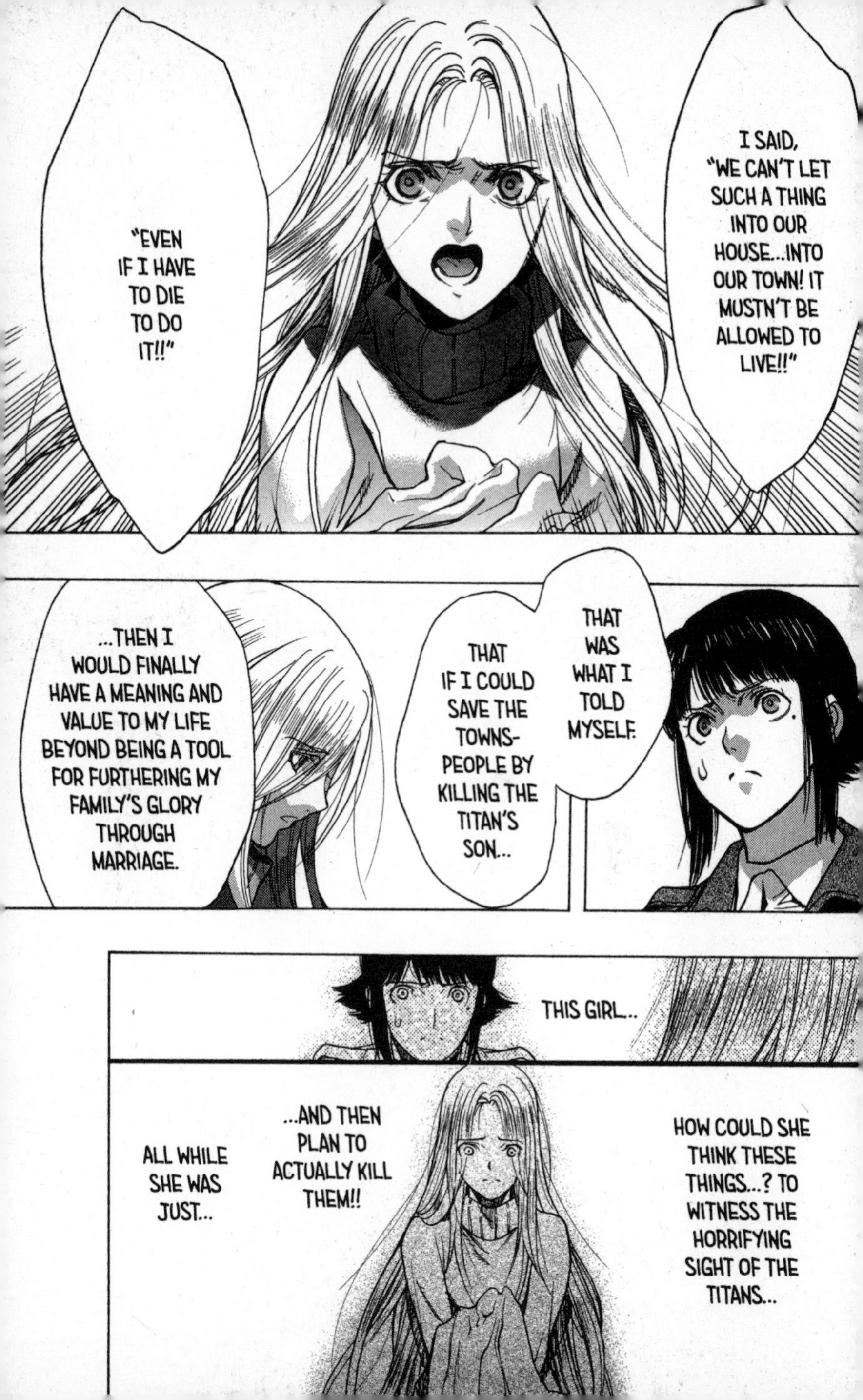
I SAID, "WE CAN'T LET SUCH A THING INTO OUR HOUSE...INTO OUR TOWN! IT MUSTN'T BE ALLOWED TO LIVE!!"
"EVEN IF I HAVE TO DIE TO DO IT!!"
THAT WAS WHAT I TOLD MYSELF.
THAT IF I COULD SAVE THE TOWNS-PEOPLE BY KILLING THE TITAN'S SON...
...THEN I WOULD FINALLY HAVE A MEANING AND VALUE TO MY LIFE BEYOND BEING A TOOL FOR FURTHERING MY FAMILY'S GLORY THROUGH MARRIAGE.
THIS GIRL...
HOW COULD SHE THINK THESE THINGS...? TO WITNESS THE HORRIFYING SIGHT OF THE TITANS...
...AND THEN PLAN TO ACTUALLY KILL THEM!!
ALL WHILE SHE WAS JUST...

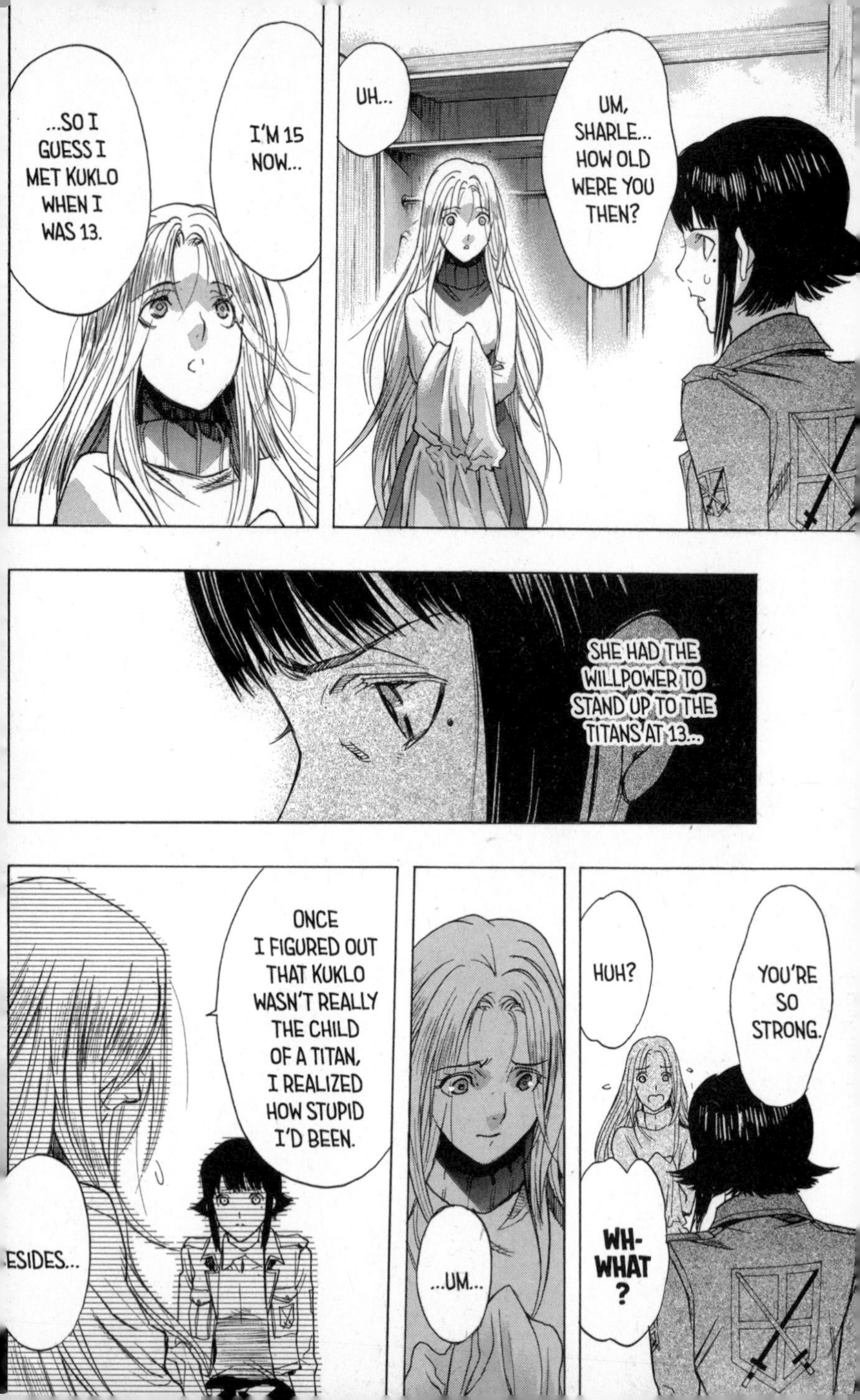

UM, SHARLE... HOW OLD WERE YOU THEN?
UH...
I'M 15 NOW...
...SO I GUESS I MET KUKLO WHEN I WAS 13.
SHE HAD THE WILLPOWER TO STAND UP TO THE TITANS AT 13...
YOU'RE SO STRONG.
HUH?
WH-WHAT?
...UM...
ONCE I FIGURED OUT THAT KUKLO WASN'T REALLY THE CHILD OF A TITAN, I REALIZED HOW STUPID I'D BEEN.
ESIDES...

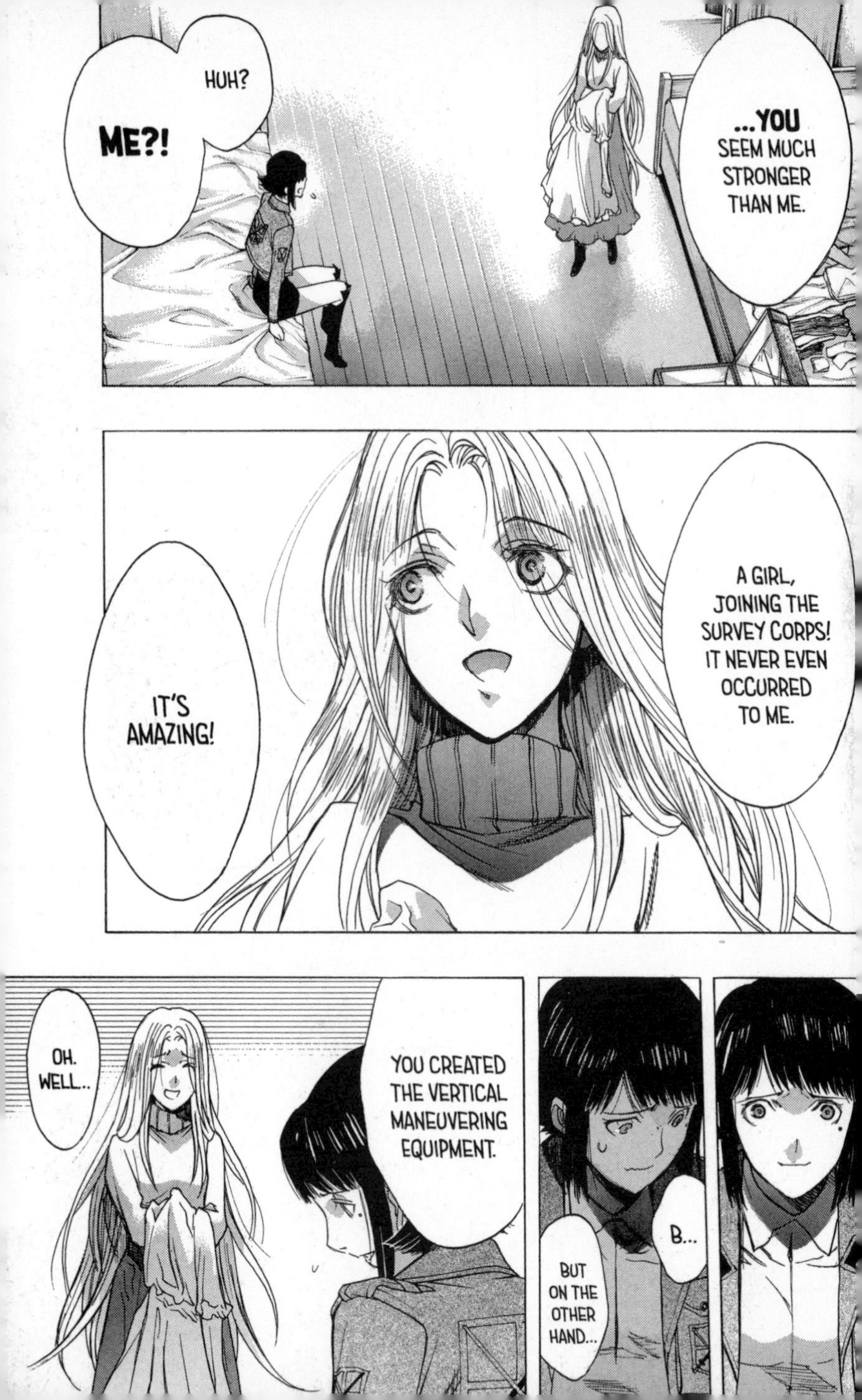
...YOU SEEM MUCH STRONGER THAN ME.
HUH?
ME?!
A GIRL, JOINING THE SURVEY CORPS! IT NEVER EVEN OCCURRED TO ME.
IT'S AMAZING!
B...
BUT ON THE OTHER HAND...
YOU CREATED THE VERTICAL MANEUVERING EQUIPMENT.
OH. WELL..

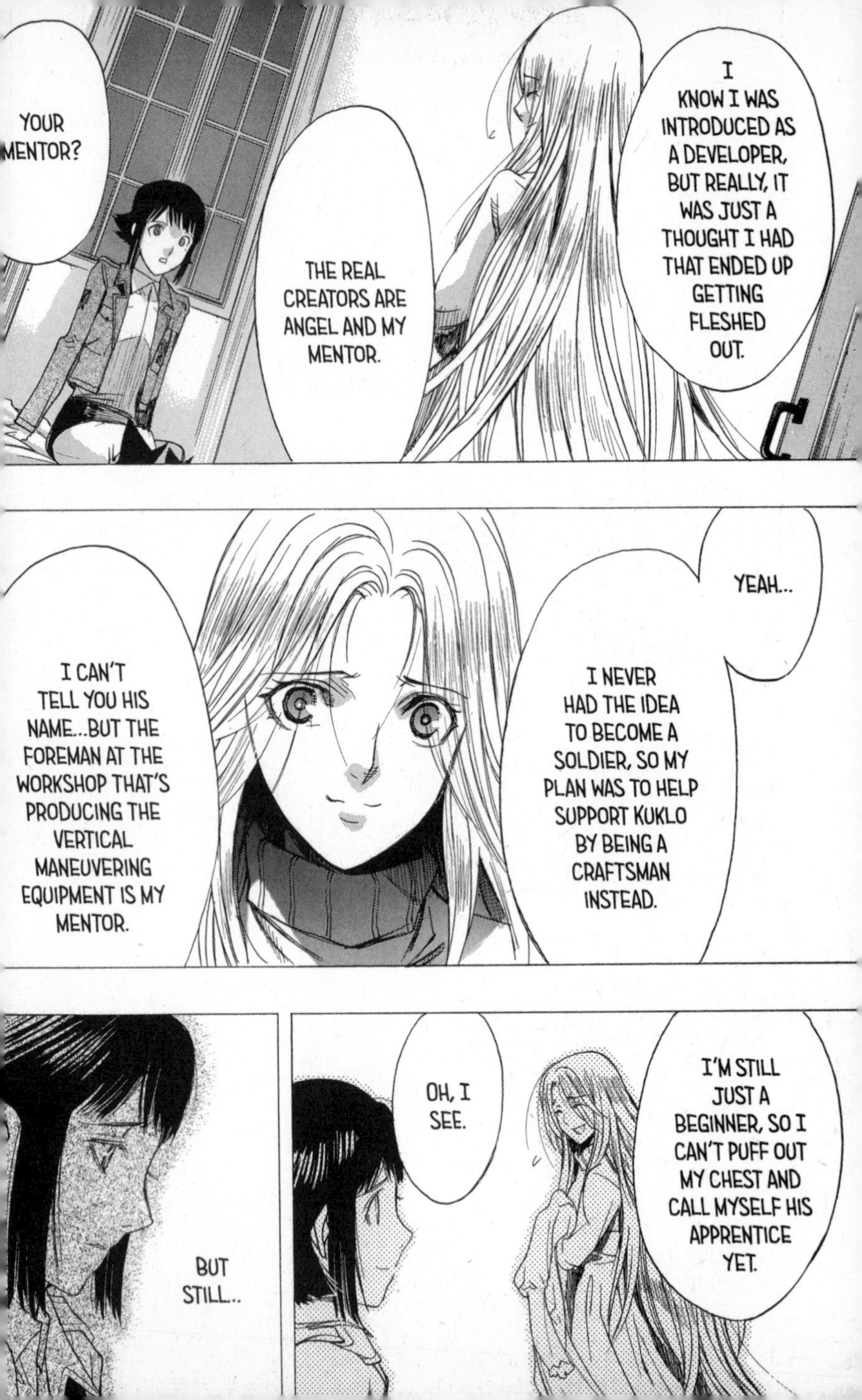
I KNOW I WAS INTRODUCED AS A DEVELOPER, BUT REALLY, IT WAS JUST A THOUGHT I HAD THAT ENDED UP GETTING FLESHED OUT.
THE REAL CREATORS ARE ANGEL AND MY MENTOR.
YOUR MENTOR?
YEAH...
I NEVER HAD THE IDEA TO BECOME A SOLDIER, SO MY PLAN WAS TO HELP SUPPORT KUKLO BY BEING A CRAFTSMAN INSTEAD.
I CAN'T TELL YOU HIS NAME...BUT THE FOREMAN AT THE WORKSHOP THAT'S PRODUCING THE VERTICAL MANEUVERING EQUIPMENT IS MY MENTOR.
I'M STILL JUST A BEGINNER, SO I CAN'T PUFF OUT MY CHEST AND CALL MYSELF HIS APPRENTICE YET.
OH, I SEE.
BUT STILL...

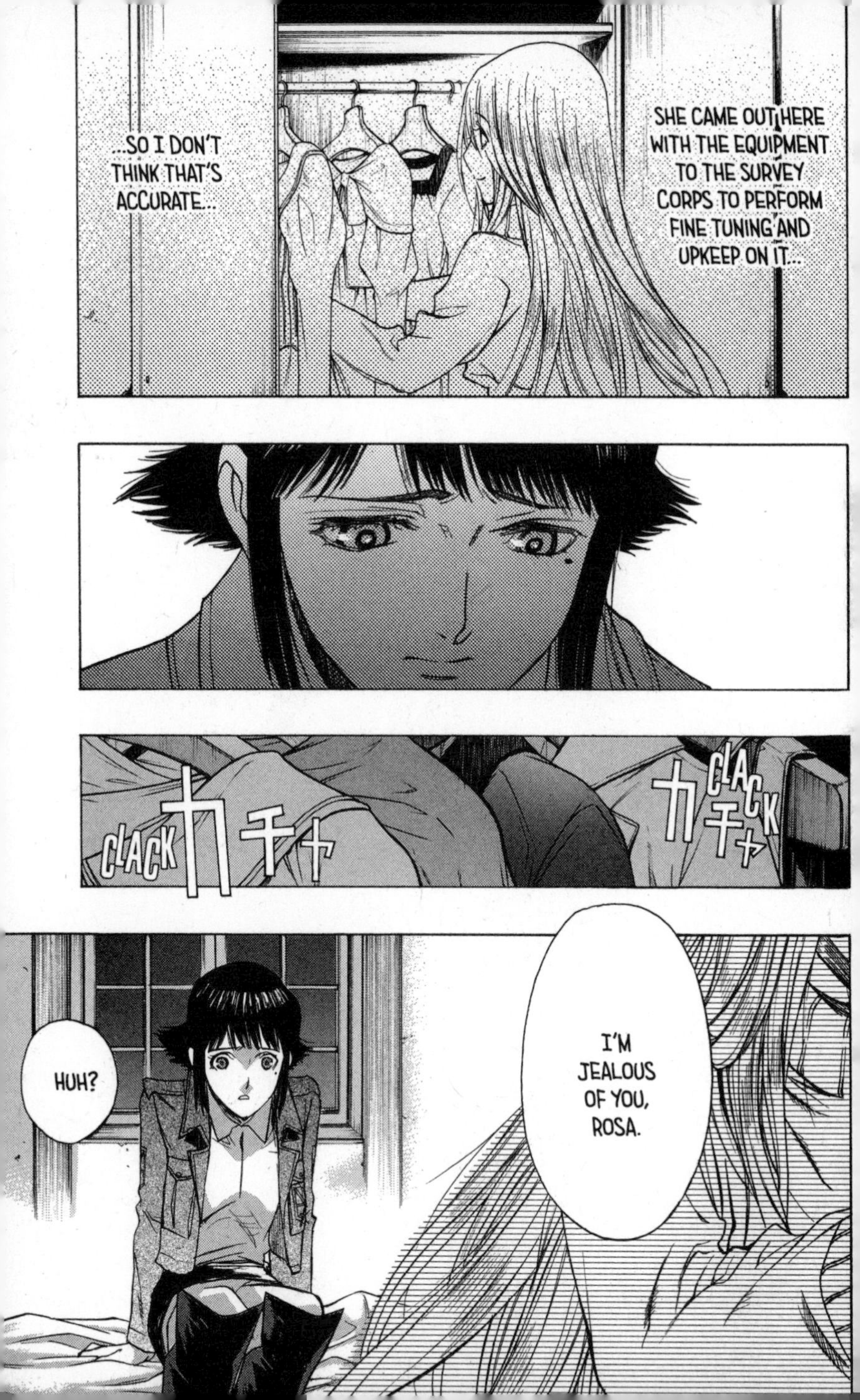
SHE CAME OUT HERE WITH THE EQUIPMENT TO THE SURVEY CORPS TO PERFORM FINE TUNING AND UPKEEP ON IT...
...SO I DON'T THINK THAT'S ACCURATE...
CLACK
カチャ
CLACK
カチャ
I'M JEALOUS OF YOU, ROSA.
HUH?

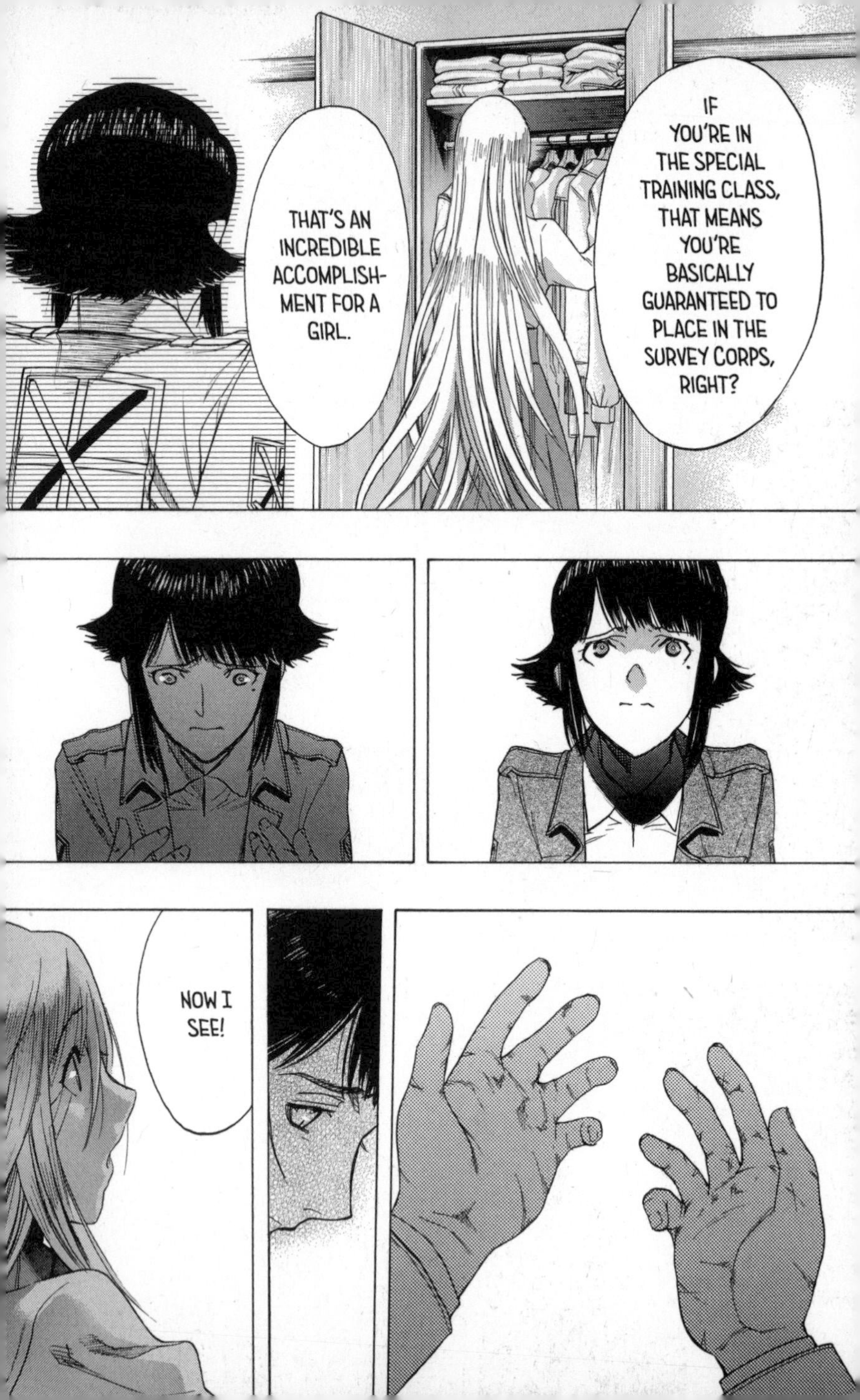
IF YOU'RE IN THE SPECIAL TRAINING CLASS, THAT MEANS YOU'RE BASICALLY GUARANTEED TO PLACE IN THE SURVEY CORPS, RIGHT?
THAT'S AN INCREDIBLE ACCOMPLISHMENT FOR A GIRL.
NOW I SEE!

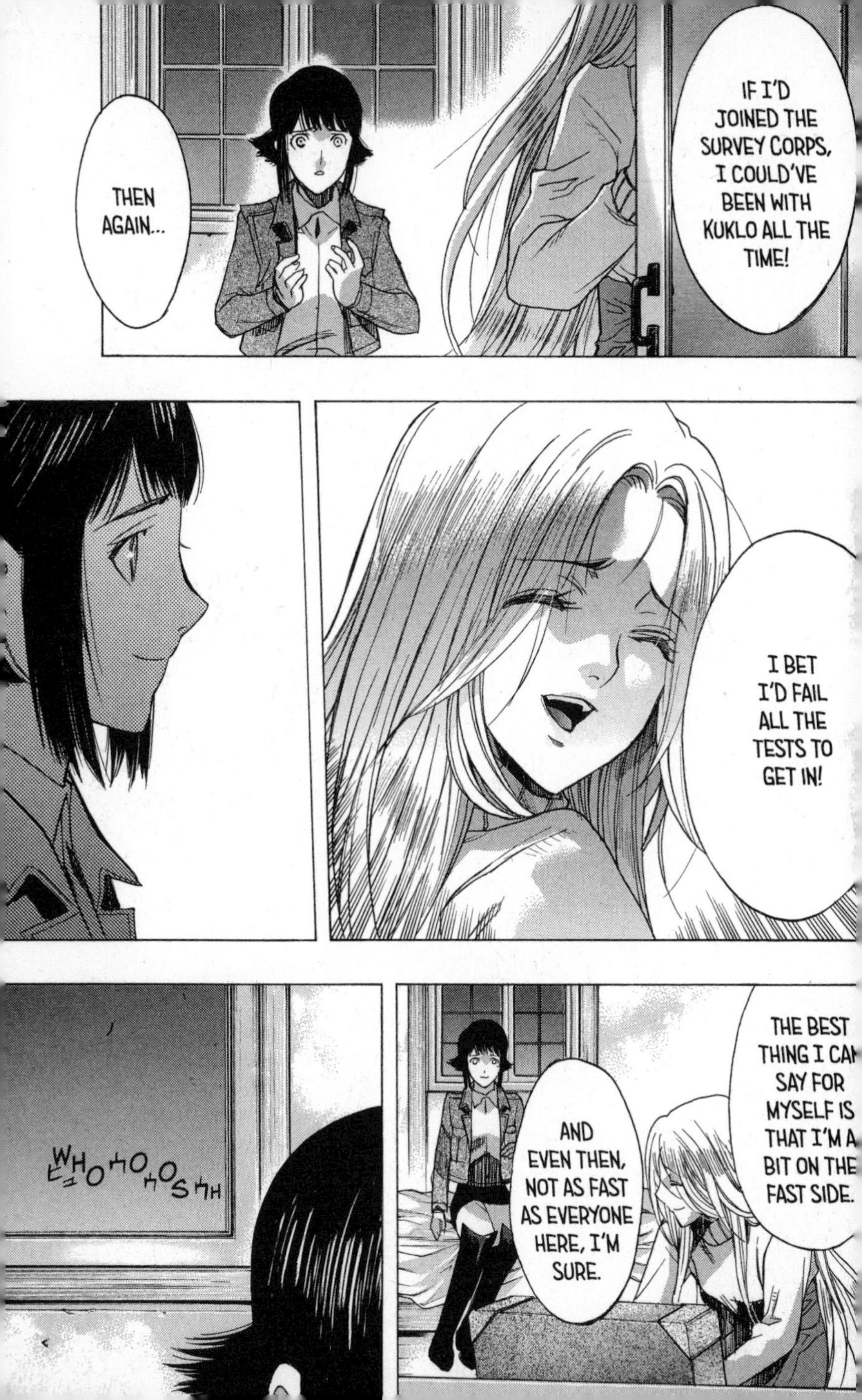
IF I'D JOINED THE SURVEY CORPS, I COULD'VE BEEN WITH KUKLO ALL THE TIME!
THEN AGAIN...
I BET I'D FAIL ALL THE TESTS TO GET IN!
THE BEST THING I CA SAY FOR MYSELF IS THAT I'M A BIT ON THE FAST SIDE.
AND EVEN THEN, NOT AS FAST AS EVERYONE HERE, I'M SURE.
WHOOOOOSHH

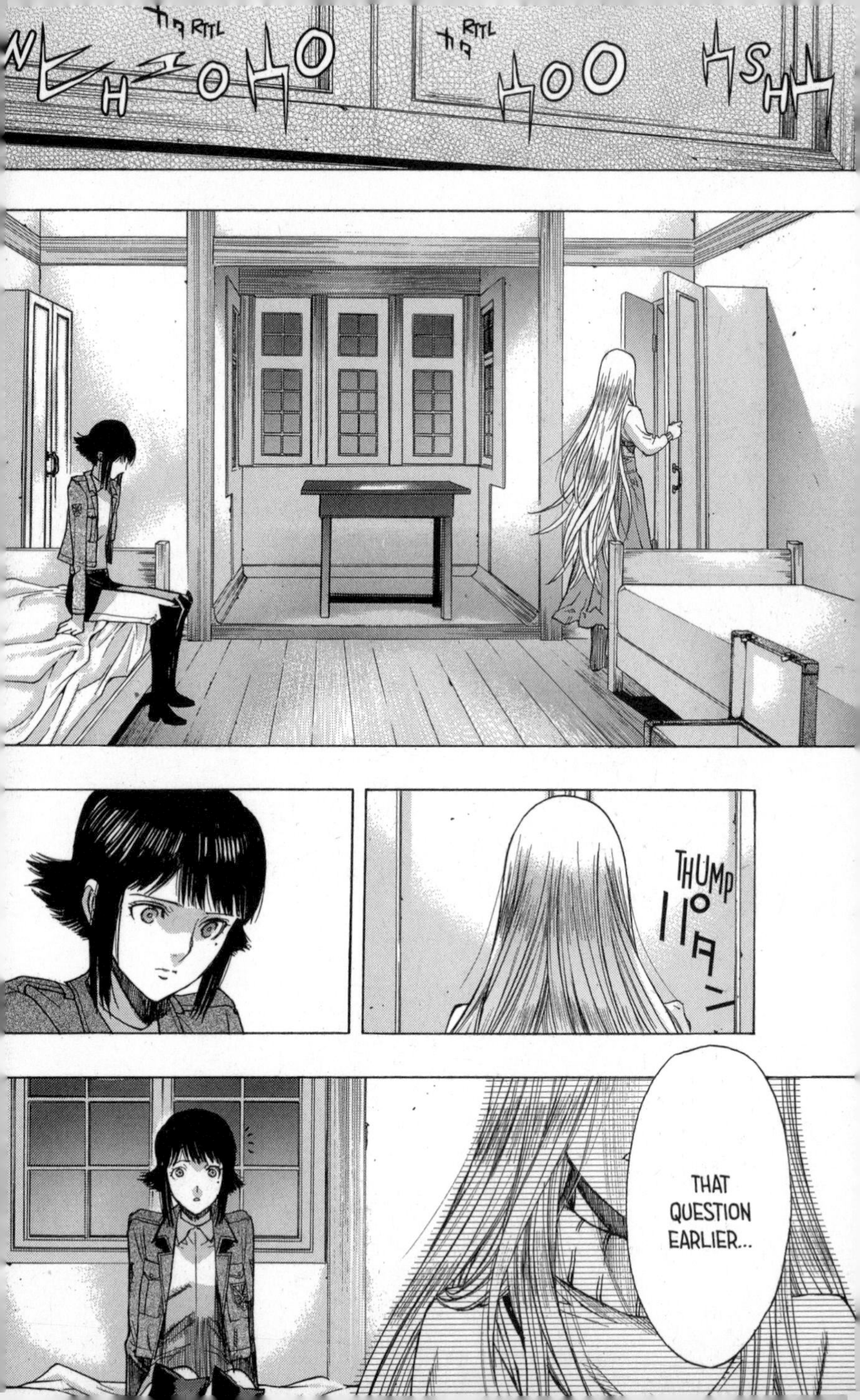
RTTL
RTTL
THUMP
THAT QUESTION EARLIER...

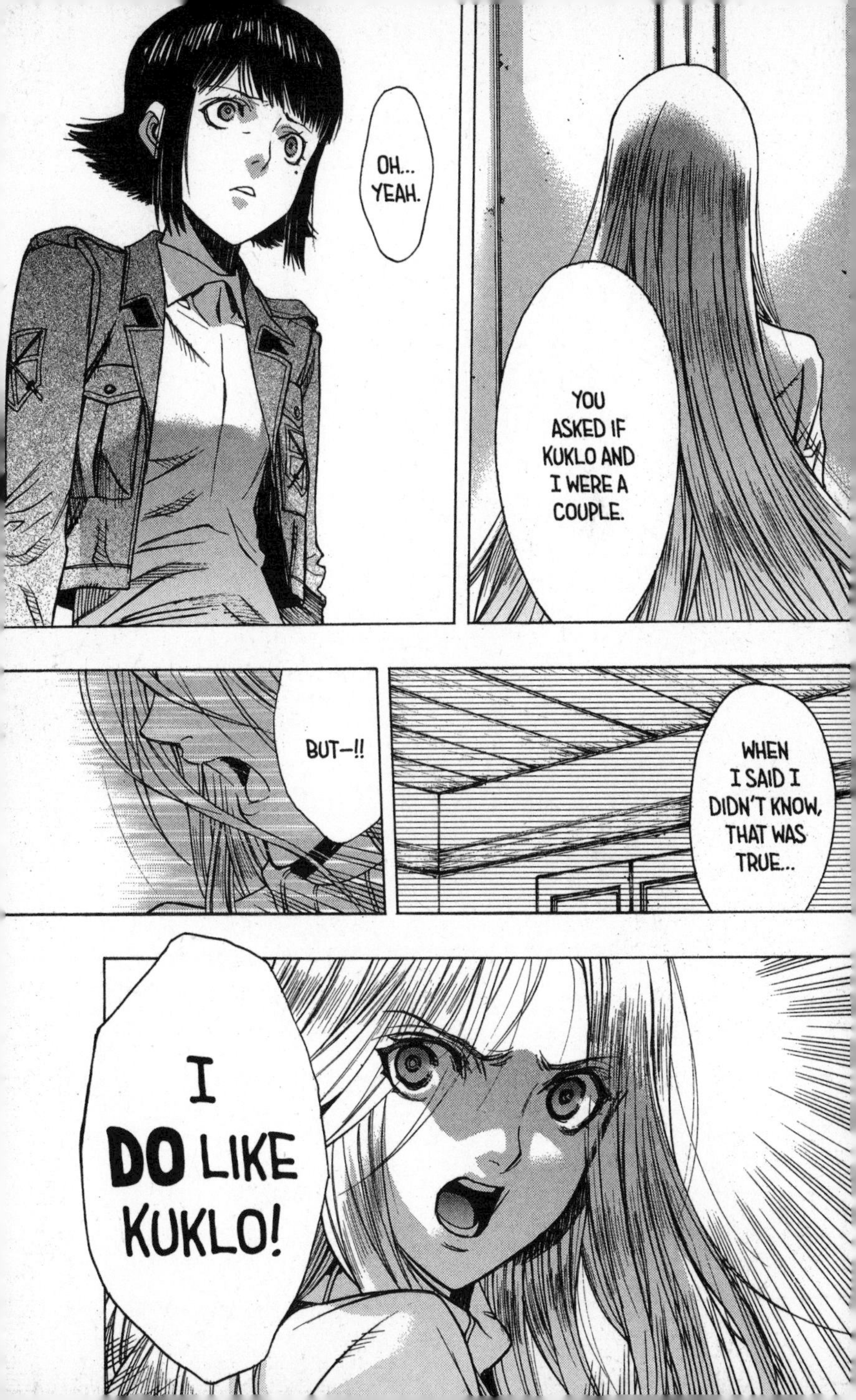
YOU ASKED IF KUKLO AND I WERE A COUPLE.
OH... YEAH.
WHEN I SAID I DIDN'T KNOW, THAT WAS TRUE...
BUT—!!
I **DO** LIKE KUKLO!

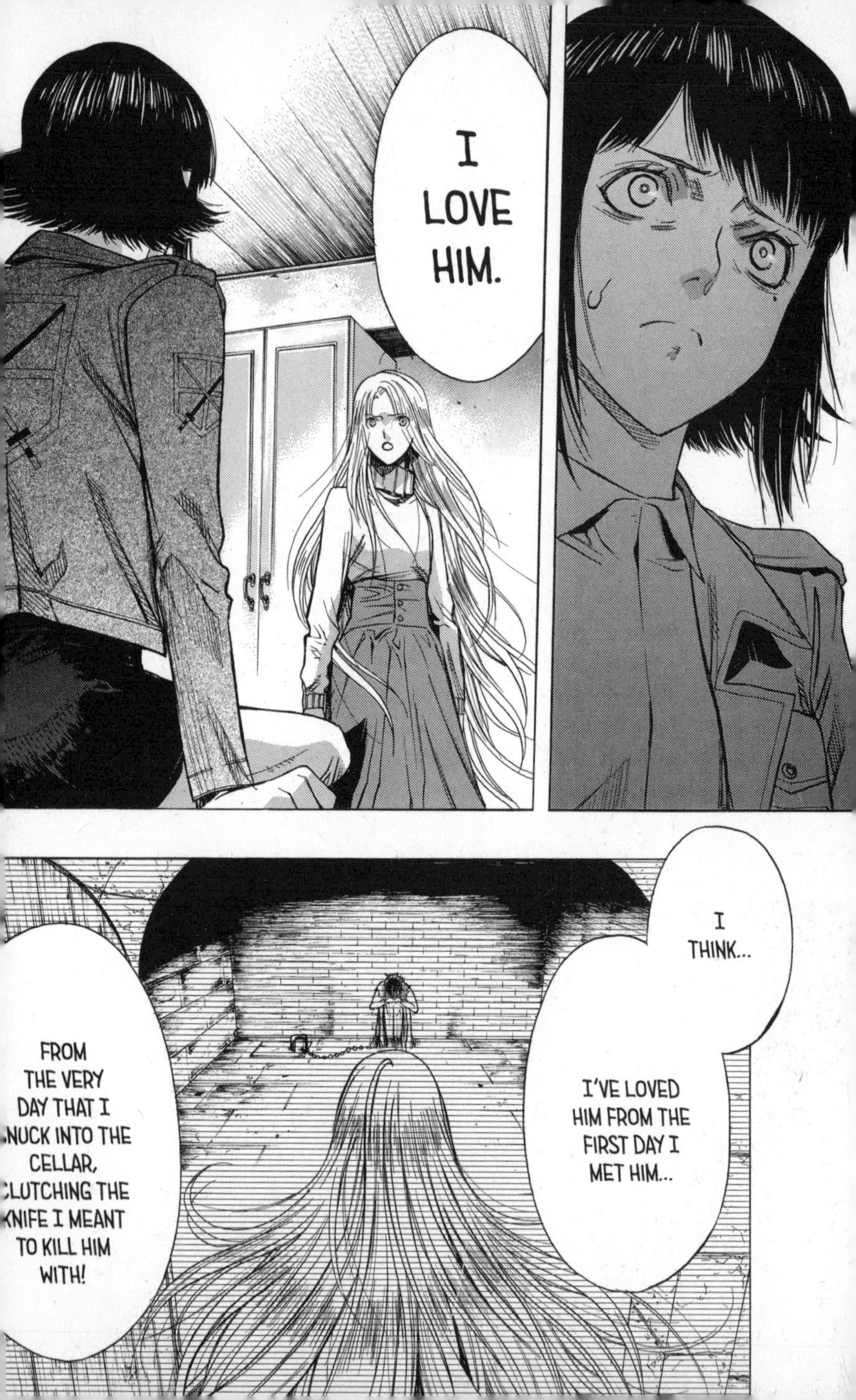
I LOVE HIM.
I THINK...
I'VE LOVED HIM FROM THE FIRST DAY I MET HIM...
FROM THE VERY DAY THAT I NUCK INTO THE CELLAR, LUTCHING THE NIFE I MEANT TO KILL HIM WITH!

GULP

AND...

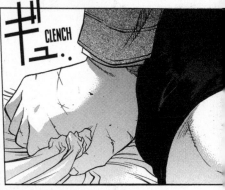

CLENCH

!!

...I THINK THAT KUKLO LIKES ME, TOO.

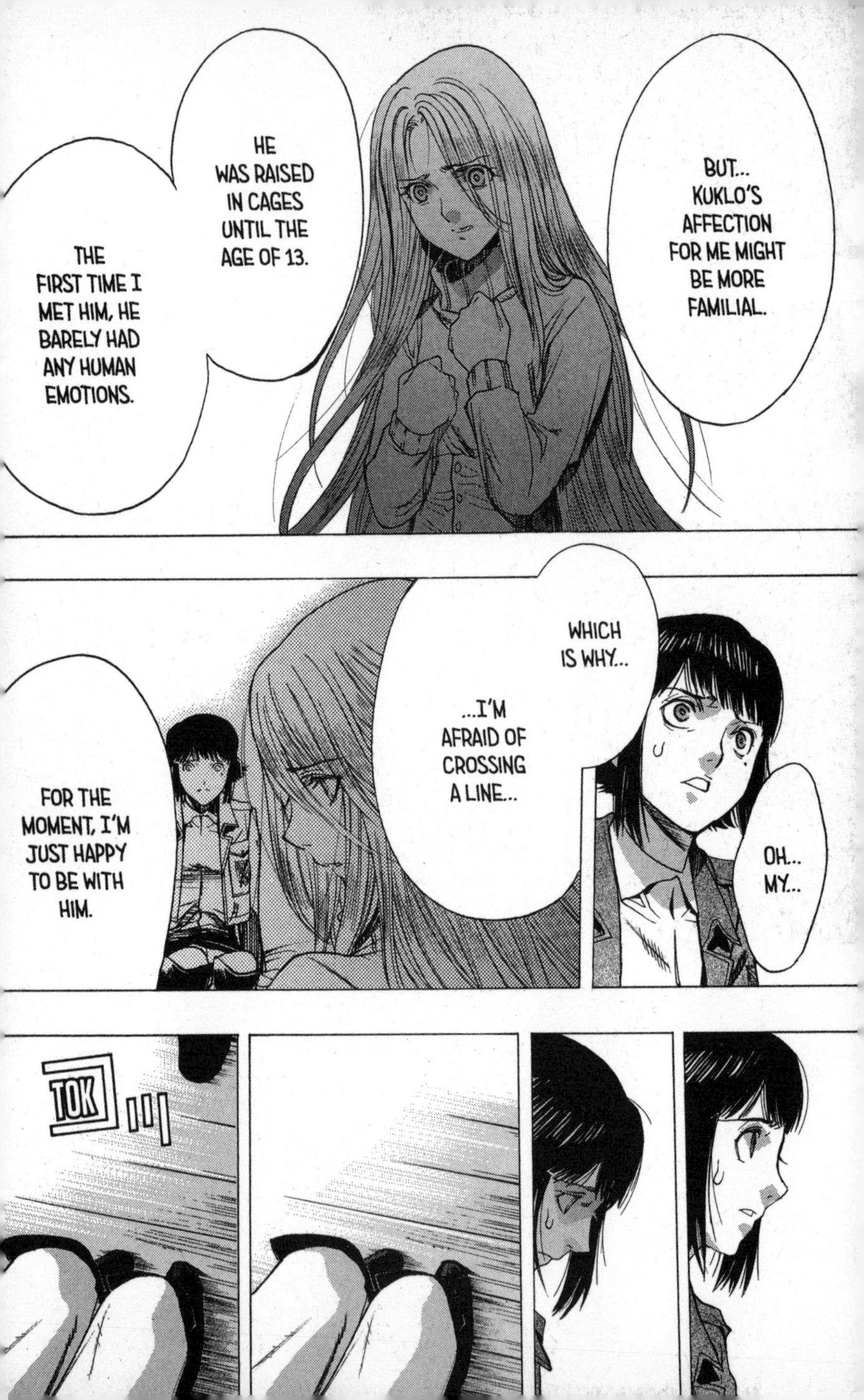
BUT... KUKLO'S AFFECTION FOR ME MIGHT BE MORE FAMILIAL.
HE WAS RAISED IN CAGES UNTIL THE AGE OF 13.
THE FIRST TIME I MET HIM, HE BARELY HAD ANY HUMAN EMOTIONS.
WHICH IS WHY...
...I'M AFRAID OF CROSSING A LINE...
OH... MY...
FOR THE MOMENT, I'M JUST HAPPY TO BE WITH HIM.
TOK

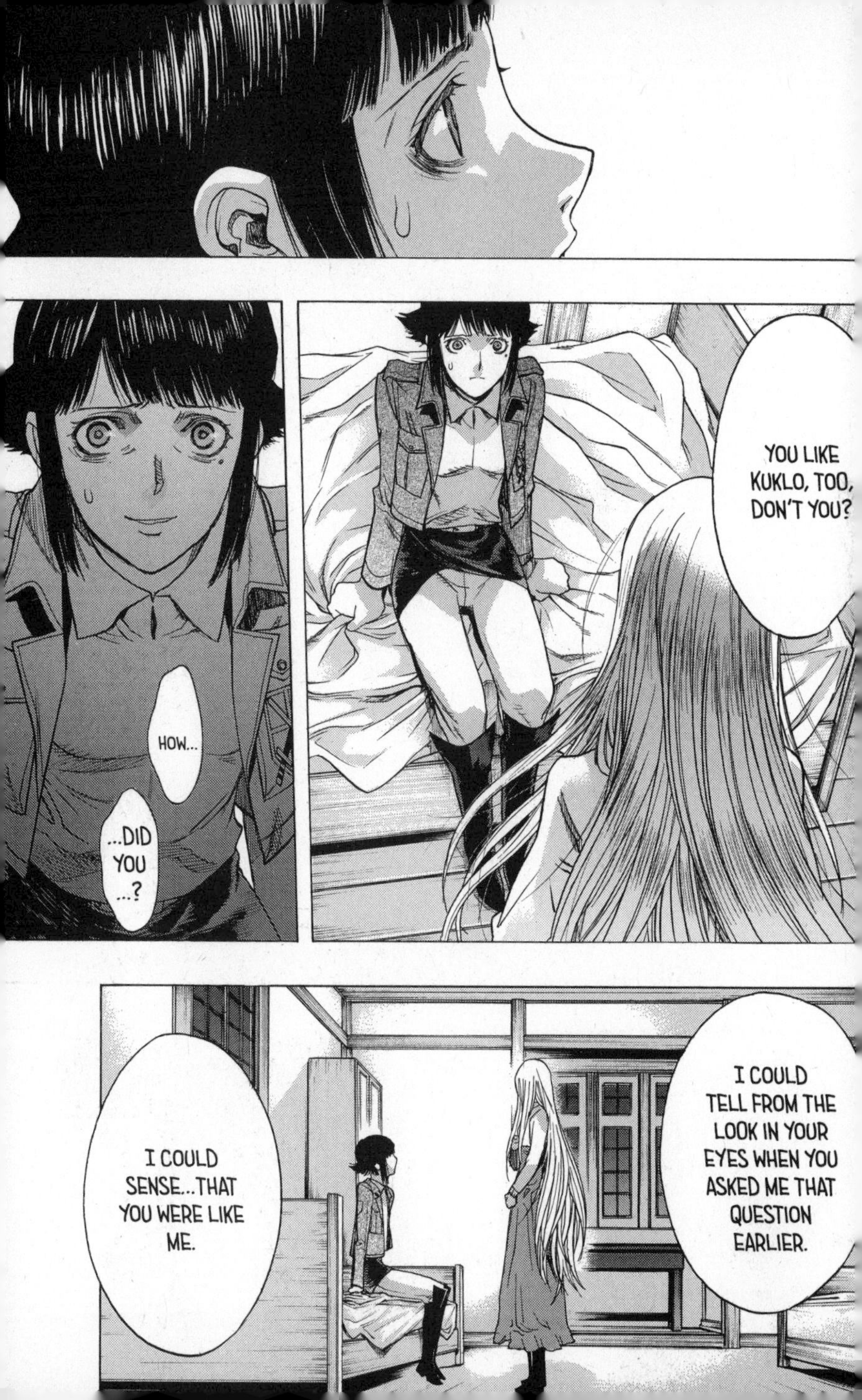
YOU LIKE KUKLO, TOO, DON'T YOU?
HOW...
...DID YOU ...?
I COULD TELL FROM THE LOOK IN YOUR EYES WHEN YOU ASKED ME THAT QUESTION EARLIER.
I COULD SENSE...THAT YOU WERE LIKE ME.

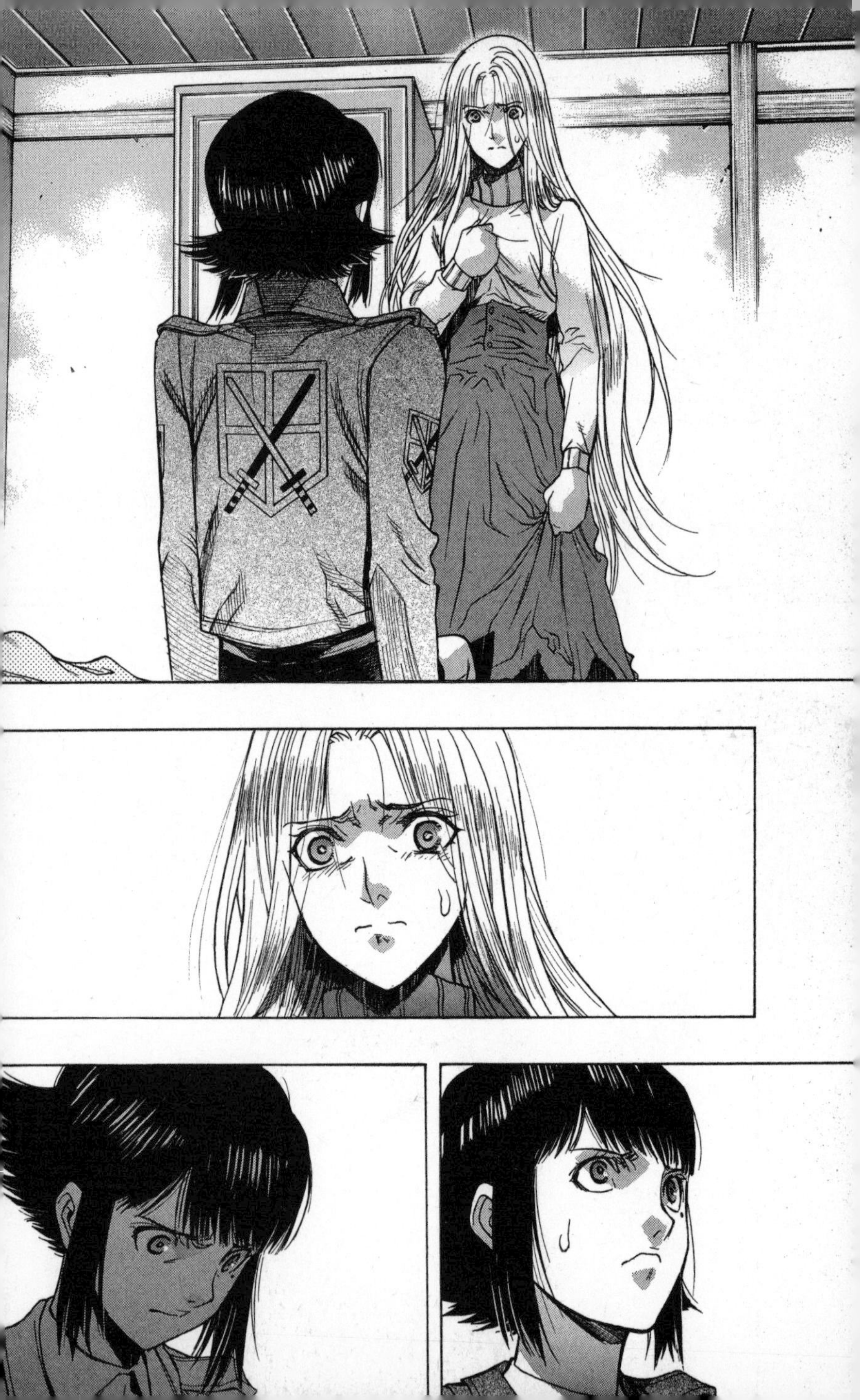

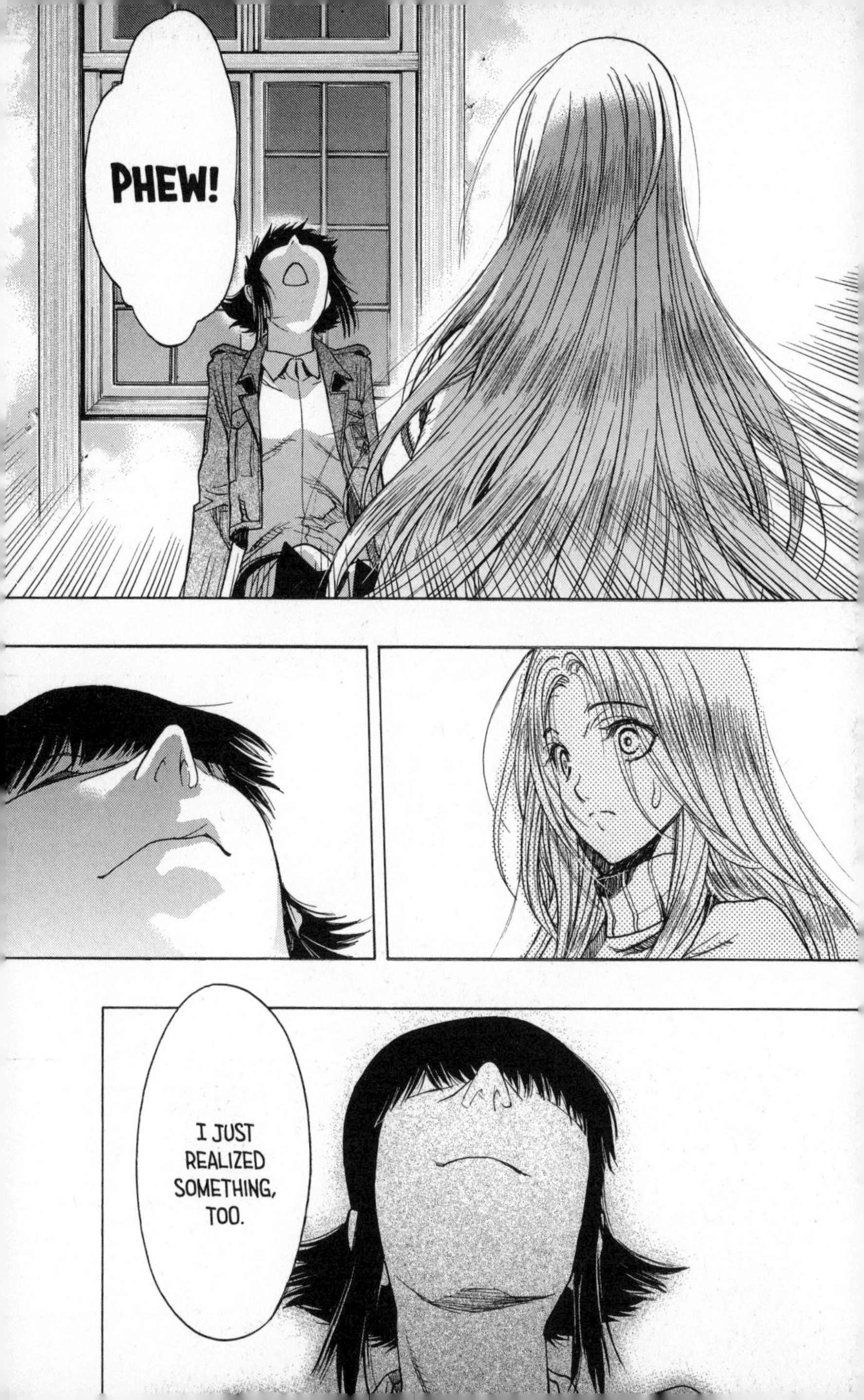
PHEW!
I JUST REALIZED SOMETHING, TOO.

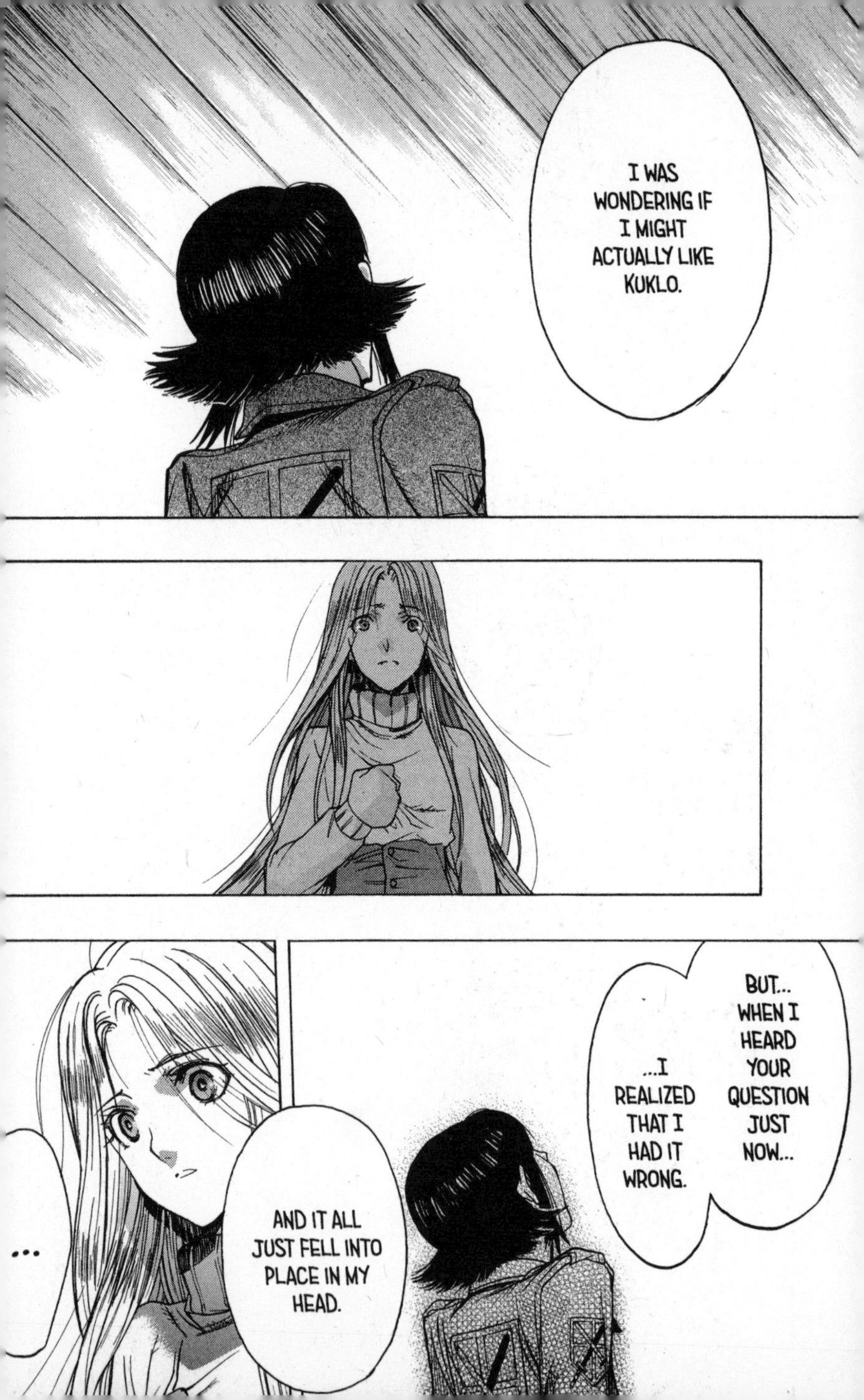
I WAS WONDERING IF I MIGHT ACTUALLY LIKE KUKLO.
BUT... WHEN I HEARD YOUR QUESTION JUST NOW...
...I REALIZED THAT I HAD IT WRONG.
AND IT ALL JUST FELL INTO PLACE IN MY HEAD.
...

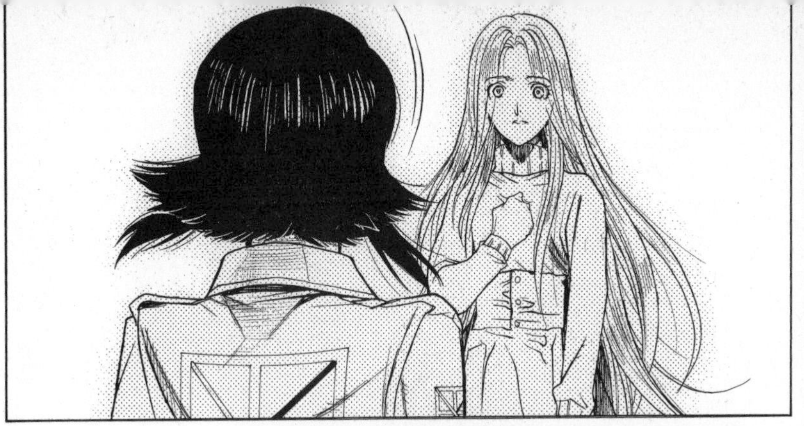

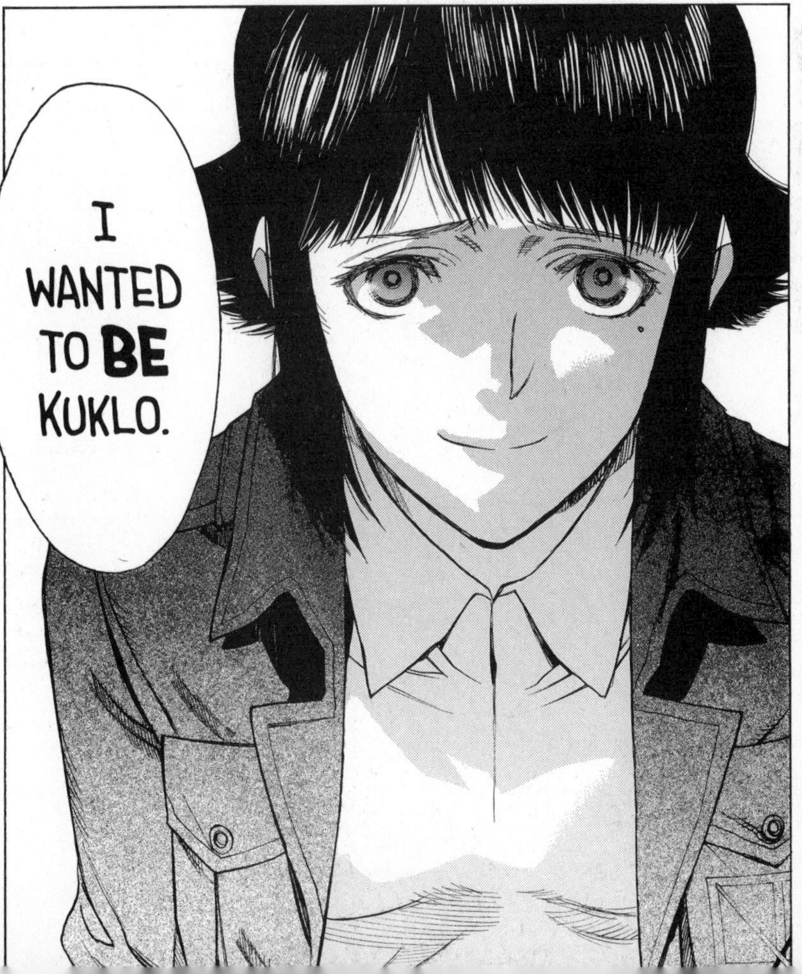
I WANTED TO **BE** KUKLO.

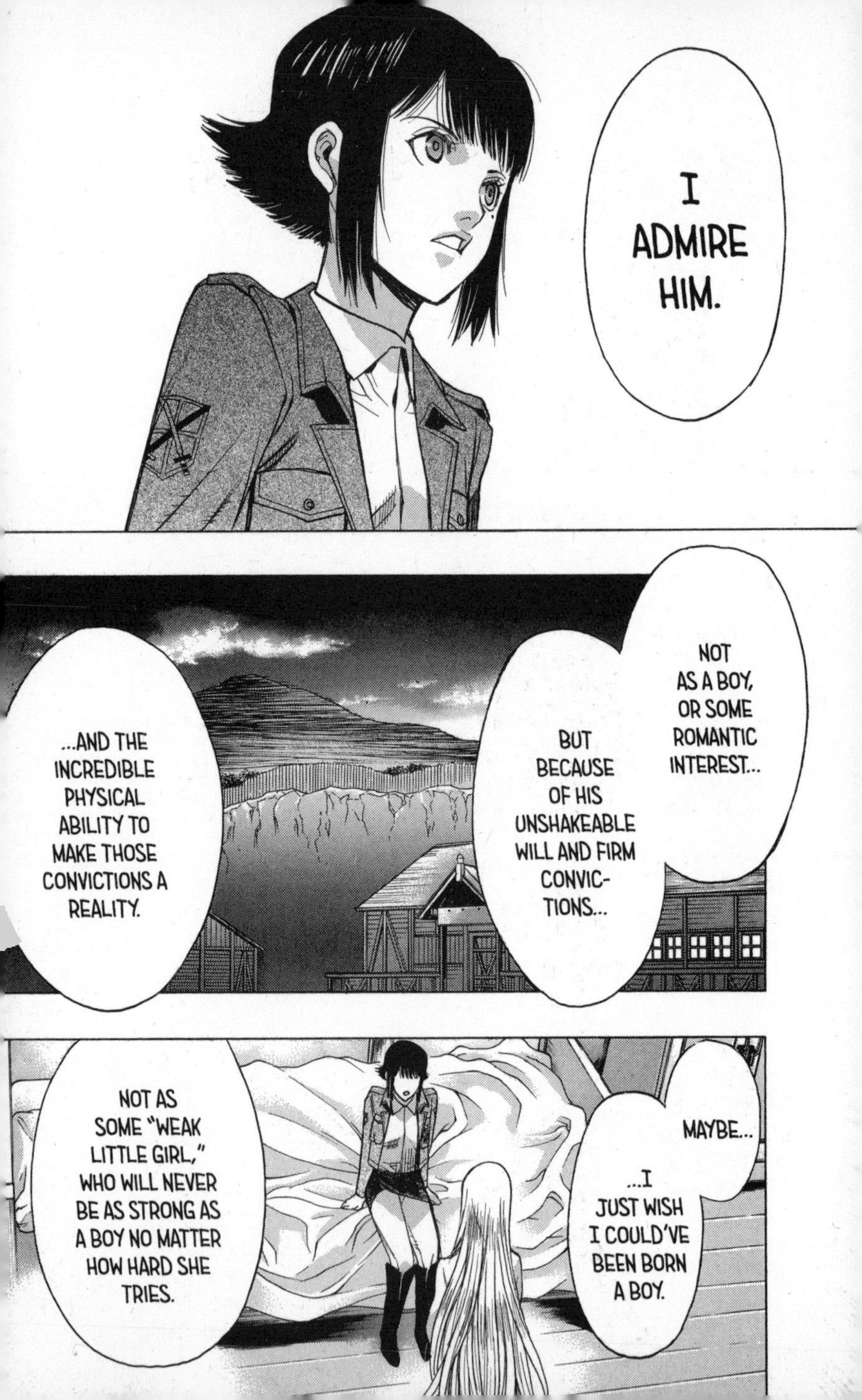
I ADMIRE HIM.
NOT AS A BOY, OR SOME ROMANTIC INTEREST...
BUT BECAUSE OF HIS UNSHAKEABLE WILL AND FIRM CONVIC- TIONS...
...AND THE INCREDIBLE PHYSICAL ABILITY TO MAKE THOSE CONVICTIONS A REALITY.
MAYBE...
...I JUST WISH I COULD'VE BEEN BORN A BOY.
NOT AS SOME "WEAK LITTLE GIRL," WHO WILL NEVER BE AS STRONG AS A BOY NO MATTER HOW HARD SHE TRIES.

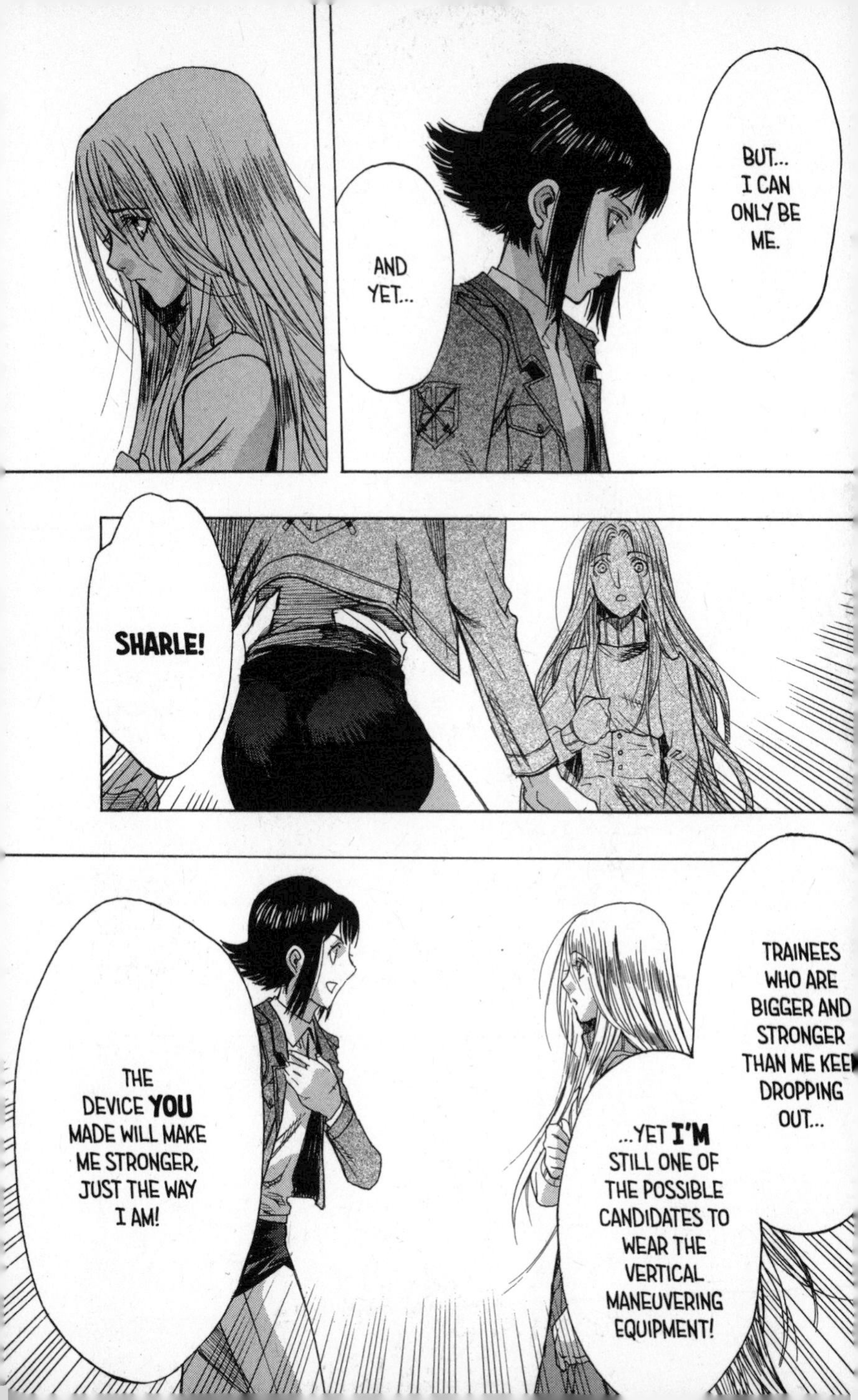
BUT... I CAN ONLY BE ME.
AND YET...
SHARLE!
TRAINEES WHO ARE BIGGER AND STRONGER THAN ME KEE DROPPING OUT...
...YET I'M STILL ONE OF THE POSSIBLE CANDIDATES TO WEAR THE VERTICAL MANEUVERING EQUIPMENT!
THE DEVICE YOU MADE WILL MAKE ME STRONGER, JUST THE WAY I AM!

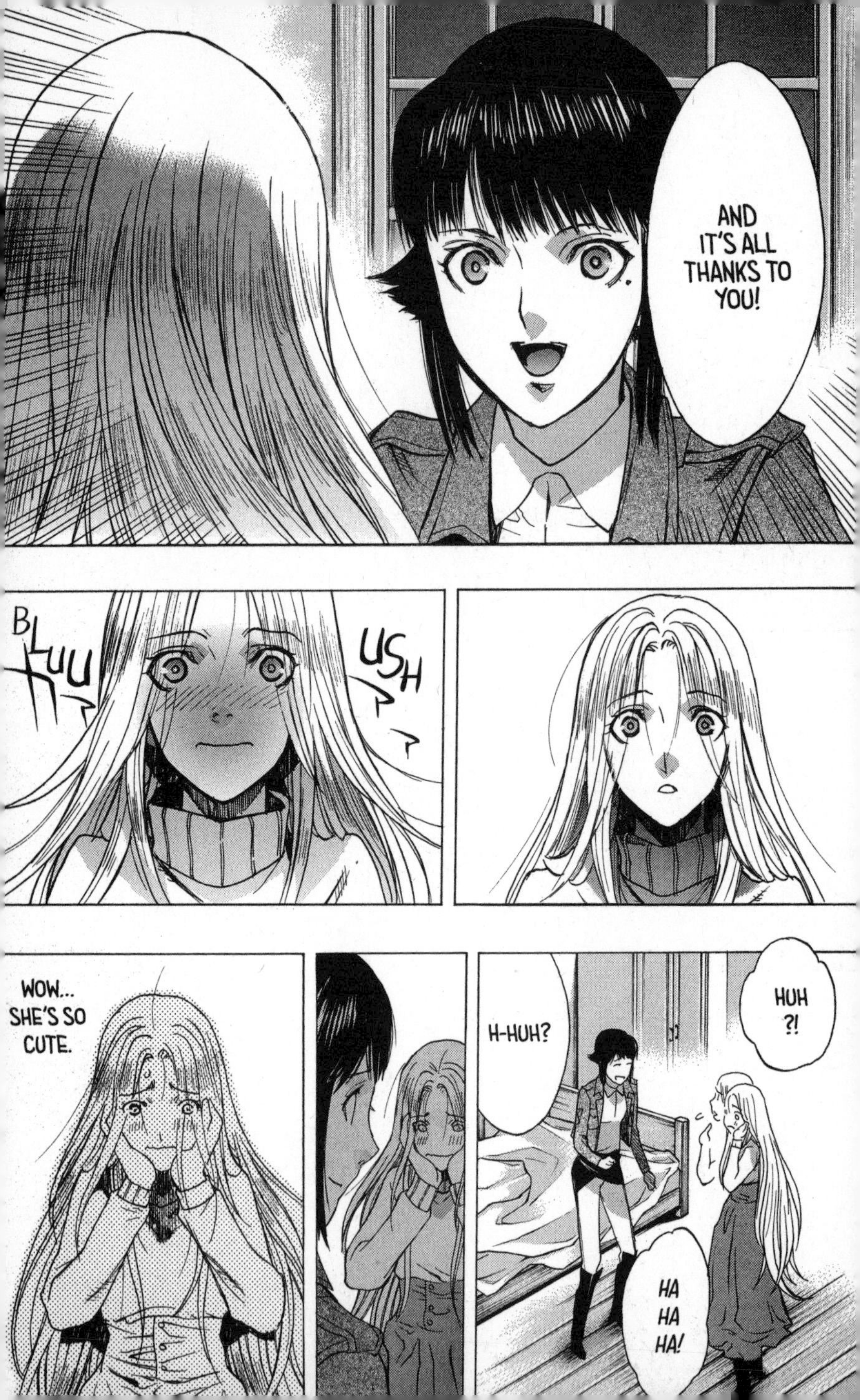
AND IT'S ALL THANKS TO YOU!
BLUU
USH
HUH ?!
H-HUH?
HA HA HA!
WOW... SHE'S SO CUTE.

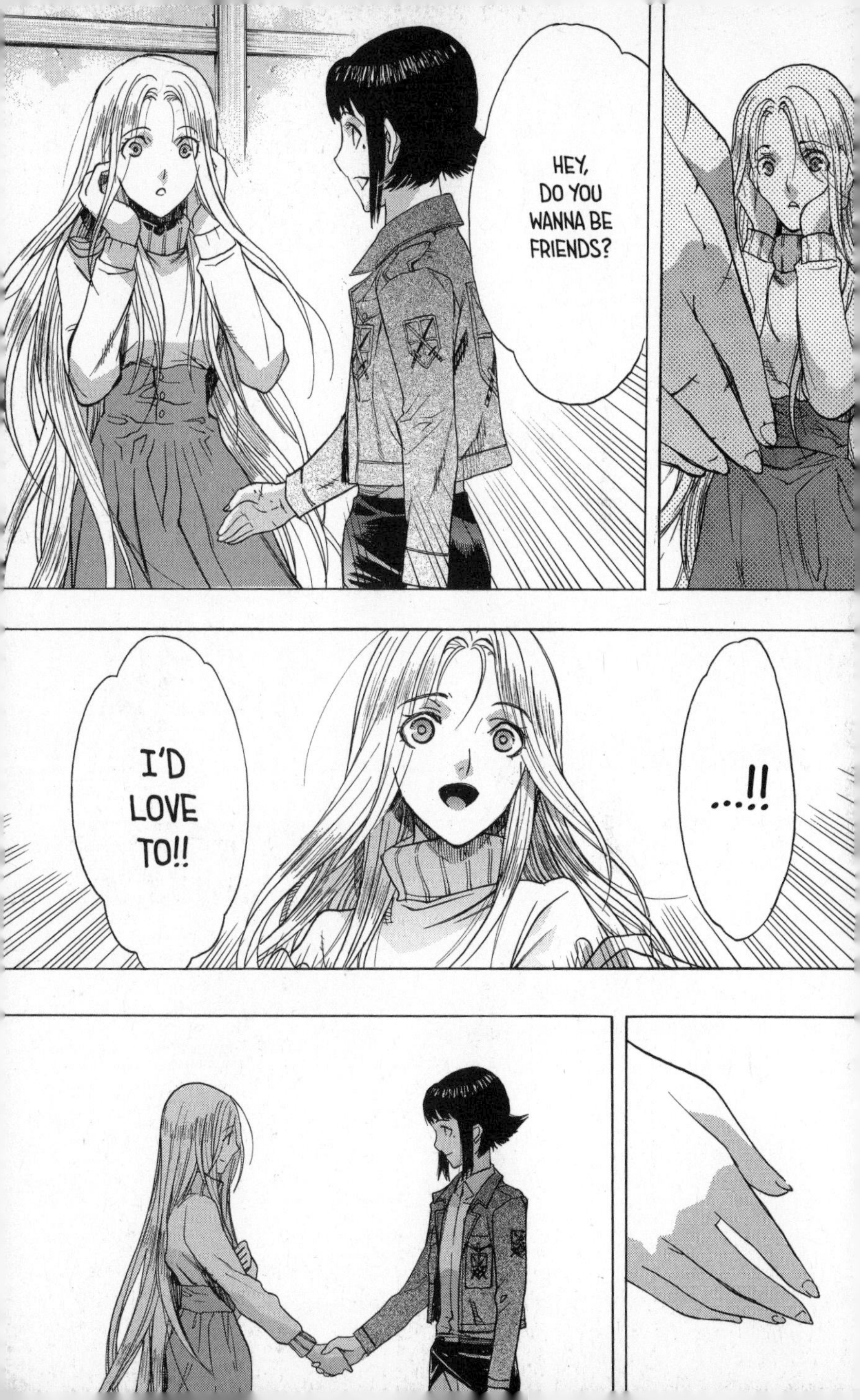
HEY, DO YOU WANNA BE FRIENDS?
...!!
I'D LOVE TO!!

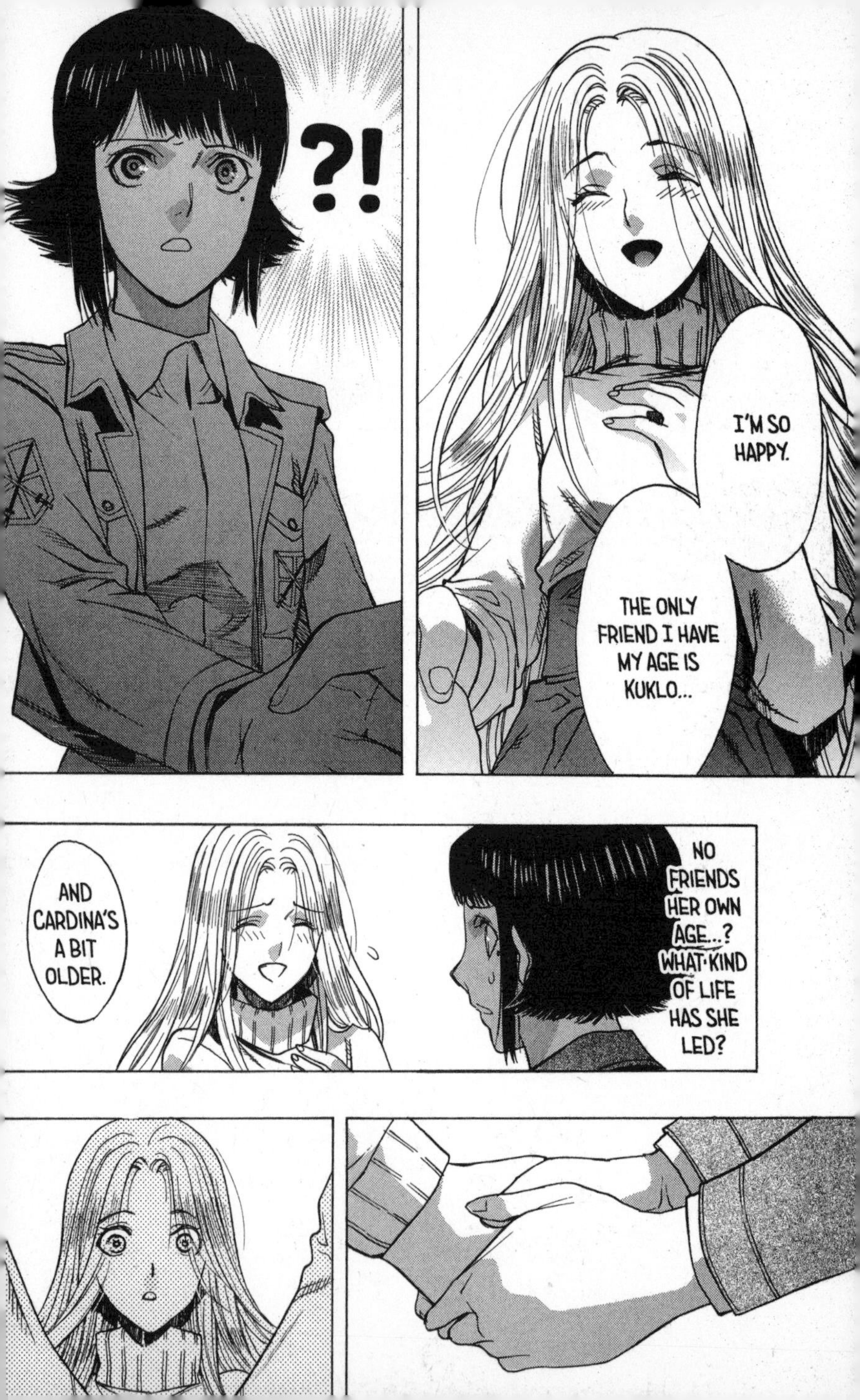
I'M SO HAPPY.
THE ONLY FRIEND I HAVE MY AGE IS KUKLO...
?!
NO FRIENDS HER OWN AGE...? WHAT KIND OF LIFE HAS SHE LED?
AND CARDINA'S A BIT OLDER.

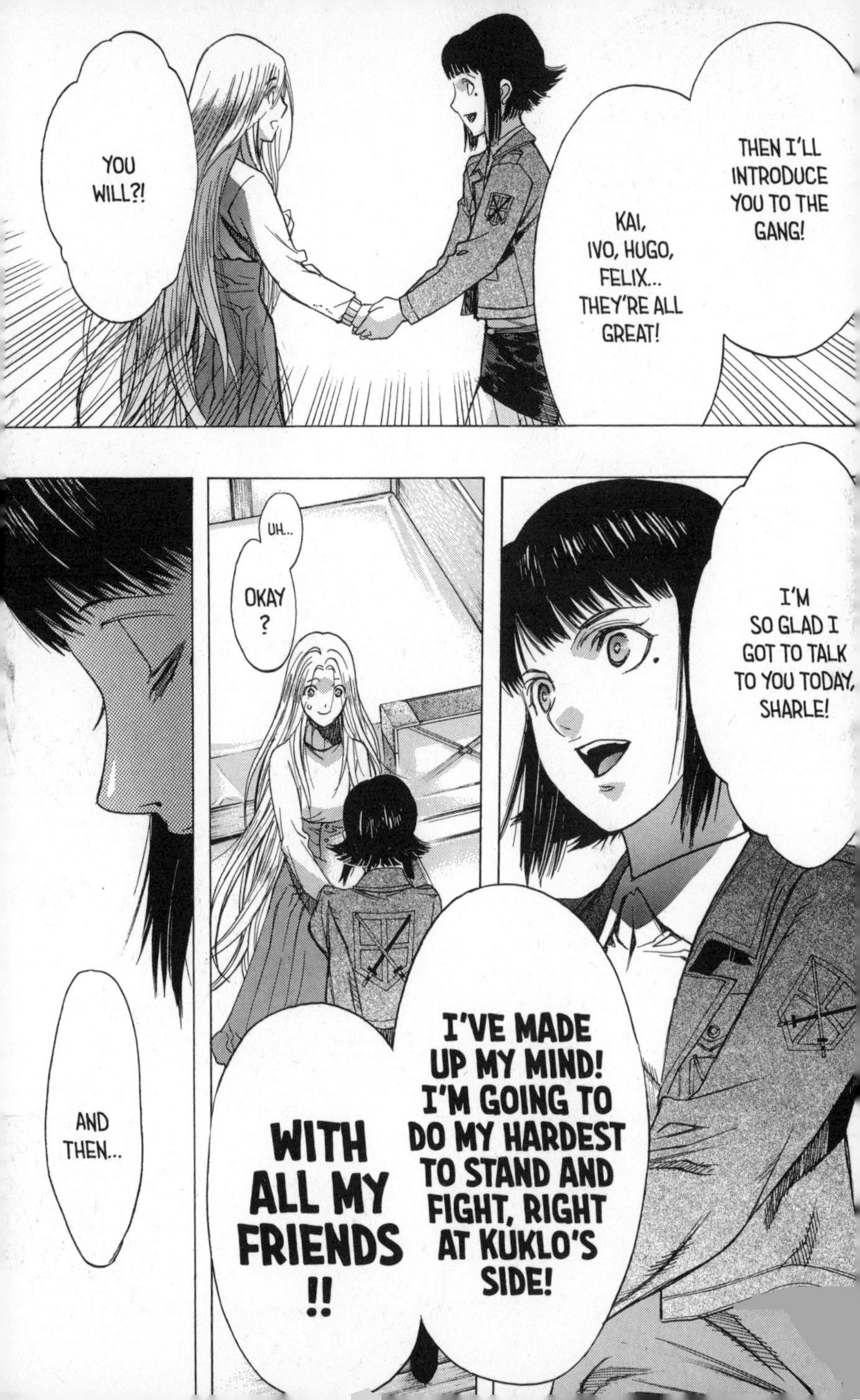
THEN I'LL INTRODUCE YOU TO THE GANG!
KAI, IVO, HUGO, FELIX... THEY'RE ALL GREAT!
YOU WILL?!
I'M SO GLAD I GOT TO TALK TO YOU TODAY, SHARLE!
I'VE MADE UP MY MIND! I'M GOING TO DO MY HARDEST TO STAND AND FIGHT, RIGHT AT KUKLO'S SIDE!
WITH ALL MY FRIENDS !!
UH...
OKAY ?
AND THEN...

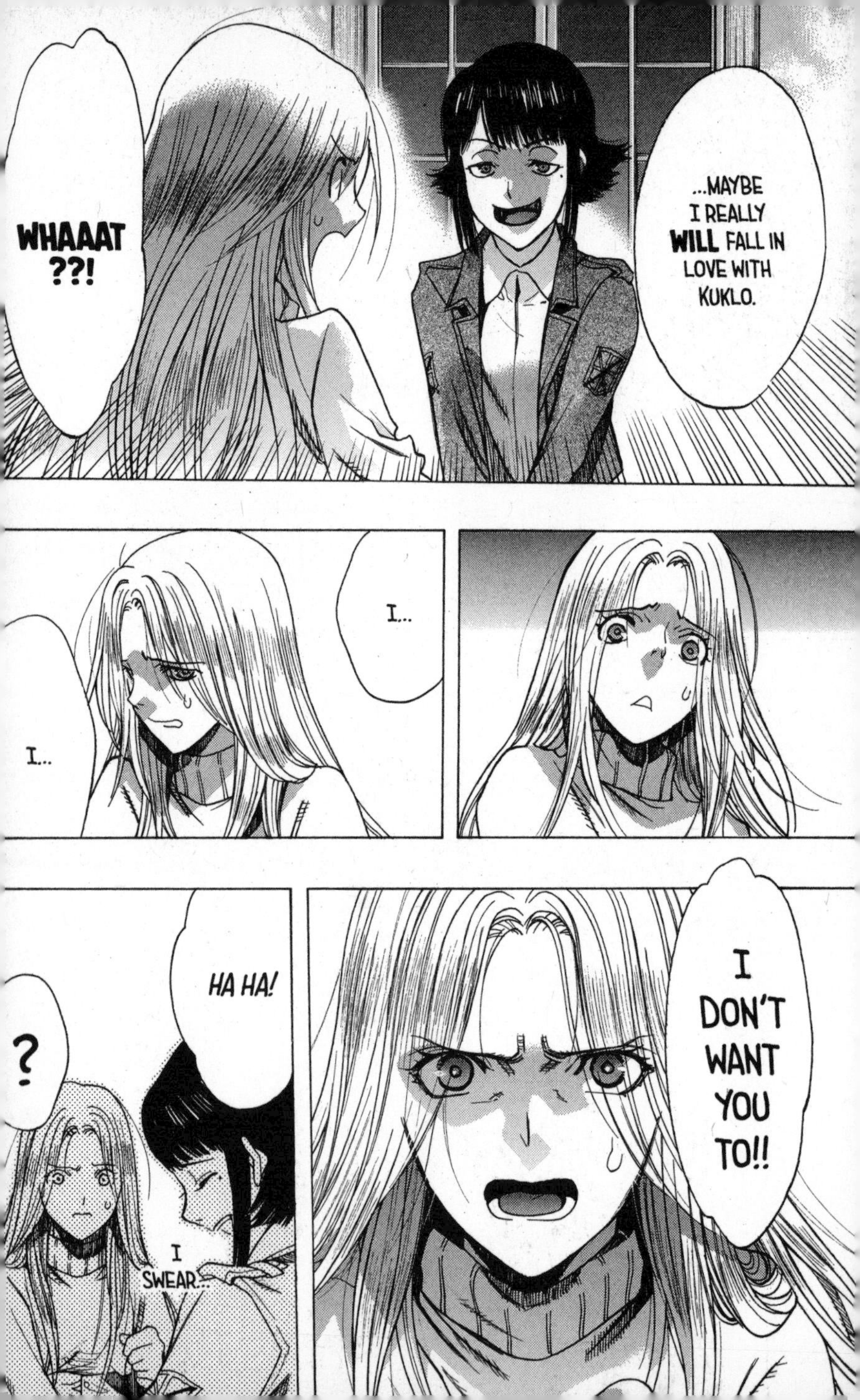
...MAYBE I REALLY WILL FALL IN LOVE WITH KUKLO.
WHAAAT??!
I...
I...
I DON'T WANT YOU TO!!
HA HA!
?
I SWEAR...

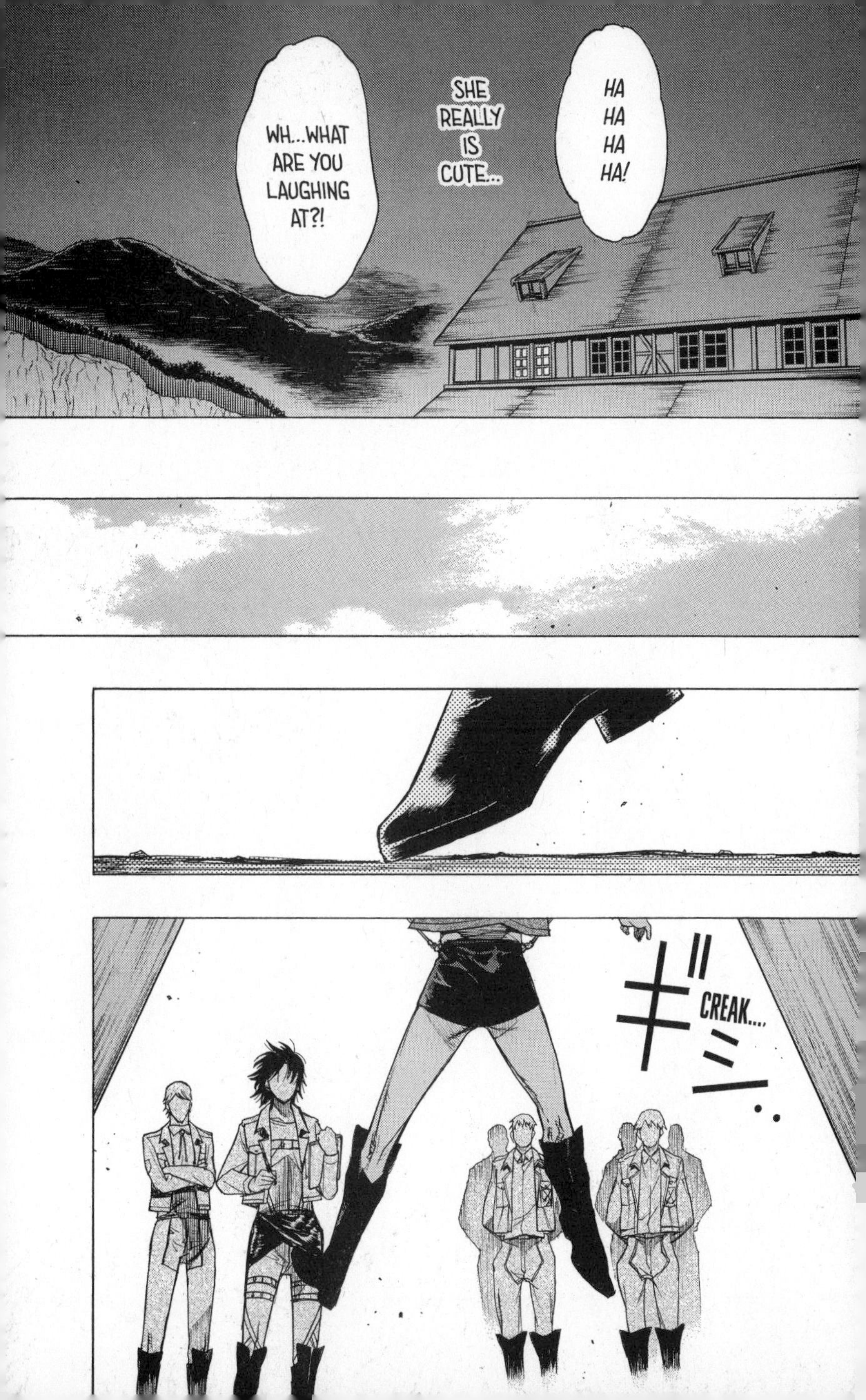
HA HA HA HA!
SHE REALLY IS CUTE...
WH...WHAT ARE YOU LAUGHING AT?!
CREAK....

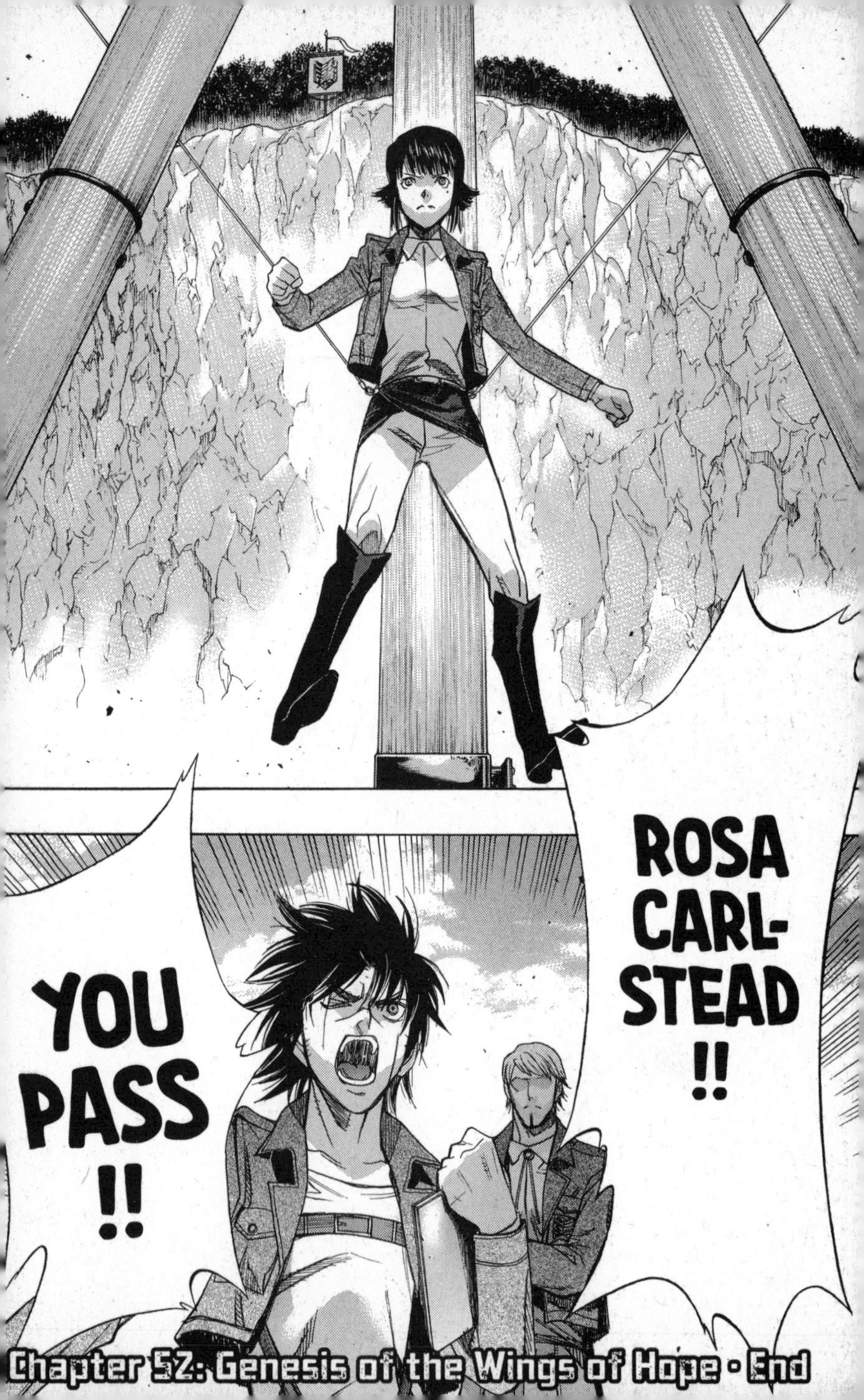
ROSA CARL-STEAD !!
YOU PASS !!
Chapter 52: Genesis of the Wings of Hope • End

ATTACK ON TITAN
BEFORE THE FALL

TO BE CONTINUED

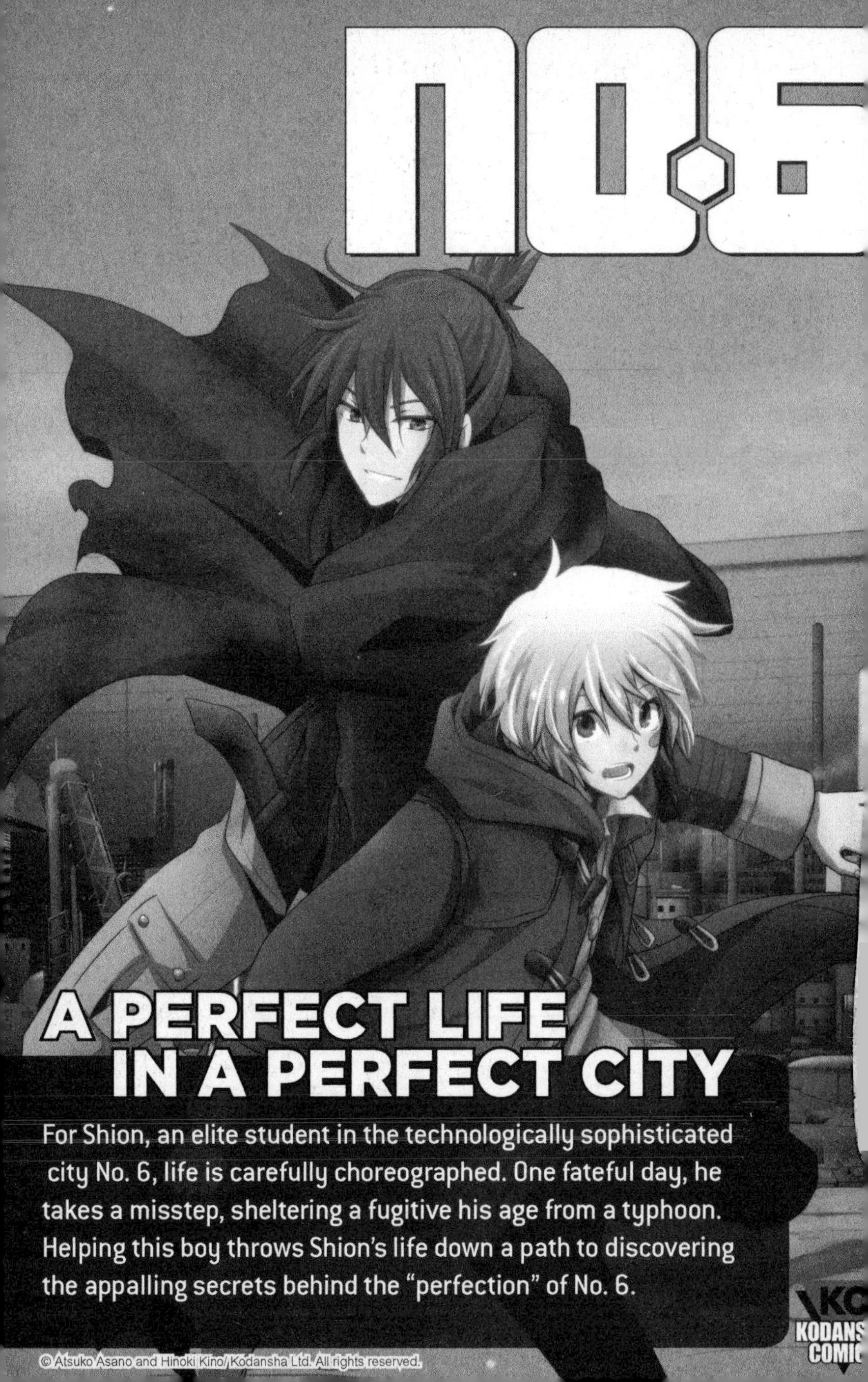
NO.6
A PERFECT LIFE
IN A PERFECT CITY
For Shion, an elite student in the technologically sophisticated city No. 6, life is carefully choreographed. One fateful day, he takes a misstep, sheltering a fugitive his age from a typhoon. Helping this boy throws Shion's life down a path to discovering the appalling secrets behind the "perfection" of No. 6.
KC
KODANSHA
COMICS
© Atsuko Asano and Hinoki Kino / Kodansha Ltd. All rights reserved.

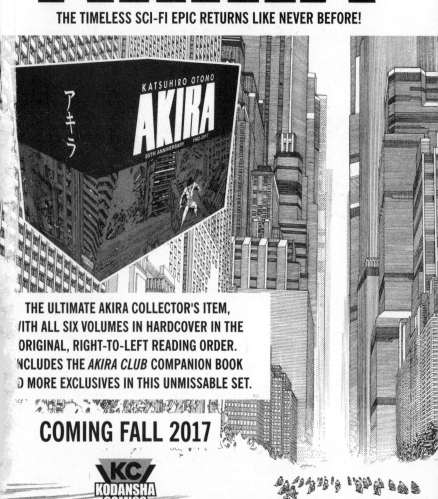

OTOMO
大友克洋

A GLOBAL TRIBUTE TO
THE MIND BEHIND AKIRA

A celebration of manga legend Katsuhiro Otomo from more than 80
world-renowned fine artists and comics legends
With contributions from:
- Stan Sakai
- Tomer and Asaf Hanuka
- Sara Pichelli
- Range Murata
- Aleksi Briclot
And more!
168 pages of stunning, full-color art

DON'T MISS THE MOST ACCLAIMED ACTION MANGA OF 2013!

"Gripping doesn't begin to describe Vinland Saga. 5 stars."
—ICv2

"Deeply engrossing... If you have any interest at all in Vikings, the Medieval period, or pirates, this is not a series you want to miss."
—Anime News Network

"The art is gorgeous, a combination of beautiful cartooning and realistic backgrounds. Yukimura is also a master of pacing, both in frenetic battle scenes and charged emotional moments."
—Faith Erin Hicks, *Friends With Boys*

"For those who love Berserk, you'll love this too... Worth the long wait."
—A Case Suitable for Treatment

"It will be impossible to stop watching this story unfold."
—Japan Media Arts Awards jury

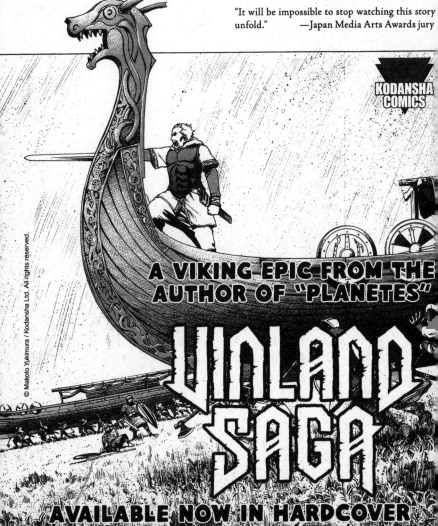

KODANSHA COMICS

A VIKING EPIC FROM THE AUTHOR OF "PLANETES"

VINLAND SAGA

AVAILABLE NOW IN HARDCOVER

MARDOCK
マルドゥック・スクランブル
SCRAMBLE

Created by
Tow Ubukata

Manga by
Yoshitoki Oima

"I'd rather be dead."

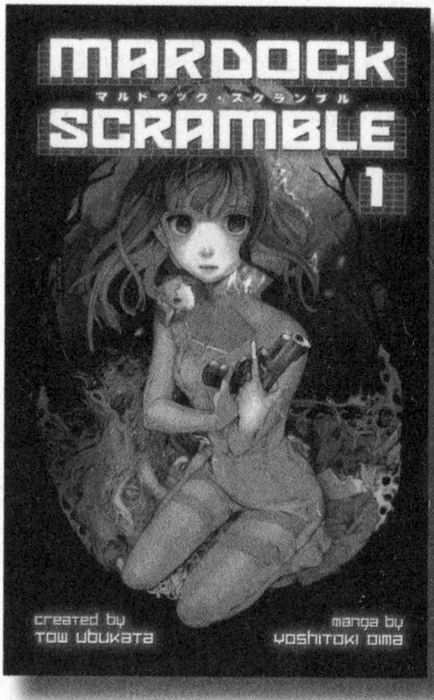
MARDOCK
マルドゥック・スクランブル
SCRAMBLE
1
created by
TOW UBUKATA
manga by
YOSHITOKI OIMA

Ages: 16+

Rune Balot was a lost girl with nothing to live for. A man named Shell took her in and cared for her...until he tried to murder her. Standing at the precipice of death, Rune is saved by Dr. Easter, a private investigator. He uses an experimental procedure known as "Mardock Scramble 09" on Rune, and it grants her extra-ordinary abilities. Now, Rune must decide whether or not to use her new powers to help Dr. Easter bring Shell to justice. But, does she even have the will to keep living a life that's been broken so badly?

KC KODANSHA COMICS

VISIT KODANSHACOMICS.COM TO:

- View release date calendars for upcoming volumes
- Find out the latest about upcoming Kodansha Comics series

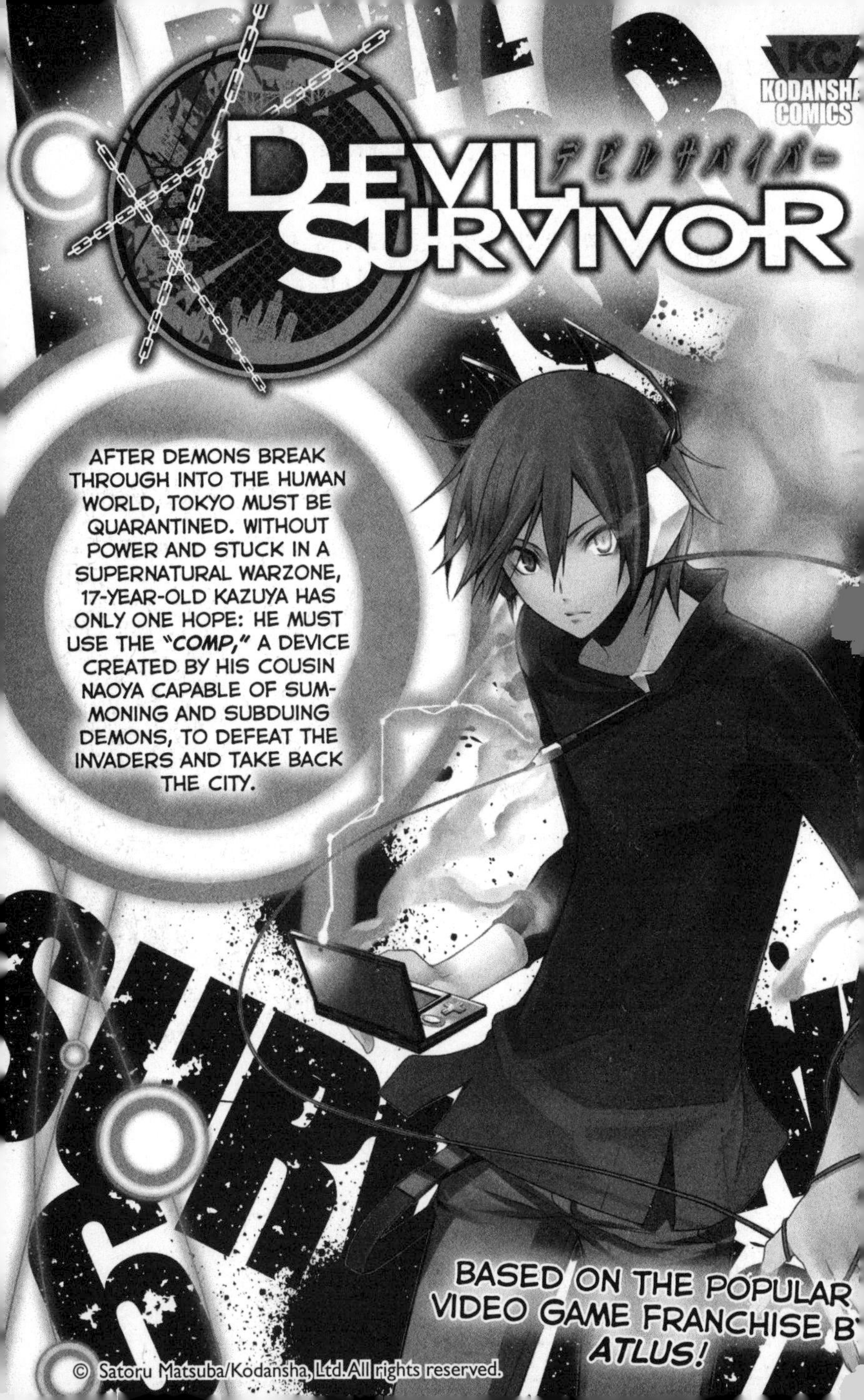
KODANSHA COMICS
DEVIL SURVIVOR
AFTER DEMONS BREAK THROUGH INTO THE HUMAN WORLD, TOKYO MUST BE QUARANTINED. WITHOUT POWER AND STUCK IN A SUPERNATURAL WARZONE, 17-YEAR-OLD KAZUYA HAS ONLY ONE HOPE: HE MUST USE THE "COMP," A DEVICE CREATED BY HIS COUSIN NAOYA CAPABLE OF SUMMONING AND SUBDUING DEMONS, TO DEFEAT THE INVADERS AND TAKE BACK THE CITY.
BASED ON THE POPULAR VIDEO GAME FRANCHISE B ATLUS!

"I'm pleasantly surprised to find modern shojo using cross-dressing as a dramatic device to deliver social commentary... Recommended."

-Otaku USA Magazine

The prince in his dark days

By Hico Yamanaka

A drunkard for a father, a household of poverty... For 17-year-old Atsuko, misfortune is all she knows and believes in. Until one day, a chance encounter with Itaru–the wealthy heir of a huge corporation–changes everything. The two look identical, uncannily so. When Itaru curiously goes missing, Atsuko is roped into being his stand-in. There, in his shoes, Atsuko must parade like a prince in a palace. She encounters many new experiences, but at what cost...?

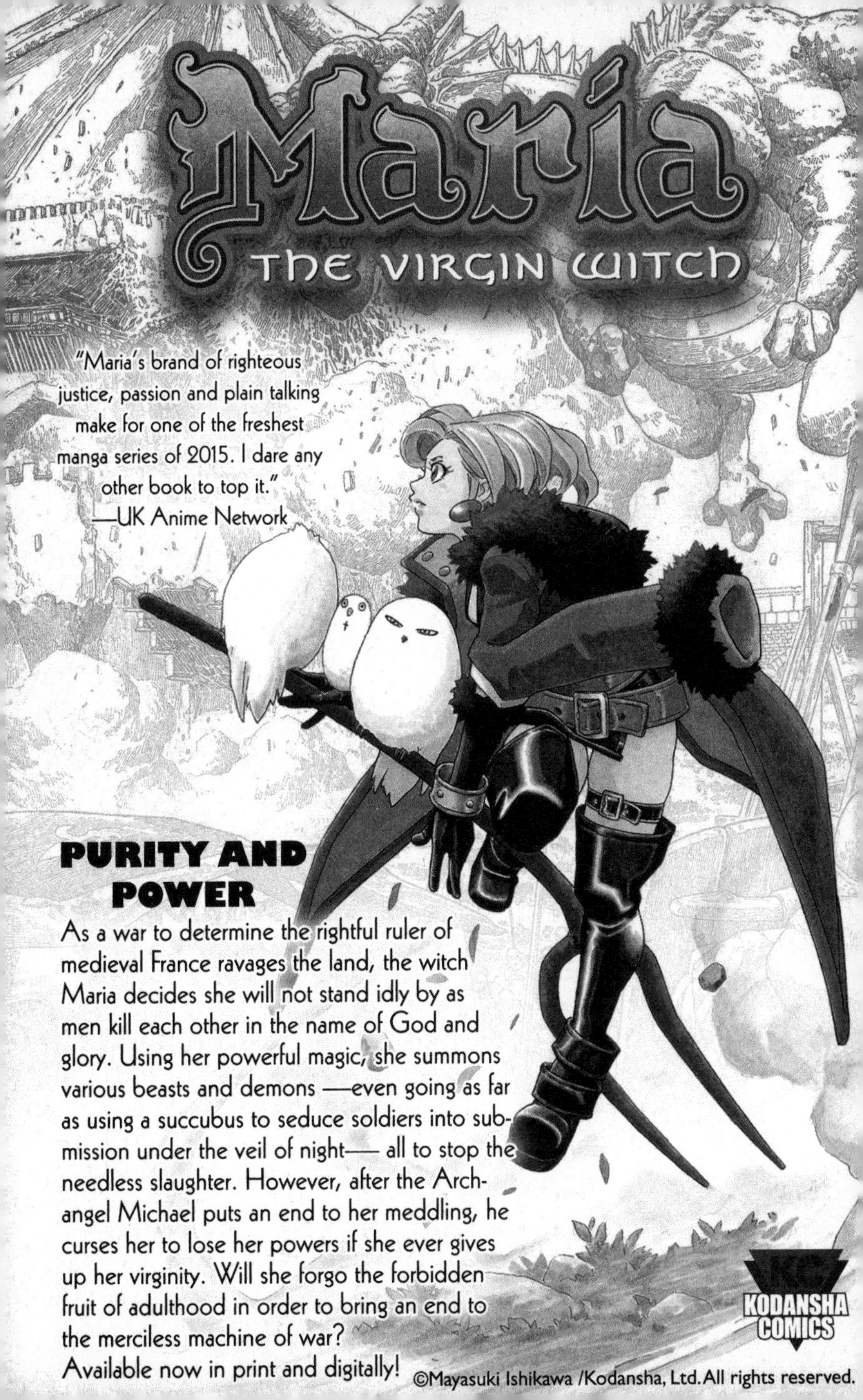
Maria
THE VIRGIN WITCH
"Maria's brand of righteous justice, passion and plain talking make for one of the freshest manga series of 2015. I dare any other book to top it."
—UK Anime Network
PURITY AND POWER
As a war to determine the rightful ruler of medieval France ravages the land, the witch Maria decides she will not stand idly by as men kill each other in the name of God and glory. Using her powerful magic, she summons various beasts and demons —even going as far as using a succubus to seduce soldiers into submission under the veil of night— all to stop the needless slaughter. However, after the Archangel Michael puts an end to her meddling, he curses her to lose her powers if she ever gives up her virginity. Will she forgo the forbidden fruit of adulthood in order to bring an end to the merciless machine of war?
Available now in print and digitally!
KODANSHA COMICS
©Mayasuki Ishikawa /Kodansha, Ltd. All rights reserved.

THE STORY STARTS **HERE!**

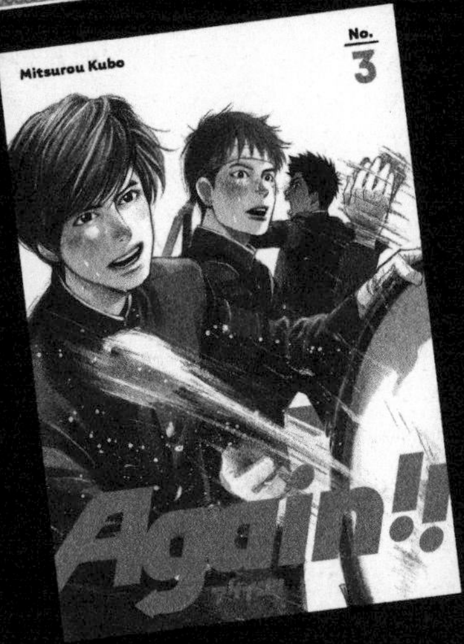
Mitsurou Kubo
No.
3
Again!!

Again!!

アゲイン!!

Kinichiro Imamura isn't a bad guy, really, but on the first day of high school his narrow eyes and bleached blonde hair made him look so shifty that his classmates assumed the worst. Three years later, without any friends or fond memories, he isn't exactly feeling bittersweet about graduation. But after an accidental fall down a flight of stairs, Kinichiro wakes up three years in the past… on the first day of high school! School's starting again—but it's gonna be different this time around!

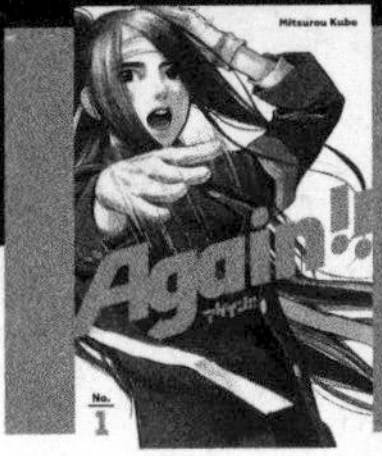
Mitsurou Kubo
Again!!
No.
1

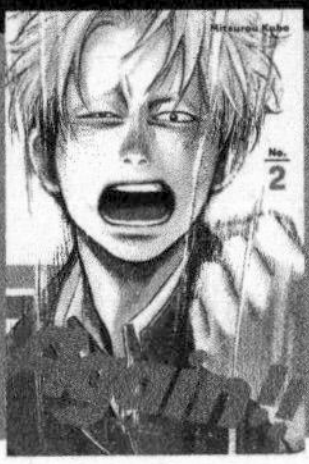
Mitsurou Kubo
No.
2

Vol. 1-3 now available in **PRINT** and **DIGITAL**!
Vol. 4 coming August 2018!

Find out **MORE** by visiting:
kodanshacomics.com/MitsurouKubo

ABOUT MITSUROU KUBO

Mitsurou Kubo is a manga artist born in Nagasaki prefecture. Her series *3.3.7 Byoshi!!* (2001-2003), *Tokkyu!!* (2004-2008), and *Again!!* (2011-2014) were published in *Weekly Shonen Magazine*, and *Moteki* (2008-2010) was published in the seinen comics magazine *Evening*. After the publication of *Again!!* concluded, she met Sayo Yamamoto, director of the global smash-hit anime ***Yuri!!! on ICE***. Working with Yamamoto, Kubo contributed the original concept, original character designs, and initial script for ***Yuri!!! on ICE***. *Again!!* is her first manga to be published in English.

KODANSHA COMICS

Kodansha COMICS

A Kodansha Comics Trade Paperback Original
Attack on Titan: Before the Fall volume 14 copyright © 2018 Hajime Isayama/
Ryo Suzukaze/Satoshi Shiki
English translation copyright © 2018 Hajime Isayama/Ryo Suzukaze/Satoshi Shiki

Published in the United States by Kodansha Comics, an imprint of
Kodansha USA Publishing, LLC, New York.

Publication rights for this English edition arranged through
Kodansha Ltd, Tokyo.

First published in Japan in 2018 by Kodansha Ltd., Tokyo
as *Shingeki no kyojin Before the fall*, volume 14.

ISBN 978-1-63236-614-6

Character designs by Thores Shibamoto
Original cover design by Takashi Shimoyama and Kayo Hasegawa (Red Rooster)

Printed in the United States of America.

www.kodanshacomics.com

9 8 7 6 5 4 3 2 1
Translation: Stephen Paul
Lettering: Steve Wands
Editing: Haruko Hashimoto
Kodansha Comics edition cover design by Phil Balsman

You are going the *wrong way!*

Manga is a *completely* different type of reading experience.

To start at the *BEGINNING*, go to the *END!*

That's right! Authentic manga is read the traditional Japanese way-from right to left, exactly the opposite of how American books are read. It's easy to follow: just go to the other end of the book, and read each page-and each panel-from the right side to the left side, starting at the top right. Now you're experiencing manga as it was meant to be.